AN EMOTIONAL GAUNTLET

AN EMOTIONAL GAUNTLET

FROM LIFE IN PEACETIME AMERICA TO THE WAR IN EUROPEAN SKIES

Stuart J. Wright

Maps and formation plans by
Grant Wright

Pen & Sword
AVIATION

First published in Great Britain in 2004 by
PEN & SWORD AVIATION
an imprint of
Pen & Sword Books Limited
47 Church Street
Barnsley
South Yorkshire
S70 2AS

Copyright © 2004
The Board of Regents of the University of Wisconsin System

ISBN 1 84415 120 4

Published in the USA by
The University of Wisconsin Press

The right of Stuart Wright to be
identified as Author of this Work has
been asserted by him in accordance with
the Copyright, Designs and Patents Act 1988.

A CIP catalogue record for this book
is available from the British Library.

Printed and bound in Great Britain by
CPI UK

Pen & Sword Books Ltd incorporates the imprints of
Pen & Sword Aviation, Pen & Sword Maritime, Pen & Sword Military,
Wharncliffe Local History, Pen & Sword Select,
Pen & Sword Military Classics and Leo Cooper.

For a complete list of Pen & Sword titles please contact:
PEN & SWORD BOOKS LIMITED
47 Church Street, Barnsley, South Yorkshire, S70 2AS, England.
E-mail: enquiries@pen-and-sword.co.uk
Website: www.pen-and-sword.co.uk

DEDICATED TO
Crew 25 and all the Liberator men of Old Buck'

IN MEMORY OF
my godfather, Howard Allies Johnson,
25 May 1938–27 November 2003,
a wonderful pianist and humorous storyteller (an anecdote
about the American GIs in Norfolk, which he told to me when
I was five years old, will always be with me!)

ON BEHALF OF WAYNE AND MAY LIM,
this book is also dedicated to the memory of their daughter,
Diana Patricia Lim-Garay, born 15 August 1952,
who lost her battle against cancer 23 April 2001

Out of our sufferings, we should learn something. . . . The well-being of "this" is the well-being of "that," . . . Every side is "our side"; there is no evil side. Veterans have experience that makes them the light at the tip of the candle, illuminating the roots of war and the way to peace.

Thich Nhat Hanh

TABLE OF CONTENTS

ILLUSTRATIONS

FOREWORD

I am the sister of Donald Lawry, the original navigator on the crew of *"Corky" Burgundy Bombers*. For me this book has been a journey from the faded memories of a kid sister to the enormous pride of an adult sister. I remember both of my brothers spending hours making model airplanes. Donald, my eldest brother, had always wanted to be a pilot, but from what I've learned, I think navigating was what he was meant to do and he did it well. Next to his picture in the high school yearbook, *The Class of '42*, it said: "The Air Corps for me." He went off for training when he was eighteen years of age and was able to realize his dream, but it cost him his life.

The letters Don wrote to my family told that Jack Nortridge was the only pilot he felt safe flying with. Jack brought home the young men that flew with him, just as he always said he would—how different it might have been if my brother had not volunteered to fly a mission with another crew in the place of a sick navigator.

Many remarkable things have happened since Stuart first located me and sent me an early draft of his manuscript. I have been privileged to meet two of Don's crew—Bill, the bombardier, and Pete, the nose turret gunner. Talking to them has been very special. In the past I have said that I lost a brother in World War II. I don't say that anymore, as Bill was quick to assure me that Don is not lost, but is remembered.

I also learned the significance of the name *Corky*, written on a drawing of a boat in Don's serviceman's folder that was sent home from England with the rest of his belongings. I think the experience that I found most emotionally rewarding was when Bill handed me the good-luck cork that hung at Don's place, as navigator in *Corky*. I treasure it and all the comradeship and true friendship that it represents.

An Emotional Gauntlet is a remarkable tribute to the crew who flew *Corky* and to all of those "boys" who fought so valiantly and gave so much. How selfless those young men were. I appreciate this opportunity to say thank you to them, and to Stuart for his tireless job of researching and writing this book.

BETTY LAWRY ALLEN

ACKNOWLEDGMENTS

So many people have contributed to this book in different ways. Some have shared accounts of their lives, of both joyful and painful memories, and without them this book would never have happened. Others have contributed information and photographs. And then there are those who have offered ideas, enthusiasm, and encouragement (as well as a great deal of patience!) as I slowly improvised, found, and followed my intuition, and through trial and error I got closer to writing the book that I felt it should be. More often than not the process felt out of control and I struggled to keep up with it as it snowballed . . . and more than once I even gave up. For two-and-a-half years after finishing the first draft, I lived in denial of its existence, but it seemed to haunt me, needing to be finished. But as for the people I most want to thank, it seems that at no time did any them ever give up on me, or the idea of this book.

First of all, thank you to Bill and Dorothea Eagleson. I value your friendship and I will always have fond memories of happy times in New England, of sailing along the Massachusetts coastline and flying in the B-24 over Florida. Thank you, Bill, for sharing your memories with me and for letting me turn them into this book. Thank you also for allowing me to be, in some way, part of the history of *Corky*'s crew. Thank you to Betty Lawry Allen—I knew there was a reason for writing this book, and I'm sure that you exemplify that reason. Donald Lawry was at first a mystery, just a name and a few details—"Killed in Action, 22 February 1944" and "Wisconsin." For some reason I was sure that somewhere there was a sister, who probably knew practically nothing about what happened to him. Having managed to trace Betty, between us we were able to share information and complete the picture. Thanks also to Don Allen, Dorothy and Clarence Taplin, and Arthur and Joan Sands for sharing their memories and enthusiasm for this book.

Thank you to Wayne Lim for driving several hundred miles from Houston to Baton Rouge to meet me in 1997; thanks also to his wife, May Lim, for endless e-mail correspondence in researching the Lim family. I think that Wayne wondered what to make of me on our first meeting, and perhaps thought it strange that I should be writing a book about his crew. But by the time of our second meeting, it was clear that I had made a good friend and, like Bill Eagleson, Wayne made me feel like one of the crew. Well, we only had one hour together in Houston airport in February 2002, but at least Wayne and May got to meet Nadine Witmer Gibson and I am thankful that through this book she was able to learn about her brother's wartime experiences, of which he never spoke. Thank you, Nadine Witmer Gibson and Hazel Witmer for providing the Witmer family story.

I am indebted to Ruby Jo Roberson Faust and her husband, Eddie, who shared so much of their research into the Roberson family prior to its publication. I am also thankful to the late Perry Roberson, whose correspondence was invaluable. Thank you also to Bill LeRoy, and to Pete and Eleanor Veilleux for their correspondence and contributions. Thanks to Anita Cohen for enthusiastically sharing the history of the Cohen family and memories of her husband, Seymour. Jack Nortridge's brother Vale contributed a great deal to this book, but regretfully didn't live to see it completed. Jack's son, John Nortridge Jr., appeared literally out of the blue and provided more background information. His tremendous enthusiasm inspired me to rewrite the manuscript at a time when the whole project seemed to be in limbo. I am sorry that John also passed away before this book reached publication.

I am thankful to George White for compiling a series of notes in answer to my questions, at a time when he was suffering from ill health, just prior to his death. His brother, Don White, contacted me just as I finished the second draft and was searching for a publisher. Don provided information that would transform Chapter Five, and he then passed away—he had been involved in this project for just three or four months prior to his death, but his contribution was invaluable. Once again, like so many others, I regret that George and Don White did not live to see the book published.

Thank you to Harvey Nielsen's great-nephew, Kenneth James. Only days after I posted a request for information on a genealogy message board on the Internet, Ken appeared by e-mail as if to prove the theory of synchronicity! He also provided the Nielsen family history—another example of the generosity of other researchers who without hesitation shared the results of their endeavors with me and let me incorporate them into this book. On that note, I am especially thankful to Tom Brittan. As far as the 453rd Bomb Group and 2nd Air Division are concerned, Tom can only be described as a research genius! I appreciate his patience and willingness to answer what seemed like a million questions, and his generosity in sharing copies of wartime documents and excerpts of his own work. Whenever I found myself stuck in a research cul-de-sac, with conflicting information or just generally confused, Tom was always willing to help. Pat Ramm kindly provided photographs, memories, and information while Don Olds, the official historian of the 453rd Bomb Group veterans' association, provided missing details and trusted me with numerous wartime photographs.

I am indebted to Philip H. Meistrich for his account, *A Crew Goes to War—the Hard Way!* This proved to be a vital source of both information and inspiration for Chapter Six. Thanks to Hubert Cripe for his fascinating account, *Mission 250—Berlin 6 March 1944*, which brought Chapter Ten to life. Ian McLachlan's excellent book, *Night of the Intruders*, was an inspiration for Chapter Fourteen, and Ian kindly provided photographs for use in this book. Thanks also to James Straub for memories and to the late Frank Kyle for help with photographs. Wilbur and Jeane Stites deserve a big acknowledgement for helping me on many occasions through their newsletter. Thanks to Vince and Marge Pale for dinner and a lovely evening on their trip to London; thank you, Vince, for sharing memories of your crew, your experiences at Old Buckenham, and that fateful mission to Brunswick. Roger Stein kindly shared his account of the Jones crew, and James N. Workman and his daughter Lou Workman Souders shared diary excerpts, flight log details, and photographs relating to the McCrocklin crew. Thank you to Irwin Stovroff for some valuable insights into the 8th Air Force experience from a Jewish airman's perspective.

Thank you to Robert B. Bieck, Jim Kotapish, Eugene McDowell, Ramsay D. Potts, Nick and Marilyn Radosevich, Abe Wilen, and Robert E. Victor for sharing memories of both Jimmy Stewart and Joe Miller, and for discussing morale and leadership issues. It seems that everyone I spoke to had a different perspective, different memories, and different impressions! I hope I managed to present a balanced and objective view. Thank you also to the Jimmy Stewart Museum.

I would like to express my appreciation to Bob and Rob Collings, and all at the Collings Foundation, for a wonderful flight in the B-24 — memories I will never forget! Martin W. Bowman enthusiastically offered to take time out from his own writing schedule to assess my manuscript for the University of Wisconsin Press. Thanks, Martin, and thanks also for your help with photographs. The second reviewer commissioned by the publisher was Jerome Klinkowitz, whose comments made me realize that I had somehow achieved what I had set out to achieve — thank you for "getting it" and reflecting this so enthusiastically in your review. Thank you to both Raphael Kadushin and Sheila Moermond at the University of Wisconsin Press for taking an interest in the first draft, for so encouragingly rejecting it (in this case that's not a contradiction in terms!), yet still maintaining interest until the end. Thank you also to outreach director Sheila Leary, editor Susanne Breckenridge, indexer Nina Roy, and to all the staff at the University of Wisconsin Press, and to Henry Wilson and Peter Coles at Pen and Sword Books.

Thank you, Joanne Blake, my former school friend and "New York genealogy research correspondent" for taking on the task of searching for the DeMay family with energy and enthusiasm. Even though we never tracked them down, I know I can sleep at night because I guess we tried everything, and with only a couple of vague clues as a starting point! Thanks, Joanne, for your help. (No thanks at all to the VA and various other government institutions, not to mention the privacy laws, which became an obstacle that have so far prevented the DeMay family from being aware of this book.)

A very big thank you must go to John P. Durborow (nephew of Crew 34's copilot, Lt. John Durborow), for taking such a great interest in this project, and for information, photographs, a refreshing forward-thinking attitude, and an open mind! Thank you especially for your tremendous help with proofreading, editing, and sharing ideas—always objective, enthusiastic and very encouraging. John, you were an excellent copilot *and* navigator during the race to the finish line and for that I can't thank you enough!

Thank you also to good friends: especially, Lee Hooker and Lo, Andy French, Nigel Perrin, Beulah Garner, Nick and Sharon Lock, Marsha Brown, Jess Whittall, Shawn and Jane Whelan, Karyl Nairn and Steve Monti, Pete Bennett and Emma Shaw, and everyone at TIN. Thank you, Graciela Romero Vasquez.

Special thanks to my family—Mum, Dad, and my brother, Grant. To elaborate on your contributions would be to fill another book! Thank you, I know that I am very, very lucky.

The following people and organizations have also contributed a great deal and helped in the creation of this book: Steve Adams, John Archer, Mike Bailey, Yvonne Barnett, Janet Bennett, Doug Birkey, Stewart Bragdon, Willa Cohen Bruckner, Rollo E. Brunsell, Patrick and Christeen Bunce, F. C. "Hap" Chandler, Robert Chenard, Diane Christensen Haagensen, Fred Christensen, Forrest S. Clark, Wilbur Clingan, Judy Cohen, Francis Conlon, Mary Lee Crowe, Ted Damick, Dan Davis and his 453rd BG Web site, Philip L. Davis, Ivo de Jong, Albert de la Garza, Kathleen Dempsey, Phyllis DuBois, East Anglia Books, *Ex-POW Bulletin,* John Farrington, Peter Fleming, Mark Forlow, Roger A. Freeman, Frank Gierhart, Harold Glover, Christy Goodman and the Courier-Life newspapers of Brooklyn NY, Bob Gormley, Harriett Gustason and the *Freeport Journal-Standard* newspaper in Illinois, Frank Hammett, Larry Hansen, Greg Hatton and the b-24.net Web site, Pam Ingram, Gloria Johnson, Randy Johnson, Robert and Betty Jordan, George D. Kasparian, Rainer Kliemann, Ed Keuppers, Thompson Kreidler, Dr. Aaron Kuptsow, Virginia Kyle, Delbert D. Lambson, Donelson Lawry, Helen Low, Will Lundy, Luther Valley Historical Society (Wisconsin), Christopher MacLehose, Mighty Eighth Air Force Public Message Board, Keith Money, Hunton Morgan, Lloyd Morris and his 453rd BG Web site, Letha Marie Mowry and the Nodaway County Genealogical Society (Missouri), Ken Nellis and his 453rd BG Web site, Lola Nielsen, Wiley and Earline Noble, Norfolk Record Office, Hank

North, Tony North, Clarinda Nortridge, Judy Nortridge, Susan Nortridge, Merle Olmsted, Jerry Penry, Lloyd W. Prang, Harlan Price, Hershel Prince, RAF Cosford Air Museum, Peter Randall, John Harold Robinson, James A. Schoenecker and the American Military Cemetery (Cambridge), Second Air Division Memorial Library (Norwich), Mike Simpson, Marvin H. Spiedel, Jim Sterling, the Stokes family, Becky Toyne, Debbie Vosburg and Col. James H. Delaney at the Air Force Aid Society Headquarters, George Wear, Barbara White, Erwin L. White, Jerry D. White, Mary White, Chuck Williams, Andrew Wilson, Bill Wilson, James W. Wint, and Terry Woods.

Many thanks to you all.

INTRODUCTION

I recall being five or six years of age and driving through the Norfolk countryside with my parents and brother in our car. My father told us that the narrow lane ahead had once been the runway of an American airfield. My first thought was one of amazement as I imagined an airplane speeding along in front of us and taking to the skies! But since Americans were to me, at that age, seemingly make-believe characters from a faraway land, seen only through television, my second thought was a question: Who was the American pilot flying the plane and what was he doing *here*?

Almost every five miles in every direction from my childhood home is a deserted and derelict airfield of the Second World War. In fact, our village had been entirely encompassed by an American base some forty years previously, when several thousand American airmen outnumbered the small community. By the time I was born, memories of these legendary flyers, the "Yanks," had become an inseparable part of the local folklore.

Thinking back, I was never particularly interested in airplanes or war—and I believe that perhaps the biggest debt we owe our war veterans is our determination to find new ways to solve our human problems, so that their endeavors may not have been in vain. This is not so much a book about airplanes or war, but a book about people.

One Saturday afternoon just a few weeks before my fourteenth birthday, while browsing along the shelves of books in the 2nd Air Division Memorial Room at Norwich Central Library, I happened to meet an American couple who were visiting England on vacation—Bill and Dorothea Eagleson. Bill explained that in 1944 he had been based at Old Buckenham, Norfolk, from where his aircrew had flown a tour of missions in a B-24 Liberator named *Corky*. And so began years of correspondence and friendship; it was Bill's colorful letters, his humorous anecdotes and stirring memories of deeply challenging times that inspired the idea for this book. And what a journey it has been!

In October 1997 I arrived in Boston on a trip to see Bill and Dorothea. That evening as we sat drinking tea and chatting, Bill asked me if I had thought of a definition for an aircrew, such as his crew or any other that flew from England or elsewhere more than fifty years previously during those dark days of war. How to sum up so much in such a concise form as a definition? No, I hadn't even thought about thinking of one! (Instead I had set myself this huge challenge of writing a whole book, totally underestimating the workload!) "What about you? How would you define your crew?" I asked. Bill's face turned into a mischievous grin as he paused, maybe bringing to mind one of their more joyful, reckless experiences, and then with great affection and humor he replied, *"Loveable Bastards!"*

PART ONE

The Meeting of
the "Loveable Bastards"

CHAPTER ONE

Shadows on the Horizon

You are training to become soldiers. You are young and inexperienced and do not have a complete understanding of what is best for you, or what will best train you to become fighting Aircrew members that you will *have* to be in order to meet the antagonist against which you will be pitted. Our enemies are cruel, vicious, ingenious, trained, and disciplined, and hard in the extreme. In order to meet them on a parity *you* have to be trained, disciplined, and hard. No one can "suddenly become anything." You can't suddenly become disciplined of mind and body. You can't suddenly become hard fighting Aircrew members. That is what you're training for.

In January 1943 a new group of cadets arrived at Santa Ana Army Air Base in California. They were strangers to each other but shared many common experiences of growing up in a world of increasing instability, enduring the era in the United States of America's history remembered as the Great Depression, only to find themselves facing a world at war. One of the cadets arriving at Santa Ana that January was twenty-two year old William "Bill" Eagleson. The base was over two thousand miles from his home in New England.

Bill Eagleson was born on Saturday February 7, 1920, and raised in Watertown, Massachusetts, where he lived with his parents and sister. The Eagleson name might suggest a connection to distant and unknown ancestors in Scotland or Ireland, but there was talk of a link to Sweden. Bill grew up surrounded by the legacies of as much recorded history as seemingly possible in the United States, for Watertown was founded under British rule during the colonial days of the seventeenth century, and developed into a suburb of Boston. Some three hundred years before Bill's childhood, British ships sailed as far upriver as Watertown, the furthest navigable inland point of the Charles River for seafaring ships of the time.

Bill's father, William Eagleson Sr., had served in the Massachusetts National Guard on the Mexican border and was a veteran of the Great War. During the 1930s he rode mules from Cambridge armory to Commonwealth armory on the other side of the Charles River. As a schoolboy aged eleven, Bill spent Saturday mornings earning pocket money by delivering weekly orders to customers from a local grocery store. World events seemed like another world away. At the age of twelve Bill learned to ski and New England winters provided plenty of opportunities to spend time on the slopes, while during the summer he enjoyed camping trips in the "wilderness" west of Watertown around Route 128.

After graduating from Watertown High School in 1938, Bill enrolled at Boston University. The university campus was spread across the city, and Bill attended the School of Physical Education at 84 Exeter Street, just west of Boston Common in the heart of the Back Bay. During the second half of the nineteenth century the Back Bay had been reclaimed from the Charles River; as the bay was filled in a new neighborhood emerged that was soon famed for its "brownstone" townhouses, reflecting the architecture of Victorian London. The neighborhood was built upon a neat grid of streets named alphabetically from Arlington through to Exeter through to Newbury, names transplanted from places in "Old" England. Running through the center, Commonwealth Avenue was laid out as a tree-lined Parisian-style boulevard. The Back Bay became a very desirable district of Boston and an exciting environment in which to be attending college during the late 1930s.

Situated five miles down river from Bill's home in Watertown, the School of Physical Education building in Back Bay was a stone's throw from Copley subway station, Boston Public Library (the world's first free municipal library), and numerous shops, bars, and restaurants. For the students at Exeter Street, the Moosehead Tavern on nearby Stuart Street was a popular hangout, and the journey west to Fenway and the main university site on Commonwealth Avenue was worthwhile considering the ten-cent beers available at the Dugout. After classes, Bill and some of his fellow students sometimes traveled over to Boston's North End, an Italian neighborhood that was popular for affordable beer and great pizza. More than half a century later, Bill Eagleson recalled his college days in Boston:

> During my college experience I was working my way through college, through the ski business, and I was teaching skiing through several locations throughout Greater Boston, finding a way to meet the bursar's demand at the college which I believe would be around $320 per year. . . . (I guess tuition at Boston University now is around $20,000 a year).
>
> It was not easy to come up with the tuition for college so, as I remember it, most of the fellas in my class all were busy working as elevator operators, bus boys . . . we all had other means of getting an income. Of course at that time to ride the Boston elevator [rail network] to classes cost five cents, today it costs a dollar, so, things change.

During the winter months Bill taught skiing at both the Commonwealth Country Club and the Oakley Country Club near Watertown. In

1939 a local newspaper reported: "Public ski classes at Oakley began officially last weekend. Bill Eagleson, head instructor, announced his plans for the current winter season. Special classes for junior skiers climaxed with a beginners' ski race, plus fundamental and advanced ski techniques for older skiers, are a few of his ideas. Bill is now a student at Boston University School of Physical Education and was formerly connected with the Newfound Region Ski School, also coach and captain of the Watertown Outing Club racing team. Assisting Mr. Eagleson will be Jack Andrews, crack racing skier, and William Gagnon, coach of the Sargent College ski team. These instructors will be on the Oakley slopes every Tuesday, Saturday and Sunday afternoon from 2 to 4." During

Bill Eagleson enjoying some skiing in front of the Oakley Country Club, Watertown, Massachusetts, in 1939. (Bill Eagleson)

warmer weather Bill taught swimming and conducted junior and senior Red Cross life saving classes at Dedham Bath House located south of Watertown.

Following the collapse of the New York Stock Exchange in 1929, Massachusetts did not escape the hardships of the Depression. In Boston's North End for example, during the months following the Wall Street crash, wages were halved as unemployment reached almost forty percent. Elsewhere in Massachusetts, unemployment levels rose dramatically as industrial output plummeted during the Depression years of the 1930s.

> We were not rich, we worked—we worked hard for just the necessary things that we *needed*, to *live*. So it was a desperate type of situation in our country at that time. As I remember it, the Depression phase put my family in rather dire straits.

Before reaching graduation at Boston University, life was about to take a significant change of direction not adhering to any long-term plans or ambitions. The generation of young Americans born in the years of peace that were intended to be "safe for democracy" following the so-called Great War now looked to a world under the threat of another global war—and they suspected that they would eventually become involved with the events across the Atlantic and Pacific Oceans. On 3 September 1939, two days after Germany's invasion of Poland, Britain and France declared war on Germany. On that day, U.S. President

Franklin D. Roosevelt addressed his nation—through the airwaves he reached the homes of the American people: "When peace has been broken anywhere, the peace of countries everywhere is in danger. But, let no man or woman thoughtlessly or falsely talk of sending its armies to European fields. . . . I have seen war and I hate war . . . as long as it remains within my power to prevent it, there will be no black-out of peace in the U.S."

Almost a year later while the Battle of Britain was being fought in the skies over England, Bill Eagleson recalls that he was home in Boston:

Bill's father, William Eagleson Sr., in the Massachusetts National Guard, Mexican border 1916. During the First World War he served in Europe. (Bill Eagleson)

in college with the threat of a world war. We were in the midst of the Depression. There was not too much to cheer about—it was more like trying to get a living done and find out what living was all about.

During the closing stages of the presidential election campaign of 1940, in which Roosevelt was voted for an unprecedented third term as president, he made a public appearance in Boston and pledged to parents: "I shall say it again and again and again: Your boys are not going to be sent into any foreign wars."

But with a diverse population of "hyphenated citizens" (Anglo-, Irish-, Italian-, Franco-, Chinese-, Japanese-American, and so on) there would always be Americans to whom a "foreign war" was a war back home. Even many second- or third-generation Americans felt a natural affinity with their ancestral homes, even though first and foremost they regarded themselves as Americans. The idea of neutrality of opinion during those early days of the Second World War was somehow unrealistic. Roosevelt himself had acknowledged this at the outbreak of the war in Europe when he announced: "This nation will remain a neutral nation, but I cannot ask that every American remain neutral in thought as well."

As a soldier in the Massachusetts Regiment, Bill Eagleson's father had been sent to Europe during America's involvement in the First World War during 1917 and 1918. He fought from the trenches in France and survived a German gas attack. Despite Roosevelt's assurances to Boston's parents that their sons would not be sent into foreign wars, the Eagleson family anticipated the day when Bill would be called to duty and directly involved with the war in Europe. He recalls:

> Certainly the loyalties at the time of the outbreak of war in Europe were closely associated with England, no doubt about it in my mind. . . . Our ties are very close to Britain, and they're always going to be very close. We're English speaking, we think very much alike, and I know that as Britain goes, so goes the United States and vice versa.
>
> If you take the map of Massachusetts you'll find that our ancestral links are very, very close. . . . The Pilgrims landed in Massachusetts. You'll find Plymouth, Taunton, Norfolk, Norwich, Salisbury, Winchester; you'll find all of your [English] towns—all of our towns named from the ancestral beginnings of our own ancestors.

New England is old by American standards. History records that back in 1620 the Pilgrims (Puritan separatists escaping religious persecution) departed Plymouth, England, crossed the Atlantic on board the *Mayflower* and landed at Plymouth Rock, Massachusetts. In 1630, with a Royal Charter promoting trade and colonization, several hundred Puritans followed, eventually settling on Shawmut Peninsula (a Native American burial ground) as the location for their "city upon a hill," which they named after the English town of Boston. Third to London and Bristol, Boston's port was once one of the largest in the British Empire. But Anglo-American relations were not always cordial.

When British troops, the Redcoats, arrived in Boston in the eighteenth century to enforce heavy taxes on the colony, a skirmish resulted in the Boston Massacre. A revolutionary activist group known as the Sons of Liberty expressed their contempt for Parliament by boarding ships in Boston Harbor and throwing crates of tea overboard in what is remembered as the Boston Tea Party. Battles were fought in nearby Concord and Lexington followed by the Battle of Bunker Hill, across the mouth of the Charles River from Boston. The battlefield moved further south, and in 1783 the War of Independence, otherwise known as the American Revolution, ended with an American victory. The United States was born; however, this was not the end of Anglo-American conflicts.

Britain provoked the United States into the War of 1812 over territory issues, specifically the Great Lakes region and Canada, and by refusing to recognize American maritime rights. Britain was simultaneously fighting a war against France, and American ships became caught in a

British naval blockade. Anglo-American hostilities ceased early in 1815 with both sides realizing they had more to gain from understanding and agreement.[1] A mutually beneficial relationship developed as diplomatic and trade relations were maintained despite occasional times of friction and imperialist competition.

In 1914, a conflict in the Balkans became a European war and escalated into the World War. Retrospectively renamed the First World War when the second such worldwide conflict erupted a few decades later, the so-called Great War was known also as the "war to end all wars" because, ironically, it was intended to make the world "safe for democracy."

Having been neutral at the time of the outbreak of hostilities in Europe, the United States at first intended to trade with both sides, but the British naval blockade in the North Sea hindered trade with Germany.[2] Americans generally sympathized with Great Britain, France, and Belgium. A sense of cultural affinity and solidarity was evident in Anglo-American relations: France was still favored for assisting in the American Revolution, but Imperial Germany was deeply distrusted.[3] In 1917 the United States was drawn into the conflict.

While the origins of the First World War remain controversial among historians, economic rivalry between capitalist and imperialist nations was a significant factor, along with what one historian described as, "an almost mystical belief in nationalism—a commitment on the part of the masses to fight for their nations, whether right or wrong, and a belief that loyalty to the flag came before all other loyalties."[4]

In 1918 the Allies achieved victory. At the subsequent Paris Peace Conference, the United States, Britain, France, Italy, and Japan dominated negotiations. The Treaty of Versailles dealt with the defeated Germany, which was forced to accept the blame for starting the war and consequently made to pay over six million pounds in reparations, surrender its colonies to the League of Nations, and significantly reduce its military power in terms of men and hardware—tanks, heavy artillery, aircraft, and submarines were not permitted. Germany signed the treaty under duress. Franklin Roosevelt, assistant secretary of the U.S. Navy during the First World War and future president of the United States, was critical of the treaty. He argued, "the effort to make the world safe for democracy had resulted in making the world safe for the old empires."

One evening in October 1938, thousands of radio listeners panicked to the point of hysteria as they heard reports that America had been invaded by Martians! But they were listening to a work of fiction, the *War of the Worlds* by H. G. Wells, broadcast by Orson Welles on a CBS drama series. Undoubtedly, radio was a profoundly powerful and emotive medium in those times, and for many people it was their primary source of information from home and abroad. Along with national newspapers and the newsreels shown at the movies, radio was a significant determinant of opinion—even the unbelievable became believable and anything was possible.

Throughout the 1930s, the American public followed news reports of German Chancellor Adolf Hitler's violent anti-Semitic policies—the oppression of Jews in Germany and Austria who were dispossessed, forced into ghettos and poverty, displaced as refugees, or sent to concentration camps as forced laborers. The Nazis were clearly ruthless and evil tyrants. In violation of the terms stipulated in the Treaty of Versailles, Hitler was rebuilding the German military in preparation to take on the world.

During 1940 and 1941 the CBS news correspondent Edward R. Murrow was instrumental in reporting life in London during the days of the German "Blitz" attacks (*Blitzkrieg,* or "lightning war") on English cities, which commenced in September 1940. Americans heard Murrow's nightly reports from London's streets beneath the howling of air-raid sirens and the thunderous pounding of bombs exploding around him. He announced, "This, is London . . ." and then described the devastation as fires raged in offices, shops, and homes, and innocent civilians scurried to air-raid shelters and subway stations. These broadcasts made a significant impact on the American people who were able to follow the experiences of those suffering the might of the German Air Force. From a government office in Washington, Murrow received a letter that encapsulated the profound reaction to his broadcasts: "You laid the dead of London at our doors and we knew the dead were our dead—were all men's dead, were mankind's dead."[5]

The American public was shocked by the reports of suffering inflicted on the civilian populations of English cities, with women and children among the many thousands of casualties. Bill Eagleson recalls:

> At that time, short-wave radio was the only means of getting information from Europe. Edward Murrow, I can remember his broadcasts, I can remember the "Bundles for Britain" campaign, I can remember the tots from London coming to the United States to avoid the terrible air attacks that London and other places in England were being subjected to. So we *did* have a feeling that we *were* going to be involved, in the European war.[6]

The United States was at first a reluctant ally, and the question of intervention in Europe was controversial. The United States' citizens considered theirs to be a peaceful nation built upon sound principles of freedom and democracy: that all men are created equal and that each nation has a right to self-determination. But the United States, born out of the British colonization from which it successfully won its independence, was also built upon the victory of conquest—of wars against the Native Americans, of violent territorial expansion condoned as "Manifest Destiny," and of manipulating other nations for its own gain.

Texas had been brought into the Union after the United States assisted in its struggle for independence from Mexico. The United States instigated the Mexican–American War of 1846 to 1848, which cost Mexico half of its territory (six of the present day southwestern U.S. states) and cost the United States fifteen million dollars (to clear its conscience of the issue of conquest). Half a century later U.S. forces invaded Cuba and Puerto Rico during the Spanish–American War. During the nineteenth century there were over one hundred incidents in which the United States intervened in the affairs of other countries, from Argentina to Nicaragua, Angola to Hawaii, Japan to China and the Philippines. The United States achieved the status of a powerful imperial force in both the Atlantic and Pacific oceans and set about creating the Panama Canal in an area that was then part of Colombia. Before the digging commenced, the United States broke a treaty with Colombia and financed a revolution in the Colombian province; in 1903 Panama became an independent country and granted the United States permission to build and control the Canal Zone—essentially a colony bridging the gap between U.S. interests in the Pacific and the Atlantic.

The sentiments of the 1823 Monroe Doctrine were still evident one hundred years later. This declaration from the era when Latin Americans were overthrowing Spanish rule and when North Americans were suspicious of British intentions, asserted the existence of a separate political system for the Western Hemisphere—a political system of U.S., rather than European, dominance in Latin America. In short, the Monroe Doctrine warned the European powers to "keep out of our back yard." With its own interests at heart, the United States assumed the role of leader and protector throughout the Americas, an assertion seen as patronizing, and therefore resented, by most of the countries in question that viewed the United States as the "Colossus of the North."[7]

The Monroe Doctrine also declared nonintervention by the United States in European affairs, but in 1917 the Great War brought Americans back to Europe to assist their allies. During the postwar era, the U.S. government continued to pursue policies of intervention in the affairs of other countries, not necessarily upon invitation. Troops were sent to Nicaragua, the Dominican Republic, Haiti, Cuba, Guatemala, and Honduras with various intentions ranging from protecting business interests, military installations, and consulates, to intervening in revolutionary unrest and "assisting" in elections. By the mid-1920s, the United States had significant influence over the economies of half of the Latin American countries. This modern form of imperialism allowed free access to world markets, but without the responsibilities of colonies or the wars of conquest of olden times.[8]

While the U.S. government looked outwards for opportunities of economic expansion, the American people focused their attention on domestic affairs. The victory of the Great War soon dissolved into cynicism and disillusionment within the United States. The war cost more than ten million lives, with many thousands of Americans among the dead. Furthermore, the war had significantly strained the U.S. economy, it had not brought democracy to the world or, as it would later transpire, lasting peace. The prevailing mood among the disillusioned American public was that the United States should in future not intervene in what were considered by many to be "other people's wars." Instead, the United States should concern itself with internal matters. Europe, the "Old World," should in future settle its own disputes and was no longer to be a concern, as long as it didn't pose an economic threat.

The American nation attempted to distance itself from outside influences. Amid fears of a flood of immigrants escaping war-scarred Europe, restrictive immigration quotas were implemented. There was an alarming resurgence of the Ku Klux Klan in the southern United States, in Indiana, and across the rural Midwest, where black Americans, Jews, and Catholics suffered prejudice and bigotry. Meanwhile, labor struggles existed and strikes were organized; but unionism, solidarity, and class consciousness were terms widely regarded as un-American.

The nation thrived upon production and profit. There was great demand for consumer and material goods such as radios, gramophones, refrigerators, and automobiles, while the world of mass media and the movies became an increasingly important part of American life. The 1920s saw the first real estate boom, while entrepreneurial prospectors speculating on the New York Stock Market created the Stock Exchange frenzy as risk and initiative became the keys to success. Some of these entrepreneurs were wealthy business people; others were ordinary working people with high aspirations and money borrowed for investment. From buying stocks when the prices fell and selling them when they rose, many individuals made their fortunes overnight. Individualism was revered; in his 1925 novel, *The Great Gatsby*, F. Scott Fitzgerald created a title character who epitomized this lifestyle.

The 1920s are remembered as the Jazz Age and the Golden Twenties. It was an age for Americans to live life to the fullest—but soberly, for alcohol was outlawed by Prohibition (although cocaine and marijuana were both legal). The Prohibition laws led to alcohol bootlegging and organized crime by gangsters such as Chicago's notorious Al Capone. Meanwhile, the heroes of the day included aviation pioneers such as Charles Lindbergh who flew his monoplane, *The Spirit of St. Louis,* nonstop from New York to Paris in 1927, the first solo transatlantic flight. The following year Amelia Earhart became the first woman to fly across the Atlantic (in 1932 she became the first woman to fly alone across the Atlantic). In the world of sports, baseball player Babe Ruth sealed his reputation as a living legend when he hit sixty home runs for the New York Yankees in 1927.

For the majority of Americans, the idea that the era was a time of prosperity was something of a myth. Subsistence living left little in the way of a disposable income with which to indulge in the party of the Jazz Age. Factory workers were often unable to afford the goods they produced, while in New York City two million people lived in tenements condemned as firetraps. Unemployment levels were low, but the wealthiest five percent of the population enjoyed one third of all personal income.[9]

American industry and agriculture became overproductive during the 1920s, leading to increasing quantities of surplus produce that could not be sold at profit. The Stock Exchange frenzy peaked toward the end of the decade when the actual value of stocks was far less than their market value, and inflated stock prices reached ever-higher levels. What had amounted to an artificial boom in the country's economy based upon a foundation of speculation led to panicked selling of some twenty-nine million shares within a six-day period in October 1929, culminating in the Wall Street Crash. Bankruptcy became widespread and unemployment levels soared. Looking for explanations, many Americans blamed the Great War for the collapse of the economy. The Golden Twenties were over; the Great Depression had begun. Subsequently, interconnected worldwide economies were in increasing states of turmoil. American loans to Europe were ended, coinciding with the collapse of a major Austrian bank and the destabilization of much of central and eastern Europe.

In the November 1932 presidential elections, the Democratic Party achieved a landslide victory. Democratic leader Franklin Delano Roosevelt promised a "New Deal" for the people of the United States. His policies of national recovery would, like the Depression itself, span the 1930s. To compound the problems of the Wall Street Crash, the agricultural industry suffered from relentless drought, heat waves, and the repercussions of intensive farming. The former grasslands of the Midwest and Great Plains were reduced to a "dust bowl." Domestic affairs were the priority, accentuating a climate of determined isolationism. However, in 1933 Roosevelt attempted to improve relations with Latin America, pledging to be a "good neighbor." Occupying U.S. forces were withdrawn.

In the neo-imperialist climate where wars of conquest were unnecessary, there had been little cause for expanding the military. Subsequently, during the isolationist climate of the 1930s, the military fell into decline—what need did an allegedly peaceful, politically isolated, neutral country have for a powerful military force? After all, the isolationists believed, the United States was insulated from international conflicts by the Atlantic and Pacific Oceans. The United States responded to Japan's yearning for economic expansion in the Far East with economic sanctions, and when Japan invaded China, several gunships were sent across the Pacific to protect American shipping. However, the United States refused to take military action when Japanese aircraft attacked an American ship in 1937. It seemed as if America was living in the shadow of a cloud constantly looming on the horizon.

In 1938, the U.S. Cavalry trained for war. Equipped with artillery hardware that had been declared inadequate in 1918, the Army had not even had a pay increase in almost as long. In 1939 the Army Air Corps had just three hundred aircraft.[10] Apprehensions increased at the prospect of America being involved again in "other people's wars." According to a 1939 poll, sixty-seven percent of Americans believed that America should remain neutral in the European situation, and the prevailing mood in the United States continued to be one of isolationism.[11] Advocates and critics of isolationism stemmed from both sides of the political spectrum, from both Republican and Democratic political parties.

Eventually, even those Americans who had previously believed the war between the Allied and the Axis powers to be an imperialist war began to see it in a different light. Unlike past conflicts, this seemed somehow to be a "just war," a "people's war" against oppressive Fascist regimes. From the perspective of the average American, it seemed that this war was not about securing empires or national gain, but about securing freedom for the people of the world. As a self-appointed protector of others, defender of liberty, and advocate of democracy (in theory if not always in practice), many Americans believed that the United States should not sit back and let tyranny prevail in Europe — the question of whether or not the United States involved itself in the European war was increasingly viewed as a moral issue.

By the end of 1940, President Roosevelt had begun to indirectly commit himself to the cause of America's allies and a gradual reversal of America's isolationism. During a radio broadcast from the White House in December 1940, Roosevelt declared: "One hundred and seventeen years ago the Monroe Doctrine was conceived by our government as a measure of defense in the face of a threat against this hemisphere by an alliance in Continental Europe. Thereafter, we stood guard in the Atlantic, with the British as neighbors. If Great Britain goes down, the Axis powers will control the continents of Europe, Asia, Africa, Australia, and the high seas — and they will be in a position to bring enormous military and naval resources against this hemisphere. It is no exaggeration to say that all of us, in all the Americas, would be living at the point of a gun — a gun loaded with explosive bullets, economic as well as military."

An invasion of Britain seemed imminent until June 1941, when Germany turned its attention towards Russia. Meanwhile, British resources were almost exhausted. The U.S. Congress revised the Neutrality Acts and passed the Lend-Lease Act, allowing arms, aircraft, and food consignments to be supplied to Britain on "loan" rather than by sale. The United States pulled itself out of the Depression and into prosperity by large-scale military spending.

American filmmakers, actors, entertainers, and musicians made a point of promoting the U.S. armed forces at every opportunity as the nation prepared for the possibility — or the inevitability — of war. Among the celebrity ranks promoting the forces was Glenn Miller. His hugely successful orchestra performed on live radio broadcasts during 1941, with segments of some shows catering specifically for the requests of young soldiers tuning in from Army and Navy camps all over America. Request time commenced with the rendition of a song, "It's Great to Be an American," which continued, "Live in the land of the free, be proud that you're an American, you stand for life, you stand for love and liberty!"[12] With an increasingly concerned and altruistic worldview, patriotism was paramount.

Those Americans who were destined to fight on the front lines of the war generally knew little about international politics, were too young to comprehend the history of nations or the traditions and past conquests of empires. Instead they were compelled by a sense of urgency for the present moment. To the majority of this generation of Americans, born and raised in peacetime, maturing to face a world war, it was clear to see that Fascism, particularly in Nazi Germany, was an evil threat to the world and had to be stopped.

By December 1941 the city of Boston, like the whole United States, seemed to be waiting in anticipation. In Watertown there were troops stationed in the town maintenance buildings while anti-aircraft batteries had been placed across the surrounding hills close to the Oakley Country Club where Bill Eagleson had previously taught skiing. He recalls:

> We at college, of course, we were working to get our grades and, we were aware that there would be a war, and we were aware that we would be involved. And our professors seemed to, as I remember, convey to us the correct meanings of what was happening in the world with the concern for Adolf Hitler and his quest for *Lebensraum* (room for living) in Germany and throughout the world.

Then on 7 December 1941 the Japanese attacked the U.S. Naval base at Pearl Harbor in Hawaii at a cost of two thousand lives.

> That was almost like a complete surprise because early on in the 1930s, I remember as a kid we were thinking of the Japanese invasion of China and the atrocities that were going on in that country. Then it was sort of covered over or *dimmed*, by the activities in Europe and our papers and everything were oriented to Europe and not to the Pacific. So Sunday December 7 was a very surprising day for all of us. It was a day that brought about . . . *anger*. It did change our lives—all of us—and of course on Monday we declared war and we were in it with your guys [the British].

On 8 December 1941 the United States declared war on Japan and three days later Japan's allies—the Axis powers, Germany and Italy—declared war on the United States.

On the Monday following Pearl Harbor, I remember that the School [of Physical Education, Boston University] and the city of Boston was evacuated due to possibilities of an enemy attack! The following day our class met again, and almost unanimously we talked about which service we were going to join, when we were going to join, and at the guidance of our professors and others, we decided that we would be out of college after our final exams in January. To my recollection, January finals were the final phase of this part of our education, and my class did split up at that time, going to the Navy, Air Force, Marines. Even later on our professors were involved with reserve training, and 84 Exeter Street, Boston University was a rather desolate spot even six months after Pearl Harbor.

So the motivation for me was to join up with the ski troops, and I applied through the National Ski Association, enlisted February 1942, and went off to Camp Roberts for basic infantry training.

Located over two thousand miles away from Boston, Camp Roberts, California, was a vast training center for infantry and field artillery troops with a parade ground the length of fourteen football fields. Many of the thousands of troops that populated the camp at any one time were quartered in large "tent cities." The camp facilitated an intensive seventeen-week training cycle, and on completion of his time there, Bill Eagleson was assigned to the 87th Mountain Infantry at Fort Lewis in the state of Washington.

The 87th Mountain Infantry Battalion was the first U.S. Army mountaineering unit and had been activated three weeks prior to the Japanese attack on Pearl Harbor. An intensive recruitment campaign followed. The National Ski Patrol was the official recruiting agency — the president of this civilian organization had previously lobbied the War Department to train troops for winter and mountainous warfare. With several years of college, skiing and ski instructing experience, as well as having reached the mature age of twenty-two, Bill Eagleson was destined to be an officer in the 87th.

At the time of the unit's activation there was a shortage of officers with winter and mountain experience. There were however, a significant number of German, Austrian, and Swiss recruits, many of whom had received training in mountainous warfare during their military service prior to settling in America — however, the U.S. Army wasn't prepared to make officers out of recent immigrants. Notably, the personnel assigned to the 87th Mountain Infantry also included world-famous skiers, mountaineers, forest rangers, and horsemen along with a regular Army cadre. From Fort Lewis the 87th was moved to Jolon, California, in November 1942 for maneuvers — personnel who had enlisted to ski found themselves learning to ride mules:

> We trained in mountain transport with mules and I was rather disillusioned as a ski instructor to find myself as a mule jockey. So I

saw my First Sergeant and said, "Sarge, I'd like to go down to King City and take the Air Force exam. What do you think?" He said "Go ahead!" So I got a pass and went down to King City and took the I.Q exams and so forth.

Meanwhile a brand new camp named Camp Hale had been constructed in Colorado and was situated 9,480 feet above sea level. The 87th moved there in December 1942 and rock-climbing classes were established as the unit commenced extreme cold-weather and high-altitude training. They tested new equipment such as laminated skis, release bindings, rucksacks, jackets, stoves, sleeping bags, combined ski-mountain boots, and nylon ropes. There was so much skiing and mountaineering to do that Bill almost forgot about flying:

> Our ski troops were moved to Camp Hale, Colorado—and we had snow, we had skiing and, all of a sudden, early January my orders came through to get to Santa Ana Air Base in California to go through the cadet preflight.
>
> Of course, I was happy to get the raise in pay. . . . When we started in the army it was $21 a month, then it went up to $50 a month I believe in July of '42. And when I went into cadet pre-flight, we were getting the big sum of $75 a month. So all of a sudden I was rich and I could afford cigarettes and chewing gum and all that good stuff.

Under the jurisdiction of the West Coast Army Air Force Training Command, there were no aircraft at Santa Ana—the base provided preflight training to pilots, navigators, and bombardiers. On arrival the cadets were each given "an informal personal letter" signed by Colonel W. A. Robertson, the commanding officer of Santa Ana Army Air Base. Tackling the issues of training and discipline the letter was addressed to "All aviation cadets of this command": "This letter is written with the hope that it may inspire within you a more earnest desire to prepare yourselves to more effectively serve your country in this her hour of gravest danger in her entire history." The letter went on to state that the cadets were training to become soldiers, aircrew members, and that they were "young and inexperienced" without "a complete understanding of what is best" for them. The letter continued: "What we are trying to do is train those qualities given you by your blessed heritage, so that you may be molded into a fighting, efficient, aggressive, and intelligent member of a smooth-functioning, fighting Aircrew. America is a peaceful nation; Americans are peaceful people. Our abilities and tremendous resources have been trained for humanitarian and peaceful purposes. The necessity for becoming tough fighting men has been forced upon us. . . . We've *got* to become tough fighting men in order to succeed. . . . Courage alone will not be sufficient. It's got to be courage made efficient by training and discipline. If you've guts enough to face your enemy, have guts enough to go through the rigorous training and discipline necessary to equip you to face that enemy. Let's don't resign ourselves to the fact that we have courage enough to die for our country. What we want to do is to have courage enough to go through the necessary stages of preparation, no matter how tough they appear to be, so that we can fight for our country and *live* for our country. All of us who are trying to train you, want everyone of you to live to go home to those loved ones who are so proud of you. We are trying to train you so that you can fight and win and go back home to the ones who love you, and there take up the task of restoring a war-torn world to peaceful enterprises and the progress of civilization and Christianity."

In the patriotic fervor of the times, for many of the cadets arriving at Santa Ana with the anticipation and excitement of adventures ahead, self-righteous comments such as "the task of restoring a war-torn world" for the "progress of Christianity" might have seemed acceptable. Others, the Jewish cadets for example, could only feel uncomfortable or bewildered by such remarks that resonated as ignorance. All of the cadets, regardless of their religion, were motivated by the urgency of the times, and felt the need to serve their country because they felt blessed to be Americans. Religious freedom was a value worth fighting for; the "progress of Christianity" was something different altogether.

At Santa Ana a challenging period of intense learning commenced. Bill Eagleson considered himself fortunate that he had gained a head start in what he described as "military orientation":

> There was a great deal of media and show business influence here in the States. We trained as cadets in Santa Ana, California, and we were right close to Hollywood and the Hollywood stars. Desi Arnaz was in our training cadre at Santa Ana, so Lucille Ball used to spend her time up there. I think Gene Raymond was an instructor at the base, Joe Lewis was a PT instructor; Joe DiMaggio, the baseball player, was a PT instructor.
>
> The civilian population around Hollywood, California, treated us very, very nicely. . . . At the time the Air Force was seen by the American public as sort of the glamour boys, particularly the cadets. The cadets were the babies of the Air Force, and people did wonderful things for us and they knew that we were working hard to get our wings. We wore semi-officer uniforms and when we went into the Ambassador Hotel in Los Angeles we always were assured of a warm reception and a good evening.

The cadets of the early 1940s had been born into the pioneering years of aviation, where flying held a particularly glamorous and adventurous appeal, especially to ambitious male teenagers. The Army Air Force offered opportunities for thousands of young men to fly, and aviation held such prestige that many young aviators believed that they were part of an elite or chosen few. Even before Pearl Harbor, many would-be American aviators went to Canada to enlist in the Royal Canadian

Lt. Bill Eagleson, 1943.
(Bill Eagleson)

Air Force, and since the days of the Battle of Britain the Royal Air Force had operated three highly successful American Eagle Squadrons. Besides being intent on fighting for a cause they believed in, the American volunteer aviators of the pre- and post–Pearl Harbor eras were eager to take to the skies.

Bill Eagleson celebrated his twenty-third birthday soon after arriving at Santa Ana—many of his contemporaries in officer preflight training were in their early twenties, others were still in their late teens—not yet recognized as being old enough to vote; some of the cadets had not yet left home or led independent lives; many of them were college students; others had been employed since leaving school and had begun to enjoy their independence, while others had experienced the hardships of unemployment. Following Pearl Harbor there was never any shortage of volunteers for the Army Air Force, which offered not only a wage and a sense of purpose, but also an opportunity to travel and to experience the vastness of the United States and the rest of the world. Most of Bill's contemporaries had never flown prior to volunteering for the Army Air Force, but he recalls:

> I had flown in a Curtis Robin over Boston—some foolish thing like that, but no serious flying.

Although at Santa Ana Army Air Base there was no flying, there was a lot of work to be completed on the ground.

> Training—Intense primary learning, many of our methods from RAF Cadre in the States and England.

Bill worked hard with a full study schedule that included mathematics, Morse code, first aid, aircraft recognition, and extensive physical training. Soon he was classified as a bombardier; the preflight studying continued and by the middle of April 1943 this stage of training had been completed. Later that month Bill was transferred to bombardier school near the town of Deming in the desert of New Mexico where flight training commenced. At Deming all bombardiers were required to take the "Bombardier's Oath":

> Mindful of the secret trust about to be placed in me by my Commander in Chief, the President of the United States, by whose direction I have been chosen for bombardier training . . . and mindful of the fact that I am to become guardian of one of my country's most priceless military assets, the American bombsight . . . I do here, in the presence of Almighty God, swear by the Bombardier's Code of Honor to keep inviolate the secrecy of any and all confidential information revealed to me, and further to uphold the honor and integrity of the Army Air Forces, if need be, with my life itself.

The Norden bombsight was famous—it became a household name, and the American public understood that it would help win the war. However, other than its existence, all other details were classified as restricted due to the advanced technology of the sight (the security classification had been reduced from "top secret" to "confidential" and then "restricted" to allow production and training). Bombardiers were under orders to destroy the Norden sight with their .45 caliber handguns in the event of a forced landing in enemy occupied territory.

The Norden was an analog computer, and the bombardier's job was to program factors such as bomb ballistics, deflection, wind drift, air

speed, and altitude. The bombs had to be dropped upwind and some
time before the aircraft was directly over the target. The type and
weight of bombs as well as wind and air resistance were key factors in
the creation of mathematic tables used to calculate "trail" adjustments,
for which the sight was set accordingly. The optical part of the sight was
a telescope with two crosshairs, one horizontal and the other vertical.
The horizontal hair related to the range to the target, and a control dial
on the right side of the bombsight altered the position of the hair across
the target aiming point; the vertical hair could be fixed to the target by a
control dial on the left of the sight, indicating the course to the identified target.

The course was relayed from the bombsight to the pilot via the Pilot
Directional Indicator (PDI) on the flight deck's instrument panel.
Therefore, as the pilot maintained a straight and level flight during the
bomb run, the bombardier dictated the required lateral movements.
This enabled the bombardier to "kill" drift by precise adjustment of the
sight as long as the pilot concentrated on keeping the PDI needle centered. Finally, the sight would indicate the exact moment that the bombardier needed to release the bombs. As an alternative to PDI, Auto-
matic Flight Control Equipment (AFCE) such as the A-5 autopilot
could be employed.

The technology of the Norden sight allowed significant potential for
accuracy, at least in training conditions. It was widely claimed in the
American media that the Norden bombsight was so powerfully accurate
that a bomb could be dropped into a pickle barrel from an altitude of
twenty thousand feet. However, skeptics often remarked that, even with
a telescope, you couldn't see a pickle barrel from twenty thousand feet!
But if nothing else, the hype and the mystery that surrounded the
Norden boosted morale.

In learning the skills required to operate the Norden bombsight
there was a scarcity of written manuals due to the bombsight's restricted
classification, as Bill Eagleson recalls:

> We did not have tech manuals on the Norden bombsights, so in the
> learning process our "notes" were most important.

Over desert ranges near Deming the bombardiers participated in
practice bombing missions in training aircraft. The "bombs" were filled
with sand and contained a bursting charge that emitted smoke that
would provide an indication of accuracy in relation to the target. A
pilot would take up two bombardier cadets at a time for these training
missions—while one bombardier dropped half the bombs the other
would film the results with a movie camera and the film would later be
evaluated. The elimination rate for bombardiers was twelve percent—
those who were "washed out" were mostly transferred for training in
other roles.

I still remember days at Deming, New Mexico: 0530, Reveille; 0600, Physical Training; 0800–1200, Ground School; 1400–1600, Ground School; 2000–2400, Night Bombing followed by Critiques. Every day was survival time, and washout boards met frequently.

There wasn't much leisure once we got to the flying phase of bombardiering. As I recall I got into Deming . . . and the first time that I left the base was the night before we graduated—I never did get to see the town at Deming, but there wasn't too much in the town anyway . . . Advanced Training (Flight) was April, May, June, and we graduated July 31st, Class 43–11.

CHAPTER TWO

Boise, Idaho

B ill Eagleson was now a Second Lieutenant and a qualified bombardier in the Army Air Force, and although several months of aircrew training were to follow, he was allowed a few days furlough, giving him the opportunity to return home to New England. When the time came in early August 1943 for him to report back for duty, he took a train one evening from Boston and woke up the following morning in Illinois. In the city of Chicago he boarded a Pullman that would take him westward to Boise, Idaho.

As the steam locomotive gathered speed out of Chicago, a fateful meeting occurred. Bill struck up a conversation with a fellow Army Air Force Lieutenant by the name of John Nortridge, who introduced himself as Jack. The two young officers enjoyed their conversations as the vast cornfields of Illinois drifted endlessly past the carriage window. Once a distant frontier, following the forced resettlement of Native American tribes to the west of the Mississippi River one hundred years previously and the subsequent Black Hawk War of 1832, large numbers of Europeans had settled in the region. To twenty-five-year-old Jack Nortridge, the Midwestern state of Illinois was home.

Jack Nortridge was born and raised in the town of Freeport, less than one hundred miles from Chicago. The town originated as a trading post on the banks of the Pecatonica River and subsequently the settlement became a significant stagecoach stop between Chicago and Galena. Although this was just one hundred years previously, to the young people of Jack's generation Freeport's olden days—when the town resembled something out of a "Wild West" movie—seemed almost like ancient history. In 1858 Freeport was the location of the second Lincoln-Douglas debate. These debates gained national popularity for Lincoln, who was elected president in 1860, just prior to the outbreak of the American Civil War over issues of slavery and states' rights.

At the time of Jack's birth, Freeport had a population of approximately twenty-five thousand citizens, mostly of either Irish or German descent. A very typical Midwestern town, during the 1930s Freeport's principal industry was the W. T. Rawleigh Company, which sold household products door-to-door. Freeport was also the home of the Burgess Battery Company, a significant local industry and employer during those times. Jack's father, John Henry Nortridge, had been the proprietor of the North Ridge Brush Company during the 1920s and 1930s, quite a

Hometowns and training bases in the United States for *Corky*'s crew.

John "Jack" Nortridge in the Army Air Corps circa 1941. (Vale Nortridge)

large company in Freeport manufacturing household brushes. These were sold door-to-door by up to four hundred company salesmen and supplied in bulk to companies such as Proctor and Gamble who used them for promotional premiums.

Jack's father, John Henry Nortridge, was born in Omro, Wisconsin. His parents were said to have been Protestant Irish, and there was also believed to be a connection with West Ham in East London, England, where there were Nortridges living during the eighteenth century. Some members of the family believed that even further back in time, their ancestors had lived in a place called North Ridge in Norway, from where the family took their name. Even so, Jack Nortridge considered himself American—but, as he would later tell his eldest son, he was half Irish, half English, and then he would lick his little finger and wipe it on something in midair and say, "and this much French." The link to France remains a mystery.

John Henry and his wife settled in Freeport in 1910 with their two children, Harold and Florence. However, following a divorce the children stayed with John Henry, who later remarried. His second wife, Sarah Austin, gave birth to a daughter, Jean, and then on 9 November 1917 John "Jack" Austin Nortridge was born in Freeport, the town that he would always call home. But then tragedy struck the Nortridge family. Jack's mother gave birth to a third child, a daughter, who died a few hours after her birth and then Jack's mother passed away days later.

Jack's father was left to raise the four children and run the family business. Legend has it that he always answered the telephone abruptly: "Busy man, be brief." He hired a live-in housekeeper and nanny named Nellie who was of German descent and was the Sunday school teacher and choir leader at his church. Soon John Henry married her, and in 1922 Nellie gave birth to a son, Vale. To all the Nortridge children, Nellie was called "Ma."

The Nortridge family. Standing: Harold and John Henry. Seated: Jean, Sarah, Jack, and Florence. (Susan Nortridge)

The children attended Harlem Grade School, at 121 North

Harlem Avenue, just around the corner from the family's home. Jack went on to attend Freeport Junior High and then Freeport High School. He had many friends, a busy social life, and even played trombone in the school band. Then, for two years he studied at Cornell College in Mount Vernon, Iowa (ten miles east of Cedar Rapids), but unfortunately he was unable to complete his course due to financial difficulties. The effects of the Depression years had taken their toll and hit the family business quite hard through the 1930s, not to mention the misfortune of a fire in one of the factory buildings. While in the cheery advertising style of the day, one of the North Ridge Brush Company brochures exclaimed with a sense of ease, "Brush away your troubles with North Ridge brushes," the reality was not so optimistic and carefree.

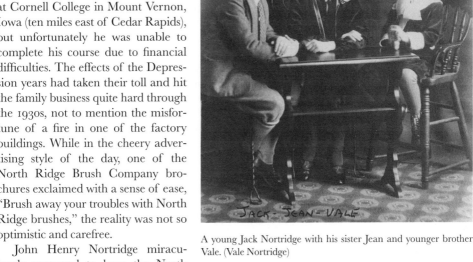

A young Jack Nortridge with his sister Jean and younger brother Vale. (Vale Nortridge)

John Henry Nortridge miraculously managed to keep the North Ridge Brush Company in business throughout the Great Depression, even though he couldn't sell the brushes that his company manufactured. Legend has it that John Henry filled warehouses with stock rather than see his employees lose their jobs. He made and lost his million — but he did it in style!

When finances for Jack's studies at Cornell College dried up, he moved out west to Los Angeles, California, where for several years he worked in drug stores and resorts, trying to make ends meet. For a while he worked in Lake Arrowhead, California, very popular at the time with Hollywood's movie stars, a number of whom Jack had the opportunity to meet. It was while Jack was in California that his father, John Henry, became ill with prostate cancer. Following his death in March 1939, the family business and family home were sold. With John Henry's life insurance, Nellie bought a duplex house on West Pleasant Street, Freeport. She lived on the ground floor and rented out the upper floor to supplement her teaching salary.

In reaction to the war that had erupted in Europe, and another step away from U.S. isolationism, a new law was passed in September 1940: the Selective Service Act. This was the United States' first peacetime conscription, and all men aged twenty-one to thirty-six were legally required to register for the draft. Jack was almost twenty-three and after registering, he volunteered for the Army Air Corps and was accepted. Jack had never really shown any particular interest in aviation, unlike his younger brother, Vale, who later joined the Army Air Force and served in the South Pacific as a control tower officer during 1944 and 1945. Jack's decision would significantly determine the course of the next few years of Jack's life. Besides education and experience, the Air Corps, as it was known at the time, offered a good wage and future prospects. It seemed as if Jack's life was taking shape—but then, Pearl Harbor.

In Sikeston, Missouri, on 26 March 1942 Jack wed Evelyn Hughes, a native of Freeport whom he had dated a few times in high school. Evelyn's grandfather, known as "Bill Chief," was the assistant chief of police in Freeport on his retirement. Following flight school in Missouri, Jack was transferred to Goodfellow Field, San Angelo, Texas, to continue flying training. On 20 July Jack left behind his cadet status when he was commissioned as a Second Lieutenant at Moore Field, Mission, Texas, and he received his wings at Kelly Field, Texas.

After being commissioned, officers were allowed to live off base, and so Jack and Evelyn lived together in rented accommodation in Texas (where Evelyn took a dislike to the scorpions) and later at Mac-Dill Field, Tampa, Florida. From MacDill Field, Jack trained in Martin Marauders, also known as the B-26—a fast, twin-engine "medium" bomber. This early version of the B-26, noted for its short wingspan became known as the "Flying Prostitute" in that it had "no visible means of support." Pilots testified that it was a volatile and merciless aircraft to fly requiring extremely high speeds for take off and landing. The frequency of serious incidents and fatal accidents involving

Detroit, Michigan, 1942. Left to right: Lt. Jack Nortridge; his brother-in-law, Dr. David Lynn; his sister, Jean Lynn; his wife, Evelyn; his eldest sister, Florence, and her husband, Bill Beatty. (Vale Nortridge)

inexperienced pilots added to the aircraft's notoriety. In Florida the Martin Marauder also became known as the "Martin Murderer" and even the "Widow Maker" as the legend followed, *One a day in Tampa Bay!* But Jack proved himself a competent pilot and was next assigned to "heavy" bombers.

On the train from Chicago, Jack told Bill Eagleson about his more recent flying experience with one particular four-engine, heavy bomber, the Consolidated B-24 Liberator—he added that he was now destined for aircrew training with a new B-24 unit. Jack and Bill compared their orders and realized that they were both destined for aircrew training at the same base, Gowen Field, Boise, Idaho. Since they seemed to get on so well, they decided that if they could they would like to be crewmates. And so the nucleus of a combat crew was formed, with vacancies for two more officers and six enlisted men.

The journey to Idaho was still young when the Pullman steam locomotive crossed the Mississippi River and proceeded across the Great Plains, all the while trailing a cloud of steam and smoke over Iowa and Nebraska, along the route of the Union Pacific Railroad. It was the railroad that finally conquered the plains for America's white settlers less than fifty years previously—the Atlantic and Pacific seaboards became just a week's journey apart, but at a tragic cost to the Native American inhabitants of the plains. The journey from Chicago to Idaho would take only a couple of days and two uncomfortable nights. The plains eventually gave way to the Rocky Mountains, which the railroad cut through toward Utah.

Eventually Jack Nortridge and Bill Eagleson found themselves in the hills of Idaho. Gowen Field near Boise was the home of the 29th Bombardment Group, which served as a parent organization responsible for the development of new Bomb Groups, the assignment of personnel and the supervision of combat crew training. Following activation in June 1943, a new unit designated the 453rd (Heavy) Bombardment Group had been established at Gowen Field under the command of Colonel Joseph A. Miller, a graduate of the United States Military Academy at West Point with thirteen years subsequent military service.

Initially the personnel assigned to the 453rd Bomb Group were drawn from the parent unit, and a detachment of flying personnel spent July training in Florida while Group Headquarters personnel remained at Gowen Field to organize the unit's development. In early August the 453rd Bomb Group was in the process of moving to their new base at Pocatello, Idaho, located two hundred miles from Boise. Destined for the 453rd Bomb Group, Bill Eagleson flew through check flights with Jack Nortridge and admired his flying skills.

> The initial cadre of pilots for the 453rd I believe came from Mac-Dill Field down in Tampa, and these people were flying B-26s, then

known as a *Widow Maker* . . . but it made damn good pilots out of these fellas.

Sgt. William "Bill" LeRoy, radio operator and waist gunner. (Bill LeRoy)

Jack Nortridge was designated a first pilot, airplane commander, and Bill Eagleson was assigned as his bombardier. While at Gowen Field, Jack and Bill met some more contenders for their crew. Sergeant William "Bill" LeRoy was a twenty-year-old radio operator born in St. Louis, Missouri, on 14 December 1922. The son of Mr. and Mrs. Charles LeRoy of 4282 Farlin Avenue, St. Louis, Bill trained as a cadet at Jefferson Barracks, Missouri, and at Miami Beach, Florida. At Scott Field, Illinois, he completed radio school and then at Gowen Field, Idaho, he attended gunnery school, developing his skills with the .50 caliber machine gun both on the ground at the gunnery ranges and in the air, shooting holes in targets towed behind aircraft. His last furlough was back in March and he did not expect further leave to return home to St. Louis for a couple more months.

Twenty-one-year-old Sergeant James Freddie Witmer joined Jack Nortridge's crew at Gowen Field, as ball turret gunner and assistant engineer. James, who is remembered as a quiet guy, was born in Dallas, Texas, on 30 September 1921. His parents, Albert and Ethel Witmer, had since relocated to Texarkana, a city that had been founded as little more than a railroad junction and had since prospered to become a major railroad center of the Southwest. Legend has it that an Arkansas railroad surveyor nailed a sign to a tree that stated, "Texarkana. This is the name of a town which is to be built here." Named for the states of Texas, Arkansas, and Louisiana, it transpired that Louisiana was twenty-five miles to the south. The Texas–Arkansas state line runs through the center of the downtown area and during the early 1920s the Texas side of the town had a population of over eleven thousand.

Many of the city's inhabitants worked for the railroads or in the processing of agricultural products, although a significant number of the local businesses closed during the Depression. However, Texarkana's fortunes recovered at the start of the Second World War with the construction of the Red River Army Depot and the Lone Star Ordnance Plant, a few miles west of the city.

James and his sister, Nadine, were raised on a dairy farm in Texas, located between Redwater and Texarkana, not far from the Texarkana city limits. Known to his family as "Freddie," his middle name, but always as James to his Air Force companions, he graduated from the Redwater School, approximately eight miles from Texarkana. However, around this time his parents were forced to sell the farm to the government upon the proposal of the two ordnance factories. Albert and Ethel purchased two hundred acres in Arkansas, approximately four miles south of Texarkana on Route 1, one and a half miles east of South State Line Road.

Following Pearl Harbor, James found employment at the Lone Star Ordnance Plant, on the site of the Witmer's former farm, which was producing artillery shells, bombs, fuses, and so on. In August 1942 he volunteered for the Army Air Force and continued working until he was called to active service. James received his military training at Keesler Field, Mississippi, and Harlingen Gunnery School, Texas, where he was awarded his gunner's wings. Following graduation James was based at Salt Lake City, Utah, and Del Rio, Texas, where he met Hazel Celum—they married on 7 June 1943.

The Witmer family in 1936, left to right: James Freddie Witmer, James Albert Witmer, Ethel Clark Witmer, and Nadine Witmer. James was almost fifteen years old when this photograph was taken. Seven years later he was assigned to Crew 25 as ball turret gunner and assistant flight engineer. (Nadine Witmer Gibson)

James Freddie Witmer married Hazel Celum on 7 June 1943. (Hazel Witmer)

Twenty year old Sergeant Perry Roberson, a Southern farm boy, joined the Nortridge crew at Gowen Field, as first flight engineer and air gunner. Born near Midland City, Alabama, on 20 July 1923, Perry was the eldest child in a close-knit family who always called him Donald since his father was also called Perry.[1] "Donald" came from Perry's middle name, MacDonald, and considering that this was also his father's middle name, it suggests perhaps some Scottish ancestry on the paternal side of the family; some of Perry Jr.'s paternal ancestors are known to have settled in America prior to the American Revolution.

On his maternal side, one of Perry Jr.'s great-grandfathers was allegedly born in Glasgow, Scotland, and traveled to America at the age of nine as a stowaway on board a ship. Other maternal ancestors traveled from Ireland and Scotland in the early 1800s, and settled in Maryland before migrating south to Alabama where they became some of the first Anglo-American settlers. Alabama was a Creek Indian name meaning "Here we may rest," but ironically, white settlers and land companies defrauded the Creeks of their land during events that culminated in the Creek Wars of the early nineteenth century—the Native Americans were pushed ever westward.

Perry Jr.'s father and Uncle Tullis were both veterans of the Great War. According to family legend, Perry Sr. served in the 81st Division and arrived on the front lines in France on the day the war ended, while Tullis served in the 115th Division and is believed to have been involved in combat. A couple of years after they returned to the United States, the two Roberson brothers married two sisters—Perry Sr. married Mattie Joe Cason and Tullis married Ruby Cason.

A few months after Mattie Joe gave birth to Perry Jr., Ruby gave birth to a boy they named Byron. They were "double-first-cousins" and being the same age, Perry Jr. and Byron seemed more like twin brothers. They started first grade together in the fall of 1930 and went all through their school years in the same classes. Meanwhile two of Perry Jr. sisters were born, Leora and Sallie, and three more cousins, Harold, Miriam, and William, before the end of the decade. Another cousin named Virgil was born in July 1931 with Down's syndrome.

During their first few years of marriage, Perry Sr. and Mattie Joe lived as tenant farmers in various places around Midland City. Mattie Joe's father, Papa Cason, lived with them while Tullis and Ruby, also tenant farmers, lived close by throughout the 1920s. At the onset of the Great Depression, Congress voted to allow the veterans of World War I to borrow fifty percent of the value of the bonds that they had been awarded as compensation. These bonds were to mature over a twenty-year period until the time when the veterans were allowed to cash them, but the loans gave them access to money sooner. Perry Sr. and Tullis put their money together and used it as a down payment on a farm, and in 1931 they purchased nearly two hundred acres in the Echo community of Dale County. The farm was located eighteen miles from the small town of Ozark in southern Alabama. The Roberson family made quite an impression on their arrival in Echo, riding in a mule-drawn wagon with automobile tires.

Roberson family siblings and cousins on the farm in Echo, Alabama, circa 1931. Left to right: Sallie Wade (Perry's sister), Byron (cousin), Leora (sister), Perry, Harold (cousin), and Miriam (cousin). (Ruby Jo Roberson Faust)

Perry Sr. and Tullis farmed their land as partners, and the two families shared all resources as jointly owned—an arrangement that would last for forty years. During the first year at Echo, the two families lived almost a mile apart with just a dirt road between them, but since the barn and the family garden were near Tullis and Ruby's house, that area became the center of activity. Perry Jr.'s family lived in an unpainted, roughly constructed tenant-type house, and soon his mother persuaded the men to move the house up the road to be closer to Tullis and Ruby.

The Robersons frequented Echo Methodist Church, where the kids also attended Sunday school—they made the journey in a cart towed by an ox or in a rubber-tired wagon. Later they purchased a used Dodge touring car with a large back-seat area—the Dodge soon gained legendary status as the men seated on the front porch of Echo Church marveled at the spectacle of seeing so many people emerge from one car. One time on a trip out of Echo they got stuck in a bog after a rain storm and a local "Negro" man (the term "African American" hadn't been invented yet) known to the kids as Mr. Rob, waded through the water to rescue them. Perry Sr. was a member of the local Baptist Church, but often he preferred long walks across the fields on a Sunday.

Perry Jr. and Byron walked to Echo School along a path through the woods and their Aunt Eunice, who stayed and worked on the farm for a while, usually walked with them to keep them out of trouble. All the Roberson children took sandwiches to school made from produce grown on the farm (scrambled eggs with sausage, homemade peanut butter and jelly), except for the flour for the large, flat biscuits, which were used in place of bread. Later Perry Jr. attended Dale County High School in Ozark where he played football and attracted many female admirers—one of Leora's classmates declared that Perry Jr. looked like a Greek god!

During the summer months, some of the Roberson children enjoyed swimming in the creek that marked the boundary of the farm, as well as the boundaries of Dale and Henry Counties. On one occasion Perry Jr. dived into the creek, hit his head and fractured three vertebrae in his neck. Luckily he survived and made a full recovery.

Getting up early to milk the cows was standard procedure prior to walking a mile to catch the bus to Ozark. Responsibilities after school included "slopping" hogs, following a mule with a plough, hoeing weeds, and gathering vegetables, peanuts, and corn. All the Roberson children grew up helping on the farm and attending to whatever needed to be done, including Virgil, a happy child who involved himself with all activities on the farm.

Alabama is inseparably part of the Deep South, characteristically the land of the cotton plantation, of the sharecropper and tenant farmer, and the home of the Blues. Although slavery had been abolished following the American Civil War, the inequalities of Jim Crow Laws continued to prevail across the South, where blacks were segregated from whites in schools, transport, and most other public and social areas. One million African Americans served in the United States' armed forces during World War II, but even the military was segregated.

Some of the land around Echo, Alabama, was farmed by African American tenant farmers; many other farms were run by white farmers and employed black laborers. The Roberson farm generally employed no laborers, white or black, since there were so many family members to share the workload and often not enough money to pay for outside labor.

The Robersons' land was notably sandy and difficult to grow crops on. They attempted for a few years to grow cotton, but gave up. Still, the farm was theirs (despite almost losing it at one point in the early 1930s when it was put up for auction) and it was successful enough to ensure that there was always food to eat, even throughout the Depression years. However, for extra income during the 1930s both Perry Sr. and Tullis joined the Civilian Conservation Corps, one of Roosevelt's New Deal employment programs, and worked away from home for varying lengths of time, leaving the rest of the family to manage the farm.

Mattie Joe gave birth to another daughter, Ruby Jo, in 1938 and then to another boy, Jimmy, in 1940—by the time Jimmy was born the farm had expanded significantly when Perry Sr. and Tullis bought some land from an adjoining farm. This land included two houses situated three hundred yards apart and separated by a barn, some pine trees, and a slope in the landscape. The families moved into them and everyone agreed that the "new" houses were more comfortable despite having no interior doors. For privacy, blankets and quilts were hung across the doorways, fireplaces provided heating in the winter months, and food was cooked in wood-burning stoves. There was no electricity or indoor plumbing. Water was fetched from a well and bathing was done in a washtub, except during the summer when a fifty-five gallon drum with a short piece of hose served as a shower. There was an outdoor toilet and a kerosene lamp was used for late night visits.

During the mid-1930s, thirty percent of Americans still lived on farms—most were without electricity. Another one of President Roosevelt's many New Deal programs, the Rural Electrification Administration, acknowledged the importance of the farmer and provided millions of people with electricity. In 1941 electric power lines reached the Echo community and on the Robersons' farm an electric pump was installed in the well, providing the houses with running water.

Electricity allowed radio broadcasts of both American and world-wide events—landmarks in time which pronounced the era—to reach and touch the lives of a young generation who matured to face a world at war. As Europe and the Far East were being swallowed up by totalitarianism, whichever way one looked, these were unsettling times of increasing anxieties. Until the Rural Electrification Act, national and international news came to the Roberson farm via the daily *Montgomery Advertiser*. Published in the state capital almost one hundred miles away, it arrived by mail a day later. Local news came from the weekly *Southern Star*, published in Ozark since the 1800s. But now the Robersons could keep up to date with world events by tuning in their new radio—it was around this time that Japanese planes attacked Pearl Harbor and the United States entered the war.

Five months after Pearl Harbor, Perry Jr. and Byron graduated from high school. This was a significant time for Perry Jr., who also started dating a girl named Elizabeth Fields. Having recently moved to Echo, Elizabeth's father was an officer in the Army and had been sent as finance officer to the new base in Dale County—Camp Rucker.

By September 1942, Perry Jr. was living in Mobile, Alabama, where he worked in the shipyards. It wasn't his first away-from-home experience since he and Byron had spent the summer of 1941 working with the Civilian Conservation Corps (CCC) in Alabama and Florida, when the New Deal program was broadened to find employment for young people. On 22 September 1942 Perry Jr. wrote home from Mobile saying that he had found a better place to stay:

> The place I can get is a private room in a family. Where I am now there are three more men in the same room with me while the place I can get will be just me and one more in the room and that is a boy I work with out at the shipyard. The man who is renting it also works out at the office. I can get the room for $4 a week but I don't know how much it will cost me to eat.
>
> I want you to send my football sweater and coat because it's real cool down here in the early morning. You might send my jacket if daddy didn't wear it out and some of those best CCC undershirts if there are any left that aren't worn out.

At the end of October Perry Jr. wrote:

> Mr. Fisher, the man I board with said he would buy all the meat
> you could send me. If you have some sausage or a ham I sure
> would like to wade into some sausage some of these cool mornings.
> Meat is hard to get down here. The market just can't get it.
>
> We are putting another ship in the water Sunday. That makes
> six they've launched since I've been with the Gulf. The number of
> employees have increased from 10,000 to 12,000 since I started. I
> guess by the time I leave they will have a real shipyard here.
> They've got it now where we have to lay off during the week for
> working on Sunday. Won't let us make but 54 hours a week now.
> We have to lay off just as many hours as we make on Sunday.
>
> I guess you gave my address to the local [draft] board so I've
> decided to work until I get my notice to be examined and then quit
> and go home and join the Navy Air Corps.

Two of Perry Jr.'s cousins served in the military during the war.
Byron joined the Army Air Force in August 1942 and trained as a tech-
nician (bombsight maintenance) at stateside B-24 and B-17 bases and
later served as part of a training cadre with a Brazilian Air Force Squadron. Harold joined the U.S. Navy in 1943, prior to completing his final
year at high school. He qualified as a flight engineer and air gunner and
served with Navy Patrol Bombing Squadron 102, flying twenty-eight
combat missions in PB4Y1 aircraft (the Navy version of the B-24) off the
coast of Japan.

Perry Jr. was the first of the three boys to enlist. Having considered
the Navy Air Force, he decided to enlist in the Army Air Force. A few
days before Christmas 1942 he wrote home from Keesler Field, Biloxi,
Mississippi:

> We got here about 4:30 this a.m. We didn't get much sleep last
> night. . . . We left Atlanta at 2:00 yesterday . . . the post is located
> right on the Gulf so it's pretty warm even in December . . .
>
> I made good enough on my I.Q. test to be eligible for officers
> training school if I get a chance to apply. I'm planning to ask for
> and try to go to school to train to be a navigator. Don't know how
> I'll make out though. I thought if I could get the training then I
> could use it after the war. Where I couldn't use aerial gunnery in
> peacetime.

In his next letter he wrote:

> I took all the exams that they offered and qualified for all the tech-
> nical schools but made better on the mechanical scores so I chose
> Airplane Mechanics. You may not approve of the aerial gunnery
> part but the Captain talked like I would start to gunnery school
> sometime within the next ten days or before without finishing my
> basic. I will get my rating as sergeant at the end of five weeks. With
> a chance like that I can't afford to miss it. He said that we will get

our rating and then go to Airplane Mechanics school and altogether it will be at least six months before I have to go across.

On 11 February 1943:

Well I'm in. I got my required amount of hits in the air firing so all we have to do now is wait for Saturday, graduation, and the all important wings. It doesn't seem right for me to be in the army only two months and getting a sergeant's rating. Seems as if it were just given to me.

I've gotten to where I like flying fine. I made my last two runs here today and really enjoyed them. We've learned Morse code by signals and radio so if we ever need that we'll have it. . . .

They gave us some of the best equipment that I ever saw today . . . a winter flying suit with fur lined boots. The suit is leather with sheepskin lining. They gave us the summer flying suit which is just

Sgt. Perry Roberson modeling the latest flying gear at Keesler Field, Biloxi, Mississippi, in February 1943. (Ruby Jo Roberson Faust)

cotton with cotton helmet to match. They gave us our own goggles and an individual parachute with collapsible life preserver. They gave us a nice leather jacket just like the ones officers wear for dress, and a dress sweater with leather gloves for dress. They even gave us a pair of sunglasses that sell for $5. I think that the whole outfit is considered $600 at least.

They tried to make an instructor out of me but when they found out my age they thought it best that I didn't try it. They want men about twenty-two years old at least so I didn't try it.

On 8 March:

Dear Mother . . . We are to start to school at 12:00 tonight and will be on the graveyard shift for the entire fourteen weeks. I guess it will be alright after we get used to it . . . we haven't been paid yet . . . I don't guess we'll need much money until I get out of this school except to go to shows. They have a show at 10:00 in the morning for the boys who go to school at night. . . .

Did Byron get home or was his furlough cancelled? . . . As for myself it will be at least five more months before I can even hope for one.

Some time soon after Perry Jr. was awarded his sergeant's stripes the family drove over to Biloxi in the family's new car, a 1942 Chevrolet. When Perry Jr.'s three-year-old brother, Jimmy, saw him in his uniform he exclaimed gleefully, "He's not a sergeant! He's still a soldier!"

Perry and his immediate family following his return from overseas. Back row: Sallie Wade, Perry, and Leora. Front row: Jimmy, Mattie Joe, Perry Sr., and Ruby Jo. (Ruby Jo Roberson Faust)

CHAPTER THREE

A League of Nations

Twenty-three year-old Sgt. Aurèle Veilleux joined Lt. Jack Nortridge's crew as nose turret gunner soon after he completed aerial gunnery training. His home in the small industrial city of Waterville in the New England state of Maine, a wilderness of pine forests that extend into Canada. The Veilleux family had been one of the original twenty or so French Canadian families to leave a community in Quebec and settle in Waterville, way back in the 1830s. Many of the early settlers that followed were farmers and lumberjacks, and over the following hundred years small towns in Quebec were depopulated as hundreds of thousands of French Canadians settled in New England.

Waterville soon accommodated the rail center for the largest railroad in Maine while the city's industries—including its sawmills, match factory, paper mill, woolen mill, cotton mill, shirt factory, and foundry, grew rapidly in the late nineteenth century, attracting further settlement of large, Catholic, French Canadian families. Up to half the combined population of Waterville and neighboring Winslow was Franco-American by the time Aurèle was born. To his French-speaking family he would always be Aurèle, but to his new aircrew the curly-haired gunner became known as "Pete."

Sgt. Aurèle "Pete" Veilleux, nose turret gunner; home on leave in Waterville, Maine. (Pete Veilleux)

Twenty-three-year-old Sgt. Harvey Nielsen was assigned to the crew as top turret gunner and assistant flight engineer. Harvey was a first-generation American; his parents were immigrants from Denmark.

Harvey's father, Johan Nielsen was born in Vorning, Denmark, in August 1878, but was orphaned by the time he was two years old. His father died of liver disease, his mother of kidney disease. So Johan and his two sisters were raised by foster parents. Johan served in the King's Guard in Copenhagen and in 1900 he was a member of the special unit. He was a large, strong man and there were even stories in the family, although questionable, that the Nielsens left Denmark and settled in America because Johan had killed a man.

Johan Nielsen married Maren From in Copenhagen toward the end of 1900. Maren was born in November 1878 in Haderslev, in what is now southern Denmark. However, at the time of her birth, Haderslev had become part of Germany, and was only returned to Denmark in 1920. Therefore, Maren and her siblings were raised in an area influenced by German culture and language, and she spoke both Danish and German. Two of Maren's sisters married Germans, and three of Maren's brothers immigrated to the United States, two in 1890 and one in 1905, to avoid being drafted into the German army.

Maren gave birth to two children in Copenhagen, son Oage in 1902 and daughter Olga in 1903, and then a third, Charles, was born in 1905 in Haderslev. The following year, the Nielsens set sail for the United States, where they arrived in July 1906 and settled in the Midwestern state of Missouri. They ran a farm in the Bedison community, near Conception Junction in the northwestern part of the state. Johan and Maren Americanized their names, changing them to John and Mary. In 1908 Mary gave birth to Hans, and soon after, the Nielsens moved to a farm in the vicinity of Pickering, Nodaway County. Pickering was a farm town known for its horse shows, which attracted folk from miles around.

In Pickering, Mary Nielsen gave birth to five more children—Anna, George, James, and Mary (who died at three months of age) and then the ninth child was Harvey, the youngest, born on 17 July 1920. Harvey was less than a year old when the family moved to a farm at Polk Township, located approximately three to four miles southwest of the city of Maryville, Nodaway County. The four-hundred-acre farm was rented from a landowner named George Baker, and the Nielsens bred short-horn cattle. In those days, farming four hundred acres would have taken many hands, and consequently the Nielsen's four eldest children never finished high school, either quitting after eighth grade at the local rural school or during their high school years.

Harvey attended a one-room rural school located about a mile's walk away from the farm, and legend has it that one day he was run over by a horse during his walk home from school in the snow! Harvey's school experience was similar to that of most farm kids growing up in rural Missouri during the Depression years—they had it pretty rough. The work on the farm was hard; they had food to eat from the farm, but they had little else. John and Mary lost all their savings twice in bank failures during the Depression, and although the amount lost each time was a small sum, it was much more than they could afford to lose.

In 1933 the Nielsens moved into the town of Maryville, set in the midst of rolling hills and farm country. Mary's health wasn't good enough to endure the farm work any more, although it turned out that she lived to reach ninety-five years of age. Harvey was thirteen years old that year and had to change schools. There were approximately ten thousand residents in Maryville at that time and so the experience of moving there was quite an adjustment for the younger Nielsen children; by this time their older siblings had left home. Following the move into town, John worked for the Carnation Milk Company, drove a truck, worked as a night watchman at a Catholic girls' school, and did various other jobs before having to claim social security benefits when work opportunities dried up.

Harvey graduated from Maryville High School in 1938 and moved to St. Joseph, forty miles south of Maryville and sixty miles up the Missouri River from Kansas City, to find work. By this time his brothers Oage, Hans, and Jim, were also living in St. Joseph. Less than a century previously, St. Joseph had been a Wild West cow town that prospered as a supply depot for the California Gold Rush. Years later the town became the eastern starting point of the legendary Pony Express, famed by such riders as Buffalo Bill who delivered the mail by horseback relay to places as distant as Sacramento, California. The notorious outlaw Jesse James was shot dead by one of his own gang members in St. Joseph in April 1882.

Harvey was stocky, shorter than his brothers, fair skinned, and with very blond hair that inspired the nickname Cotton Top when he was a kid, and which already showed signs of receding by the time he reached his early twenties. Oage and Hans owned a trucking and grain haulage business in St. Joseph, which at times proved successful and they were able to help out their parents during hard times. All five of Harvey's brothers turned out to be truck drivers and Harvey followed suit. He started working for his brothers, driving trucks all over the Midwest. Traveling was an exciting and new experience for the young Harvey Nielsen. He lived so many hundreds of miles inland that like most of the kids he grew up with, traveling far enough to see the ocean for the first time was an experience reserved for adulthood (if at all). Denmark must have seemed a very distant place to the young Harvey if not for the news of the worsening situation in Europe.

The Army Air Force offered opportunities of travel and new experience like these young men would never have imagined possible, but there were of course complex personal motivations for Harvey. He

Harvey and Bonnie Nielsen's wedding photograph. (Kenneth James)

had many relatives—uncles, aunts, and cousins—still living in Denmark and under Nazi occupation since 1940. But he also had two aunts living in Hamburg, and married to Germans, who were still in correspondence with his mother up until the beginning of the war.

Harvey's brother George later became a staff sergeant in the Army Air Force and spent the last months of the war stationed in North Africa and Italy, assigned to an ordnance unit. While away in the service, both Harvey and his brother George wrote letters to cheer up their niece Iris Barton in Conception Junction. Iris was twelve years old and in and out of Maryville Hospital for about a year with a hip infection. Harvey also wrote to Bonnie Lou Smith, whose sister Edith was married to Harvey's brother Charley. Upon Harvey's return from overseas service, Harvey and Bonnie Lou were to be married.

In the spring of 1943 Harvey wrote to his niece Iris from Tyndall Field, Panama City, Florida:

> Dear Iris . . . I am going to a gunnery school down here learning to shoot machine guns from an airplane. All we do is shoot machine guns for a half day and then we go to the classroom and study how to fix them if something goes wrong with them. We have to be able to tell what is wrong with them and repair them blindfolded.
>
> You should be down here, you would have a lot of fun. You could walk two blocks and go swimming in the ocean. We have a fine beach right by the camp. We are usually so busy that we don't get to go swimming only on Sunday though.
>
> How is everything up on the farm? Have these floods I have been hearing about washed all your daddy's crops away? I hope

not. I bet John and Lawrence are big boys by now. Tell them I hope to come up and wrestle with them someday. I don't know when it will ever be though. Furloughs are really hard to get. If I ever do get one I am sure going to come up and eat chicken with you. Well this is about time to go to school so I will have to sign off. Tell your mother, Daddy, Lawrence and John all hello.

On 11 August Harvey wrote to Iris from Gowen Field, Boise, Idaho. By this time he was a sergeant and assigned to the 52nd Bomb Squadron:

This is really nice country out West here. The camp is located in a valley. Every way you look you see mountains. They are really pretty scenery. Even though it is so nice out here I would still a lot rather be in Missouri. Where ever it is if it is home that is the best place in the world.

I am still going to school out here a little bit. When I finish here I will be first engineer on one of those big four motor air planes that they use to drop bombs with. When that happens I will go to another field and do some practice flying there. My job, is to take care of every thing on the airplane while the airplane is flying. If anything goes wrong up there I am supposed to be able to fix it. Boy I sure hope I can.

The letter was signed, "As ever, Your Uncle Harvey." It transpired that Harvey became the top turret gunner and assistant engineer on his aircrew. On 30 August 1943 Harvey wrote again from Gowen Field:

How is every thing going with you folks on the farm. I bet you and John will soon start to school. I bet you are sure glad you can go this winter instead of being all crippled up like you were last winter. Say have you throwed that cane away yet. I hope so.

It has certainly started to get cold out here in this part of the country. We already have to wear a coat out here. Winter seems to start a quite a bit earlier out here than it does back in Missouri.

Sergeant Lim Wing Jeong was assigned to the Nortridge crew as tail gunner, at the age of just eighteen. As a Chinese American he was certainly a minority figure in the 453rd Bomb Group, and the more the crew got to know and like him, the more their respect for him increased as they heard about some of his remarkable past experiences.

Both of Lim Wing Jeong's grandfathers had left China and traveled to the United States during the second half of the nineteenth century when many Chinese citizens crossed the Pacific Ocean in search of new prospects. Practically all of the Chinese in America at the time were males and the majority of them had no intention to stay, but had come to earn money to support their families in China. Some sought their fortune while others just a modest standard of living.

Lim Wing Jeong enlisted in the Army Air Force when he was seventeen years old. At eighteen he was assigned to Crew 25 as tail turret gunner. (Wayne J. Lim)

Perhaps first of all, thousands of Chinese were drawn to California in the mid-nineteenth century by the allure of the Gold Rush; others found employment in the West Coast's canning and timber industries; and most significant, thousands more came to work as laborers on the Central Pacific and other railroads. Carving through the Sierra Nevada Mountains on the route of the Central Pacific Railroad cost the lives of over one thousand Chinese laborers. One historian wrote, "Men of China . . . built whole or part of nearly every railroad in the West . . . thousands of these young men gave their lives . . . the dead were never counted, nor have they been memorialised."[1]

However, soon California hit hard times and endured high levels of unemployment compounded by the influx of European immigrants. The reliable, hard-working Chinese were seen as a threat by the European arrivals that feared for their own futures—tensions frequently led to violence against the Chinese. The introduction of a state constitution prohibited Chinese immigrants from owning property in California and significantly restricted their sphere of employment. Anti-Chinese discrimination was implemented on a national level in 1882 when Congress passed the Chinese Exclusion Act that restricted further Chinese immigration.

Lim Wing Jeong's father traveled to the United States, in the footsteps of his own father, in search of employment and new prospects; however, he became frustrated by federal laws that prevented Chinese immigrants from financial investment and property ownership. He decided to return to China where he worked in the banking business and subsequently was married—in 1925 Lim Wing Jeong was born in the southern province of Canton, where the Lim family lived in a small village called Hoy Saeng.

However, China was in turmoil during the early 1930s with conflicts between Nationalists and Communists. Nationalist leader Chiang Kai-Shek responded to the rise of Communism with force, almost annihilating the Communists between 1930 and 1934. Under the leadership of Mao Zedong, one hundred thousand Communist supporters set out on the "Long March" and relocated to the Northwest. While Chiang focused his attention on the Communist threat, the Japanese were making inroads into China via Manchuria.

It was around this time that Lim Wing Jeong's parents decided to send him off to America to live with his paternal grandfather as his guardian. They hoped that he would have a better life and a more secure future in America. And so when Lim Wing Jeong was a ten-year-old boy he set sail on an amazing but daunting journey. Unable to speak a word of English, he traveled alone on a ship full of strangers, across the Pacific Ocean to San Francisco and the uneasy reception of U.S. immigration officials. Because Chinese names are written with the family name first (in this case, Lim), followed by the first and then second given names, Immigration registered him incorrectly as Lim (first name) Wing (middle name) Jeong (family name), and subsequently this sequence was used during his military service.[2]

Ten-year-old Lim Wing Jeong was met in San Francisco by his grandpa, Lim Bow, who had allegedly been admitted into the United States for business reasons, and therefore Lim Wing Jeong was able to obtain dual citizenship. From California they traveled to Tucson, Arizona, where Lim Wing Jeong settled into a Chinese community.

The Southern Pacific Railroad had brought the majority of early Chinese settlers to Tucson, when they were employed for the back-breaking task of extending the railroad across the Arizona desert, and some also found work in the copper mines. Following completion of the railroad, many of the Chinese laborers chose to stay in Tucson despite being subjected to hostility. Their employment prospects were extremely limited, but some leased land and became Tucson's chief source of fresh vegetables; others worked as cooks and servants, and eventually modest businesses such as Chinese laundries, grocery stores, and restaurants were opened by the former railroad and mine workers.

Grandpa Lim Bow ran a restaurant in Tucson, where he was a prominent figure in the Chinese community, but he tragically died during surgery less than a year after Jeong arrived. Lim Wing Jeong was just eleven years old and was sent to San Antonio, Texas, to live with his maternal grandfather, William King. King's family name was really Lew, but somewhere he had adopted a new name. Back in 1906 an earthquake and a fire struck San Francisco, causing immense damage to and destruction of the city. Archives of immigration records were lost, including any that might have shown that William King passed through U.S. immigration to work in America. Following the disaster in San Francisco he claimed that he was born in the United States and was therefore a legal citizen. However, King is remembered by his descendents as a "wetback" (derogatory term for illegal immigrants from Mexico, many of whom swam across the Rio Grande river). A number of Chinese workers went to Mexico when they were unable to find work in the states of the Southwest. But King had crossed back into Texas with no documentation and no shoes—legend has it that he was pulling cactus spines from his feet on the journey.

During the mid-1930s there was a close-knit Chinese community of several hundred individuals in San Antonio. Almost all of them, like Lim Wing Jeong, were from the Canton region in southern China and spoke Cantonese. The history of Chinese settlement in Texas corresponds with that in Arizona—the Chinese first arrived in Texas to build the railroads and some remained when the work was completed.

A group of five hundred Chinese men remembered as "Pershing's Chinese" arrived in San Antonio in 1917. The *San Antonio Express* reported that they were, "Speaking in Spanish, smiling in Chinese." They had come from Mexico, having assisted U.S. General John J. Pershing on what turned out to be a failed military venture south of the boarder in search of Francisco "Pancho" Villa, the man responsible for an attack on New Mexico during the Mexican Revolution. The only exception to the exclusion law, Pershing arranged for this group of Chinese to settle in the United States where they were registered as legal immigrants in 1922. Many of them remained in San Antonio.

Over time, Chinese communities were formed in San Antonio despite the exclusion laws preventing the Chinese from legally bringing their wives to America. In the early 1920s Chinese women were not permitted to join their husbands in the United States, even if their husbands were U.S. citizens. However, their children who were born in China were given U.S. citizenship through the father and some were sent to America, although a trip across the Pacific could cost nearly a year's salary for a laborer.[3] The Chinese found employment in areas where they were not initially seen as an economic threat and little capital was required, such as hand laundries, restaurants, or grocery retail.

Founded by Spanish missionaries in 1691, San Antonio remained a predominantly Hispanic city in the 1930s, despite years of settlement in the area by Anglo-Americans. The primary requirement for securing any kind of employment in San Antonio at the time was fluency in speaking Spanish. Lim Wing Jeong studied both English and Spanish in school during the day, while each evening he attended classes at San Antonio's Chinese school. At the age of just thirteen, he learnt to drive an automobile.

Meanwhile, the situation went from bad to worse back home when the Sino-Japanese War broke out in 1937. Soon the Japanese controlled most of northern China. San Antonio's Chinese community followed attentively the shocking news reports of the "Rape of Nanking" as Japanese planes flew raids against the capital city and reduced much of it to rubble. Fifty thousand Chinese citizens were slaughtered by Japanese troops in Nanking, more than twenty thousand Chinese women were raped.[4] The Japanese swept through most of China's east coast and occupied the cities of Shanghai and Canton.

In response to Japanese aggression, a branch of the Chinese National Party, the Kuomintang, was established in San Antonio. When China became an ally to the United States during World War II, anti-Chinese feelings in the United States were significantly calmed and in 1943

Sgt. Harvey Nielsen and Sgt. Lim Wing Jeong. (Wayne J. Lim)

the Chinese Exclusion Act was repealed. For Lim Wing Jeong, the situation in China was the primary motivation to enlist in the Army Air Force on 11 November 1942, rather than waiting in anticipation of eventually being drafted into the regular army. But since he was only seventeen years old, as his guardian his grandfather, William King, had to go along with him to sign the papers. Jeong hoped that he would serve in the China-Burma-India or Pacific theaters—just so long as he was helping fight the war against the Japanese.

CHAPTER FOUR

Pocatello, Idaho

On Tuesday 7 September 1943 Lt. Jack Nortridge's fledgling crew arrived at Pocatello, an Idaho railroad town, ready to commence "Phase" training. Pocatello Army Air Field was a new training field shared by the 453rd Bomb Group and another unit in training. Therefore facilities and space were limited, and the 453rd's headquarters resumed Group operations from the Officers' Club, while close to the flying field Squadron Operations were established under canvas alongside medical and technical supply tents.

Jack Nortridge's crew was assigned to the 733rd Bombardment Squadron. The 453rd comprised four bombardment squadrons, the 732nd through 735th, and at Pocatello it was determined that each squadron would eventually be assigned eighteen crews (732nd Squadron, crews numbered one to eighteen; 733rd Squadron, twenty-one to thirty-eight; 734th Squadron, forty-one to fifty-seven; and the 735th Squadron, sixty-one to seventy-eight).

However during the first of the three phases of aircrew training the 733rd Squadron would comprise just six crews. Crew 21 became the 733rd Squadron's model crew under the command of the Squadron Operations Officer, Lt. William McCrocklin. Lts. White, Kimball, and Wilder had been assigned on 26 August and designated Crews 22, 23, and 24 respectively (White and Wilder were subsequently replaced). Jack Nortridge's crew was designated Crew 25, and Lt. Stock's crew became number 26. The squadron had just two B-24 E-model aircraft for flight training purposes.

Following Crew 25's arrival at Pocatello, twenty-three-year-old 2nd Lt. Francis "Frank" Conlon was assigned to Jack's crew as copilot. He was born in southwestern Wisconsin, in Cuba City, just fifty miles from Jack's home. In 1924, when Francis was four years old, the Conlon family moved fifteen miles to the city of Dubuque, Iowa, on the banks of the Mississippi River, across from both Wisconsin and Illinois.

Francis Conlon enlisted for military service on 3 January 1942, less than a month after Pearl Harbor. He was assigned to the Corps of Engineers and in July 1942 he received his officer's commission. With an ambition to fly, Lt. Conlon attended flight school from January 1943 onwards, and in August he was assigned to the 29th Bomb Group at

Crew 25 at Pocatello, Idaho, on 14 September 1943. Left to right: Witmer, Nielsen, Roberson, Eagleson, Nortridge, Conlon, LeRoy, Jeong, and Veilleux. The following day, Lt. Donald Lawry was assigned to the crew as navigator. (Ruby Jo Roberson Faust)

Gowen Field Army Air Base, Boise, Idaho. From the parent organization, Francis was transferred to the 453rd at Pocatello, and assigned to Crew 25.

On Wednesday 15 September nineteen-year-old 2nd Lt. Donald Lawry was assigned to Crew 25, having just been transferred from Gowen Field, Boise. Like Lt. Francis Conlon, Donald Lawry was born in the state of Wisconsin. Donald's father, Charles E. Lawry, was an Englishman born in January 1889 and raised on a farm named Tremorkin in Liskeard, Cornwall. The Lawry ancestors are buried in the churchyard at nearby St. Neot. In 1911 Charles Lawry arrived in New York and then settled in Wisconsin where the green valleys and rolling farmland filled with grazing cows must surely have reminded him of his home in England's West Country. When one of his sisters married in 1912, the newlywed couple set sail on the doomed *Titanic* for a honeymoon in America, never to arrive. A few years later Charles Lawry returned to

Europe, but as an American. In June 1917, just two months after the United States entered the Great War in Europe he enlisted in the army and served as a cook in the 331st Machine Gun Battalion.

Following the war, Charles married Myrtie L. Fletcher, born in Green County, Wisconsin, in February 1894. Together they ran a farm near the rural town of Oregon, ten miles south of the state capital, Madison. Their first son, Donald Charles Lawry was born on Thursday 27 March 1924 in Oregon, Wisconsin. Donald's brother Raymond Gordon was born in February 1926 and his sister Betty Lou was born in January 1934—just three weeks later their father died in a hospital in Madison. The family later suspected that the cause of his death was related to his exposure to a German gas attack during the war in Europe.

Myrtie Lawry was left alone to raise three children and manage a farm in the middle of the Depression, and by the spring of 1935 she decided to sell the farm. While she might have moved into Oregon to be closer to relations there, she chose to move to the town of Evansville, Rock County, Wisconsin. Located approximately twenty-five miles south of Madison, the town of Evansville was founded back in 1839, and during the 1930s it remained a small rural community with a population of less than three thousand inhabitants. The Lawrys moved into a house close to the center of the town, 409 Almeron Street, and Myrtie Lawry began a new job teaching in an Evansville private school, Leota School for Girls. The family attended Sunday services at the local Methodist church and the three Lawry children all went on to graduate from Evansville High School.

During his childhood, Donald spent much of his free time around Evansville hunting and fishing with friends. It was a very short walk from the center of town to the surrounding fields and countryside. He also shared a keen interest in aviation with his best friend, Arthur "Artie" Sands, who had been fortunate enough to take a flight in an airplane when he was just eight years old.

Donald and Artie spent time building model aircraft from balsa wood, with elastic bands to power the propellers. Donald was particularly skilled at making these and his always flew really well. Model making usually took place at Artie's house on Main St., because there the two boys were able to secretly smoke cigarettes with nobody finding out. At one point they had amassed such a stockpile of model aircraft that they decided they could spare one for the sake of having some fun. They dipped the nose of an aircraft into some kerosene from the stove, set fire to it, and sent it flying out of Artie's window. It eventually crashed in flames on the brick-paved road, much to the amusement of the older guys hanging out in the pool hall across Main Street.

Then came news of wars breaking out around the world. The radio brought reports of the Japanese bombing of Pearl Harbor and the German bombing of English cities including Plymouth, twenty miles from

Lawry, Donald
"Charlie"

"The Air Corps for me.'

Boxing 4; Boys' Tumb. 2; Boys' Intra. 1. 2, 3, 4; Band 1; Sr. Hi-Y 3, 4; Jr. Hi-Y 1, 2; Safety Club 1, 2; Class Officer 4.

From the Evansville High School yearbook—the Class of '42. (Betty Lawry Allen)

Donald's father's home in Liskeard. During his summer vacations, Donald worked long, hard hours in the canning factory in Evansville and during term time he worked at night in the bowling alley, setting pins. In June 1942 Donald and Artie graduated from high school. The Class of '42 book included a quote below Donald's portrait: "the air corps for me." He was already eighteen and about to enlist; however, Artie was not eighteen until July and so they both waited patiently until Artie's birthday on 8 July. The following day they set out from Evansville, walking and hitchhiking the twenty-five miles from Evansville to the city of Madison to take the Air Force test.

Artie Sands later completed training as a nose turret gunner and togglier-bombardier, and he was assigned to a B-24 Liberator aircrew in the 98th Bomb Group, 15th Army Air Force, based in Italy. His missions commenced in January 1945 and he flew fourteen combat missions prior to the end of the war in Europe in May 1945.

But back in 1942, as the weeks turned into months and as the summer turned into the fall and winter, both Donald and Artie found ways to pass the time and earn some money until they were called for active service and commenced their training. Donald went to work in Madison at the Oscar Mayer Company, which processed beef and pork. He still lived at home in Evansville, contributing money from his wages to help the family, and getting a ride each day to Madison with some of his co-workers. Donald got his driving license despite not having a car in the

Donald Lawry (far left) with his mother, Myrtie, and siblings, Betty and Gordon, at home in Evansville, Wisconsin. Donald was eighteen and waiting to be called to active service in the Army Air Force; he is seen here wearing spectacles, a necessity that he feared might spoil his chances of becoming a pilot and instead have him restricted to ground duty. (Betty Lawry Allen)

family, but of course the test was less demanding in those days. He also started dating a local girl named Dorothy Brunsell, who lived on a farm one-and-a-half miles out of town. She recalls:

> We more or less got together with other friends. . . . I thought he was perfect, wonderful, everything to me. He didn't say too much about the Air Force except that he would like to have been a pilot.

Dorothy played piano and was self-taught—living out in the country there wasn't really anyone to teach her. Donald and Dorothy occasionally went to barn dances where there was usually a small band of musicians playing piano, violins, harmonicas, and guitars. Otherwise, music was supplied by nickelodeons in the places they frequented around Evansville. Several months passed and then Donald was called to active service via a telegram received on Sunday 10 January 1943.

The following Sunday, Donald wrote home from Texas. He was stationed at the San Antonio Aviation Cadet Center (SAACC), a classification center at Kelly Field. Basic training commenced for Air Cadet Lawry, Squadron 112, Flight G, who dreamed of becoming a pilot. However, Donald wore glasses and feared that this might prevent him from pilot training—and of course, everyone wanted to be a pilot and so there was a great demand for navigators and bombardiers. Perhaps if he had been a couple of years older and a little more experienced in life then he would have been selected for pilot training. He was academically intelligent, with a natural aptitude for mathematics, perhaps this was also significant. Often it's been said that the navigators were the brainy ones.

Donald wrote home saying that he might be able to train as a navigator, but was worried about being restricted to ground duty. More than anything he wanted to fly. A few days passed and then on 26 January he wrote home to wish a happy birthday to his sister Betty, and with the news that he had been classified as a navigator.

Donald arrived at Ellington Field near Houston, Texas, on 17 February, and preflight training commenced the following day. In a letter dated 25 March, he mentioned that the Squadron was going down with the measles and the following day he wrote again saying that *he* was in hospital with measles. On 13 April, he took a test to complete the course at Ellington Field and from there he expected to move to another base for navigation flight training. Donald had completed three months of active duty in the Army Air Force, but still he had not left the ground!

On 22 April, Donald arrived at Hondo Field, Texas, a little west of San Antonio, for advanced training. A couple of days later the first letter from Hondo, Texas, arrived in Evansville:

> I guess we start to fly about the second or third week. That will be
> a new experience for me. I only hope I don't get washed out for air
> sickness, some of the boys did.

The navigators at Hondo Field were issued with their navigation equipment—a wristwatch and stopwatch, a flashlight, a pair of dividers used for measuring distances, and an E-6B flight "computer" which would become one of their most vital pieces of equipment. The E-6B was a handheld instrument, an analog computer, used for a method of navigation they were about to learn called "dead-reckoning." This involved plotting a course based on variables such as altitude, air speed, atmospheric conditions, distance, compass direction, and time. Donald also learned the age-old tradition of celestial navigation—navigating by the stars. Therefore a considerable amount of this study took place late at night. Classes were also held in radio navigation (using radio beacons and a radio compass) and pilotage navigation (map reading and identification of landmarks).

On Sunday 9 May Donald Lawry wrote home:

> I was flying last Thursday. We had a three hour, forty minute flight, we did pilotage (flying by land marks) to Corpus Christi, then to Brenham, and then back to the field. By some chance of fate I didn't get sick, most of the guys that went up did get sick.

There was not much time to get home to Wisconsin, and passes were a rarity anyway. Donald had resigned himself to the fact that he was in Texas for the duration:

> I'm going to stay on 'till I graduate, we only have about fifteen-and-a-half to sixteen weeks left. The time really goes fast when they keep us so damn busy.

Donald was ambitious and he had big dreams. He read a great deal and enjoyed learning about the world, thinking, and making plans. At home, whenever one of the two Lawry boys was required to look after their kid sister, Betty, she always liked it when Gordon was given the responsibility of child minding. Gordon was playful and kept Betty occupied with fun and games, but Donald was quiet and liked to sit, absorbed in a book, while keeping a watchful eye on Betty.

In a letter written late June to Gordon, Donald reflected on all the things that they had planned for when the war was over. They had discussed these dreams many times on past occasions: of building a small cabin beside Lake Michigan, near enough to reach by plane or car for weekends and hunting seasons; and of building a boat, thirty to thirty-two feet long, something sturdy but not necessarily too fancy. Not anticipating the postwar economic boom that later occurred in the United States, he anticipated hard times and a scarcity of jobs, just like the era in which he had grown up. He remarked:

> Then, if a depression hits we probably wouldn't have a job anyway, and that would be the ideal time for a cruise like I suggested.

There were also wilder dreams of exploring the South American jungle, of a plane with floats, wheels, and extra gas tanks. Maybe they wouldn't need to worry about struggling to find conventional jobs if they could get some movie equipment and film their explorations, have success, and get names for themselves! The letter was signed, "Your brother and future partner, Don."

Navigation training was completed after eighteen weeks and Donald then received his commission in August—he had earned his wings and was now, at the age of nineteen, an officer (second lieutenant) in the

Army Air Force. At around this time he was given some leave to return home to Evansville.

Donald reported to Gowen Field, Boise, Idaho, in early September. Considering that there were B-24 Liberators stationed there, he anticipated becoming the navigator on a B-24 crew. He spent only a few days at Gowen Field before being transferred to the 733rd Bomb Squadron, 453rd Bomb Group at Pocatello, Idaho, on 15 September. At Pocatello he met his new crew, under the command of pilot Lt. Jack Nortridge.

Donald was growing accustomed to the Air Force life and flying. He was kept so busy during his training that he hardly had time to think too much about anything else or to get too homesick. Having recently returned to Evansville to see his family and Dorothy, he had to leave home all over again. He was no longer one guy in a classroom full of navigators—instead he was the *only* navigator on a real aircrew. There were nine other guys whom he didn't know too well, who were all depending on him. It was a test for his confidence and his ability. Knowing that soon he would be going overseas to encounter the daunting realities of war, maybe he was feeling a little homesick when on 18 September he wrote in a somber tone to Gordon, who couldn't wait to follow in his brother's footsteps:

> After you graduate from High School there is still plenty of time to join the air corps. This place isn't the best place in the world to be as you would soon find out once you get into the army . . . but you want to make the most of what you have while you are at home. I'm sorry I didn't talk to you more while I was home but I wanted to be with Dorothy whenever I could.
>
> This war will last long enough for everyone to see all they want of killing or be killed.
>
> Maybe after it is all over we will be able to do some of the things we planned like sailing the face of the Earth in some small boat, but take my word for it and stay out of the war for as long as possible.

Jack Nortridge, it turned out, was from Freeport, Illinois—just forty miles south of Evansville. Don and Jack discovered that they had a lot in common, and this helped to make Don feel at ease on Crew 25.

Bill Eagleson recalls those early days of Phase training:

> Phase training—With the comfort of our aircrew we supported each other, and knowing goals were in sight, we shared and developed as a team. We were newcomers, untested but *trained* and disciplined to meet unknown factors—ten guys on our crew all fresh out of Air Training Command schools.

The first phase included local area familiarization flights in the squadron's two B-24 bombers, "shooting" landings, practice of emergency procedure, instrument flying, practice bombing, and aerial

gunnery. Additionally there were classes to attend on the ground, organized on a group basis. Toward the end of September, seven more crews
were assigned to the 733rd Bomb Squadron. On 26 September Donald
wrote a more cheery letter to his brother, Gordon:

> Are you still hot for the idea of a boat? I hope so. I think I'll like
> boats just as good as airplanes, there is something fascinating about
> them.

As the first phase of crew training neared completion seven more crews
were assigned to the 733rd Squadron. Meanwhile it was rumored that
the 453rd Bomb Group would leave Pocatello for the second phase. An
advanced echelon of four officers and thirty enlisted men left Pocatello
on 22 September and traveled by train to the 453rd Bomb Group's new
base at March Field, Riverside, California, where they arrived on 24
September. The main body of the Group left Pocatello on 30 September
and proceeded to California by troop train, while a few crews of mostly
officers and a few enlisted men flew the Group eight B-24s to California.

At March Field the 733rd Squadron received five more crews following their transfer from the parent group at Boise, Idaho, and were subsequently designated crews 34 through 38. Under the command of
Captain Robert H. Kanaga the 733rd Squadron commenced Phase
Two training with an additional seven B-24E Liberators—the Squadron
now had nine B-24s to share between eighteen crews.

When President Roosevelt called for an increase in American military air power in January 1939, the Boeing B-17 Flying Fortress was the
most modern aircraft that the United States Army Air Corps possessed.
The Consolidated Aircraft Corporation was contracted to design and
build a prototype of a long-range bomber, superior in performance to
the B-17—the prototype of the B-24 bomber made its debut flight in
December 1939. The B-24 went into production and commenced service in Europe with the Royal Air Force's Coastal Command, and later
with Bomber Command, whose personnel named it the Liberator.

The B-24 Liberator hardly improved on the design of the B-17 Flying Fortress, and some pilots claimed it to be less stable and harder to fly.
However, the Liberator carried more bombs and flew a little faster,
much to the frustration of its pilots, who were often placed in formations behind their counterparts during combat missions. The B-24 Liberator was scheduled for mass production as the United States Army Air
Force's major heavy bomber, although the aircraft was subsequently
overshadowed in media fame by the B-17 Fortress. In reality, the B-24
was far more versatile, used for a wider variety of roles and operated on
every fighting front in the Second World War, serving with the air forces
of fifteen Allied nations.

The United States' aircraft manufacturers had not escaped the economic depression of the 1930s, and the recession did not end for the

industry until Britain's demand for aircraft was met under the "Lend-Lease" Scheme. Subsequently the industry was projected into unprecedented levels of production during the expansion of U.S. air power. In addition to the aircraft plant in San Diego, California, Consolidated Aircraft Corporation opened a new mile-long plant at Fort Worth, Texas, for Liberator manufacturing. Both North American Aviation at Dallas, Texas, and the Douglas Aircraft Company at Tulsa, Oklahoma, began manufacturing the Liberator under license—and then when the U.S. government banned civilian auto production following Pearl Harbor, the Ford Motor Company began manufacturing B-24 Liberators.

At its peak, Ford's Willow Run plant near Detroit produced one Liberator per hour. The B-24 was built in considerably greater numbers (over eighteen thousand, compared with less than thirteen thousand B-17s) and became significant to more American lives than any other aircraft in aviation history. By 1944 there were over 180,000 people employed in the production of Liberators.

Bill Eagleson considers:

> Tonight I wonder who trained our aircraft makers right down to the last mile of wiring—the training command was without glamour but it sure accomplished its mission . . . meeting that objective has been so overlooked. . . . Consider how many trades had to be trained, mostly housewives, to produce one B-24 every fifty minutes—just the riveting! Take it from there!

As a result of large-scale military spending, by the end of 1943 there were over eighteen million more people in employment than four years previously in the United States. Finally the Great Depression had ended, but ironically it had been replaced by war.

CHAPTER FIVE

Riverside, California

R iverside was a lively town located just east of Los Angeles. March Field was an old and established Army Air Corps base with outstanding facilities that certainly would not be found in a war zone. The 453rd Bombardment Group had enough room and facilities to operate and train efficiently, and each of the four squadrons was assigned a hangar in which classrooms were established. Roads and sidewalks were paved, the flight line and hangars were just a couple of hundred yards from the barracks, which were heated and located close to the mess halls, orderly, and supply rooms. There were two theaters showing the latest movies, a gymnasium, bowling alley, swimming pool, and a PX serving ice cream, milk shakes, and other snacks.

At first, ground school was conducted under Group organization but eventually each squadron became responsible for its own course of training. Specified classes were conducted for pilots, navigators, bombardiers, radio operators, flight engineers, and gunners. Phase training allowed the Group to develop with an emphasis on more intensive aircrew training, and the crews began clocking up hours of flying experience. They flew cross-country training missions covering instrument flying, formation flying, navigation, target practice over bombing ranges, and aerial gunnery.

During one of their cross-country training missions over desert and mountain ranges, Jack Nortridge's crew encountered some engine troubles. Things were not looking too good for Crew 25. Jack sent Bill Eagleson back to the waist section of the aircraft to give the bail out order to the rest of the crew, who were not wired into the intercom system. Bill opened the escape hatch in the floor of the waist section of the B-24, and he sat perched on the edge, his parachute on his back and his legs dangling out of the belly of the aircraft. But then Jack announced over the intercom that it might be a false alarm and advised Bill to hold on. Jack, Frank, and flight engineer Perry Roberson might be able to sort out the problem after all. Bill waited, while some of the enlisted men gathered around him waiting for their turn to jump, uncertain as to why Bill was hesitating. Bill enquired, "Should we go now, Jack . . . ?" Jack advised him to hold on a moment longer, and this was taken as an order. Meanwhile, thick black smoke from the troubled engine began to pour through one of the open waist hatches, filling the waist section of the aircraft. The crew was eager to breathe, and therefore eager to jump. Bill enquired again, but choking this time, "Jack, are we jumping today or not?!"

Donald Lawry found them a place to land, and between the pilots, flight engineer, and navigator they decided that they could just make it to a nearby airfield. They sure were glad to get on the ground, where they stayed overnight while their Liberator received some attention from the ground crews. To the crew's amusement, their bombardier had flown the mission in his ski suit! This was not considered suitable attire for the Officers' Club, and Bill spent the evening restricted to the billet while Jack, Frank, and Donald enjoyed a glass or two of beer and the enlisted men hung out at theNon Commissioned Officers' (NCO) Club. The following day they attempted to return to Riverside and despite experiencing further engine problems en route, they managed to make it back to March Field without having to test their parachutes.

That night the crew relaxed and let off some steam at their favorite haunt, the lively Mission Inn in Riverside. For some reason, their co-pilot Lt. Frank Conlon started unscrewing light bulbs above the bar. As the rest of the crew propped up the bar, the bemused barman asked, "What's he doing!?" So one of the crew called out, "Hey, Frank! What are you doing?" He replied, "I'm going to turn out the last light and yell 'FIRE!' and see what happens!" Maybe it was Frank Conlon's reckless sense of humor that set the precedent for Crew 25.

Crew 27, piloted by Lt. Thomas Purcell, also ran into some difficulty during one of their training missions when they overshot the Fucinitas calibration range and approached downtown San Diego. They promptly corrected their course, encouraged by ten bursts of anti-aircraft fire! This was all the training in dodging "flak" that a crew could expect, and it gave Crew 27 an insight into what was to come in the months ahead. It also gave them a good story to tell at the Mission Inn.

Early in October Lt. Francis Conlon was transferred to a unit at McChord Field, Washington, destined to be the first-pilot on his own crew. On 11 October 1943 Lt. Robert Holberg Jr. was assigned to Crew 25 as copilot, but was soon replaced by Lt. John McCue, who was subsequently transferred to Crew 26.

During the second half of October 1943, twenty-year-old 2nd Lt. George White was assigned to Crew 25 as copilot. His very arrival was something of a statement about his strength of character, for this young pilot walked in with a very noticeable limp and, it later transpired, he ran with a skip and a hop.

George White came from Oklahoma. His maternal grandparents originated in Illinois but moved to a homestead in Coon Hollow, Arkansas, approximately seven miles northwest of Gentry, Benton County, Arkansas. George's mother, Sophia Jenks, and her eleven siblings were born and raised on the homestead. In 1905 Sophia Jenks married Walter

White, who then moved in with the Jenks family and worked on the farm. George's eldest sister, Jessie, and eldest brother, Cecil, were born in Coon Hollow.

Although the family was quite poor, George's parents managed to save enough money to allow them to relocate to Joplin, Missouri, close to the Oklahoma and Kansas borders. George's father went to work as a shoe cobbler before finding work with the Frisco Railroad, a company that later transferred him to Sapulpa, Oklahoma, just fifteen miles from the city of Tulsa. The family relocated to Sapulpa, and George's father worked as a fireman on a train crew.

What had originally been the Atlantic and Pacific Railroad reached Sapulpa some thirty years previously. Sapulpa was named after the area's first settler, Chief Sapulpa, a Creek with whom some of the railroad men boarded during the construction period. Oklahoma, once a reservation for Native Americans forced west of the Mississippi River, had became an area of white settlement during the free-for-all Oklahoma Land Rush back in 1889.

In that year a post office was established in Sapulpa. For the white settlers, one of the first major industries was logging. The railroad allowed timber to be easily shipped out of Sapulpa and then sold to a European market. Meanwhile, the region became infamous for gangs of wild outlaws, but a great deal changed during the three decades prior to the arrival of George White's family. Oklahoma's economy depended largely on both agriculture and oil. In 1905, oil was discovered seven miles southeast of Sapulpa at Glenpool, and this soon became one of the most important oil fields in the world. Consequently, Sapulpa prospered.

Soon after the White family moved to Oklahoma, more children were born—James, Aleene, Donald, and then three years later on 1 February 1923, George Lewis White was born. By this time, his sister Jessie was already seventeen. Three years after George's birth, a baby brother was born and named Dale. Don, George, and Dale were always known as the "little boys" of the family.

George White with his brother Don (standing) at home in Sapulpa, Oklahoma, in 1926. (White family)

For the town of Sapulpa, the 1920s were the really good times, when the oil boom, the railroad, and the brick and glass plants turned Sapulpa into a bustling community with twenty thousand inhabitants. However, Oklahoma's economic boom ended in misery during the Depression years. Historic Route 66 runs through Sapulpa; during the Great Depression it carried "Arkies" and "Okies" westward from the drought-stricken "dust bowl" to greener pastures.

The White family regularly attended their local Baptist church, and they lived at the edge of town in a house on the north side of Lincoln St. They bought a pasture on the south side of the street, adjacent to the remains of a disused oil well service facility. This included a two-story house, along with a smokehouse, a feed room, and a big barn where they butchered pigs, smoked them, and then stored them in a freezer.

The family lived right beside the railroad tracks, and only a short walk of half a mile or so down the tracks led to an area known for good rabbit and squirrel hunting. Don, the eldest of the three "little boys" of the family, was held responsible for George, the future pilot, and Dale. Don was generally allowed to go off hunting on the stipulation that he took his two little brothers with him. Sometimes he was allowed to go alone just as long as he could sneak out without George and Dale noticing, which was quite unlikely since they followed him almost everywhere.

On one occasion, a young Don White was trying to go off hunting alone when his two little brothers, George and Dale, came out of the house and saw him with his rifle. Don dived into some long grass and weeds at the edge of their property. George called out, "I kin see where yur at, cuz I kin see the weeds movin'!" When Don refused to give in to his brothers' demands, either George or Dale declared, "If y'don't come out I'm gonna throw this rock!" Both George and Dale were deeply shocked when Don emerged from the undergrowth, screaming, and with blood pouring from his head—it was a game, and this wasn't meant to happen! Years later, nobody could quite remember if it was George or Dale who threw the rock, but the three brothers would laugh about the incident for the rest of their lives.

The family was considered to be very lucky during the Depression years, but like everyone they worked very hard to get by. Although George's father was eventually laid off in 1937, until that time he was able to work a few shifts each week on the Frisco Railroad, which provided some money for the family. But it was their home-based livelihood that became their saving grace during the end of the 1920s and throughout the hard times of the 1930s. They kept cows, chickens, turkeys, and pigs. All members of the family were involved in their gardening activities, growing potatoes, beans, and corn, and they were able to provide a great deal of food for themselves and for their neighbors.

Highlights of life in those days included their school vacations. Because George's father worked on the railroad, they could get free transportation to anywhere in the United States. So each summer, the first month of their school vacation was spent working overtime, getting the vegetables in and canning them. Then, after the harvest was complete, with three or four weeks remaining until they had to return to school, they would set off on a traveling vacation.

George's father would get them passes and the three brothers would then head off to California to see their older brother, to Florida to play on the beach, to Colorado to see the mountains, to New York City, and to the 1933 World Fair in Chicago. They would go anywhere that the railroad would take them, sometimes making a big circle around the United States from Sapulpa to El Paso, Texas, and beyond, just spending their whole vacation riding the trains from one place to another. They considered it to be a great and blessed life.

Perhaps inspired by their traveling experiences, George became interested in photography. He had always played with model airplanes and this led to a keen interest in aviation. George and his friend, Dan Dower, were always busy building model airplanes. George and his buddy, James Hopkins, used to go fishing quite frequently (James later introduced George to his wife, Barbara). Meanwhile, George's elder brother Don and James's elder brother Freddie used to go hunting together. George and Don shared many friends throughout their childhood and adulthood.

Some weekends George and his brothers Don and Dale would get other family members to fill in for them with their chores of milking, feeding the animals, and so on. They would head out into the woods, ten to fifteen miles west of Sapulpa, for an overnight camping and hunting trip. They would take nothing but salt and pepper and would survive off the left, hunting rabbits, squirrels, bullfrogs, fish—whatever they could find. They enjoyed many such times together, until the prospect of war separated them.

Don White left home in 1939 and went to Alaska where he spent a large part of the war years building airfields. Meanwhile George continued at Sapulpa High School. One day in May 1940 when George was cycling home from school, he turned a corner about one block east of Lincoln Street, just as a gas company utility truck thundered along the residential street towards him at fifty miles an hour. George and the truck both swerved to miss each other but they swerved in the same direction! George was knocked quite a distance, through the top of a tree, before landing in a neighbor's yard. The truck stopped and the driver ran to call an ambulance. The damage could have been worse—George had broken his right leg, two inches above his ankle.

At the hospital, George's right leg was set in a cast but the tendon in the back of his leg was caught in the fracture. Every time he moved his right foot he would rebreak the bone and it refused to heal. George suffered with this for almost a year, during which time he relied on crutches to get around. For several months he kept trying to convince the doctors that he knew what the problem was, and finally the X-rays revealed that he was correct. George went in for surgery during the spring of 1941 and the tendon was removed from the fracture. A bone graft was necessary and so the doctors cut some splints from his shin and grafted them to his ankle to join the gap.

The operation was a success, but George ended up with his right leg at least half an inch shorter than his left leg. During the many months that he was absent from school, he pursued his interest in aviation in a practical manner, taking an aircraft sheet metal mechanic's correspondence course with an aviation company. By August 1941, George was back on his feet and he went off to Glendale, California, where he spent two months working for the company with whom he had completed the correspondence course.

Then between October and December, George was employed by North American Aviation and worked at the company's plant in Englewood, California. His work involved the assembly of the belly radiator systems of the A-36, which at the time was being supplied to the Royal Air Force in Britain—the later version of this aircraft was named the P-51 Mustang and would play a vital role in George's future.

George was working for North American Aviation when the Japanese attacked Pearl Harbor and the United States went to war. George returned to Oklahoma for six months and meanwhile he checked with his doctor regarding the progress of the recovery of his right leg. Despite the injury and with the help of his doctor, George managed to pass the Army fitness test and in April 1942 he was sworn into the Army Air Force. He then waited for an opening at a cadet school and soon he was packing his bags and leaving Oklahoma to go and begin his training.

During basic training he endured tremendous pain at times during the physical exercise and the marches. Many of his friends and half his family didn't believe that George was going to make it through his basic training on account of his short leg and the trouble it caused him. But nonetheless, everyone was impressed with his determination and all were very proud of him. At times even George himself wasn't sure that he was going to make it. But more than anything in this world, George wanted to be a pilot and so he was determined to at least try to fulfill his dream.

George *did* complete his basic training. A few months passed and then in late summer 1942 he completed preflight at Santa Ana Army Air Base, California. During the fall of 1942 George commenced primary flying training with Ryan PT-22 Recruit aircraft at King City, California. January to March 1943 were spent at Chico, California, training on Vultee BT-13 Valiant aircraft, and then in April and May he trained on North American AT-6 Texan advanced trainer aircraft while stationed at the Army Advanced Flying School, Yuma, Arizona. On Friday 14 May 1943, George was commissioned as second lieutenant, USAAF, and graduated with the Class 43-E. Despite the short leg that would

Lt. George White in the Yuma graduation book, 1943. He was assigned to Crew 25 as copilot. (White family)

WHITE, GEORGE LEWIS
Sopulpa, Okla. Hobby: Model Airplanes and Hunting. Ambition: Aeronautical Engineering. "Take me back to Tulsa".

cause him problems for the rest of his life, he was now an officer in the Army Air Force and a qualified pilot.

Next to his portrait in the class graduation book, his biography reads, "White, George Lewis. Sapulpa, Oklahoma. Hobby: Model Airplanes and Hunting. Ambition: Aeronautical Engineering," and then as a quote, the title of a popular Western swing-style song of the era, "Take me back to Tulsa."

Indeed, George was Tulsa-bound for a period of deserved leave, which he spent at home in Sapulpa—just fifteen miles from Tulsa, where the Douglas Aircraft Company was manufacturing B-24 Liberators under license from Consolidated. George's next assignment was at Randolph Field, Texas, where he trained to become a BT-13 Valiant instructor. However, he began experiencing problems with his spine caused by his short right leg and he was subsequently washed out of instructor school and sent back to Yuma. His health problems settled down and off he went to Fresno, California, assigned to the 396th Bomb Squadron, 47th Bomb Group. This unit was equipped with B-25 Mitchell twin-engine bombers. The unit moved to Sacramento, California, and George was assigned temporary duty at a naval air station at Arcata, California, and was involved with coast patrols. His next assignment was Alaska and the Aleutian Chain before returning to Sacramento and on to Fresno, California.

The 47th Bomb Group was then shipped to China, but George was left in California as part of a pool of personnel intended to form a new B-25 Bomb Group. This never happened and instead, George was shipped to the 453rd Bomb Group at Riverside. He walked with a limp and ran with what his brother, Don, would later describe as a "skip-hop," but George was an exceptional pilot. However, since he was only twenty years old, five years younger than Jack Nortridge and with less experience having been in the military for only one year, George was assigned as copilot to Crew 25.

Just a week or two after George White was assigned to Crew 25 the 453rd Bomb Group completed Phase Two of aircrew training. Phase Three commenced on 6 November 1943 with an emphasis on group formation flying and increasing the efficiency of each crew member in their individual specialties. Practice missions lasting six hours were devised to comprise actual bombing at the Muroc Dry Lake Range, camera bombing of targets (such as the Consolidated plant and docks at San Diego), fighter interception, and navigation. Gunnery was eliminated from these missions and a squadron roster was established allowing three squadrons to participate in each of the twice-daily missions. The squadron excluded from the Group mission roster on any given day made independent bombing practice flights and practiced aerial gunnery over the Pacific, west of Santa Maria. Meanwhile, each of the four squadrons continued to organize ground school independently.

On Tuesday 9 November Jack Nortridge celebrated his twenty-sixth birthday with Evelyn, who was living with him in Riverside (officers were allowed to live off base but most lived on the base in the BOQ, Bachelor Officers' Quarters). Also on that day, the first of six additional B-24E bombers was assigned to the 733rd Squadron, and the rest arrived over the following few days. The 733rd now possessed a total of fifteen B-24s

Crew 25 at March Field, Riverside, California, in November 1943. Donald Lawry wrote on the back of his copy of this photograph, "The best crew in the 453rd Bomb Group" and sent it home to Wisconsin. Back row, left to right: Sgt. Lim Wing Jeong, Sgt. Harvey Nielsen, Sgt. Aurèle "Pete" Veilleux, Sgt. James Freddie Witmer, Sgt. Perry Roberson; Front row, left to right: Sgt. Bill LeRoy, Lt. George White, Lt. Jack Nortridge, Lt. Donald Lawry, and Lt. Bill Eagleson. (Ruby Jo Roberson Faust)

Donald Lawry (far right), Bill Eagleson (second right), and unidentified personnel at 733rd Bomb Squadron Operations, March Field, California. Bill was the best man at Donald's wedding. (Bill Eagleson)

for their Phase training. Jack gave Bill Eagleson and Donald Lawry some elementary flying lessons, as he was keen for them to be familiar with the rudiments of flying a B-24. In the event of both pilots being badly injured on a mission, it would be reassuring to know that other crew members stood some chance of getting them home. Bill and Donald exchanged the fundamentals of bombsight operation and navigation and the crew became increasingly versatile and dynamic.

Throughout his training Donald was regularly sending money home to his mother who he knew was struggling to make ends meet. He wrote home frequently, and his letters to his mother were reassuringly confident and mature, as he didn't want her to worry. However, he often revealed more realities in the letters to his brother, such as the time when he and some friends went AWOL one night. They had gone into Hollywood to experience the high life and didn't get back to March Field until 4:30 a.m., just in time for a training flight at 6 a.m. In his letters he often referred to his desire to travel the world and also to maybe learn to play the piano some day, like his kid sister, Betty Lou.

Donald knew that the Group had almost completed Phase training at March Field, and that soon they would be sent overseas. His high school girlfriend, Dorothy Brunsell, had been out to California to visit him on a number of occasions. She was a year younger (eighteen) and had graduated just a few months previously. Donald confided in his crew a couple of times, unsure if getting married was a responsible thing to do under the circumstances. Bill assured Donald that, if that's what he and Dorothy wanted then they *should* get married. Bill and Lt. Samuel "Sammy" Borenstein, a navigator from the Squadron and one of Donald's closest friends, went out and bought a wedding present and a card.

Meanwhile, on Saturday 20 November, Donald wrote a letter to his mother, explaining that Dorothy was there visiting him, and that they were hoping, if all went to plan, to get married the following Monday. He also wrote about the pilot of the crew:

> He went through Cadets before the war, when it was really tough, and he's been flying army planes for two years now. The last time up he started to teach me how to fly, it sure is a funny feeling. . . . Did you know that Nortridge is from [near] Rockford, Illinois. He knows all the places I used to go, and some of the people. He is also the only pilot that I feel safe riding with.
>
> PS, Jack brought in a picture so you can see what the best combat crew looks like.

On the back of the photograph was written, "The best combat crew in the 453rd Bomb Group." Two days later at 7 p.m. on 22 November, Donald and Dorothy were married at March Field post chapel, by the 453rd Bomb Group's chaplain, Lt. Lester Liles, with Bill Eagleson as best man. Sammy Borenstein and some of the other officers from the 733rd were also present. A couple of days later, on Thanksgiving, Donald got

Lt. Lester Liles, 453rd Bomb Group chaplain (on the left), with Dorothy and Don Lawry on their wedding day, March Field, 22 November 1943. (Dorothy Taplin)

some time to write home and share the news. The *Evansville Review* reported the wedding: "The ceremony was performed by Lieutenant Liles, post chaplain. The bride was given in marriage by Captain Robert Kanaga. The only other attendant was Lieutenant William Eagleson, a friend of the groom. Mrs. Lawry wore a light blue wool jersey dress with brown accessories and three gardenias. The ceremony was followed by a party at the Officers' Club."

Fifty-eight years later Dorothy reflected:

> We had so little time together. When I left California, the only thing he could tell me was that he thought he was leaving from Florida.

The Group POM (Preparation for Overseas Movement) inspection had been successfully passed on 16 November, and finally on 28 November, the end of Phase Three marked the completion of training. The ground echelons departed March Field on 2 December for New Jersey, leaving the shores of the United States on 13 December. The air echelon of forty-eight crews awaited further orders to collect their new aircraft from Hamilton Field, California. Meanwhile the Nortridge crew celebrated the completion of their training during an evening at Lake Arrowhead, as Bill Eagleson recalls:

> We did have quite a celebration at Lake Arrowhead when we finished our crew training at March Field. . . . That night we broke ten bottles of burgundy wine in a sort of a farewell to the Phases party.

PART TWO

"If You Fly with Me, I'm Going to Bring You Home"

CHAPTER SIX

On the Road to
the Big League

On 5 December, while driving west along Highway 60 from March Field to Riverside, Jack Nortridge was stopped by the California Highway Patrol for driving at an average speed of 65 mph, allegedly passing all other traffic. After flying B-24s every day, Jack probably didn't realize he was breaking the speed limit!

During the first few days of December 1943, with Phase training completed, the 453rd Bomb Group aircrews awaited further orders as they passed the time in Riverside. Meanwhile, Crew 25 celebrated Bill LeRoy's twenty-first birthday on 14 December. Then, the air echelon received movement orders to travel by troop train to Hamilton Field, San Francisco. Arriving on Saturday 18 December, most of the crews were issued their brand new H-model B-24 Liberator aircraft.

Bill Eagleson:

> December found us picking up a $250,000 aircraft . . . I remember
> my pilot's remarks when he had to sign for one EA B-24H Consoli-
> dated aircraft (with four engines) . . .

The aircraft, serial number 42–52234, was a Ford version of the B-24, manufactured under license from the Consolidated Aircraft Corporation, at the Ford Motor Company's Willow Run plant in Michigan. It had been delivered to the USAAF on 29 October 1943 and flown to the Birmingham Modification Center in Alabama, being arriving at Hamilton Field on 25 November. It was the aircraft that Jack Nortridge's crew expected to fly into combat upon reaching some overseas theater of operations. With its four 1,200 horsepower Pratt & Whitney radial engines mounted across the wingspan of 110 feet, this aircraft would become the icon of all their hopes and fears, and they hoped that it would serve them well and bring them good luck. However, there was significant disappointment for the bombardiers of the 453rd Bomb Group when they climbed aboard their new aircraft for the first time, as Bill explained:

> The irony of the whole situation was—I was trained on Norden
> bombsights . . . we worked hard, we trained to become proficient on
> the Norden bombsight, we *were* proficient on the Norden bombsight

and when we picked up our airplanes at Hamilton Field we found
Sperry bombsights in them. Everybody's excited about being is-
sued all this new equipment, .45s, binoculars . . . and there [in the
B-24] I look and there's this thing that looks like a toaster.

We did drop two bombs out over the Pacific, and that was the
training I had on the Sperry bombsight. We were a little short-
handed on that kind of a deal to have spent all that time training on
one instrument and then finding we had a different situation. . . . I
never, never had the confidence in that bombsight that I had in the
Norden.

The bombardiers of the 453rd Bomb Group couldn't help feeling
that months of training with the Norden bombsight had been in vain.
There had been so much mystery and intrigue surrounding the famous
Norden bombsight, not only in the media as a morale-boosting exercise
but also during bombardier training when the bombardiers were sworn
to secrecy with the "Bombardier's Oath."

On arrival at Hamilton Field, Donald Lawry wrote home with news
of their grueling train journey from Riverside. He wrote that his crew
had been given their new "ship" and that he had spent the day calibrat-
ing the navigational instruments, and they had been up for a flight so Bill
could drop some bombs over the ocean, to familiarize himself with the
Sperry bombsight. Donald added that he suspected that they might be
destined for England, however nobody knew for sure. He advised his
family that from now on, all mail should be sent to a New York address
from where letters would be redirected to him at his overseas destination.

Crew 25 decided that they should personalize their brand new B-24,
as was the aircrew tradition. Following their recent end of Phase training celebrations at Lake Arrowhead, they decided on a name for their
aircraft: *"CORKY" BURGUNDY BOMBERS*
Perry Roberson:

> The name came to us during the celebration we had after comple-
> tion of flight training. We each bought a bottle of [burgundy] wine
> and saved the corks for luck. We then hung these at our stations on
> the plane.

At Hamilton Field the 453rd Bomb Group's air echelon became the
responsibility of Air Transport Command (ATC) under which the crews
went through processing. This entailed procedures for flying into
strange lands and unfamiliar airfields with limited communications, as
well as over-water and ditching procedures. The crews prepared to fly in
broken formations across the southern sector of the United States. Each
crew was assigned several stopover points before arriving at Morrison
Field, West Palm Beach, Florida. The journey to Florida was scheduled
to take several weeks, due to the endless flow of aircraft and crews en
route overseas.

A number of the crews had been disappointed on their arrival at Hamilton Field to find that the Group had not yet been assigned its full quota of aircraft and so most of the aircraft flew with additional passengers on board, either flying personnel or ground staff. Four passengers were assigned to *Corky:* 2nd Lt. William H. Powell Jr. (copilot from Lt. Bertrand's crew), Sgt. Pasqual A. Gicale (flight engineer and gunner from Lt. Hamilton's crew), T/Sgt. Richard N. Brennan (crew chief of one of the ground crews), and Sgt. Arthur Schacht (radio mechanic).

Air Transport Command gave Jack Nortridge orders to fly first to southern California and on Tuesday 21 December Crew 25 and their four passengers were on their way in *Corky*. After a three-hour-and-forty-minute journey they touched down at Palm Springs, known as the "Capital of the Desert," where *Corky*'s green camouflage guise seemed somehow inappropriate.

Bill Eagleson:

> We had just left Hamilton Field, California and we stopped in at Palm Springs. Of course we were under ATC orders at that time, and flight clearances were all backed up as there was a stream of aircraft going overseas, and so at Palm Springs we were stood down.

At Palm Springs, *Corky*'s crew met a British ferry pilot with a single-engine fighter aircraft that the crew would come to appreciate during the months ahead. "She was flying a sleek machine . . . known as the P-51," Eagleson recalls.

During their conversation with the female ferry pilot, George White told of his experiences at the North American Aviation plant in Englewood, California, where he worked on the A-36 assembly line—the A-36 was subsequently redesignated the P-51.

The crew anticipated that they would spend Christmas in Palm Springs, where late each afternoon Mount San Jacinto shades the town from the hot desert sun.

> Christmas Eve in Palm Springs was very, very beautiful. It was quite a place for Christmas Eve—palm trees, and then you looked off and you had snow-covered mountains. Jack and I spent the evening right up to going to church at the Desert Inn, in Palm Springs . . . went to twelve o'clock Communion and the pastor very kindly sent the program home to my folks, and they had first knowledge that I was no longer at March or Hamilton Field, and that we were possibly en route to *somewhere*—because at that time we didn't know.

On Tuesday 28 December the crew was alerted for their next flight, to Midland, Texas. Crossing the Joshua Tree National Park and leaving California behind them, the 453rd Bomb Group crews continued over the vast desert landscapes of Arizona and New Mexico and across the

Rio Grande that passed beneath them in seconds. From the air, faces looked down at the moving shadows—a miniature formation of aircraft cast across the sandy terrain below them. After a flight lasting five hours and forty-five minutes *Corky* landed at Midland, Texas, where the crew was to spend three nights waiting for their next flight clearance.

On 31 December *Corky* departed Midland, Texas—next stop: Memphis, Tennessee. The five hour flight took them across some four hundred miles of Texas until eventually the state of Arkansas consumed the horizon and the view below, at first nearing James Witmer's home town, Texarkana. Two hundred and fifty miles later and the aircraft crossed the mighty Mississippi River at a point over two-thirds of the way along its two thousand three hundred mile route to the Gulf of Mexico. The city of Memphis was in sight, the Mississippi Delta's cotton-trading centre and the location of one of the country's largest inland ports.

The 453rd Bomb Group's crews were authorized to leave the base that night to celebrate the arrival of the New Year, and *Corky*'s crew headed into the downtown area of the city, to the Hotel Peabody on Union Avenue. Despite their youthful confidence and their pride in their achievements of graduation and crew training, they knew that their greatest challenges and uncertainties lay ahead of them still. Speculation was pointless, for they could only hope and pray that they would make it through the following months, and that the year ahead would bring an end to the war. But that night was about having some fun—after all, it might be their last night out on the town for some time.

Jack assumed a responsibility for his crew. At twenty-six years of age, he was the eldest member of the crew—Donald Lawry was nineteen and Lim Wing Jeong was only eighteen. Jack knew he had to be a good leader and that his crew had to have faith both in him and in each other if they were to have any hope of surviving. Every crew believed they were the best, but not necessarily because they *knew* they were the best, but because their sanity depended on the hope and the belief that they could survive. Jack told them what they needed to hear, and his positive attitude was contagious. At the Hotel Peabody, toasts were made, songs were sung, and the drinks flowed steadily as the celebrations ascended to midnight. Jack Nortridge vowed to his crew that, "If you stay with me you're going to come back and we're going to come back together." Together they looked to 1944.

Bill Eagleson:

> New Year's Eve we were in Memphis, Tennessee—the Hotel Peabody—and all of my crew have different recollections of that evening—but we were together. I believe we met up with Skitch Henderson who was *back* from England and there, at the Hotel Peabody.[1]

Six nights were spent in Memphis, awaiting ATC flight clearances.

> We saw Frank Sinatra's *Higher and Higher* at Memphis. . . . Frank did
> a great job with "A Lovely Way to Spend an Evening"—and there
> we were, confined to the base. But that's a great wartime song . . .

Finally on Thursday 6 January 1944 the orders were given for the Group to make their last North American flight, and that day Bill Eagleson wrote in his diary:

> Today it looks as though we're on the last hop in United States:
> Memphis to Miami. Glad to leave the coal-dirty air of Memphis.
> The Red Cross at Memphis has been very kind to us, everyone in
> our crew had a lunch to eat that was very good.

Leaving Tennessee, *Corky* flew southeast over the state of Mississippi and then through the heart of Alabama, eventually nearing Perry Roberson's hometown, Ozark. They crossed a corner of Georgia before reaching northern Florida. After a five-hour flight they landed at Morrison Field, West Palm Beach, a base surrounded by alligator-infested swamp and everglade. A diary entry preserved the experiences:

> Flying over Florida, much more interesting than anything thus
> far—everglades, winding canals, and we finally saw the Atlantic
> Ocean. Landing at Morrison Field we found the weather warm,
> food good, and the realization that we were all having our last
> twenty-four hours in the United States.

Jack Nortridge's crew had now flown several thousand miles in *Corky* in just four flights over a period of sixteen days. At Morrison Field there was a reassignment of passengers on *Corky*. The two flying personnel, Lt. William Powell and Sgt. Pasqual Gicale, were to continue with Crew 25 for the flights to the Group's overseas destination. But the two ground personnel were replaced by Sgt. William E. Hawkins (flight engineer and gunner from Crew 51, 734th Bomb Squadron) and Sgt. Floyd Evje (crew chief of one of the ground crews).

To where they were going was still a subject of speculation. Bill Eagleson recalls their departure from Florida:

> We were, I think, sort of relieved to get out of Morrison Field. It
> was a lonely feeling; we had no communication with our family,
> and just waiting in anticipation of "Where do we go?" At Morrison
> Field we had no idea as to whether we were going to the Far East,
> the 15th Air Force in Italy, or England. England at that time was
> known as the "Big League"—That was a baseball expression I
> guess.

On the night of Friday 7 January 1944, he added to his diary:

> It was a long day—record checks, final pay, physical examination,
> and one thing and another that lead us up to takeoff time. The

> biggest thrill tonight was at the Officers' Club, while just sitting
> around writing and getting some letters off, somebody played Bos-
> ton Symphony Orchestra *Overture to Romeo and Juliet* (I think they
> called it "Our Love"). The food at Morrison: very good. We had
> breakfast at midnight and (I hate to say this, but) I ate ten eggs!
> (These were our last look at real eggs as we were told that every-
> thing would be powdered.)[2]

The crew did not sleep that night. *Corky* taxied out at a darkened
Morrison Field in the early hours of Saturday 8 January for a flight to
Puerto Rico. As *Corky* climbed away from the base the crew looked
down and saw a burning wreck at the end of the runway—the preceding aircraft had crashed on takeoff.

Another diary entry recorded:

> After waiting all night for a flight clearance *Corky* finally lifted her
> nose to the southeast and we all said, "See y'later America!" I
> crawled back to the tail for a final glimpse of the peninsula: "Next
> time we see you Florida, may the lights be a lot brighter than they
> are tonight!"—The lights of Florida were dimmed and dulled and
> yellow.

Following the United States' entry into hostilities, American coastal
cities at first refused to impose blackout regulations for fears of the effect
that this would have on the tourist trade. Over the course of three
months, German U-boats sank over two hundred ships off the East
Coast of the United States. The victims were visible for sinking because
they were silhouetted against the glow of the illuminated cities. Eventually the enemy threat was acknowledged; blackout regulations imposed
and the lights along the Atlantic coast were dimmed.

Crew 25 looked back at Miami's half-hearted glow and felt as if they
were leaving behind their lives. Three members of the crew were married and four of them had already found the women they were to
marry—if they survived the war. They faced endless possibilities of
what Bill Eagleson later described as "unknown" factors.

The crew and their four passengers were now flying the Southern
Ferry Route to *somewhere*, but still nobody knew exactly where—perhaps
with the exception of Donald Lawry. The navigators were given more
information than the pilots, as they were briefed in advance on the
routes they would most likely be taking and the airfields they must find
for their stopovers. From San Francisco Donald had already written to
his family and mentioned that he suspected he was heading for England. But nothing was carved in stone. The first leg of this journey took
them between two points that make up one side of what was to become
known as the Bermuda Triangle! Eyes kept returning to their watches
as they counted down the minutes. One hour into the flight and Jack
would be opening his secret, sealed orders containing their overseas

assignment. Finally the moment of truth arrived and all listened closely
to their pilot.

Bill Eagleson remembers:

> We got a little bit south of Miami and Jack opened the orders . . .
> called us up on the flight deck and said "Well, we're headed to the
> European Theatre"—we discovered that we were destined for the
> Big League.

Lim Wing Jeong resigned himself to the fact that he would not be
fighting the war against the Japanese, but instead would be fighting the
Germans—but still, Germany, Italy, and Japan were in it together as the
Axis powers.

The ground echelons of the 453rd Bomb Group had already completed the journey by sea and had since begun establishing the 453rd
Bomb Group at a base, to use the familiar media expression of the time,
"Somewhere in England." As *Corky*'s crew began to focus their thoughts
and expectations of the 8th Air Force and of England, the Bahamas
passed beneath them. After a six-hour flight *Corky* touched down at
Borinquen airfield, in the American colony of Puerto Rico. "Before
sunrise," Eagleson recalls, "we landed in Puerto Rico to realize, Home
Was Away, England Ahead!"

The crew spent five nights in Puerto Rico while some engine problems on *Corky* were rectified and while they anticipated further flight
clearances. This gave the crew some time to relax and experience their
first glimpse of life outside the United States, and provided a few
thoughts for personal diaries, such as Bill Eagleson's:

> Borinquen has been swell. Thus far this overseas business has been
> fun! Met some civilians our third night here and managed to play a
> round of golf. The native caddies charge thirty cents for doing
> their chores.

The crew left Puerto Rico on Thursday 13 January and looked down
over the pale green waters of the Caribbean Sea until the island of
Trinidad came into view. *Corky* crossed the coastline over sandy beaches
and palm trees, skimmed over a thick carpet of jungle, and dropped
down into the American base at Waller Field. The flight had lasted four
hours plus forty-five minutes.

Some of the crews were beginning to personalize their aircraft, turning the olive drab camouflage finish into a backdrop for brightly painted
colors of "nose art." Typically American bombers displayed colorful
artwork featuring cartoon characters and pinup girls often based on the
work of the illustrator Alberto Vargas. In Trinidad, Jack's crew made
some negotiations with a ground crew mechanic who, through his own
artistic skills ran a sideline enterprise of painting aircraft nose art. *Corky*'s crew suspected that the guy had never seen a day sober, and so they

offered him a bottle of Bacardi rum as payment for some artwork on their aircraft. He remarked, "For that, I'll paint the whole plane!"

In big, bright, burgundy and orange letters below the copilot's windows he painted *CORKY* and plugged the *O* with a painted cork. Below *CORKY* he added *BURGUNDY BOMBERS* in smaller letters. Below one side of the nose turret he painted *MISS ELLA MAE*, for Pete Veilleux (his girlfriend's name was Eleanor Mae). Below the nose turret and above the bombardier's sighting window he added *Bill's Bar* for bombardier Bill Eagleson; below George White's side window it said *Whitey*; while the bomb bay doors were decorated with the words *bomb cocktails*. Alcohol was the recurring theme.

That night the crew billeted in barracks raised above the ground on poles. Lectures on malaria control soon made the American visitors appreciate the mosquito netting which covered their beds. The following morning they attended ATC briefings for the day's flight. Aircraft were to leave Waller Field at five-minute intervals—next stop: Brazil. The flight of seven hours and thirty minutes took the crew over water and coastline until reaching Guyana, and then over miles of jungle, the Amazon Delta, and the equator. These long flights were strenuous and took a high level of concentration from Jack and copilot George White. Behind the flight deck, flight engineer Perry Roberson closely monitored his instruments and fuel levels. Donald Lawry had little opportunity to relax in the nose compartment of *Corky* as he studied his maps and navigational instruments in order to keep the aircraft on course over seemingly endless miles of unfamiliar terrain. *Corky* had been designed for combat, with little thought spared for comfort. Bill Eagleson recalls the long hours for the rest of the crew during these Southern Ferry Route flights:

> The crew was not very comfortable but they adjusted well, and usually they huddled up in the flight deck and they huddled back in the waist section. Sometimes if it were daylight they'd play a little poker.

Eventually Val de Gaens (Valley of Dogs) airfield came into view amid the jungle, close to the large Brazilian city of Belem. The crew spent one night there, billeted in white plaster barracks adjacent to the airfield. The drinking water was brown, although, the crew was assured, water supplies were purified by U.S. engineers. The tropical climate in Brazil was a new experience. The bluest skies would suddenly blacken in a downpour of torrential rain, and then, as quickly as they had turned black the skies would fade to blue again. From South America, Donald Lawry sent silk stockings to Dorothy in Evansville, which were impossible to find in the United States at that time. All letters were censored so Dorothy had very little idea about what Donald was doing or where he was going.

During the morning of Saturday 15 January the crew attended a briefing for their next flight. The ATC flight briefings provided details of their route and other information of interest, and instructions that received serious attention. All bomber crews flying this route over Brazil were warned not to stray too far inland. They understood that if they did and they got into trouble, nobody would go looking for them. The crews speculated upon reports that the vast tropical forests and jungle were inhabited by unfriendly natives—according to the colorful rumors on the base at Belem, some of them were cannibals! Certainly the indigenous peoples were unlikely to send welcoming parties to greet any U.S. airmen who happened to crash-land their B-24 in this unspoiled part of the Earth. Some crews remarked that they would rather fly over the water of the coastline instead of over land, for if they got into trouble, the prospect of drowning was somehow preferable to facing the locals!

Leaving Belem behind and beginning a four-hour-and-forty-five-minute flight over mile upon mile of dense Brazilian jungle, Donald Lawry was actually fulfilling some of his wildest dreams of exploring the South American jungle, of flying from place to place on exciting adventures. He had even bought a pair of Brazilian boots on his travels, and was beginning to look the part. However, Donald was particularly cautious to navigate close to the coastline. After several hours the jungle became increasingly sparse, opening into more interesting terrain. Following a railroad they approached their last stop in the Americas—Fortaleza, Brazil. Bill Eagleson recalls:

> Trinidad, Belem, Fortaleza—The country did not seem too friendly. It was jungle and this really was our first taste of "away from home" so to speak. We were in a stream of planes in the ATC South Atlantic route, and the length of time that we spent at each of these stations was dependent upon the planes that were backed up. As I remember there were B-24s, B-17s, there were C-47s on this route, all waiting for clearances to get across the South Atlantic.

In 1944 this long South Atlantic journey was quite an adventure, especially to a young aircrew whose high school days were only a couple of years behind them. They all knew that the South Atlantic flight would be an unnerving journey full of more uncertainties than they could imagine: Would the aircraft make the next flight without mechanical or technical failure? Would their navigation be accurate and would they find land safely? Would the fuel load hold out long enough for them to reach their next base? If anything was to go wrong, then there would be little or no hope for them, for there was almost two thousand miles of U-boat infested ocean to cross before they would see land again—only just within the range of a B-24.

The Sunday morning ATC preflight briefings were detailed and extensive. Dakar, French West Africa, was the next destination. The flight

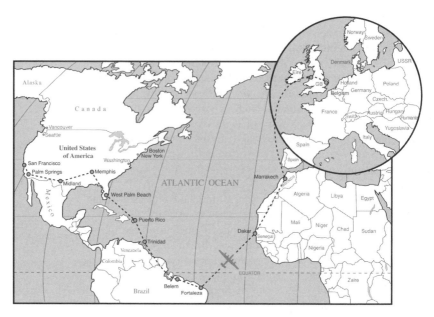

Corky's crew departed San Francisco on 21 December 1943, spent Christmas in Palm Springs; New Year in Memphis; proceeded to South America; West Africa; Valley, Wales, and finally arrived at Old Buckenham, England, on 30 January 1944.

was estimated to take around ten hours, and they would fly through an Equatorial Front. The South Atlantic crossing was scheduled to be a night flight to allow the use of celestial navigation (navigating by the stars) and so that landfall would be in daylight. Bill Eagleson recalls:

> We left Fortaleza on another night flight—just made takeoff because of load conditions . . . we damn near didn't get off the ground at Fortaleza.

Perry Roberson:

> A nervous time for me was the flight from South America to Dakar, Africa. . . . On the trip to England we had four passengers—two flight crew and two ground crew. We had all their gear as well as ours. We also had two bomb bay fuel tanks for added range to get from South America to Africa. With all that weight we had a gross weight of 62,000 lbs., which was maximum for the plane. It was standard practice on takeoff for the pilot to apply brakes after lift-off to stop the landing gear from spinning. On our takeoff from South America, just as the brakes were locked the plane hit the runway again and could have caused a crash but our luck was good; we bounced and got off okay, even if a little rattled.

Weighed down with baggage, fuel, a cargo of mail (on behalf of the U.S. postal service), and several cases of rum (for personal consumption),

Corky climbed away from South America and out over the Atlantic Ocean. In the darkness the "New World" seemed to fade away behind them. A couple of hours later and the weather deteriorated as they approached the Equatorial Front that they had been warned about in their ATC briefing. *Corky* endured thunder and lightning as rain poured into the aircraft, and the crew marveled, albeit with uncertainty, at the sight of St. Elmo's fire flashing and flickering around the aircraft and along the bomb bay catwalk.

Jack and George struggled at the controls, battling with the elements to keep a straight and level flight. As cadets the crew had marveled at how something so huge as a B-24 could fly. But in these stormy and turbulent conditions, the aircraft seemed hopelessly small, fragile, and precarious. Below them was seemingly endless and certainly perilous ocean, for hundreds of miles in any direction. The heavens above had opened up, throwing at them all they could take. It seemed like at any moment they might be washed away.

Perry Roberson:

> We had been told to fly at 9,000 feet but we had some rough air and thought by going higher it would be better. We climbed to 15,000 feet and by this time it was all that both pilots could do to keep us on level flight.

Bill Eagleson:

> We had a horrendous night flight out of Brazil to Dakar—by horrendous I mean the weather was *God-awful*—very turbulent. We were flying in fronts most of the night. . . . We had an overloaded plane, we were full of gas, and we just made it off the runway and we went into this horrendous weather front that just threw us around the entire night.

No stars could be seen throughout most of the flight, and when stars were visible it was impossible to focus on them for long enough, due to the violent turbulence that shook the aircraft. Therefore celestial navigation was not an option. There were no facilities on board for radio navigation and with no landmarks out at sea, Donald's skills in pilotage navigation were redundant. The last resort was dead reckoning (DR) navigation. Considering the weather information provided at the preflight briefing, recording the prevailing wind direction and velocity throughout the flight, and bringing the factors of altitude and airspeed into the equation, Donald calculated accurate headings and times. Bill Eagleson recalls:

> Don did not have an opportunity to do celestial navigation during the night flight. We were bouncing too much. . . . Don and I were up in the nose trying to do a little navigating. It was strictly all DR, trying to record air speeds and headings and altitudes . . . passing information onto the pilot. It was quite a scary-type situation.

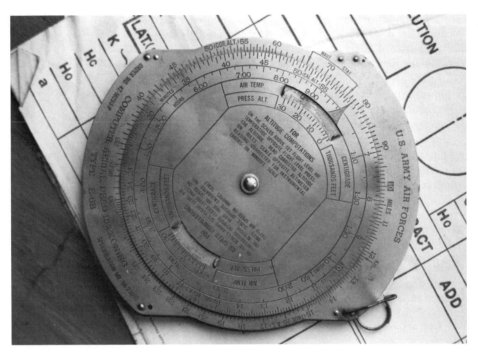

An E-6B computer used for dead reckoning navigation. "This computer is really the business, I don't know where I would start if I didn't have one," wrote Donald Lawry. (Ian McLachlan)

Finding land again depended solely on the precision of Donald's navigation skills. From Hondo Field navigation school in Texas only eight short months previously, his training curriculum had covered dead reckoning navigation, and on Sunday 9 May 1943 he had written home to his mother with an insight into his studies:

> The time really goes fast when they keep us so damn busy. We have started the most important phase of the first nine weeks, it is called dead reckoning, drawing vector diagrams, and then working out problems on our E-6B computer.

The E-6B dead reckoning computer was a manually operated, handheld device made of concentric brass discs of different diameters, each engraved with figures pertaining to altitude, air speed, atmospheric conditions, distance, and compass direction. Essentially it was a circular slide rule that enabled a skilled navigator to calculate all relevant factors in order to navigate with precision.

> This computer is really the business, I don't know where I would start if I didn't have one. They are so efficient that we can take a reading from all our instruments and make an entry in our log

every five minutes. If it wasn't for that it would take about fifteen to twenty minutes to take all the readings and calibrate them for instrument error, changes in altitude and temperature. It's a lot of fun though.

In contrast, during the long night flight across the South Atlantic it was no fun at all. It was a survival situation as the aircraft and crew was shaken by turbulence and storms. In the confined nose compartment of the aircraft, Donald Lawry tried to remain perched on his swivel seat while hunched uncomfortably over his chart table—with his back to the front of the aircraft it seemed to him like they were flying backwards. Donald studied his maps and notes with a sense of eagerness and urgency, assisted by Bill Eagleson:

> Think about it, the age, the experience—here we are over the South Atlantic, trying to get through turbulence that we never had experienced, anywhere in our lives, doing DR navigation with Don Lawry up there in the nose.

The maps were illuminated by the red glow of a lamp that cast shadows across the inside of the nose compartment—a red lamp was used because red light least affects night vision. From the flight deck Jack Nortridge and George White could see the dim red light leaking into the black skies from the Plexiglas astrodome window above the navigator's compartment. The rest of the crew were in darkness. Bill Eagleson recalls:

> Jack was rather strict on night flying. He did not like any lights in the aircraft, and I can understand that because he wanted to keep his night vision to a maximum. We flew one tropical front after another. Maintaining 15,000 feet was difficult.

Eventually Donald announced that they had reached the "point of no return," which meant they were closer to Africa than South America—hopefully enough fuel to reach Africa but certainly not enough to make it back to South America. Regardless of all eventualities—weather conditions, engine failure, navigation error, fuel leak—there was no going back, no matter what.

Bill Eagleson later added to his diary an account of the events of the crew's South Atlantic flight from Fortaleza:

> Midnight GMT we took off on a night of hell—the next stop Africa. Two hours out we hit turbulence caused by an occluded front. I was all over the plane nose bouncing whichever way the plane wanted to throw me. Jack and White worked together all night trying to keep the ship level. Don Lawry couldn't do anything but dead reckoning navigation—no moon, no stars, just thick "soup" accompanied by hail, strong winds, and lightning. Don and I worked the DR together that night and it was an unforgettable evening. Dawn came up and we still couldn't find land.

As the weather conditions cleared at the break of dawn, Donald Lawry began to see the waves in the Atlantic below them and at last he became confident that they would soon be approaching land. However, the flight was estimated to take ten hours, and by now they were flying into the eleventh hour. The crew was anxious that their fuel supply would last them to their destination at Dakar, and flight engineer Perry Roberson made adjustments to balance the levels in each fuel tank. By distributing the depleted fuel supply evenly to each engine, Perry was able to keep all four engines running. He recalls:

> Sweat was pouring from both pilots so we let back down to 9,000 feet and the trip was routine from there.

Donald's navigation had turned out to be flawless, and the crew's sprits were lifted when they saw Africa on the horizon. In the hazy early morning light like a majestic bird, *Corky* swooped down to the landing strip at Eknes Field, Rufisque, Dakar, in the French colony of Senegal, West Africa. The flight time had reached eleven full hours. The crew was startled to find they were landing on a steel mat runway submerged on the landing strip. As they touched down a cloud of sandy dust was raised behind the aircraft. Bill Eagleson:

> It was our first landing on steel mat runway—the noise surprised us. . . . That's quite a sensation when you think you're going into grass and all of a sudden under the grass is steel.

The shaky takeoff from Fortaleza had first caused tension on the tires and the surprise steel mat landing in Dakar added to the strain, as Lim Wing Jeong recalls:

> When you hit that runway, man it sure was noisy . . . the pilot told us to look out the waist to see how the tires were, and a tire was torn.

Perry Roberson:

> On landing in Africa we checked the tires on the main gear and found the rubber burned off to the fabric on both tires—one had to be replaced.

Lim Wing Jeong:

> When we flew over from South America to Africa, I wasn't wearing a life jacket and when we got to Africa Jack Nortridge said, "Next time you do that I'll ground you!" So, anyway, I wore the Mae West after that.

Dakar's cool sea breezes were welcome after the humid heat of South America. Twenty times each day the sound of a bugle was heard from the French garrison on the hill. The colony, although commanded by the French, was guarded by native Senegalese troops carrying old bayoneted rifles and who kept watch over each aircraft on the airfield at all times. They wore shoes by night but were barefooted during the daytime. The food at Dakar was not too good and neither was the beer, but the French Cognac was enjoyed by most. Bill Eagleson's diary preserved the feeling of relief of being safe on the ground in Africa:

> Our gas supply was damn low when we finally arrived at Dakar. Our crew is exhausted. Come hell, fatigue, or famine—Nothing could keep Jack and I away from the Officers' Club! Tonight we had a swell time singing songs and getting acquainted with the French. The food here is good, coffee drinkable, and the short time we're at this base our army has fixed it up swell. The natives speak French and are quite fortunate in that the only clothing they wear is a long night-gown—must make it easy for them to get up in the morning! All in all, Dakar has been right to us. It sure was a welcome sight.

The South Atlantic flight had been the most harrowing experience the crew had shared in their few months together. Through these experiences a greater level of dependency and unity surfaced within the crew. Reflecting on the trials of the night flight to Dakar, the bombardier remarks:

> That was a night I don't think we as a crew can ever forget. I have a [diary] note here: "*Corky* turning over beautifully—sure is a wonderful ship, and every man on the crew is proud of her. Every man on the crew is capable, well trained, and *ready!*"

At Eknes Field conditions were particularly overcrowded as a continual stream of American aircraft and crews were arriving there daily, awaiting weather and flight clearances for the next leg of the journey. However, the Nortridge crew spent just one night in Dakar. In the billets the beds were uncomfortable, and the night was cold. The following morning, Tuesday 18 January, the crew was briefed for their next flight. Their destination was Marrakech, Morocco, over one thousand and three hundred miles northeast of Dakar, and under 150 miles south of Casablanca. The minutes ticked by that morning and soon it was take off time.

The first navigational checkpoint for Donald Lawry was the town of St. Louis on the coast. The next checkpoints were the oasis at Atar and then Black Mountain, visible for some fifty miles. Continuing over desert sand and dune, *Corky* crossed the Western Sahara—like flying over an ocean of sand, there was nowhere to land in an emergency. The next checkpoint came into view, Tindouf, and then *Corky* skimmed over the foothills of the Atlas Mountain range, cautiously avoiding Spanish Morocco. Jack Nortridge and George White steered carefully through the narrow Scoura Pass in the Atlas Mountains at the briefed 9,000 feet, as the rocky and snow-capped peaks passed by eerily at the end of each wingtip. Clearing the Atlas Mountains, the city of Marrakech, French Morocco, was in sight. From the air the city appeared magnificent; large and clean, and full of white buildings that reflected the sun. The flight had totaled eight hours and thirty minutes when the wheels touched down at Marrakech.

The base had been a French army and commercial airfield before the war and around the field were many abandoned French aircraft. The resident Free French Army and Air Force personnel still flew aerial patrols in old British Wellington bombers and American A-20s; however with the large American presence on the base, the French now occupied just one corner of the flying field. The United States Army Air Forces had turned the field into a vibrant American base, inundated with aircraft and crews en route to England, the Middle East, and Italy. At each point of the journey, the Nortridge crew was reunited with other 453rd Bomb Group crews and they shared their experiences of the long adventurous flights. Along with hundreds of airmen on their ways overseas, there was what Bill Eagleson described as "all kinds of north-south-east-west traffic parked up at the field there."

In Marrakech, *Corky*'s crew met the veteran aircrew of the B-17 *Hell's Angels*. This aircraft had completed forty-eight missions from England with different crews assigned to the 303rd Bomb Group. It was now being returned to the United States with a veteran combat crew who were to fly *Hell's Angels* around the country on Victory Bond tours to promote the sale of war bonds. Hundreds of signatures of the Molesworth-based Americans covered the aircraft. Bill Eagleson recalls:

> We were locked in with great envy to every word from its combat crew members.

At Marrakech the American airmen endured more cold nights. Some slept in modern stucco houses, once the dwellings of French officers and their families, while many of the crews experienced very little in the way of comfort:

> We spent a few days in Marrakech and *it was cold!* We were in tents, six man tents, and I can remember using a number ten tin can to warm my hands with, burning the wrappings of K-rations. This was our first experience of seeing the actual effects of war. There were Italian war prisoners who were staffing the camp. (Bill Eagleson)

The majority of the American aircrews in Morocco made at least one visit to downtown Marrakech, where a number of French families lived and ran their businesses, and where determined Moroccan peddlers would offer various leather goods such as shoes, bags, and wallets for high prices. Experimenting with a little haggling, the American tourists could secure a deal for a third of the original asking price.

Donald Lawry later wrote about these experiences in a letter to his mother:

> It sure is a heck of a job trying to make the people of the different countries understand us. Every time you want to buy anything the first price they set is a good ten times too much, so you divide by about fifteen and start bargaining.

The GIs also marveled with horror at some of the sights and the history of Marrakech, where for a thousand years sultans had bestowed the city with palaces, mosques, and citadels. Allegedly, the remains of thousands of enemies of the Muslim faith had been baked into the bricks used in the making of the fortifying city walls, while the captives' blood was used in the cement and their heads in the foundations of the city gates.

Before they were issued passes to leave the base, the GIs were given lectures on VD and warned that the "forbidden city" of Medina was strictly off-limits. But to many of the young, adventurous Americans, sometimes the rules were there to be broken as the bombardier remembers:

> Marrakech was quite a place, and we did one night break some rules and the crew went down into the Medina and we saw all of the horrors of that place.

From the air the white buildings of Marrakech had appeared clean, neat, and tidy, but those first impressions soon proved deceiving. The Americans found the native quarters of the Medina to be dirty, smelly, overcrowded, and quite depressing. Flies and maggots plagued the food in the marketplaces and Djemma el Fena Square, where among the food sellers there were snake charmers, beggars, and boys as young as ten years of age pimping for the prostitutes of the Medina.

Bill LeRoy:

> We had a gunner named Harvey Nielsen, he had a fixation on monkeys. He bought his first one in South America and it was a mean son of a gun, and he sold it back to the guy for half the price he paid for it.

In Marrakech, Harvey looked out for another monkey. At least one of the monkeys that Harvey tried to buy was trained to bite the buyer and run back to the seller, who would then go and sell the same monkey to someone else. But Harvey was a happy-go-lucky guy, and undeterred, he was determined to own a monkey. He bought another in Africa, which one night wrapped itself in a blanket to keep warm on the darkened flight deck of *Corky*. The aircraft was guarded at all times while on the ground and one night while Bill LeRoy was on guard duty dressed in bulky flying clothes, he unknowingly sat on the monkey, "sending him to monkey heaven!" The crew were saddened the following morning to learn of the death of the monkey, and Bill LeRoy tried to calm them by explaining that the monkey was so cold that it had frozen to death.

The crew spent eleven nights in Marrakech, and on the morning of Saturday 29 January they were briefed for their next flight, to Wales, Great Britain. For the first time, *Corky*'s guns were loaded with ammunition. The crew would be flying into a war zone, and the gunners would need to keep alert at their combat stations. The aircraft was still without radio navigational aids, but Donald Lawry kept their course as they flew back out over the Atlantic around Portugal, Spain, and out over the Bay of Biscay around France.

Harvey Nielsen had bought yet another monkey while in Africa. This one developed a liking for chewing gum and it befriended Jack, who would talk to the monkey while it sat on his shoulders in flight. While descending from altitude Jack would hold the monkey's nose to try to clear its ears, telling the monkey to swallow. But the monkey would just sit there screaming, perched on the pilot's shoulders. The journey to Wales turned out to be uneventful—no enemy encounters. *Corky* turned over the Irish Sea and swooped down into Valley airfield, Holyhead, Wales, after eleven hours flying time.

B-24 *"Corky" Burgundy Bombers* at Old Buckenham early in 1944. The legs and boots visible underneath the aircraft suggest that discussions were being held in the open bomb bay. (Bill Eagleson)

The crew spent one night in Wales, and the following day, Sunday 30 January, they embarked on the last leg of their journey. They received their last ATC orders, which detailed them to fly to a new airfield located in East Anglia (eastern England), a region that was home to the bomb groups and fighter groups of the 8th Air Force. Two hours and thirty minutes out of Valley, *Corky* touched down at Old Buckenham airfield, Station number 144, near Attleborough in the county of Norfolk.

Since collecting *Corky* at Hamilton Field the crew had spent seventy-five hours and twenty-five minutes in the air. Throughout the long journey to England, Jack Nortridge's crew had become familiar with the aircraft they had christened *"Corky" Burgundy Bombers*, and as an aircrew and as friends the journey had provided them with their biggest challenges so far. They had been without letters from home, isolated from friends and family, and uncertain as to what lay ahead of them. On Sunday 30 January 1944 they were glad to arrive at Old Buckenham—at last they had reached the 8th Air Force, England—the Big League.

Bill Eagleson:

> Looking back . . . must remark on our very lucky flights, United States to England. We were without radio navigational aids and had limited skills—however our training and team work brought us through.

On arrival in England he updated his diary:

> The trip across has been thrilling but held long hours of work for pilot, copilot, navigator, and engineer. My respect and admiration for these guys grows deeper each day.

CHAPTER SEVEN

Somewhere in England

Theground echelon of the 453rd Heavy Bombardment Group sailed across the Atlantic during December 1943. Disembarking in Scotland, they continued their journey by rail to the county of Norfolk in eastern England. The train took them to the small market town of Attleborough, and from there they continued on foot for one mile to the brand new base at Old Buckenham, Station 144. They arrived in the midst of winter, just in time for a cold and lonely Christmas far away from home. Subsequently a stream of aircraft and aircrews had made their way along the South Atlantic route just as fast as the Air Transport Command could allow them flight clearances to Europe.

Located one hundred miles from London and eighteen miles from

Ankle deep in mud! 453rd Bomb Group ground personnel line up outside one of the mess halls at "chow" time in December 1943. Note the Royal Air Force liaison staff in the doorway. (Donald Olds, 453rd BG Association Collection)

the city of Norwich, Old Buckenham airfield was exclusively the home of the 453rd Bomb Group. Many of the American airmen arriving in England were issued with a small book, *A Short Guide to Great Britain*. The opening lines were: "You are going to Great Britain as part of an Allied offensive—to meet Hitler and beat him on his own ground. For the time being you will be Britain's guest."

To the frustration of the local farmers who had no choice in the Air Ministry's purchase of their land, farmland in the parish of Old Buckenham had been earmarked for use as a bomber base almost two years previously. During the initial days of construction, the people of the rural villages and hamlets in the vicinity of Old Buckenham airfield, or "aerodrome" as many of them called it, anticipated that their peace and calm would soon be shattered by the din of aircraft engines. They expected that the narrow lanes would become congested with military vehicles that would span the width of the road no matter which side they were trying to drive on—for it was rumored that the new aerodrome would be a base for "the Yanks."

It was an ideal location for an airfield. The terrain was mostly as flat as a pancake, and apart from a few narrow farm tracks that crossed the site there were no public roads. The occupants of Abbey Farm were forced to sell up and leave. Their farmhouse and outbuildings were demolished to make way for the western end of the main runway (Castle Farm to the south was later renamed Abbey Farm). Woodhall Farm,

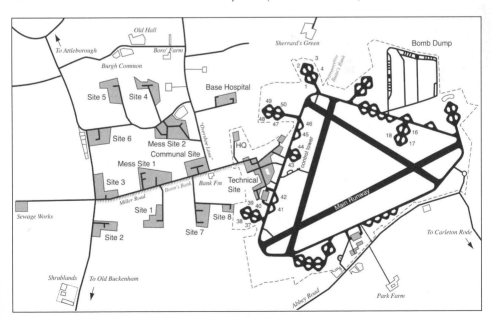

Station 144: Old Buckenham, England.

453rd Bombardment Group Headquarters at Old Buckenham. (Donald Olds, 453rd BG Association Collection)

located beside a plantation of trees in the very center of the airfield construction site, was also demolished, and Island House, set back from Abbey Road, was reduced to rubble to make way for the southeastern end of one of the secondary runways. Right across the site earmarked for the flying field, all trees were felled, hedges removed, ditches filled in, the land levelled.

Taylor-Woodrow Limited undertook construction of the airfield during 1942 and 1943, adhering to the specifications of a Class A bomber base, with the finishing touches being applied early in 1944 with the Americans in residence. These requirements necessitated the construction of a main runway of 2,000 yards in length and two secondary runways each of 1,400 yards, all 50 yards in width. The three runways were encircled by a concrete perimeter track—a taxiway for aircraft en route to takeoff or for landed aircraft on their way back to one of the fifty concrete "hardstand" dispersal points scattered around the airfield. On the northwestern perimeter, a row of terraced farm laborers' cottages escaped the wrecker's ball; they became almost surrounded by the 733rd Bomb Squadron aircraft dispersal area.

Two metal T2-type hangars had been erected. Number One hangar was positioned adjacent to the control tower and Technical Site on the western side of the flying field. The Technical Site was also the location

A view across part of the Technical Site with hangar number one on the right and the control tower visible at the top left. To the right of the tower, fire, and ambulance buildings is a visiting B-17 and (center) an RAF Halifax bomber undergoing major repair work (a bomb dropped by another aircraft fell through part of its fuselage, but somehow it made it back to England. A large section of the rear fuselage was replaced and the aircraft returned to combat!). One of the secondary runways is seen running horizontally at the top of this photograph. (Pat Ramm)

Looking toward part of the Technical Site, with the taxiway running diagonally across the photograph and the "removed" section of the Halifax fuselage visible furthest left. Three B-24s are parked around the hangar; a fourth is being stripped for spare parts (topmost center of photograph), and the fuselage shell of another can be seen among the Nissen huts and "slit trenches," which offered limited protection from air attack. (Pat Ramm)

Turning swords into ploughshares; the metal window frames, balcony railings, and exterior stairway had been removed from the derelict two-story control tower at Old Buckenham by the time this photograph was taken in 1975. The control tower was demolished just months later for no apparent reason, while the adjacent fire engine and ambulance buildings remain standing, although derelict, in 2003. (Pat Ramm)

of the Operations buildings, briefing halls, parachute and equipment stores, repair and engineering workshops, a carpenter's workshop, bomb and turret trainers, and a photo laboratory. Number Two hangar was located on the southern perimeter of the flying field adjacent to Abbey Road.

In case of air attack the rest of the base was divided into thirteen dispersed sites situated among farmland across Burgh Common to the west of the flying field (additionally there was a station sewage works still further to the west). The dispersed sites included the accommodation and living areas, mess halls, Group Headquarters, the station hospital, as well as communal and recreational buildings. The Officers' Club and later on, the Aero Club (for the enlisted men), the Post Exchange (PX), the chapel, the base cinema, and gym were all located on the Communal Site. There was also a living site earmarked as a WAAF Site (Women's Auxiliary Air Force, the British equivalent of the WACs) but in the absence of any women, British or American, stationed at the base, this site was occupied by 735th Bomb Squadron flying and ground personnel. The buildings were mostly Nissen, Quonset, and Maycrete huts, designed to last only the duration of the war, after which time the buildings could be easily dismantled and the whole area returned to agricultural use.

The western boundary of the base area was determined by Buck-enham Road, which connected Attleborough and the village of Old Buckenham. Between December 1943 and January 1944, the small pop-ulation of the village became outnumbered by the ever-increasing con-tingent of American airmen. Completion of the airfield construction program coincided with the arrival of nearly three thousand troops dur-ing those winter months of rain and snow, and any area of the base not covered in concrete had been reduced to thick, deep mud.

The troops were issued overshoes to help cope with these muddy conditions, and one of the worst unpaved roadways on the base became known officially as "Overshoe Lane." The name was inscribed on a piece of wood as a street sign and nailed to a telegraph pole where Overshoe Lane joined Miller Road. This intersection in front of Bank Farm was usually flooded with muddy water and so it became known as the "Old Swimming Hole."

Prior to the construction of the air base, Miller Road was a narrow public lane running alongside a watery ditch and an unkempt hedgerow of trees and bushes upon a slight ridge, a legacy of Saxon earthworks known as "Bunn's Bank." Miller Road was given the name "Riverside Drive" by the Americans, possibly after Riverside Drive in Manhattan, but more likely after Riverside, California, where the 453rd Bomb Group completed their Phase training. Old Buckenham, the airfield, and the village, soon became known affectionately as "Old Buck'" to the Americans who made it their home. Flying what were often terrify-ing combat missions into enemy-occupied Europe, the aircrews would hope and pray to survive and make it back home—to Old Buck'.

During the long journey to England, *Corky*'s crew was literally flying in the face of the unknown and each day had brought new experiences. Meeting the veteran crew of the B-17 *Hell's Angels* in Marrakech had provided a few insights into the reality of war-torn Europe. But it was their arrival at Old Buckenham that was most enlightening, as Bill Eagleson recalls:

> Finally to Old Buck'. . . . We were relieved—Better than one month on the "road" separated from friends—the "unknown" fac-tor partially eliminated.

Corky's crew spent their first afternoon at Old Buckenham reuniting themselves with friends, some of whom they had not seen in many weeks. There were many stories to share of their adventurous journeys to England. Sgt. Robert Victor, the radio operator from Lt. Nick Rado-sevich's crew, recalled an incident that occurred while he was guarding their aircraft at the base in Marrakech. Suddenly a large troop of horse cavalry, several automobiles, and soldiers on motorcycles appeared. They came to a halt close to the B-24 Sgt. Victor was guarding, and to the sound of a military band the leader of the free French, General Charles De Gaulle, stepped from one of the cars. Then an aircraft circled overhead, landed, and taxied up to the French contingent. Some legionnaires rolled out a wide red carpet and out stepped British Prime Minister Winston Churchill. De Gaulle greeted him with a kiss on each cheek and the shaking of hands, before leading Churchill away into a waiting limousine. The entire group drove away behind some hangars, and ten minutes after it had begun the event was over. Robert Victor was left sitting alone in the sun on top of the B-24 with little else to do except watch the clouds roll by and consider that he had just witnessed a historic moment.

Although the crews were relieved to have arrived at their final overseas destination, they were far from enamoured by the conditions on the base.

Bill Eagleson:

> Our first impressions of England were that we were in war. . . . I remember that after our flight from Wales, we went to our living site and it was most shocking. Actually it was a concrete walkway surrounded by mud, and I looked at the mud and I thought, "This must be war!"—Just what my family told me about [World War I], because mud was a very common sight at Old Buckenham at that time. This was January 1944; the station was still in the process of building.
>
> I guess for our demands at the time it was just miraculous how they could put all this together, all these accommodations for us. Building an airfield is a major task—these hundred or more air sites we had in Britain sprung up overnight in the *middle* of a war.
>
> When we did go back and forth to the flight line there were trucks on the concrete slabs, and the roads were very narrow roads, and often times we were forced into overshoe country in the deep mud that bordered the roads. So Old Buck' was *not* a pleasant environment in the earlier days.

As a reminder of his father's experiences in the muddy trenches of French battlefields during 1917–18, Bill Eagleson had with him his father's wartime mess kit and hoped that it would bring him some good fortune in Europe. Two days after his arrival in England, Bill felt reassuringly closer to his family than he had since departing the United States:

> We had been without communication to home and family. Our APO [Army Post Office] was [Station] #144 and what a Christmas we had, February 1, when mail and packages caught up with us.

Tuesday 1 February 1944 was a double celebration—not only had Christmas arrived but Jack Nortridge, Bill Eagleson, and Donald Lawry celebrated their copilot George White's twenty-first birthday in the Officers' Club. Two days later the nineteen-year-old navigator, Donald

Lawry, wrote his first letter from England to his family in Evansville, Wisconsin. To avoiding having his letter smeared by the black ink of the censors, he kept details of his location to minimum:

> Dear Mom, Well we all arrived safe, and sound, somewhere in England. It doesn't seem to be such a bad place except that it always rains, and the mud is up to your ankles.

The four officers of *Corky*'s crew, Lts. Nortridge, White, Eagleson, and Lawry, were billeted in a Maycrete hut on Site One, located south of Miller Road, or "Riverside Drive." They shared their hut with the officers of three other crews, including the one piloted by Lt. Gustav "Bob" Johnson, of Minnesota. The other officers assigned to Johnson's crew were Lieutenants Gilbert Stonebarger, Paul Olson, and Edward Bebenroth.

Bill Eagleson:

> Originally we had four crews in the hut; that meant sixteen people. It wasn't a Nissen hut, it was more like a long shed. . . . There were two stoves in it, coal burning stoves, and coal was a very precious item because those huts were cold. . . . Actually, in spots you could see through openings to the ground. At both ends of the hut there was a door, and there were windows in the hut. I slept at one end, my pilot Nortridge, he slept at the opposite end of the barracks, and I guess we communicated with Verey [flare] pistols!

The 733rd Squadron's enlisted personnel were billeted on Site Four situated on Burgh Common. These huts were slightly less spacious than those occupied by the officers and were equally lacking in luxury. Similar in design to the officers' huts, the buildings were asbestos-roofed with rendered brick walls. Barely comfortable, the inhabitants endured draughty windows with metal frames, cold concrete floors, and uncomfortable bunk beds. When snow fell it would drift under the single wooden door at one end of the hut. Heating was limited to a couple of potbellied stoves and with any luck a week's coal ration would last half as long. At Old Buck' the Americans' winter existence constantly reminded them of how far away they were from the creature comforts and the familiarity of their homes back in the United States.

Perry Roberson:

> Arrival at Old Buck' showed us mud like some of us had never seen before. I grew up on a farm in South Alabama that was sandy soil. Also we learned to live with the cold and rain. The officers and enlisted men had separate quarters but both were Spartan to say the least—coke fired heaters and community showers with latrines in separate buildings.

The accommodation huts appeared to have been randomly placed within each living site. Narrow concrete paths or wooden plank boardwalks interconnected each hut and concrete pathways linked each site to the wider base network of concrete roadways and muddy lanes. Each accommodation site included an area of latrines and a washroom, otherwise known as the "ablution center." Personal hygiene depended on running out through the cold to take a cold shower and then back through the cold and the mud into cold barracks—there was no escaping the cold and the mud! However, compared to the conditions experienced by many American soldiers fighting elsewhere in the world, Old Buckenham wasn't so bad. At least there *were* showers and mess halls and at least the base was located in a relatively peaceful environment.

While the officers of the Nortridge and Johnson crews were billeted in the same hut, the enlisted men assigned to the Nortridge crew (Sergeants Jeong, LeRoy, Nielsen, Roberson, Veilleux, and Witmer) shared their hut with Johnson's enlisted men (Sergeants Peter Becker, William Cleary, Frederick Derolf, Albert Eihausen, Salvatore Giombarrese, and Corporal Henry Landry).

Bill LeRoy recalls:

> We were in a Quonset hut (two crews, twelve enlisted men). We billeted with Lt. Gustav R. Johnson's crew at Old Buck' for all our stay.

The Johnson crew had flown to England in a Liberator named *Stinky* after the pet skunk that belonged to the crew's tail gunner, Bill Cleary. The skunk had flown to England with the crew as their adopted mascot, and lived with the enlisted men in the hut, along with Peter Becker's dog and Harvey Nielsen's monkey!

On Sunday 13 February, Harvey Nielsen caught up with some correspondence and wrote to his niece Iris Barton back home in Missouri:

> It has been a long time since you have heard from me. Well I haven't even been allowed to write home for a long time. Well I have arrived at my destination I am now stationed in England. I had a quite a long trip. I am still doing the same thing I was doing, only here it is to be for the real thing if you know what I mean. There are two crews living in our barracks. I bought a little monkey on the way here for a mascot for the crew. It is getting to be quite a pet. The other crew in the barracks have a pet skunk that has been deodorised and a little dog. You see we have a regular menagerie. The weather is pretty wet over here. . . .
>
> There isn't much I can write about because you know they don't allow us to say much about what we are doing. Tell every body hello and write soon. As mail is about the only thing we get for enjoyment. . . .

Following their arrival at Old Buckenham, many of the American personnel took advantage of their very limited off-duty hours to investigate the local area. Issued with British currency and, in the case of the

Once the homes of the 733rd Bomb Squadron enlisted men, a number of derelict buildings remained on Site Four until the late 1990s. They have since been demolished—history swept aside for the sake of a truckload of rubble! The enlisted men from *Corky*'s crew shared one of these huts with the enlisted men from Johnson's crew, a dog, a monkey, and a skunk! (author)

enlisted men, a pass to leave the base, the American GIs set about their recreational explorations and encountered the natives who talked with peculiar accents as if a different language to that spoken by the king and queen.

The Americans made use of the bicycles that many of them were issued for local transportation, and they soon discovered the local villages and market towns where the public houses, or "pubs," served unfavorably warm beer. The Norfolk village and town names were often intriguing to the Americans, and foreign were the local pronunciations of places such as Old Buckenham *(buck-un-um)*, Wymondham *(win-dum)*, and Deopham *(deef-um)*. Consultation of *A Short Guide to Great Britain*, reminded the Americans that: "The British are often more reserved in conduct than we. On a small crowded island where forty-five million people live, each man learns to guard his privacy carefully. . . . The British have phrases and colloquialisms of their own that may sound funny to you. You can make just as many boners in their eyes. It isn't a good idea, for instance, to say 'bloody' in mixed company in Britain—it is one of their worst swear words. . . . Our common speech, our common law, and our ideas of religious freedom were all brought from Britain . . . parts of our own Bill of Rights were borrowed from the great charters of British liberty."

All signposts had been removed from the roadsides of wartime England, to confuse the enemy in the event of an invasion, and so finding one's way back to base by bicycle along the narrow lanes could become quite an eventful journey. The Americans found the county of Norfolk to be a rural, agricultural district. The consistently flat landscape and geographic location proved ideal to the Air Ministry. Across most of the Norfolk countryside and the neighboring counties, an airfield was constructed almost every five miles and many of them became American bomb group and fighter group bases.

In getting to know the local area, many of the Americans were struck with fascination by the modest scale, the "quaintness," of everything English. They were often intrigued by the history and antiquity evident in almost everything they encountered—the villages with their timber-beamed pubs, the houses and thatched cottages, the village greens, and the flint churches that were already historic buildings when the first white settlers arrived in the Americas.

Thomas Paine, the political writer who in 1776 challenged the British government and monarchy with his *Common Sense*, which became a manifesto for the American Revolution, was born in 1737 in Thetford, fifteen miles west of Old Buckenham (upon the publication of *The Rights of Man* following his return to England, Paine was outlawed for treason). For those Americans from New England, the town and village names were sometimes more familiar. President Abraham Lincoln's

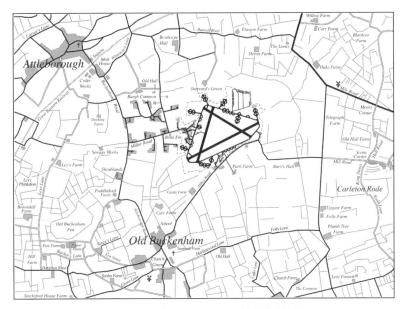

Old Buckenham Village, airfield, and surrounding area. Norfolk, England.

ancestors originated from the Norfolk village of Hingham (pronounced *hing-um* by the locals), just eight miles from Old Buckenham. In the early seventeenth century, thirty-five families (including Lincoln's ancestors) left the village and settled in America, where they founded Hingham, Massachusetts.

The Massachusetts town of Attleboro was named after the town of Attleborough *(attlebur-ruh)* just one mile from the base at Old Buckenham. In the seventeenth century Reverend William Blackstone arrived in the New World where he became the first white settler on Shawmut Peninsula; the Puritans of the Massachusetts colony arrived later and renamed the peninsula after the English town of Boston, Lincolnshire. Blackstone is believed to have lived in Attleborough, Norfolk, prior to his departure to America.

Attleborough's origins are rooted in Saxon times. Located on the main London to Norwich road, it had been a staging post for the Royal Mail and stagecoaches. For the past ninety-nine years the town had been connected to the Great Eastern Railway and was known for both turkey sales and cider production — part of Gaymer's Cyder factory had been bombed earlier in the war by a German intruder aircraft. By 1944 Attleborough existed within a triangle of American bases (Old Buckenham, and the B-17 bases at nearby Deopham Green and Snetterton Heath). The public houses in the town (most notably the historic Griffin

Hotel, a former stagecoach inn) became frequent haunts of the American airmen. The Red Cross ran an Anglo-American Club in Attleborough where the airmen could enjoy sandwiches, tea, and coffee; it was also the venue for regular dances.

Arrival in England was something of a culture shock to the Americans who witnessed and experienced first-hand the effects of four years of war and uncertainty on every aspect of British life. Even the unappetising British food provisions fed to the American personnel during their first days at Old Buckenham induced both homesickness and empathy for the British.

Perry Roberson:

> We learned to dislike Brussels sprouts since we had them so often.

Bill Eagleson:

> Our early eating situation was not too pleasant at Old Buck', it was difficult to adjust to. I believe that we were on British rations and the constant serving of lamb and mutton and Brussels sprouts . . . to this day I can't eat sprouts or lamb—canned grapefruit juice (highly acidic), greasy Spam. Later our Group opened a Combat Mess for flying crews. Much better—good hamburgers and Coke.

Like Americans, the British had also endured an economic depression during the 1930s, but Britain had not had the opportunity to recover before war came. People were poor, or at least lived under extremely low living standards. Most foods were rationed, allowing each person only a few ounces of sugar, butter, cheese, and meat each week. There were few luxuries available—powdered eggs became the norm, and many children grew up having never seen bananas. Even the wealthy upper classes had to adhere to the ration book system for purchasing their weekly allowance of food, clothes, and all other consumables—their money could only afford them extravagances if spent illegally on the black market.

Every man, woman, and child carried a gas mask at all times. There were strict blackout regulations after sunset, leaving every street, every town, and every village in darkness until dawn. The reality of deadly air attack was highlighted in *A Short Guide to Great Britain:* "Don't be misled by the British tendency to be soft-spoken and polite. . . . Sixty thousand British civilians have died under bombs, and yet the morale of the British is unbreakable and high. . . . The British are tough, strong people, and good allies. . . . Use your head before you sound off, and remember how long the British alone held Hitler off without any help from anyone. . . . Britain may look a little shop-worn and grimy. . . . There's been a war on since 1939. . . . The British people are anxious for you to know that in normal times Britain looks much prettier, cleaner, neater."

In this period of subsistence living, recycling was a way of life, from material for clothes to pots and pans for Spitfires. Meanwhile, houses and public buildings remained in need of redecoration, most automobiles remained stationary due to the shortage of gasoline, and village greens, private and public parks were now used for growing vegetables. For the Americans, the similarities and the differences of each new experience were continually compared to life at home, the primary reference point for any homesick traveler. Sometimes they were just confused and bewildered, wondering, "Why the hell do these Limeys drink warm beer?" The guidebook advised tact and diplomacy: "It is always impolite to criticise your hosts. It is militarily stupid to criticise your allies. Use common sense on all occasions. By your conduct you have great power to bring about a better understanding between the two countries after the war is over."

History has since recorded that there were often misunderstandings, and that the English of East Anglia responded uncomfortably to many a GIs brash assertion that everything in America was in some way bigger, or even better. Perhaps the English believed this attitude to be rooted in arrogance, not appreciating how miniature the British Isles seemed to the Americans. Surely most British people were unable to comprehend the geographic magnitude and vastness of the United States, where the scale of the automobiles, the road networks, and skyscrapers were perhaps fitting. With their pay considerably higher than their British counterparts in the RAF, the GIs seemed comparatively rich. According to the unavoidable cliché, the Americans were perceived as "overpaid, overfed, oversexed, and over here!" — "The British dislike bragging and showing off. . . . They consider you highly paid. They won't think any better of you for throwing money around."

Prior to the war, the people of Norfolk had almost no contact with outsiders, with people from far away with different ideas about life, and many of them had never any need to travel, even as far as London. They learned about the world from books, newspapers, and the radio, if they learned about the world at all. Then the war brought Czechoslovakians, Norwegians, Frenchmen, Dutchmen, Belgians, Poles, West Indians, Australians, and Canadians to East Anglia from where they flew with or alongside the Royal Air Force. And then there were the many thousands of North Americans from the United States, otherwise known as the "Yanks."

British preconceptions of the Yanks were often based on Hollywood movies that had been shown at cinemas in each city and small town — Americans were cowboys, gangsters, or sophisticated romantics. And here, in the flesh they had attitude, were confident and seemingly larger-than-life characters. They were simultaneously arrogant, outspoken, loud, and polite, charming, endearing, even exciting. They walked into town with a kind of swagger, often interpreted as arrogance. In comparison, the British were, on the surface, modest and reserved with an inability to show their emotions. Across Norfolk and the neighboring counties, the natives felt at times as if they had been invaded by their American allies, albeit a friendly invasion, especially in contrast to the threat of a German invasion, which Britain had longed feared. The countryside became something of a giant aircraft carrier densely populated by thousands of GIs.

In those days the United States Army was segregated. In the entire United States Army Air Force during the Second World War, there was just one operational flying squadron of African Americans. This unit was a highly successful P-51 fighter squadron based in Italy. There were ten thousand black GIs based in Great Britain during 1944, but the majority of these men were assigned to engineer battalions working as laborers in airfield construction and development or transporting bombs and supplies to the airfields. The Norfolk natives had never encountered black people before, but following initial curiosity they generally viewed them no differently from all the other Americans, as well as the Canadians, Poles, and Czechs who had arrived to help win the war.

However, there were attempts by the media to discourage English women from dating black servicemen, partly as a means to prevent provocation and fighting between white and black troops, but such attempts were largely ignored. The British public were sometimes intrigued, not by the sight of black men, but by the Army-imposed social distinctions based on these racial differences—segregation. It seemed as if a little bit of the Deep South had been imported into England. The prejudices held by many white southerners now based in this foreign, nonsegregated environment, mixed with alcohol and in the presence of black GIs associating with white women, were feared to be a recipe for trouble, especially since interracial relationships were something not seen or accepted in the southern states. Certainly in the city of Ipswich, Suffolk, as a precautionary measure, black and white Americans were allocated different pubs where they could drink during off duty hours. In Norfolk, black and white Americans were sometimes allowed into the city of Norwich on alternate evenings. Relations between black and white Americans in England were generally harmonious even where segregation was not enforced, and pub fights were more frequent among white troops, or among black troops, but not between the two. Generally speaking, the idea of segregation seemed strange to the British people. On at least one occasion, an African American choir was invited to attend a service at St. Mary's church in Attleborough, where the congregation was inspired by the gospel singing style.

Although there were no African Americans assigned to any level of the 453rd Bomb Group, the personnel based at Old Buckenham came from diverse backgrounds, but the overall majority was considered to be white and were of European descent. There was a very small minority of Native Americans, Mexican Americans, and Chinese Americans

serving in the bomb groups, fighter groups, and support units of the 8th
Air Force in Norfolk—but African Americans were totally excluded.

During the first few weeks at Old Buckenham before most of the
crews commenced their combat missions, the enlisted men found themselves on the point of boredom at times, especially when they were without passes to leave the base and go into town. Some of the enlisted men
found an empty Nissen hut on a quiet corner of one of the accommodation sites, and for a while it seems this hut became something of a secret gambling den, where alcohol was consumed if available.

Back in 1942, Gaymer's Cyder mill in Attleborough had been
bombed during a German intruder attack and part of the factory had
been destroyed. Subsequently, most air-raid alerts in Attleborough
turned out to be false alarms. One night as the air-raid siren howled its
chilling warning, several Americans (unidentified, although allegedly
one or two of *Corky*'s enlisted men were among them) liberated a barrel
of cider from the back of the Gaymer's factory and rolled it home to the
base where they drank it before the cloudy sediment had time to settle.
But the Americans paid the price, and all were sick.

One or two enlisted men from *Corky*'s crew sometimes attended the
poker games, including Lim Wing Jeong, the only Chinese American on
the base. Sgt. Vince Pale, the radio operator from Lt. August "Gus" Ber-
man's crew, lived in the hut next door to the enlisted men from *Corky*'s
crew, and he also attended a few card games. Vince Pale remembers
Lim Wing Jeong as a quiet guy, who was nevertheless always sociable
and cheerful. Vince was an immigrant himself, born in Italy and raised
in Pennsylvania, and so his attitude to his Chinese acquaintance was optimistic: "Well, we've got a 'melting pot' right here!"

However, there were others who lacked this sense of openness. An
Italian radio operator from another crew (his name intentionally with-
held) pushed Jeong's patience to the limit by consistently making racial
slurs and derogative comments, which almost resulted in a fight—or
worse. Jeong's calm temperament momentarily snapped and he lost his
cool, challenging his antagonist to a duel! The Italian was surprised and
unprepared for the reaction. Perhaps picturing the scene of a duel at
dawn on Burgh Common with .45 caliber pistols, he backed down and
from then on he kept his mouth shut and avoided such confrontations!

The Americans had a sense of conviction and optimism: they were
here to win the war! The British had heard that once before, when the
Americans turned up late the last time around. Attleborough's ninety-
six casualties from that former conflict had not been forgotten, and once
again many men would not be returning home to the towns and villages
of Norfolk. But the sight and sound of hundreds of bombers departing
in the early mornings and then returning hours later, often badly damaged and firing flares to indicate wounded and dying on board, soon

English kids, George Cooper (front left) and Pat Ramm (right) befriended some of the "Yanks" at Old Buckenham. (Pat Ramm)

dispelled any preconceptions about the Americans. In time the English locals and the American flyers warmed to each other.

Far from home, the Americans talked about their families, their lives at home, their "Old World" ancestors, for many were of English, Irish, Scottish, French, Italian, Scandinavian, Polish, and even German descent. They were at all times generous, always sharing their food and cigarettes with their English hosts and their candy rations with the children. Chewing gum had never been experienced before, and kids would greet the GIs with the enquiry, "Have y'got any gum, chum?" At Christmas time the Yanks entertained the local kids with parties on the bases. Local woman in the vicinity of Old Buckenham ran laundry services. Three children, whose mother did the laundry for a number of Americans, were responsible for the collections and deliveries—Julie, John, and Ernie Rider pulled a red wagon full of clean GI uniforms all the way from Attleborough to the base each week.

Some of the children in Old Buckenham and Carleton Rode congregated along Abbey Road to view the Liberator bombers parked at the roadside and to chat to the Americans. An eleven-year-old boy named Pat Ramm lived in Carleton Rode under the main runway flight path. In fact, his grandfather owned the windmill used as a landmark by the American navigators to identify Old Buck' from all the other bases in the area. Each morning Pat cycled along Abbey Road to school in

Old Buckenham, often stopping to watch the bombers depart for missions. Sometimes he made his way back to Abbey Road in time to watch
the Liberators return. Having befriended some of the 735th Bomb
Squadron ground crews, Pat and his friend, George Cooper, seemed to
have a free rein over the 735th aircraft dispersal area: "We used to just
walk onto the airfield—that was our airfield! We didn't think we were
trespassing; we never got into trouble. We just looked, listened; we sat in
the planes; we had the candy."

Many of the English children had not seen their fathers for several
years, many would never see them again, and they idolized the Americans, just as women adored them. The impact of the Americans on
British society, especially the towns and villages in sleepy Norfolk, was
profound. Today the legendary Yanks are remembered throughout the
region with great affection.

CHAPTER EIGHT

In the Air and
On the Ground

The role of the Allied bomber offensive in Europe during the Second World War was an around-the-clock assault upon Germany's means to continue fighting. While the Royal Air Force's heavy bomber force flew missions over Europe by night, the United States Strategic Air Forces in Europe operated two heavy bomber forces in Europe (the 8th Air Force from bases in England and the 15th from Italy), and flew their missions by day. To undermine the enemy's physical means to wage war, the German industrial infrastructure was to be crushed and so targets were primarily of strategic significance—rail systems, electrical power installations, synthetic petroleum plants, aircraft factories, and Luftwaffe airfields.

The concept adopted by the Americans had initially been "precision bombing" of strategic targets. This method originated in the military planning during the uncertain and uneasy peacetime days of the mid-1930s. The term "precision bombing" suggested accuracy and a scientific approach, and the faith in this strategy depended significantly upon the technology of the American bombsights, notably the famous Norden bombsight, which provided the capacity for precision with minimum loss of civilian life. It also allowed the bombers to fly at very high altitudes, compromising the accuracy and the effectiveness of the enemy's anti-aircraft artillery, known to the Americans as *flak*. In short, it was widely claimed and exaggerated that the Norden bombsight could facilitate the dropping of a bomb into a pickle barrel from an altitude of 20,000 feet. According to this theory, aerial bombardment could be aimed accurately at industrial areas with pinpoint precision, while the enemy civilian areas would be left untouched.

However, the impressive accuracy achieved on desert bombing ranges was invariably much harder to reproduce in combat conditions where numerous factors interfered. Improved anti-aircraft defenses forced the American formations to higher altitudes than had been anticipated, and just as this compromised the flak gunners' aim it also reduced bombing accuracy. The flying altitude meant that even on a summer's day, the aircrews encountered harsh winter conditions. The weather frequently interfered, cloud and smoke screens obscured targets, enemy fighter attacks disrupted the bomber streams, equipment malfunctioned, stress and inexperience often led to human error in navigation and bomb aiming—so much for the "pickle barrel" concept of "precision bombing." In reality, pinpoint accuracy was frequently unachievable; at times it was not even attempted. Far from being a humane, scientific approach to warfare, where there was destruction there was always death.

The British bomber squadrons had suffered terribly, enduring heavy losses during their attempts at daylight bombing. Without advanced navigation and target sighting technology, attempts at precision bombing had been in vain. Subsequently the RAF bombers were assigned night missions and conducted the desperate and controversial concept of "area bombing." Targets were still largely strategic, but with less emphasis on accuracy. While all methods of bombing would cause human casualties, the implications of area bombing were that unlimited numbers of civilians would perish. During a RAF raid on Hamburg, Germany, on 27 July 1943, 40,000 Germans were killed in the firestorm that spread through the city. Speaking from Los Angeles, Chet Huntley underplayed the horror and announced on CBS radio: "It was not a terror operation as has been suggested in some quarters. The Germans were rebuilding very quickly after the attacks. To prevent that at Hamburg, the homes of the workers, the stores, the buildings, even the very streets had to be demolished."

On 10 October 1943, while the 453rd Bomb Group was still training in the United States, for the first time the 8th Air Force was assigned a mission to the German city of Münster, a city with a significant rail junction. Precision was not a factor—in an effort to disrupt the German civilian rail workers, Münster cathedral, surrounded by the workers' homes, was selected as the main aiming point for the bombardment.

The 453rd Bomb Group's bombardiers had been disgruntled when they were assigned their aircraft in December 1943 and found them equipped not with the Norden bombsights on which they had become skilled but with Sperry bombsights. Since the 453rd Bomb Group's bombardiers were training during the spring and summer of 1943, bombing procedures had been developed. Of particular significance was the development of the "lead crew" concept, which had become standard procedure by the time the 453rd Bomb Group commenced operations in February 1944.

A lead crew included a bomb group's most experienced or most proficient pilots, navigator, and bombardier. Often a group would fly in two formation "sections," each in trail of a "lead ship." No longer did the bombardiers in each aircraft make their own target sightings. Instead, this responsibility was given to the bombardiers in each lead aircraft. The rest of the bombardiers in the formation waited for the colored smoke markers and bombs to fall from the lead ship, and would release their bombs on this visual signal. At that instant, using the bombsight's toggle switch, all other bombardiers dropped, or "toggled" their bombs simultaneously, "on the leader." Consequently each lead bombardier became responsible for the bombing accuracy of half a bomb group. Sometimes, while the lead bombardiers sighted for range and deflection, all other bombardiers sighted for range only, with exceptions depending on the requirements, conditions, and actual circumstances of each mission. There was also a toggle switch located in the nose turret enabling the gunner to "salvo" the bombs should he be required to do so.

Flying in daylight hours the American aircraft were especially vulnerable to flak and enemy fighter attacks. To defend them from the Luftwaffe fighter aircraft, six of the crew members on each B-24 were gunners, while on each B-17 there were up to eight gunners, including the navigator and bombardier. The American bombers were arranged in tight formation to maximize their combined defensive efficiency.

Four days after the raid on Münster back in October 1943, the 8th Air Force attacked Schweinfurt. The American media reported the occasion as a tremendous victory, declaring the destruction of three ball-bearing factories, highly exaggerating claims of destroyed enemy fighters, and creatively misinterpreting the figures of American losses. But far from an example of successful precision bombing, in reality a mere 7.2 percent of the bombs dropped actually fell on the industrial plants. The rest hit streets and houses. Furthermore, sixty B-17s failed to return—six hundred missing airmen! Additionally there were the statistics of the dead and the wounded brought home on the badly damaged aircraft that returned to their bases or crashed elsewhere in England. Far from being a victory, the mission was a severe blow to the morale of the 8th Air Force.

The theory devised in peacetime had been tried and tested in combat, and high losses meant that undoubtedly the daylight bomber streams could not defend themselves sufficiently. Critics of the daylight bombing campaign accurately described the venture as suicide. Flying in large-scale formations at high altitude was not enough. Fighter escort to and from the targets was imperative. The reality of Schweinfurt amplified the sense of urgency for suitable fighter aircraft with the sufficient operational range to escort the bombers to distant targets during these deep penetration attacks on German industry.

The bomber crews referred to Allied fighter aircraft as "little friends." The RAF was famous for its Spitfires and Hurricanes—against the odds they had successfully fought off the German Luftwaffe during the Battle of Britain in 1940. The American P-47 Thunderbolt, flying from England from the spring of 1943 onwards, was recognized as a very reliable single-engine fighter. But the question of limited operational range was a significant issue.

In England throughout the spring and summer of 1943, American engineers experimented with an idea implemented by the RAF for some time—the use of wing-mounted "drop tanks" which could be discarded once the supplementary fuel supply had been exhausted. On 27 September 1943, P-47s fitted with drop tanks escorted formations of B-17s all the way to a target in Germany for the first time. But all too often the bombers were sent to distant German targets such as Schweinfurt, far beyond the range of the fighters—the little friends would have to turn back too soon, just when fighter protection was needed most.

Fighter units equipped with the twin-engine P-38 Lightnings became operational from bases in England in October 1943. Meanwhile there were rumors of the arrival of the P-51 Mustang, manufactured by the North American Aviation company. Designed for the British to an RAF specification, the RAF had operated this aircraft since 1942, but a lack of interest by the USAAF meant that the Americans initially overlooked the Mustang. That is, until the RAF successfully experimented by replacing the Allison engine with a Rolls Royce Merlin, such as that used on the legendary Spitfire. Subsequently the P-51 B-model was manufactured with an American version of the Merlin engine. The first American P-51 unit in England was assigned to the 9th Air Force, but it was an 8th Air Force pilot, Lt. Col. Donald Blakeslee, deputy commander of

Little Friends—a flight of P-51B Mustangs from the 357th Fighter Group carrying "drop tanks." The Mustang was the saving grace of many bomber crews. Later versions had a "bubble" canopy that improved pilot visibility and enhanced the sleek appearance of the "Cadillac of the Sky." (Olmsted Collection)

the 4th Fighter Group, who was assigned the task of leading the unit into combat for the first time, in November 1943.

The maneuverability, cruising speed, and acceleration of the P-51 were considered to be excellent. Fuel consumption was roughly half that of the P-47 and P-38. With an additional internal fuel tank and drop tanks under each wing, the P-51 could make a round trip from England to almost anywhere in Germany—even Berlin! The P-51 even looked good, almost like a sports car, it was often remarked, and soon it became known as the Cadillac of the Sky. Soon there were increasing numbers of American P-51 units in England. Bomber crew morale was elevated by the presence of the Mustang, which became the saving grace of many American lives.

Air superiority over Europe had long been an ultimate goal for the Allies, only now it was achievable. Not only would this allow the Americans to continue their daylight bombing campaign without such heavy losses, but also, air superiority would be imperative for the success of the forthcoming Allied invasion of Western Europe. At the beginning of 1944, the commander of the Army Air Force, General Arnold, announced the priority for the 8th Air Force during the months ahead: "Destroy the enemy air force wherever you find them, in the air, on the ground and in the factories."

Joining the 389th Bomb Group that had arrived at nearby Hethel in June 1943 and the 445th based at nearby Tibenham since November, the 453rd at Old Buckenham completed the triad of Bomb Groups designated the 2nd Combat Bomb Wing. This was one of five wings assigned to the B-24 Liberator-equipped 2nd Bomb Division. This division was one of three assigned to the 8th Air Force.

All aircraft and crews had arrived at Old Buckenham by mid-February 1944. Meanwhile, the priority for the 453rd Bomb Group was further training both in the air and on the ground. Bill Eagleson had the opportunity to become better acquainted with the Sperry bombsight in *Corky*. Bill's stateside training on the Sperry sight amounted to dropping two bombs over the Pacific Ocean, but at Old Buckenham he was able to spend some time in the bomb trainer, a primitive simulator, trying to develop his skills and confidence with the Sperry sight inside a hut at Old Buckenham.

> When we got to England we spent a great deal of time in your
> RAF bomb trainers with the Sperry sight, and when we were free
> we were down there working that bomb sight. . . . Also we took
> some flights and dropped actual practice bombs.

Group formation assembly and formation flying was given priority. The unfavorably cold winter conditions, the dense cloud cover, and limited visibility over England were quite unlike anything the Americans had experienced during training over California during the previous

September, October, and November. Furthermore, the pilots of the 453rd had to learn to contend with the formations of numerous other bomb groups flying from bases located in close proximity to one another, and therefore all forming in a concentrated area and heading in the same direction. They had to identify aircraft from their own group by the tail markings, join them, and fly in tight formation, all the while trying to avoid collisions.

Pilot Lt. Robert "Bob" Bieck had been transferred to the 453rd Bomb Group partway through its Phase Three training at March Field in November 1943, having never even flown a B-24 before. Although formation flying was at that time a priority for the 453rd, Phase Three training lasted just three weeks and was compromised by a scarcity of training aircraft.

> The group had never flown with more than six planes in a formation, and that is a heckuva lot different than forming up with four squadrons of twelve planes each and then joining some dozen other groups in the Division. At Old Buckenham . . . we began practice missions almost immediately. We were an aviation abomination. On our first practice mission, the weather was dreadful, and it took us forever to assemble. All in all we made five practice missions before we were considered fit for aerial combat, and all the practice missions were dreadful.

To assist in formation assembly over England, each B-24 Group employed a war-weary Liberator bomber known as an Assembly Ship or Judas Goat. These aircraft were brightly painted and decorated with

The gaudy paint scheme of yellow and green checkers made the 453rd Bomb Group's assembly ship *Wham Bam* easily recognizable. The aircraft's nose art featured a cartoon rabbit. (Donald Olds, 453rd BG Association Collection)

individual psychedelic colors in stripes, checkers, or polka dots enabling easy recognition by their flock of bombers. The 453rd's example was named *Wham Bam*, a veteran of the 93rd Bomb Group with a notable combat history including the legendary low-level Ploesti raid of 1 August 1943.

All armament and bomb racks had since been removed to reduce weight and increase maneuverability; the olive drab camouflage had been replaced by large, gaudy yellow and green checkers, but *Wham Bam* retained its original nose art that featured an energetic cartoon rabbit—the epitome of the "get-up-and-go" of the assembly ships. *Wham Bam* was employed to lead the Liberators from Old Buckenham during group formation assembly, en route to the 2nd Combat Wing formation assembly area where the 453rd would join with the 389th and 445th Bomb Groups. From there the Wing would proceed to the 2nd Bomb Division and finally 8th Air Force assembly lines, while *Wham Bam* returned to Old Buck.'

Bill Eagleson:

> We had constant air and ground training—RAF bomb trainer, formation and navigational procedures for assembly. Imagine assembling a 1,000 ship bombing line over the Wash. . . . That took skilled crews and solid planning—Elements, Flights, Squadron, Group, Wing, Division, Air Force.

These practice missions proved to be eventful at times. On 3 February 1944 the 453rd Bomb Group practiced formation assembly over the shallow coastal waters of the Wash, between Hunstanton, Norfolk, and Boston, Lincolnshire. On return to base, a B-24 blocked the main runway when its landing gear collapsed. Meanwhile, Lt. Hubert Cripe of the 734th Bomb Squadron was on the landing approach in his B-24, *Libby Raider*. At the last moment, the control tower instructed Lt. Cripe to land on one of the shorter runways, but it was too late for him to regain enough power to recover from his approach. *Libby Raider* stalled just short of the runway, and upon touching the ground the left landing gear broke, swinging the aircraft into the mud. The crew walked away unhurt but the aircraft was scrapped for spare parts.

The following day the group was airborne again for a formation training flight. The weather conditions were particularly bad, and one 733rd Bomb Squadron aircraft got lost in the cloud—reaching clear skies the group was nowhere to be seen. The pilot, Lt. John Turner, and his navigator were completely lost and disoriented and strayed over France where they were attacked by German fighters, seriously injuring one crew member and badly damaging the aircraft. After making an emergency landing at a Luftwaffe airfield, the crew were taken as prisoners of war.

That evening, the 453rd Bomb Group was alerted for its first bombing mission—not all crews would be participating, and Jack Nortridge's

"Poor *Libby Raider!*" recalled Hubert Cripe, who flew this ship to England and then crashed it at Old Buckenham following a practice mission: "We walked away unhurt, but the plane was scrapped." (Hubert Cripe)

crew was not assigned to fly the mission. The next morning, Saturday 5 February 1944, the Norfolk-based B-24 Liberator Groups were dispatched to targets in France; the 453rd Bomb Group was assigned Tours airfield as its primary target. All those present on the Old Buckenham flight line that morning witnessed the crash landing of a 93rd Group B-24 that had suffered technical problems following its departure from Hardwick. At Deopham Green airfield just five miles from Old Buck', a new B-17 unit, designated the 452nd Bomb Group, also became operational on this day. Both new 8th Air Force Groups completed their debut missions and returned to their bases at Old Buckenham and Deopham Green without loss.

Since late 1943 a team of Royal Air Force liaison personnel had been stationed at Old Buckenham, preparing for the arrival of the Americans and subsequently supervising and assisting the establishment of the 453rd Bomb Group at the new base. On the day of the Group's first mission, the RAF officially transferred Station 144 to the USAAF; during the ceremony the Union Jack was lowered and the Stars and Stripes was raised.

On Sunday 6 February the 453rd Bomb Group dispatched crews from Old Buckenham for an attack on an installation that was still under construction at Siracourt, France. This was to be a *Noball* mission, the code name given to targets associated with a secret German weapon. The aircrews did not know the nature of these targets at the time, and assumed that they were coastal defences. In fact they were the

A precursor to the many tragedies that were to befall the Liberator men of Old Buck' and a chilling reminder of their proximity to death. Weighed down with fuel, bombs, and ammunition, Lt. Alfred Voskian's Liberator stalled and crashed on take-off, killing eight members of the crew. (Frank Kyle)

storage and launch sites for the V-weapons, the V.1 *Doodlebugs*. These pilotless flying bombs were being prepared on the French coast in the Pas de Calais region. A few months later they were used to terrorize London and the southeast of England.

A tragedy occurred at Old Buck' on this morning of the Group's second mission. Lt. Alfred Voskian of the 735th Bomb Squadron was setting out for his second mission. The takeoff initially seemed routine but reaching seventy-five feet the Liberator, named *Little Agnes*, seemed to stall and fell earthwards onto the main runway. With the landing gear partially raised, *Little Agnes* slid off the end of the runway into a ditch and broke into pieces. Ten unarmed 500-pound bombs were on board, one of them exploded and another broke in half and started to burn (the other eight bombs were salvaged). Eight members of the crew were killed, but somehow Lt. Alfred Voskian and his engineer, Sgt. Archie Bloodworth, were both rescued. Alfred Voskian suffered a fractured spine, burns on both hands and ears, and was unconscious for a week; Archie Bloodworth later recovered from a broken leg and hip.

A precursor to the many tragedies that were to befall the Liberator men of Old Buck' during the months ahead, to them this incident

provided a chilling reminder of their proximity to death, and it was unnerving to realize that the dangers were not restricted to the airspace
over enemy-occupied Europe. As Voskian's ship burned at the end of
the runway, fifteen Liberators proceeded to their target at Siracourt. All
returned safely from what turned out to be an uneventful mission. Having been initiated into combat operations with two missions to targets in
France, what were considered to be relatively easy missions, or "milk
runs," within a few days the 453rd Bomb Group's rookie crews would be
flying over Germany itself.

CHAPTER NINE

At Dawn for Gotha

On Monday 7 February, Donald Lawry wrote home to his brother, Gordon, in Wisconsin. The long journey to Europe had provided Donald with plenty of insights into life outside of Wisconsin. For a while at least, he had seen enough of the South American jungles, the Atlantic Ocean, African deserts—more of the Earth than he had thought imaginable—and in his letter he told Gordon that he had intended to confine future traveling to the United States. He wrote that there was not much for him to spend his money on in England, and since training in California he had already managed to save over $300 as an investment in his future. Tuesday 8 February was Bill Eagleson's twenty-third birthday. Bill spent the evening celebrating and singing songs with Jack, George, Donald, and other friends at the Officers' Club.

The 453rd bombed Gilze-Rijen airfield in Holland on 10 February, and the following day the target was a construction installation near Hamburg, Germany. Early on that cold frosty morning Lt. Gus Johnson's crew, the Nortridge crew's hut mates, were awakened for their first mission, and they set off in a B-24 named *Heavenly Body*. All aircraft returned safely to Old Buck'.

Celebrations resumed in the Officers' Club on Saturday 12 February for Abraham Lincoln's birthday. Around this time, Jack Nortridge got sick with a bad case of influenza and ended up in the base hospital. During the early days at Old Buckenham there were numerous cases of sickness, which resulted in many grounded airmen as Bill Eagleson recalls:

> When we arrived at the base we were trying to adjust to your British cold [weather]. . . . I believe there was a little flu running around—bad colds—and both Jack and some of the others in our barracks did have "the bug."

Even a minor head cold could have very serious implications at high altitude in a freezing cold, unpressurized aircraft. Trouble would arise while descending from altitude, causing acute sinus pain and even blown eardrums. Donald Lawry also fell ill, and on Sunday 13 February he wrote home to his mother:

> Well the Doc finally took me off the "grounded" list but I still have
> such a cold and I can hardly breathe. . . . I haven't even gone into
> town [Attleborough] for a week or so, you can really see how I've
> been feeling. My biggest job has been to keep the fire going. This
> shack we live in is the coldest damn place I know, you can see your
> breath in any part of it. That might be the reason why over half of
> the boys are grounded that live in here.

Still suffering from sickness, enduring the bleak winter weather in a
freezing hut with rain and snow coming through under the door, trying
to keep out of the mud, and feeling particularly homesick, Donald
Lawry was not enjoying his experience of overseas life. A cold Wisconsin winter at home was significantly more preferable than life in a shack
in the middle of the English countryside. On Tuesday 15 February,
Donald, the son of an Englishman, wrote to his brother, Gordon:

> Boy, I can really see why dad never wanted to leave America and
> come back to England. This place is definitely for the birds.

During February 1944, German raids continued on London but
were unequal in strength to the around-the-clock Allied raids on Germany at the time. Sunday 20 February was the first of seven consecutive
days in which the 8th Air Force in England, the 15th Air Force in Italy,
and the Royal Air Force launched a concentrated assault to weaken the
Luftwaffe by attacking aircraft factories and assembly plants in Western
Germany. While the bombers hit the factories, the "little friends" would
offer escort protection and challenge the Luftwaffe into aerial combat.
This seven-day onslaught became remembered as "Big Week."

On the morning of Sunday 20 February, as the 8th Air Force readied
itself for the first mission of Big Week, snow fell on many of the bases in
East Anglia. At Old Buckenham the scene was bleak as the 453rd Bomb
Group dispatched twenty-four of its aircraft to bomb aircraft industries
at Brunswick, Germany. Although *"Corky" Burgundy Bombers* was the aircraft assigned to Jack Nortridge's crew, all available aircraft were needed
during maximum effort missions, and that morning Lt. Elmer Crockett,
a pilot from Grafton, Virginia, was assigned to fly the *Burgundy Bomber* to
Brunswick.

By now *Corky* was combat-ready—modifications had been made and
additional equipment such as radio and navigational aids installed.
Fourteen-millimeter armor plating had been attached to the outside of
the aircraft below the flight deck side windows. On the aircraft's stabiliz-
ers and upper surface of the starboard wing a large black letter "J" was
painted in a white circle (the "J" signified the 453rd Group and the
white circle the 2nd Bomb Division). On the fuselage of the aircraft
beside the waist window hatches, the 733rd Squadron code "F8" was
painted in large white letters.

The base hospital where Jack Nortridge was treated for the flu and where Donald Lawry received treatment for injuries suffered while cutting firewood. (Donald Olds, 453rd BG Association Collection)

The first mission of Big Week was only the second time that the 453rd Bomb Group had been assigned a target in Germany, and it was the first mission on which the crews encountered enemy fighters. When four ME-109s attacked the formation, the American air crew gunners allegedly shot down two of them, but one attacked *Battle Package* from the glare of the sun—pilot Lt. William Bates was semiconscious and almost freezing to death after his electrically heated suit failed; copilot Lt. Eugene McDowell was flying the ship and was hit in the foot by a 20mm shell. Somehow they made it back to Old Buck'. Lt. Donald Cannavaro's Liberator was badly damaged and he landed at Tibenham where the aircraft was salvaged for spare parts. Lt. Albert Lane's crew of the 734th Squadron had set out for the mission in a B-24 named *Briney Marlin*, on loan from the 733rd Squadron. This crew failed to return to Old Buck'. Four members of the crew were killed in action, and six were later reported as prisoners of war. Lt. Elmer Crockett brought *Corky* safely home to Old Buck'. The following day, an airfield at Achmer, Germany, was the target and all aircraft returned safely.

From California three months previously, Donald Lawry had written home with enthusiasm about Jack Nortridge's flying skills and added that Jack was the only pilot he felt safe flying with. But now Donald had spent three weeks in Europe without setting eyes on the enemy; he knew too well that there was a bloody war to win but the only fighting he seemed to have done so far was fight off flu and the freezing cold. He watched the other crews go out and he anxiously waited to see if they returned. Donald didn't expect combat missions to be a pleasant experience, but the sooner he started flying, the sooner he would be granted some furlough time which he planned to spend looking up some of his relatives in Cornwall. Only when he had completed his missions could he leave this bleak, austere place and return home to Wisconsin. On Monday 21 February, Donald wrote:

> Dear Mom and family, how is everybody at home? I've been in the hospital for the last few days, because I slipped when I was cutting some wood for the fire, foolish thing to do wasn't it. At least I got over my cold and can fly again. I'm as good as new now, so don't worry about me.
>
> It looks like I'll start flying against the Hun pretty soon now. Will he catch hell, ha.

Donald also wrote to his wife, Dorothy, telling her that he expected to fly his first mission very soon. That evening he was on alert for a mission scheduled for the following morning. A navigator was needed on Lt. Richard Ingram's crew for the mission of Tuesday 22 February. Lt. Ingram's original navigator, Lt. John Farrell, had been reassigned as a lead navigator and transferred to a lead crew commanded by Lt. William Penn. Ingram's replacement navigator was suffering with flu and so Donald Lawry volunteered to fly the mission.

Donald was awakened before dawn along with the other officers in the hut ordered to fly that day. George White and Bill Eagleson each returned to sleep as their hut mates prepared themselves. 22 February 1944 was a significant date for Donald—three months had passed since his wedding day; it was his brother's eighteenth birthday; and he was about to discover the horrors of war without his closest companions.

Amid the mud of the dispersed accommodation sites, the base became a scene of activity as trucks, jeeps, cyclists, and pedestrians made their way along the concrete roadways, mostly in the direction of the two mess sites. After breakfast the combat crews attended the premission briefings in the Operations area of the Technical Site. The target was announced—the aircraft assembly plant at Gotha, Germany.

Following final preparations, Don Lawry and the rest of Richard Ingram's crew were driven out to the airfield and to the hardstand where B-24 *Ginnie* awaited them. Ground crews and ordnance personnel had been working through the night preparing each of the twenty-eight scheduled aircraft dispersed around the base, and loading them with fuel and bombs destined for the German aircraft factory. This was to be Ingram's second mission, having flown *Ginnie* on the mission to Brunswick two days previously. For the mission to Gotha, four stand-in crewmembers were assigned to his crew—Donald Lawry as navigator, and the tail, top, and ball turret gunners usually assigned to Lt. George Wear's crew.

Takeoff commenced at 0915 hours. First away was the group's commanding officer, Col. Joseph Miller (flying as command pilot on board *Black Jed 654* with a 735th Bomb Squadron crew, followed by the aircraft of the 735th and the 734th Squadrons. At 0925 Assistant Operations Officer Capt. Andrew Low departed Old Buckenham (Capt. Low was flying as command pilot on board Lt. William Penn's 733rd Squadron ship named *Rooster*). The 732nd Squadron departed next, followed by the 733rd—Lt. Joseph Waiter at 0931; Lt. James Hamilton in *Shack Rabbit* at 0932; Lt. William Bertrand in *Golden Gaboon* at 0934 followed closely by Lt. Hal Kimball and Lt. Robert Catlin.

At 0936 Richard Ingram's crew in *Ginnie* took off into overcast skies—Donald Lawry was airborne for his first mission. A few ships followed and then the Group began formation assembly, hindered by the cloudy skies above Old Buckenham. The 453rd Bomb Group had scheduled twenty-eight aircraft for the mission, however three aircraft failed to join the formation over the field—evidently only twenty-five aircraft were airborne. Nine minutes after the last ship left the field, the first abort, *Queenie* of the 735th Squadron, landed back at Old Buckenham with a runaway propeller.

The 453rd formed into two sections before joining the other two 2nd Combat Wing groups. The first section, led by Col. Miller and comprising the 734th and 735th Squadrons, flew high-right to the 445th Bomb Group. In trail of the first section, the second section, led by Capt. Andrew Low and comprising the 732nd and 733rd Squadrons, flew high-right to the 389th Bomb Group. Capt. Andrew Low, whose twenty-seventh birthday was just four days away, reported upon his return to base:

> I was in charge of the [second] section and rode in the first ship. We made a rendezvous with the 389th Bomb Group as briefed and fell in as high section at 13,000 feet. We held our position until the formation went into a heavy overcast on instruments while climbing. We broke out occasionally but were not on top until 20,000 feet. In the clear there were planes of all groups in all sorts of formations.

A scattered formation of over one hundred and seventy B-24s of the 2nd Bomb Division proceeded across the North Sea. On board *Ginnie*, bombardier Lt. Michael Boehm called out for oxygen checks every ten to fifteen minutes, to make sure that the oxygen was flowing and that all crew members were still conscious. In a southern drawl a crewmember from Louisiana responded, "Radio operator okay," and other confirmations followed.

Five years after Donald Lawry set out on his first mission, his brother Gordon expressed his feelings of loss by drawing a scene he named *At Dawn for Gotha*. (Betty Lawry Allen)

Crossing the enemy coastline at 22,000 feet and flying over the Low Countries, strong headwinds caused further formation and navigation confusion. In the second formation section, Donald Lawry looked out at the powerful starboard engines through the right-hand side window in the nose of *Ginnie;* the sound was exhilarating. He could see Lt. Robert Catlin's ship, *Valkyrie,* in the right wing position of the element and he looked ahead to see the element leader turn and leave the formation; piloted by Lt. Hal Kimball, this ship returned home with supercharger problems resulting in a loss of turbo power.

A while later a 732nd Squadron aircraft named *Son of a Beach* left the second section and returned to base with similar supercharger problems. Eleven aircraft remained in each section. Group CO Col. Miller was forced to return to base with mechanical failure, and eight other aircraft from the first section followed and returned to base due to the adverse weather conditions. Two aircraft from the first section continued on the mission; *663* joined the second section formation and *Rumplestilskin II* hooked up with the 448th Bomb Group formation. Two Liberators from the second section, *Hard T'Get* and *Valkyrie,* aborted due to the deteriorating weather conditions; Lt. George Baatz's crew found themselves with the 446th Bomb Group formation and continued on the mission.

Encountering turbulence and snow squalls, Lt. Ingram's crew in *Ginnie* became separated from the 453rd Bomb Group's formation. Donald

Lawry worked frantically at his dead reckoning navigation, and *Ginnie* tagged along with the 44th Bomb Group formation. Known as the "Flying Eightballs," this was the first Norfolk-based Liberator Group, identified by their "circle-A" tail markings. Meanwhile, Capt. Andrew Low's ship continued to lead seven other aircraft from the 453rd Bomb Group towards Gotha in pursuit of the 445th Bomb Group.

At 1225 while flying approximately one hundred miles inland the Division was recalled—the mission had been abandoned. In the vicinity of Münster, Germany, the 44th Bomb Group received a recall signal and headed for home. Bombs would be dropped into the North Sea en route, as landing back at base with full bomb bays was a recipe for disaster. *Ginnie* remained with the veteran "Eightballs." Donald Lawry's first mission had turned into a non-event. The rest of the 453rd Bomb Group did not turn back immediately—Capt. Low's radio operator received the recall message but at first was unable to reach any other aircraft on VHF radio. Finally, at 1310 hours, approximately twenty minutes from Gotha the 445th Bomb Group circled west of Münster and headed home with the 453rd Bomb Group in tow.

Enemy fighters were seen but kept their distance from the American bombers. Amid the confusion, some Bomb Groups, believing that they were still flying over Germany, sought targets of opportunity and regrettably jettisoned their bombs on four targets in Holland with tragic consequences. At Nijmegen, where a factory and railroad marshalling yards were bombed, two hundred Dutch civilian lives were lost. Unfortunately, the two 453rd Bomb Group aircraft that had joined the 446th and 448th Bomb Group formations were among the aircraft that dropped their bombs at Nijmegen.

Fourteen Liberators, the early returnees, had landed back at Old Buckenham by 1249 hours and then nearly two hours passed while the personnel on the ground at Old Buckenham sweated out the return of eleven more ships. At last, ten ships landed between 1442 and 1459 hours and along the flight line all eyes were fixed skyward as air crews and ground crews waited anxiously for *Ginnie* to appear on the horizon . . . but Richard Ingram's crew never returned. At Operations, the word "missing" was chalked up on the board next to aircraft 41-28615, *Ginnie.*

At Shipdham airfield, the *Flying Eightballs* were attending mission debriefing. One 44th Bomb Group crew reported that on the way home soon after receiving the recall, they flew into a heavy cloudbank. When they emerged into some clear sky, the other two planes in their element had gone—in the cloud these two Liberators had lost their positions, but continued to follow the formation homewards. Meanwhile, a lone B-24 with the 453rd's identification letter "J" in a white circle on the tail fins had been seen to join the 44th Bomb Group's formation—this was Lt. Richard Ingram's aircraft, *Ginnie,* with Donald Lawry on board.

At 1222 hours the formation was attacked by eight FW190s; *Ginnie* and the two straggling 44th Liberators were singled out as easy prey. These three ships, badly damaged and with injured on board, struggled to keep up with formation, all the while losing altitude. Thirteen minutes after the attack, a single parachute emerged from one of the Shipdham Liberators, and ten minutes later more parachutes were seen. Eventually this ship went down near Wesel, Germany. One crew member was killed and nine became prisoners of war.

The 44th Bomb Group formation crossed the Dutch coastline and encountered sleet, snow, and a cloud base of 1,800 feet. The other badly damaged 44th Liberator was never accounted for and was presumably swallowed up by the North Sea. Richard Ingram's crew in *Ginnie* limped homewards. A 44th Bomb Group navigator recorded the fate of Ingram's crew in his logbook— somewhere off the coast of Rotterdam, *Ginnie* was seen to fall into the icy cold water of the North Sea, exploding on impact. No parachutes were seen and it was therefore believed that the entire crew of ten went down with the plane.

The eyewitness accounts from the 44th Bomb Group personnel were sent to the Operations section at Old Buckenham, where Bill Eagleson was anxiously awaiting news. He was deeply shocked to discover that along with Richard Ingram's crew, his dear friend Don Lawry was "missing in action," presumed dead.

At the Officers' Club, festivities had been scheduled in honor of George Washington's birthday. But *Corky*'s crew was hardly in a celebratory mood—sadness became paramount that Tuesday evening, and for a while there

In January 1944, Donald Lawry navigated *Corky*'s crew from the United States to England. He was killed in action on 22 February 1944, less than five weeks before his twentieth birthday. (Betty Lawry Allen)

weren't too many celebrations. The following day a replacement crew
piloted by Lt. Donald Jones arrived at Old Buck' and moved into the
huts that Ingram's crew had previously inhabited. On 24 February, the
453rd Bomb Group tried again for Gotha; this time the assembly plant
was destroyed, costing the Germans up to seven weeks of Me110 fighter
aircraft production. All the bombers returned safely to Old Buck'.

The following day, 25 February, Jack Nortridge and his crew were assigned to fly their first mission, with a navigator from another crew joining them for the trip. Their hut mates, Gus Johnson's crew, were also
assigned the mission to an aircraft factory at Fürth, near Nürnberg,
Germany. It was a maximum effort to bomb Germany's aircraft industries as a conclusion to Big Week, with eight hundred American bombers and crews participating.

The Nortridge crew was not assigned *Corky*, but instead climbed
aboard *Valkyrie* at dispersal point number thirty-nine. Gus Johnson was
assigned an unnamed Liberator (which would later be named *Shack Rabbit II*) parked at the adjacent dispersal point, number thirty-eight. The
Nortridge crew took off at 0936, and Johnson's crew followed three
minutes later. Twenty-two aircraft were airborne for the mission, but
five aborted. Jack Nortridge's aircraft developed supercharger problems, and the crew was forced to abort the mission prior to reaching the
target. Gus Johnson also suffered supercharger problems and landed at
1321; the Nortridge crew landed at 1412 hours, some four hours earlier
than those who completed the mission. One crew failed to make it back
to Old Buck'.

During Big Week, Allied bombers dropped 18,000 tons of bombs on
Germany, halving the planned fighter production for the month ahead
and significantly influencing the course of the war. But this military success came at a price—from the 8th Air Force alone, one thousand five
hundred and eighty-seven American airmen were missing in action.
Then there were the 15th Air Force and Royal Air Force casualties.
More than half a century later, Bill Eagleson reflected:

> I was very sad for quite some time regarding Don because he and I,
> we more or less depended upon each other in the nose of that B-24
> *Corky*.

On Tuesday 7 March 1944, Mrs. Myrtie Lawry received a telegram. The golden-brown envelope stated "Western Union Telegram" in large letters. The back of the envelope carried the advertise-
ment, "Money in a hurry; to send it . . . or get it, Telegraph it! Quick
and safe. Economical . . . no red tape." The telegram came from the
War Department—every mother's worst nightmare. The emotionless
and impersonal "Casualty Message" declared that Donald had been reported "Missing in Action" on a mission to Germany.

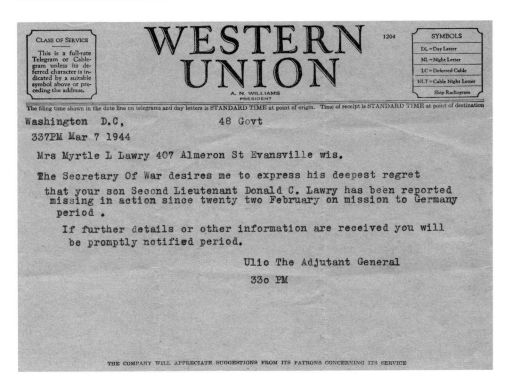

CLASS OF SERVICE

This is a full-rate Telegram or Cablegram unless its deferred character is indicated by a suitable symbol above or preceding the address.

WESTERN UNION

A. N. WILLIAMS
PRESIDENT

1204

SYMBOLS

DL=Day Letter

NL=Night Letter

LC=Deferred Cable

NLT=Cable Night Letter

Ship Radiogram

The filing time shown in the date line on telegrams and day letters is STANDARD TIME at point of origin. Time of receipt is STANDARD TIME at point of destination

Washington D.C,   48 Govt

337PM Mar 7 1944

Mrs Myrtle L Lawry 407 Almeron St Evansville wis.

The Secretary Of War desires me to express his deepest regret
that your son Second Lieutenant Donald C. Lawry has been reported
missing in action since twenty two February on mission to Germany
period .

If further details or other information are received you will
be promptly notified period.

Ulio The Adjutant General

33o PM

THE COMPANY WILL APPRECIATE SUGGESTIONS FROM ITS PATRONS CONCERNING ITS SERVICE

Myrtie Lawry told the news of uncertainty to Donald's younger brother, Gordon, his eight-year-old sister, Betty Lou, and his wife, Dorothy. Two days later the loss of Don Lawry was reported in both the *Evansville Review* and the *Janesville Daily Gazette*.

At Old Buckenham, having been informed of the eyewitness accounts, *Corky*'s crew understood that Don had been killed. But for some considerable time he was categorized ominously as "missing in action." Back home in Wisconsin, the Lawry family knew little about the fate of their loved one, and letters that Myrtie Lawry had written to her eldest son since early February were returned to her.

As Don's twentieth birthday passed on 27 March, the family could do nothing but wait for more news, and hope that soon he would emerge from the uncertain limbo status of "missing." They knew nothing of the circumstances—that the witnesses had not seen any parachutes to substantiate any possibility of hope. And so the Lawrys hoped and prayed that Don was alive and safe, perhaps even as a prisoner of war. The desperate necessity for some knowledge or reassurance led many families in these circumstances to search out their missing relatives in the pages of publications such as the *Prisoners of War Bulletin,* a monthly American Red Cross paper produced for the relatives of American prisoners of war.

In November 1944 the wife of Lt. Arthur White, Ingram's copilot, reported seeing her husband in a photograph that appeared in the August 1944 issue of the *Prisoners of War Bulletin*. Below the photograph a caption stated, "A group of unidentified American Prisoners of War at Stalag Luft III." The mother of Sgt. Charles Ross, Ingram's radio operator, believed that she identified her son as one of the men pictured in another photograph that appeared in the August edition of the *Prisoners of War Bulletin*, and also in a photograph in the October 1944 issue. Myrtie Lawry wrote to the Casualty Branch of the War Department one year after her son, Donald Lawry, was lost on the mission to Gotha:

> Recently we found Donald's picture, or so we believe, among a group of unidentified American airmen at Camp Stalag Luft III, Germany. This picture was published in the August 1944 issue of *Prisoners of War Bulletin*.
>
> Not only the immediate family, but others can readily pick him out of the group. We have also heard that four other members of that bomber crew have been identified by their next of kin as being in that picture.

In May 1945 Myrtie Lawry received a message from the War Department stating that her son, missing in action, was now presumed to have died on 22 February 1944. When airmen were captured by the Germans and became prisoners of war, invariably their families were notified and sometimes personal letters were received from the individuals via the Red Cross—but none of the ten men lost on 22 February 1944 had been reported as prisoners of war and nobody had heard from them. Unlike the majority of confirmed POWs, Richard Ingram's crew never went home.

Following the war the remains of Sgt. Richard Anderson, the tail gunner from Ingram's crew of 22 February 1944, were recovered from an unknown grave in a British cemetery at Bergen-op-Zoom, Holland, and were reburied in a military cemetery in America. It is unknown where Anderson's remains were discovered but assumed due to the proximity of the British cemetery to the sea that they were washed ashore. No known trace of the other nine members of the crew was ever found. Donald Lawry, along with the other missing crew members, was posthumously awarded the Air Medal and Purple Heart. His name is written on the Wall of the Missing at the American Military Cemetery in the Netherlands.

After Bill Eagleson returned to the United States, he and Dorothy Lawry arranged to meet in Columbus, Ohio, midway between Boston and Evansville. Less than a year earlier, Bill had been the best man at Don and Dorothy's wedding at March Field in California. It wasn't until the spring of 1945 that Don's personal belongings were returned to his wife and family. Among them was a sketch of a boat, probably the type of boat that Don had dreamt of sailing on Lake Michigan after the war,

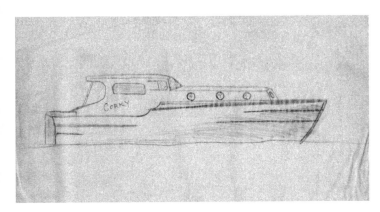

"I think I'll like boats just as good as airplanes, there is something fascinating about them." Donald Lawry's drawing was sent home to Wisconsin along with the rest of his belongings; the significance of the boat's name was a mystery to the Lawry family for over half a century. (Betty Lawry Allen)

which he referred to in the letters he wrote to his brother about their plans for when the war was over. On the side of the boat's cabin, Don had named the boat *Corky*, but for half a century the story behind the name was unknown to his family.

A memorial service for Donald Lawry was held at the Methodist Church of Evansville, Wisconsin, in May 1946. Dorothy, his widow, remarried. In the spring of 2002, Dorothy and her husband, Clarence Taplin, with the assistance of Don's sister, Betty, arranged for a permanent memorial stone to be placed in a cemetery near Don Lawry's birthplace. The memorial stone was placed next to his father's grave in Oregon, Wisconsin.

CHAPTER TEN

Prisoner of War

On Sunday 5 March, the B-24 Bomb Groups were scheduled to attack enemy targets in France. Bill LeRoy, the radio operator from *Corky*'s crew, was called upon to fly his first mission and was assigned to fly with Lt. Robert Catlin's crew. Having already lost his navigator, Jack Nortridge was not happy about his crew members being assigned to fly missions with other crews. But his protests were in vain. The 453rd Bomb Group was struggling to find its way; combat initiation had been challenging, and due to the number of cases of cold and flu that were spreading across the base, composite crews had to be formed.

Lt. Robert Catlin's crew had started out on three previous missions but had been forced to abort each of them. They had endured turbo failures in two engines on 20 February and encountered extreme weather conditions on the recalled Gotha mission two days later, and a feathered propeller necessitated an early return to base on 3 March. Then Catlin's radio operator, Sgt. Kenny Drapeau, became another victim of the cold and flu epidemic spreading around the base at Old Buckenham. Bill LeRoy's usual crewmate, Bill Eagleson recalls the situation:

> When crews were short-handed they would call for other crews that weren't flying to fill in. . . . I think in the status of the enlisted men, they didn't have quite the influence that we had as officers in trying to avoid this kind of a call up.

However, in this case Bill LeRoy was quite happy to fly with Lt. Robert Catlin's crew, as he knew them very well from Phase training in the United States. Prior to their crew training, LeRoy had studied in radio school with Kenny Drapeau, whom he was to replace for the mission of 5 March. Like all airmen listed to fly that morning, LeRoy was awakened during the early hours. He made his way to the mess halls for an early morning breakfast before attending the mission briefing for radio operators and gunners.

Following mission preparations the crews made their ways to their aircraft parked out around the airfield. Lt. Catlin's awaiting B-24, the ship named *Valkyrie* that he had flown from San Francisco to England, was parked on dispersal point number thirty-nine adjacent to the technical site. Twenty-three aircraft ran up their engines and taxied out to the

Sgt. Bill LeRoy flew his first mission on 5 March 1944; the following day he flew to Berlin. (Bill Eagleson)

Lt. Robert Catlin and his crew. On 5 and 6 March 1944 Catlin's radio operator was ill and so Sgt. Bill LeRoy from *Corky*'s crew stood in for two missions. (Donald Olds, 453rd BG Association Collection)

main runway for an instrument takeoff. The 453rd Bomb Group formation assembled over the base at 5,000 feet, prior to 2nd Combat Wing assembly at which time the 453rd took up the low-left position, the 389th the high-right position, behind the leading 445th Group. This, the 2nd Combat Wing formation, was dispatched to bomb an airfield at Cazaux, ninety miles southwest of Bordeaux in southwestern France. However, the absence of radar-equipped Pathfinder Force (PFF) aircraft prevented them from finding their primary target, which was obscured by cloud.

Following the Initial Point of the bomb run the leading 445th Group turned off the briefed route and circled the Bergerac area, east of Bordeaux. Antiaircraft gunners fired flak into the formations at several points. Two of the 453rd's aircraft attacked a target of opportunity (believed to be Bergerac airfield), while most of the group salvoed their bombs in an uninhabited field and wooded area eight miles south of Niort, en route back to the Channel. *Valkyrie* suffered some technical problems when the superchargers in number one and number four engines failed, but Catlin and crew made it back to base safely with the rest of the group. By half past four that afternoon, all twenty-three aircraft had landed back at Old Buck' and taxied to their dispersal points.

On Monday 6 March, Bill LeRoy, James Witmer, and George White were awakened in the early hours to fly with short-handed crews or to complete composite crews on a "maximum effort" mission. The Charge of Quarters officer (CQ) routinely announced scheduled breakfast and briefing times while those not assigned to fly drifted back to sleep.

For the second day running, Bill LeRoy was assigned as Lt. Robert Catlin's radio operator in *Valkyrie*. This time LeRoy had been consulted the night before and was asked if he was willing to fly again on Catlin's crew. With enthusiasm he responded, "Sure!" and was then alerted for the mission. He went to get an early night, and hoped for another trip to France—but he was sorry that he had been so obliging when he found out the target for his second mission. James Witmer was not given a choice and had not been alerted the night before. Assigned his first mission, James was to fly as ball turret gunner on Lt. Patrick Tobin's B-24, *Shack Rabbit*, in the place of a sick gunner. James was familiar with the enlisted men from Tobin's crew, for they lived in the hut next door. George White was assigned as Lt. Joseph Waiter's copilot.

Airmen congregated at the mess halls for an early morning breakfast. Soon after five o'clock, the crews waited with anticipation in the briefing hall, restlessly fidgeting on the uncomfortable wooden benches. As the room turned hazy with cigarette smoke, all eyes became fixed on the curtain that concealed the map and the target for today. Everyone hoped for a "milk run," a short hop across the Channel to a target in northern France and then home again. Major Hubbard commenced the briefing and the curtain was drawn to reveal the aircrews' worst fear—Berlin!

Lt. George White, copilot on *Corky*'s crew, at home in Oklahoma on a furlough prior to completing his training in 1943. George was assigned to fly the 6 March 1944 mission to Berlin with Lt. Joseph Waiter's crew. (White family)

Sgt. James Freddie Witmer, from *Corky*'s crew. On 6 March 1944 he was assigned to fly as ball turret gunner with Lt. Patrick Tobin's crew on board *Shack Rabbit*. (Hazel Witmer)

The German capital city had already been the target for many Royal Air Force missions—most notably, RAF night bombers had first bombed the city in August 1940; in January 1943 RAF Mosquitoes made an attack in broad daylight; and one night in November 1943 the RAF made its first large-scale raid on Berlin. In November 1943 an 8th Air Force daylight mission to "Big B" was called off before the bombers had left their bases. The next attempt by the Americans was not until 3 March 1944 but the mission was abandoned in the face of dense cloud up to 28,000 feet. The following day the 8th made another attempt but again weather interfered and the bombers were recalled—however, three Squadrons of B-17s did not receive the signal and continued alone, becoming the first American bombers to attack the German capital. And now, on 6 March the 8th Air Force was again poised in readiness for a "maximum effort" mission to Berlin.

The significance of a large-scale daylight attack on the German capital was threefold—targets, fighter opposition, and morale. Berlin was the location of vital strategic targets, the elimination of which could help the Allies win the war. A large-scale daylight attack would entice the German Air Force into battle with all its might, thus providing an opportunity for the long-range American fighters to challenge and weaken the air superiority of its adversary. If successful, such an attack on Berlin would do wonders for morale both in the UK and the United States, while delivering a severe blow to German civilian morale. But enticing the Luftwaffe into an unprecedented air battle over the German capital could potentially have a crippling effect on the American bomber force. As well as enemy fighters, the flak would undoubtedly be ferocious. High losses were a certainty in the treacherous skies over "Big B."

Tension was high in the briefing room at Old Buckenham that morning. Major Hubbard explained that the 8th Air Force was to attack industrial targets in the Berlin suburbs. The 1st Bomb Division B-17s were to lead the force, followed by the 3rd Bomb Division B-17s, and lastly the B-24s of the 2nd Bomb Division, destined for the Daimler Benz aero engine plant at Genshagen, just south of the city. The mission was to become the 8th Air Force's first full-scale raid on Berlin.

An aerial view of a "spectacle" dispersal point in the 733rd Bomb Squadron area at Old Buckenham. The B-24 in the foreground is parked at dispersal point number forty-nine, where on the morning of 6 March 1944, James Freddie Witmer climbed aboard *Shack Rabbit*, never to return to Old Buck'. Note the terraced farm-laborers' cottages at the left of the photo, surrounded by taxiways and aircraft dispersal points; beyond the cottages the cube-shaped control tower and one of the secondary runways are visible. To the right, and below the hazy horizon, the technical site and hangar number one can be seen. (Pat Ramm)

It was a cold morning and before dawn, light snow fell on parts of eastern England. George White assisted Joseph Waiter in the preflight checks in their assigned B-24 (an unnamed Liberator, serial 42–52218). North of the technical site at dispersal point number forty-nine, James Witmer climbed aboard Lt. Patrick Tobin's aircraft, *Shack Rabbit*. Meanwhile, Bill LeRoy and his assigned crew gathered on dispersal point number forty for a pre-mission pep talk by Robert Catlin. After climbing aboard *Valkyrie*, LeRoy checked in and prepared his radio equipment.

In their hut situated just a stone's throw across a meadow to the west, Jack Nortridge and Bill Eagleson tried to sleep beneath the droning din of one hundred and twelve aircraft engines. They knew that George White had been assigned the mission because they had heard his early-morning wake-up call. Of the enlisted men on their crew who were billeted on another accommodation site, Nortridge and Eagleson weren't surprised when they learned that Bill LeRoy was airborne, as he had flown the mission on the previous day with Catlin's crew. But as for James Witmer, Bill Eagleson recalls:

> Back on our site we did not know that Witmer was on a mission. He was awakened in the morning and assigned a crew, and off he went.

The Group began to taxi out to the runway soon after eight o'clock that morning. Ground visibility was better than forecast, although there was more cloud than expected as twenty-eight B-24 Liberators took to the skies over Old Buck'. Each aircraft climbed into the overcast at 3,000 feet, and then into clear sky at 6,000 feet. Patches of scattered cloud were encountered above 8,000 feet.

With the crews on oxygen, the 453rd Bomb Group circled over Old Buckenham at 13,500 feet and formed into two sections; the first section comprised the 732nd and 733rd Squadrons, while the second comprised the 734th and 735th Squadrons. From the leading three-plane element of the first section, George White looked ahead to the lead ship, *Hollywood & Vine* (Lt. Phillip Stock's crew were the lead crew with Group CO Col. Miller on board as command pilot) while immediately to the right he could see *Battle Package* (flown by Lt. William Bates). Meanwhile, the Liberators flown by Lt. Patrick Tobin (with James Witmer on board), Lt. Elmer Crockett, and Lt. Robert Catlin (with Bill LeRoy on board) arrived in the formation as a three-plane element immediately to the left.

Lt. Marshall Johnson's crew on board *El Flako* encountered technical difficulties, dropped their bombs in the countryside five miles south of Old Buckenham and returned home. Group assembly was completed at half past nine, and the formation proceeded to *Buncher 6* radio beacon at Hethel for 2nd Bomb Wing assembly. The 453rd Bomb Group took up position in trail of the 445th Bomb Group and set course for *Splasher 6* at

Scole; from there the Liberators proceeded to the *Splasher 5* beacon at Mundesley. Flying at 14,000 feet, the 2nd Combat Wing crossed the English coast at around 1030 hours, by which time the 453rd was flying abreast of the 445th, in a low-left position; the 389th flew high-right of the leading 445th. In trail of the Flying Fortress Groups, over 240 Liberators were airborne; the entire American bomber stream was over ninety miles long.

George White looked to the right out of the cockpit window and remarked to Joseph Waiter that Lt. William Bates was pulling out of the formation—*Battle Package* returned to base with turbo problems. Lt. James Parcells's 732nd Squadron crew on board *Archibald* also returned to base, with a stuck propeller governor.

Patrick Tobin and his crew had previously completed two missions during February and had set out for the aborted Berlin mission on 3 March. On board *Shack Rabbit,* James Witmer was the unenvied member of the crew, the ball turret gunner. Over the final few miles of the North Sea crossing, the retractable ball turret was hydraulically lowered beneath the belly of the aircraft, the gun barrels appearing from slots in the underside of the fuselage. James depressed the guns by ninety degrees so they were pointing downwards, thus rolling the turret forward and allowing access to the armor-plated entry hatch. He then stepped into his precarious turret—looking down through the circular plate sighting window, thirteen inches in diameter, all that could be seen was a large expanse of water, more than fourteen thousand feet below.

Once inside the spherical turret, James plugged in his electrically heated flying suit and oxygen mask and tried to make himself comfortable between the two .50 caliber machine guns as one of the waist gunners closed the hatch above him. Wearing bulky flying clothes, there was no room left inside for the ball gunner to move. Therefore, this crew station was suited to gunners who were slim and not too tall. At around five feet and eleven inches, James was certainly pushing the height limit, but he was reasonably slender. From March Field, California, back in November, James had sent a crew photograph home to Texarkana. Known as Freddie to those back home, his mother had proudly written on the reverse of the photograph, "This is Freddie's crew.

A wartime illustration of a gunner inside the Sperry ball turret, which was hydraulically lowered beneath the belly of the B-24. (Air Force Aid Society)

Freddie looks skinny but he really isn't. He weighs about 174 lbs." The front of the photograph had been autographed by Bill LeRoy ("To a real pal, Bill") and Pete Veilleux ("Good luck always, Pete").

Good luck over Berlin was what James Witmer was hoping for. Cramped into a kind of fetal position, his legs were bent at the knees and his feet in stirrups positioned on each side of the circular window. His hands clung to two control sticks at his sides, each with a thumb trigger to fire the guns. The turret was electro-hydraulically operated; the control sticks were levered sideways for 360-degree horizontal turret rotation or pushed and pulled to enable vertical movement, depressing and elevating the guns by ninety degrees. Whichever way James rolled the turret, he would physically roll with it. If the guns were kept in a horizontal position for too long, the blood circulation to James's feet would be restricted.

The ball turret on *Shack Rabbit* was in constant motion as James Witmer searched the sky for Luftwaffe aircraft. The weather conditions were reasonably clear, allowing good visibility—the cold, pale blue morning skies seemed to reach up to the heavens. Certainly the ball turret offered some breathtaking views, but it was also a lonely and claustrophobic place for a gunner to spend several long combat hours. James was isolated from the rest of the crew despite the intercom system over which a variety of accents could be heard—the pilot was from Michigan, the copilot from Tennessee, others were from New York, Ohio, Pennsylvania, North Carolina, and Massachusetts.

The ball turret's guns were fed from ammunition boxes inside the aircraft. There was not even enough room inside the ball turret for the gunner to wear a parachute, and the only physical lifeline he could depend on was a canvas safety strap that connected him to the inside of the aircraft where a parachute was at the ready. Aircrews were not given much in the way of parachute training and it was understood that in an emergency they would have to jump, pull the ripcord, and hope for the best. But first the ball gunner would have to escape the turret to which many horror stories were associated—all of them were unwise to contemplate outside of nightmares if the gunner was to maintain his sanity. The situation of being trapped inside the turret as the aircraft plummeted earthwards was, in reality, quite a likely scenario.

The gunners all fired short bursts to test their guns. James was practically deafened by the two guns on each side of his head, and spent brass cartridges and their links were ejected from the ball turret, often to the detriment of other aircraft. The formations were already being monitored by German radar, and enemy fighter and flak installations were alerted. The Dutch coastline passed beneath the 453rd Group's bombers at 1110 hours as intermittent bursts of flak exploded around them. The 445th Bomb Group led the 389th and 453rd in a 360-degree counterclockwise turn in the vicinity of Egmond (possibly to allow the last of

B-24 Liberator *Consolidated Mess* amid a sky full of contrails. On 6 March 1944 Berlin mission, Lt. Wayne McBride and his crew brought this aircraft home to Old Buck', but it was so badly battle damaged and in need of repair that it was not dispatched on another mission until 22 March. (Frank Kyle/Donald Olds, 453rd BG Association Collection)

the B-17 Groups to proceed into enemy airspace) before recrossing the enemy coast at 1120.

Four aircraft from the second section aborted in the vicinity of the coast, one of them had supercharger problems and another, *Spirit of Notre Dame*, ran into difficulties when an expended ammunition link from a ship ahead had sliced through and become lodged in an engine's rocker box cover. When the engine started leaking oil, pilot Lt. Ray Sears had to feather the propeller and return to base.

Twenty-one aircraft from the 453rd Bomb Group continued towards Berlin, still several hundred miles away. The scheduled route was designed to avoid as many of the major flak defenses as possible, but soon inaccurate bursts of anti-aircraft fire were seen among the 445th Bomb Group formation ahead. Meanwhile, like snow white streamers thrown across the sky, the single engine contrails were, to the bomber crews, a

Running the gauntlet through the first of the flak. By the time the 453rd Bomb Group approached Berlin, the aircrews from Old Buck' were filled with dread. They encountered a ferocious anti-aircraft barrage that appeared to be a solid black cloud and was visible fifty miles away. (Frank Kyle)

reassuring indication of the P-47 Thunderbolt fighters that were airborne and watching over them from on high, ready to pounce on approaching enemy fighters before they got too close. Further along the route, the double contrails indicated that twin-engine P-38 Lightnings had taken over the escort relay, while P-51 Mustangs were anticipated in the target area. Some eight hundred American fighters and two squadrons of RAF Mustangs were airborne for escort duties, to disperse German fighter forces before they could wreak havoc among the bomber formations.

Over Germany the 445th led the 389th and 453rd Bomb Groups over the town of Standal, approximately ten to fifteen miles north of the briefed route. In an attempt to resume the correct course, these three groups, the 2nd Combat Wing formation, turned towards Brandenburg in an attempt to reestablish the briefed course. Meanwhile, aircraft were shaken as flak bursts exploded around them, visible by small clouds of dense, black smoke, and audible by rumbling explosive sounds.

Absorbed into the English language since the Second World War as a word to describe adverse criticism, the word *flak* was derived from the German *Fliegerabwehrkanone*, meaning anti-aircraft cannon. A Liberator or Flying Fortress bomber could be destroyed by a direct hit from a single German 88mm flak shell. However, the large majority of flak bursts were inaccurate although still potentially deadly—it didn't require a direct hit to cause horrific damage to an aircraft, or severe injury to the crew inside. Altitude detonators caused each shell to explode, dispersing hundreds upon hundreds of steel fragments at high velocity. This shrapnel would tear through the aluminum skin of the wings and fuselage of the bombers, shredding fuel lines, hydraulic systems, damaging engines, and injuring and killing crew members. Armor plating added weight and was therefore kept to an absolute minimum. Aircrews were therefore inadequately protected, relying on their flak jackets and steel helmets.

Something appeared to be wrong with Lt. Robert Witzel's ship, *Lonesome Polecat*. During the months ahead, Lt. Hubert Cripe, a 734th Squadron pilot, found that not only did he have time on his hands (he was confined to a prisoner of war camp), but courtesy of the Red Cross, he had the rare luxury of a few sheets of blank paper on which to write. With the bitter memory of an eventful mission to Berlin still fresh in his mind, he put pen to paper:

> Witzel suddenly pulled out of formation. Well, being out of formation [less than] one hundred miles from Berlin is just like slitting your own throat but I followed him. He was definitely in trouble. And sure enough—he feathered Number three. What to do? Why didn't the dumb fool try to stay with the formation? But no, he's going home [he eventually made it]. Well, I've got to catch the formation or my goose will be cooked. I gave her full throttle and caught my Group just after they had passed the IP.

The 453rd Bomb Group had reached the IP (the Initial Point of the bomb run, where bombadiers commenced target sighting) at 1325 hours and began the straight and level run to the target. The antiaircraft barrage over Berlin was certainly the most intense opposition encountered so far on any mission by the aircrews from Old Buck', and this aerial minefield caused a great deal of confusion. Hubert Cripe wrote:

> Over the target was the most concentrated flak barrage I have ever seen. It was almost a solid black cloud with red bursts of exploding shells. We could see it fifty miles off and it filled me with dread. . . . Our bomb bay doors were open and we were going to drop our eggs when the lead plane did. Suddenly we were in the flak. It was everywhere . . . spent pieces of flak bounced off our ship like BBs [ball bearings]. Boy, a hit in our bomb bay and we've had it.

A Liberator named *Pug* lost two engines to flak over the heart of Berlin and the pilot, Lt. Richard Holman, turned, reduced altitude, and limped home alone. Six or seven enemy fighters attacked the straggler but somehow the crew managed to fight them off, shooting down two, possibly three, enemy aircraft with just the top turret and waist guns in operation. They ran into more flak over Amsterdam and then crossed the North Sea low on fuel; the crew threw ammo boxes and flying equipment out of the waist hatches to lighten the load and somehow they made it home to Old Buck' without injuries.

Relentless flak rocked Patrick Tobin's *Shack Rabbit*, too close for comfort as far as James Witmer was concerned. James was curled up against the belly of the aircraft, his guns were elevated to horizontal and facing the tail so that the armor-plated turret door shielded his behind from the flak. There was nothing for him to do except sweat out the flak barrage. An engine was hit, and the pilots and engineer shut it down and feathered the propeller blades to minimize wind resistance. Elmer Crockett's crew found themselves in a similar predicament when their aircraft also lost an engine. Both Tobin and Crockett struggled to keep up with the first section of the 453rd Bomb Group formation and subsequently found themselves in the second section during the bomb run.

The primary target at Genshagen was partially obscured by cloud cover and was too far to the right for the 453rd Bomb Group's lead ship to sway the group away from the division in order to attempt a run. The first section sighted a target of opportunity, a factory area in the vicinity of Spandau, and commenced the bomb run—two minutes later the bombs were dropped at 1337 hours from 21,000 feet. The second section proceeded to drop their bombs on marshalling yards in the immediate area of Spandau and the bombs were seen to hit the target. James Witmer watched from the ball turret of *Shack Rabbit* as the group's bombs rained down some four miles in a trail of death and destruction.

Meanwhile the 445th Bomb Group had bombed targets of opportunity in the southern and western regions of Berlin while the 389th aimed at Genshagen's aircraft engine factory, the primary target. These two groups were far ahead of the 453rd Bomb Group following "bombs away," and so the 453rd turned short of the Rally Point on a heading of three hundred degrees in an attempt to catch up, before descending to 15,000 feet and heading for home. The American bombers were out of the flak but they still had to fight their way through hostile skies back to England. Hubert Cripe saw one ship, possibly Elmer Crockett's, with gas leaking from the bomb bay, probably caused by flak damage to a gas line. Since Cripe had followed the troubled Wertzel out of the formation before rejoining the group during the bomb run, he had struggled to find a comfortable position in the formation:

> I tried to get into a position but was chased out by other planes so rather than brush wings I let them have it until I finally got on the left wing of Lt. Tobin who had one engine feathered. We didn't know then that was a mistake as he started lagging behind. Flak was negligible and neither Russ [copilot] nor I saw enemy fighters.
>
> Things were going too well. Sporadic conversations were coming over the interphone so I let Russ fly and I tuned in the [command set] radio to fighter-bomber frequency. Enemy fighters were

around. As the waves were full of frantic calls to our fighters to come
to their aid, I glanced around. Our formation was quite a ways
ahead of us and we were letting ourselves wide open for attack!

We were in the Dummer Lake area where lots of enemy fighters were concentrated. Should I leave Tobin and chance getting to
the formation, or try to give the stricken Tobin what protection we
could? The Jerries settled that question. One minute all was tranquil, the next I heard an explosion in our ship!

We were under attack and we had been hit! Almost immediately I saw a large gaping hole appear in the trailing edge of Tobin's
left wing as a 20mm shell exploded. The attack was from the rear.

It was nearly an hour and a quarter since "bombs away" and all hell
had broken loose; there was tremendous panic on board *Shack Rabbit* as
Patrick Tobin and his copilot, Lt. Ray Gilbreath, struggled to control
the aircraft. Several of the crew had been injured but in those sudden
moments of chaos, nobody was quite sure of the condition of the rest
of the crew in isolated parts of the doomed Liberator. Hubert Cripe
remained close to Tobin's ship and caught a glimpse of one of their
attackers sweep past to the left of his own ship.

> Why don't the waist gunners get him? He's a sitting duck! I got on
> the radio and called for fighters. A cool Texas drawl replied,
> "Don't get excited, Sonny, Pappa's coming." Almost immediately
> two P-47s appeared and chased the ME 109. I didn't look to see if
> they got them as more pressing business was at hand.

Hubert Cripe's left wing was on fire; a 20mm cannon shell had
pierced the wing and punctured the fuel tanks. Just as he become en-
grossed in this, his own emergency, Cripe caught a final glimpse of
Tobin's *Shack Rabbit:*

> Tobin evidently had had it. A figure appeared in his [left] waist
> window and bailed out.

Tobin's injured bombardier, Thomas Underwood, scurried to the
back of the aircraft and found Clair Kreidler, one of Tobin's regular
crew members, badly wounded. Kreidler, a thirty-three-year-old waist
gunner and former taxi driver from Scranton, Pennsylvania, was laps-
ing into unconsciousness; his left eye had been destroyed, and he also
endured injuries to his right arm and left leg. Kreidler later recalled that
as the aircraft became consumed by fire:

> Lt. Underwood returned me to my senses, attached the balance of
> my parachute and aided me in getting off to parachute to the
> ground.

Both Underwood and Kreidler escaped. Kreidler's next recollection
was waking up in a hospital at a German prison camp. Joseph Williams
escaped his tail turret and succeeded in bailing out. James Witmer

disconnected his oxygen supply and electrically heated suit, unclipped his safety harness, and then managed to escape the ball turret and climb into the aircraft (perhaps it was Thomas Underwood who assisted James also). He fastened his chest parachute pack to his parachute harness and bailed out of the burning ship. James counted to ten and pulled the ripcord; the parachute opened and slowed his fall . . . the noise and the chaos seemed to fade away, except for the explosion when *Shack Rabbit* hit the ground near Plantlunne, Germany. Six crew members were killed.

The four escapees drifted earthward beneath their parachutes. Remembering the few words about parachuting that he was told during his training ("Hit the ground, and roll . . .") James tumbled into the abyss of uncertainty. Without any of the others in sight he was alone, disoriented, and afraid.

Meanwhile, Hubert Cripe struggled along far behind the formation in his burning Liberator. Over Holland he decided to ditch in the North

Lt. Hubert Cripe's crew during training at March Field, California, 1943. On 6 March 1944 a composite arrangement of this crew went to Berlin but didn't make it home; only three of the ten-man crew survived. Standing, left to right: Sgt. Dunham (lost with another crew, POW), Sgt. McGue (KIA), Sgt. Davis (KIA 18 May 1944), Sgt. Keefe, Sgt. Edgett, and Sgt. Yoder (all three KIA). Front row, left to right: Lt. Heynes (injured in training and replaced), Lt. Cripe (POW), Lt. Fowle (survived the war with another crew), and Lt. Anderson (POW). (Hubert Cripe)

Sea and told his crew to be prepared. But when it became apparent they weren't even going to make it that far, the crew bailed out and the Liberator crashed into the Zuider Zee. On his descent towards the cold water below him, Cripe saw six other parachutes. Along with his copilot and navigator he was plucked from the drink by the crew of a Dutch fishing boat, which was later intercepted by a German harbor patrol launch. There were only three survivors of Crew 44 and all were taken prisoner.

The 2nd Combat Wing crossed the enemy coast at around 1515 hours and the English coast near Cromer forty minutes later. At 1605 the 453rd Bomb Group approached Old Buck' where crowds gathered on the flight line around the control tower. Jack Nortridge and Bill Eagleson had learned from the enlisted men of their crew that both Bill LeRoy and James Witmer were flying the mission. George White returned safely on board Joseph Waiter's ship, albeit with eighteen flak holes, after seven hours and fifty minutes flying time. Robert Catlin's ship, with Bill LeRoy on board, also made a safe return. Two aircraft returned with serious flak damage and thirteen more with moderate damage. But where was *Shack Rabbit*? What had happened to Freddie Witmer? In all, four aircraft were missing—watchful eyes stared at the horizon in anticipation of late returnees.

Battle damaged and low on fuel, Lt. Herman Meek was forced to ditch his Liberator in the North Sea. Of this 735th Squadron crew, only the bombardier survived the cold water long enough to be rescued. One of the gunners on this crew, William Koch, was from Freeport, Illinois—Jack Nortridge's hometown.

Having sustained serious flak damage over Germany, Elmer Crockett had been forced to leave the formation over Berlin with only three engines running and a gas leak. Elmer and his crew later endured severe enemy fighter attacks and another engine was shot out. Short of fuel and with injured on board, Crockett struggled across the North Sea at low altitude—literally on a wing and a prayer. When he was forced to shut down a third engine it was clear that they weren't going to make Old Buck' or even dry land. Ditching the B-24 was going to be a hazardous venture. Five miles east of the Norfolk seaside town of Great Yarmouth, Crockett put his Liberator down on the water—the bomb bay doors burst open and flooded the aircraft in seconds. Five of the crew were killed but Elmer Crockett and four others escaped and were rescued.

Soon reports of two Liberators downed in the North Sea reached Old Buck' and later the survivors of Crockett's crew returned. Within a couple of days, corpses that had been washed ashore or picked out of the sea and identified by their dog tags were taken to Old Buck' and placed on metal trays in the morgue. Elmer Crockett was given the sorrowful task of identifying the bodies of his dead crew members.

The 8th Air Force lost sixty-nine bombers on the 6 March mission to Berlin, the heaviest losses it had so far endured in one day. Worst off was the "Bloody Hundredth" Bomb Group at Thorpe Abbotts, Norfolk, with fifteen bombers missing in action as a result of enemy fighter attacks. A further one hundred 8th Air Force bombers needed major repairs and several others were scrapped on their return to England. Bombing results were considered to be moderate although it was suggested that the attack would have been more accurate if Berlin's skies had either been clear to maximize the effectiveness of visual bombing, or completely overcast so that Pathfinder Force radar techniques would have utilized.

However, the first major American mission to Berlin held particular significance, for this important city was a distant target protected by fierce anti-aircraft defenses and Luftwaffe fighters. But despite severe losses, the 8th Air Force had been successful in executing a maximum effort daylight raid on Germany's capital city. Significantly, the Luftwaffe had also suffered very heavy losses resulting in a profound effect on its morale. It was now clear that no German city was safe from possible daylight attack, and the Allies were on the verge of achieving air superiority over continental Europe.

On 27 March 1944, the *Texarkana Daily News* reported: "Staff Sergeant James F. Witmer, 22-year-old turret gunner has been reported missing since a bombing raid over Germany on March 6, according to a notification from the War Department."

Back home in Texarkana, nobody knew if James Freddie Witmer was alive or dead. Following his parachute jump from *Shack Rabbit*, Witmer was immediately captured and taken prisoner—a prisoner of war. The only respites from a few days of solitary confinement were the hours of daily interrogation. In compliance with the Geneva Convention, James was only obliged to give his name, rank, and serial number. But what could he possibly tell the Germans that they didn't know already? He harbored no military secrets, for he was just an aircrew gunner assigned to fly a mission to Berlin. Former prisoners of war have testified that somehow German Intelligence had accumulated a disturbing amount of information about them prior to their capture. The Germans even had copies of American high school records. Some prisoners stated their name, rank, and serial number, and the German interrogators responded by stating the prisoners' home towns, the names of the high schools they had attended, and so on. Of course, this had the intended effect of significantly heightening the uneasy feeling experienced by the prisoners.

Later in the spring of 1944, the *Texarkana Gazette* published a photograph of James and reported, "Card Reveals Freddie Witmer Prisoner of War": "Freddie Witmer . . . who was previously reported missing in action over Western Europe, is a prisoner of war in Germany. Witmer's wife, who resides with his parents, received a card from him Monday informing them that he was a prisoner of the Reich. Witmer wrote that he was safe and 'getting plenty to eat.' The card was written on March 11."

James was incarcerated at Stalag Luft IV, a German prison camp for Allied enlisted airmen, located at Gross Tychow, Poland, northeast of Stettin and near the Baltic coast. The first prisoners at the camp arrived in May 1944. Some survivors later testified that when they arrived at the nearby railroad station, they were forced to run the two miles to the camp at the points of bayonets—those who couldn't keep up either received flesh wounds or were bitten by the guard dogs.

Situated in a forest clearing, construction of the prison camp was never completed and with a prisoner population that exceeded the proposed maximum capacity, construction work was ongoing. Two ten-foot-high barbed wire fences ensnared the camp, and between each of these there was a four-foot-high barricade of rolled barbed wire. Around the perimeter, towers loomed high above the camp from which German soldiers kept a watchful eye with searchlights and guns at the ready; below them, guards with vicious dogs made their patrols. Fifty feet inside the perimeter fences, a warning wire served as an initial deterrent—anyone crossing this wire would be shot. Internally, yet more barbed wire fences divided the camp into five compounds.

Prisoners slept on three-tiered beds or in many cases, on the floor, in insufficiently heated wooden huts that accommodated at least twenty-five men in each. There was an absence of latrine facilities and proper showers, not to mention hot water, which didn't seem to exist. On a weekly basis each prisoner received half a Red Cross package, but otherwise they lived mostly on potatoes and soup. There was nothing to do but sit around and wait out the rest of the war. Time passed slowly; there was too much time to think and worry. James wondered how long he would spend in this hell, and longed to see his wife, Hazel, and his family and friends again.

During the summer, new arrivals brought morale-boosting news of D-Day, the Allied invasion. The German guards responded by telling the prisoners that the invasion would become another Dunkirk, with the Allies driven back into the sea. Only time would tell.

By October there were over seven thousand American and almost one thousand British prisoners at Stalag Luft IV. Then came a harsh winter of snow and ice, without enough fuel to keep the tiny stoves burning in the huts. One night in December the prisoners could hear the RAF bombing of Stettin, thirty miles away. Everyone was especially restless over the Christmas period—but it was pointless risking ones life in desperate escape attempts, for the ongoing flood of new arrivals brought exciting news reports, raising the expectation of liberation. On Christmas Eve the curfew was lifted, allowing the prisoners to socialize around the camp until past midnight. On Christmas morning, the German

James Freddie Witmer during happier days. One of four survivors from the ten-man crew on board *Shack Rabbit,* James spent the rest of the war as a POW and endured the three month, six hundred mile "death march" ordeal. (Nadine Witmer Gibson)

guards seemed cheerful with Christmas good wishes as they distributed Red Cross parcels—but the guards' display of goodwill did not last beyond 25 December.

Then came crushing news of the Battle of the Bulge—the German breakthrough and the Allied retreat. Suddenly, home seemed even further away. One former prisoner reflected many years later, "Stalag Luft IV was a lonely place of hungry men. It was as close to hell as I will ever want to be."[1] But daily life at Stalag Luft IV was a walk in the park compared to the hell that the prisoners would endure in the months to come, during the "death march."

As the Allies drew ever closer from the west in January 1945, visible by the flashing of artillery fire, and the Russian army approaching from the east, the Germans evacuated Stalag Luft IV. The sick and wounded prisoners were moved by rail, and then on 6 February an estimated six to eight thousand American and British prisoners set out on foot, loaded down with Red Cross parcels which the Germans had been keeping from them, and which many prisoners soon discarded to lighten the load. After all, the prisoners were told, the march would last just three days—but for many the journey lasted three months. Divided into groups that traveled along different routes to the west and then south, the prisoners walked some six hundred miles. Everywhere there were people on the move heading in all directions—displaced and dispossessed people, disoriented refugees, European prisoners who had been kept alive just to be used as forced labor, and homesick Allied prisoners of war.

Food rations provided by the Germans were minimal and Red Cross rations were scarce. The Allied prisoners were often forced to steal potatoes, grain, or the food given to pigs from the farms they encountered throughout the countryside. Many of the prisoners ate grass at the roadside, some even ate uncooked rats; most prisoners suffered from malnutrition. They slept in barns or in fields, inadequately clothed for the snow and the subzero temperatures of one of the coldest winters ever recorded in that part of Europe. Many of the prisoners endured dysentery, pneumonia, tuberculosis, trench foot, and frostbite; and without medical care, injuries turned gangrenous. Virtually everyone was crawling with fleas and lice. The stronger men helped the more fragile prisoners along, sometimes with the use of carts or wagons, but as the ordeal continued, nobody escaped exhaustion and hundreds are believed to have died as a result of starvation and ill health. All the while the vicious guard dogs were present to force the men to continue. Some prisoners were beaten for trying to escape and it has been reported that in some instances, those too weak to continue were taken by the guards and shot in nearby woods.

The knowledge that the Allies were steadily advancing and the hope that soon they would be liberated was all the prisoners had to sustain them throughout the ordeal. For many of the prisoners, the death march seemingly ended on 30 March 1945 as they approached Hanover, Germany. From there the prisoners were transported in railroad boxcars as Allied bombs fell all around them. Reaching another camp, on 6 April they immediately set out again on foot. Most were liberated by Allied forces east of Hamburg on 2 May 1945. Six days later brought Victory in Europe, VE-day. The war was over!

The *Texarkana Gazette* published an article titled, "Sgt. James Witmer Sends Cablegram after Liberation" in which it was reported: "Mrs. James F. Witmer, 601 Texas Avenue, has received a cablegram from her husband, Staff Sergeant James F. Witmer who was liberated from a German prison camp. The telegram was the first word she had received from him since last November 19."

The reporters in Texarkana had no knowledge of the death march and assumed that James Witmer had remained confined to a prison camp until liberation. On 1 July 1945, the *Texarkana Gazette* reported: "Staff Sergeant James F. Witmer, who was liberated from a German prison camp May 2 by the British, has returned to his home at Route 1, Texarkana, Arkansas. Son of Mr. and Mrs. Albert Witmer of Texarkana, Sgt. Witmer was shot down while on an Eighth Air Force mission March 6, 1944. At the time of his liberation he had been prisoner 14 months."

James Freddie Witmer had been away from his home and family for almost two years. Changed forever, in the summer of 1945 he set about rebuilding his life with his family around him, working on the family dairy farm alongside his father, and spending time relaxing with his wife, Hazel.

On 6 March 1944, Crew 25 waited in vain for James Witmer to return from "Big B." Within the space of two weeks, two men from Jack Nortridge's crew had been lost, as Perry Roberson recalled many years later:

> Lt. Lawry went down when he flew with another crew. We heard that Lawry was killed. Sgt. Witmer . . . we heard he was a prisoner of war. This is the last I heard of him.

The officers of the 733rd Bomb Squadron were always able to express their opinions, grievances, and requests to Capt. Robert Kanaga, the squadron CO, and his successor Capt. Robert Coggeshall. With regard to the loss of two of his crew members, Jack Nortridge voiced his complaints to his senior officers, making his feelings clear that he was opposed to members of his crew being assigned missions with other crews. He felt strongly that because they had trained together as one crew and worked well as a team, then they should fly together and remain together and not be separated. Later, while under the command of Capt. Robert Coggeshall, it became the norm in the 733rd Squadron that as far as possible, aircrews stayed together.

Bill Eagleson:

> One of our crew philosophies was that our pilot kept telling us, "If you fly with me, I'm going to bring you home," and we believed that. Unfortunately, the people that we lost from our crew were people that were assigned to fly other missions with other crews . . . my dear friend Don Lawry and James Witmer, our gunner, were lost on other crews.

PART THREE

Flak/Fighters

CHAPTER ELEVEN

Hosts in the Sky

The Jack Nortridge crew did not have much time to contemplate the whereabouts and the experiences of James Witmer or to mourn the loss of Don Lawry, for they anticipated commencing a "tour" of twenty-five combat missions. From January to June 1944, the time period in which the Nortridge crew flew their missions, less than forty-one percent of airmen in the 8th Air Force survived fifteen missions; the rest were either known to have been killed or were regarded as "missing in action" (in time, all men declared missing would be recategorized as either "killed in action" or "prisoner of war," while a very small minority escaped death and evaded capture). Less than twenty-eight percent of men would survive twenty-five missions.

High-altitude combat missions were physically, mentally, and emotionally exhausting, and therefore aircrew morale depended significantly upon the quantifiable combat tour, which offered at least some hope of survival. However, some time around March 1944 the quota was increased to thirty missions. Those who survived a tour of duty could expect to return home to the United States for thirty days R&R, rest and recreation, recuperation time before further assignments either in combat or training roles. Experienced combat personnel were in great demand to train new crews back home where there seemed to be an unlimited number of volunteers in need of training, thus enabling the U.S. Army Air Force to operate this rotation system of combat personnel.

Jack Nortridge was assigned a replacement gunner, twenty-one-year-old Sgt. Joseph DeMay. He was assigned to Crew 25 as ball turret gunner in place of James Witmer. Joe's family were Russian but like many immigrants in that era, they adopted a foreign name—DeMay is French and dates back to the fifteenth century. The years 1880 to 1914 had brought a large influx of Russian immigrants to the United States, including many poor peasants and persecuted Jews, in reaction to the Russian government's attempts to eliminate the diversity of ethnic groups within the country. They traveled to America in search of basic human rights, employment opportunities, and the dream to of living freely.

Joe was born on 10 January 1923 and raised in the New York City borough of Brooklyn. Throughout Brooklyn, most parents and many children were immigrants. Life was hard, and although jobs were generally available, incomes were low and many people lived on the borderlines of poverty. But for most, life was better than in the "Old World." Apartments had indoor plumbing and running water, although for most it was cold water necessitating the heating of water on the stove, but still considered a luxury. Then came central heating for the winter, while during the summer months, in those days before air conditioning, screened apartment windows were left open on warmer evenings.

In Brooklyn, the streets seemed safe to walk at night and crime wasn't feared. Brooklyn's residents at the time included Russians, Eastern European Jews, Italians, Irish, and Scandinavians, predominantly Norwegians. By the 1930s there were approximately two million residents in Brooklyn. To the south they could enjoy Brighton Beach and Coney Island where kids enjoyed the roller coaster rides, ate hot dogs, walked barefoot along the sand, and swam in the ocean. To the west across Brooklyn Bridge were the bright lights and the skyscrapers of Manhattan—libraries, museums, theaters, and myriad other attractions as well as employment opportunities.

When Joe DeMay was assigned to the crew he made himself at home in the hut shared by the other enlisted men of *Corky*'s crew, Johnson's enlisted men, the dog, the skunk, and the monkey. Joe was a very likeable character, remembered as a "real nice guy" with a characteristic Brooklyn accent.

On Monday 13 March, Lt. Gus Johnson's crew flew the *Golden Gaboon* on their second mission, already one month since their first. This was a *Noball* mission to a V-weapon site at Ponthion in the Pas de Calais region of France. The 453rd Bomb Group dispatched twenty-five aircraft but all returned to base without attacking the target, which they could not locate because it was obscured by cloud. The following day the base at Old Buck' was visited by the Luftwaffe with a delivery of incendiaries—a few brush fires resulted but fortunately there were no casualties and no damage to buildings or aircraft.

That evening the Jack Nortridge crew was alerted for what would become their first mission, scheduled for the following day, Wednesday 15 March. Enlisted men alerted to fly were restricted to base, and therefore not issued passes for trips into town. Given the choice, most would willingly opt for an early night anyway prior to a mission, but sometimes a crew might have already gone for an evening in town, only to return to base and find that they had been alerted. Sometimes these alerts were false alarms, as often missions were scrubbed due to unfavorable weather at the last minute. Sometimes crews were awakened for practice missions when they expected the day off and sometimes people were unexpectedly woken to fill in on another crew in place of someone who fell ill. Nothing was certain until the Charge of Quarters (CQ) officer did his early morning rounds from hut to hut, but meanwhile all alert warnings were taken seriously, as Bill Eagleson recalls:

> The night before our first mission we were not aware that we were
> to fly the next day. We were alerted as I remember, but our first ex-
> pectation to fly would be when the CQ woke us up in the morning.

In the predawn darkness of that Wednesday morning, the Quonset
hut's door swung open and a beam from the CQ officer's flashlight projected across the billet. He read from his clipboard the names of the
officers of that hut who were ordered to fly that day—Lts. Nortridge,
White, and Eagleson. In the enlisted men's quarters shared by twelve
men from the Nortridge and Johnson crews, Sgts. DeMay, Jeong, Le-
Roy, Nielsen, Roberson, and Veilleux were awakened to the announcement of breakfast and briefing times.

While trying to adjust to the early morning adrenaline and apprehension, the airmen dressed and went to the washrooms situated in an
adjacent hut. There they washed and had an essential shave to reduce
irritation caused by wearing an oxygen mask. The first cigarettes of the
day were lit and glowed in the half-light. Thirty minutes after waking,
amid a burst of activity from jeeps, trucks, bicycles, and pedestrians,
crews began congregating at the mess halls, some of them nervously
talkative and confident, others still sleepy or quiet in thought. Breakfast
was served. Bill Eagleson comments:

> Food: Not very good, or designed for long hours at high altitude. . . .
> Coarse bread constituted prebriefing breakfast, sometimes [at]
> 4 a.m. . . .

The combat crews were provided a specialist diet, different from the
food served to the ground crews, with consideration for the consequences of some foods that caused notable discomfort at 20,000 feet—
but the nonflatulent foods provided as part of the airmen's diet did little
to encourage a healthy appetite at such an early hour. Nerves and butter-
flies in the stomach prevented some from even contemplating eating the
cereal, hot cakes, toast, and powdered eggs; rather than the highly acidic
canned grapefruit juice, many opted for coffee, a welcome stimulant.
Lim Wing Jeong learned quickly to skip the food and just drink coffee
before missions; he couldn't stand the smell, let alone the taste of powdered eggs. Since the aircrew officers received higher wages and paid for
their food, usually they were served real, fresh eggs prior to flying missions. The enlisted GIs' wages were lower, and although their food was
provided at no cost, they usually had to make do with powdered eggs.
Breakfast was the last opportunity to eat a meal for many hours, as only
candy and gum rations were available on the long mission ahead.

Perry Roberson:

> Our breakfast before missions was most always powdered eggs and
> canned sausage.

Half an hour later the airmen made their way to the briefing rooms, and all would learn of the eagerly anticipated "target for today." At the end of the briefing hall the curtain was drawn to reveal the European map—eyes followed the red ribbons leading deep into Germany, to the city of Brunswick. No easy target for Nortridge's first mission! Operations and Intelligence staff provided pilots, bombardiers, and navigators with vital information for the mission and target ahead, including start-engines times, taxi times, takeoff times, formation plans, assembly procedures, and so on. Navigators studied maps and drew flight plans while bombardiers scrutinized target information and reconnaissance photographs. The pilots and copilots checked and double-checked the details of their mission orders and awaited further instructions.

The gunners attended a separate briefing which commenced elsewhere on the technical site, where they were informed of all known enemy defenses in their flight path, and when and where on the mission to expect encounters with enemy fighters. At the radio operators' briefing, Bill LeRoy was given top secret signals information, including the day's wireless codes, radio call signs, and frequencies written on rice paper protected by two sheets of celluloid—the paper could be eaten in the event of capture.

At the equipment store the gunners exchanged their personal belongings for flight rations, electrically heated flying suits, steel helmets, flak jackets, oxygen masks, Mae Wests, parachute harnesses, and parachute packs, before dressing in the locker rooms. Many of the aircrews attended a short service at the station chapel. Jeeps, trucks, pedestrians, and cyclists made their ways to their aircraft dispersed all around the field. *"Corky" Burgundy Bombers* was parked on dispersal point number forty-four, a concrete hardstand adjacent to the control tower.

Corky held a full load of bombs in the bomb bay. Although assisted by the ground crews, the gunners were responsible for checking and arming their guns with ammunition and extra rounds were stowed on board. The crew climbed inside the aircraft through the hatch in the floor near the waist gun position, through the open bomb bay or via the nose wheel doors.

Bill Eagleson, Pete Veilleux, and a stand-in navigator made final preparations in the nose of the aircraft. The nose section was never occupied during take offs or landings because if the plane crashed on take-off undoubtedly its underside would be compressed and the nose compartment access tunnel would be blocked, leaving no way out. So Eagleson, Veilleux, and the navigator gathered behind the flight deck with the rest of the crew, ready for takeoff. They waited as long, anxious minutes passed—a few silent moments were spared to gather thoughts, and then . . .

The sound of gunfire echoed across Old Buckenham airfield as a green flare arched into the sky from the control tower. A monotone drone of aircraft engines commenced, shattering the early morning silence.

Ten minutes passed as pilots ran up their engines making last minute checks, and flight engineers observed their instruments and fuel gauges. Finally *Corky* rolled away from the dispersal point and joined the other 453rd bombers in single file along the perimeter track. Each aircraft paused for a few minutes until a flare was fired from the checkered van parked at the side of the main runway— *Wham Bam* roared down the runway followed by twenty-six bomb-laden aircraft.

Jack hit full power and hurled *Corky* along the full length of the runway before finally pulling back on the controls. Weighed down with fuel, ammunition, and a bay full of bombs, *Corky*'s wheels left the tarmac and

Lt. Jack Nortridge. (Vale Nortridge)

began the ascent to 3,000 feet for group formation assembly over Old Buckenham. Following takeoff, the assigned navigator and Pete Veilleux climbed down through the nose wheel well, situated underneath the flight deck, and crawled out from under the chart table into the navigator's compartment. Pete stepped over the ammunition boxes that were fixed to the floor and climbed into the nose turret.

The 453rd Bomb Group was airborne by 0700 hours and formed into the briefed two sections of thirteen aircraft. Lt. James Bingamen flying in *Rooster* led the first section where Jack Nortridge and George White found *Corky*'s assigned position. Reaching 10,000 feet, George White announced over the intercom that the crew were to go on oxygen and the group continued to 16,000 feet over Old Buck'. At 17,000 feet over *Buncher 6* radio beacon at Hethel, the 453rd Bomb Group was absorbed into the 2nd Combat Wing formation. Crossing the coastline at Lowestoft, Suffolk, the bomber stream continued over the North Sea.

Nearing the enemy coast, Joe DeMay stepped down into the ball turret, lowered beneath the belly of the aircraft. Perry Roberson left the flight engineer's station behind Jack's seat on the flight deck and went back to the waist where he would spend much of the mission, keeping guard with the two hand-operated .50 caliber machine guns mounted at the left and right waist hatches. For the time being, Bill LeRoy remained at his desk behind the copilot's seat and vigilantly listened over the radio waves as the mission began to unfold. Usually the radio operators in lead and deputy lead aircraft were given most responsibilities. Otherwise, when enemy fighters were anticipated, LeRoy would go back to the waist section to assist Perry by manning one of the waist guns. When the pilots required Perry's assistance on the flight deck for flight engineer duties, LeRoy would cover for Perry at the waist guns.

Each member of the crew checked into his position over the intercom. Over the North Sea all gunners fired a few rounds to test their guns. Carrying a portable oxygen bottle, Bill Eagleson stepped along the bomb bay catwalk and pulled the pins from the bombs. Bill had acquired an 8mm movie camera and several times took it along on missions and filmed the formation heading towards Germany and into flak-filled skies. At 0950 hours the 453rd Bomb Group crossed the enemy coastline and received a little attention from the enemy flak gunners, as Bill Eagleson recalls:

> Usually over the coast we got our first signs of combat—tracking flak—and that was most accurate.

In the event of overcast skies, which to the aircrews was considered an "undercast," German anti-aircraft gunners implemented the use of radar for their aiming. Each aircraft carried bundles of aluminum foil called "chaff," which the gunners would throw out of the waist hatches over the flak zones. These strips of reflective foil produced spurious echoes on German radar screens, and consequently jammed their reception. Bill Eagleson:

> I remember one time we got into tracking flak and there was an undercast and the guys in the waist were throwing out "chaff." They decided to throw it out by the box, not by the bundle, but that's understandable. After tracking flak (usually we found that at the coast and over some of the cities), then we'd sweat out the fighters.

The waist gunners standing at the open hatches were exposed to high-altitude winds that could reach forty degrees below zero. In the tail turret, Lim Wing Jeong endured the worst of these drafts that whistled through the length of the aircraft. Most tail turret gunners left their turret's tambour doors open for two reasons. When closed, they hindered the possibility of a fast exit, making the tail more isolated from the rest of the crew; and because when they were left open the aluminum protection at each side of the turret was doubled. While aluminum hardly suffices as armor plating, leaving the doors open at least made the gunners feel a little less vulnerable.

Lt. Bill Eagleson. (Bill Eagleson)

Despite the confines of the turret, Lim Wing Jeong had to wear the standard electrically heated flying suit, sheepskin flying jacket, flying boots and gloves, parachute harness, and flak jacket, with a Mae West life preserver and parachute at the ready. The electric suits were often unreliable and prone to failure. On a later mission, Jeong's heated suit failed. He spent the rest of the flight with icicles on his eyebrows and a blanket wrapped around his head as he continually pounded himself with the palms of his hands in an attempt to keep his blood circulating.

Bill Eagleson:

> Flying over enemy territory, we didn't seem to mind the heavy flying clothes—we were probably "adrenalized" and "souped up"

and ready for it. Long hours at high altitude *were* a strain. You take maybe four to six hours on an oxygen mask—it was not fun. The difficulties were the freezing of the moisture from the breath, and this was a problem. We had to watch each other and beat the ice from the oxygen masks when we got to altitude, particularly back in the waist. The gunners in the waist, they were covered with shammy and goggles and they had to really protect themselves from the wind.

Twenty-two 453rd Group aircraft continued to Brunswick's industrial areas. Reaching the IP, the three groups of the 2nd Wing turned into the briefed course of the bomb run in trail, flying a straight and level approach to the target at reduced speed with bomb bay doors rolled open—suddenly the tail and waist gunners felt even colder and more windswept. On the bomb run the Liberators could not take evasive action from enemy fire due to the precision necessary for sighting—there was no alternative but to make a straight and level flight through the barrage of exploding flak shells.

Ten-tenths cloud cover over the target prevented visual bombing and so the bombardier on the leading Pathfinder Force (PFF) aircraft made a radar sighting. At 1106 hours the 453rd Bomb Group's bombardiers dropped their bombs on a smoke streamer from the PFF Liberator. The bombs fell from the Liberators and disappeared through a curtain of cloud. Several miles above the earth the crews were significantly removed from the damage and destruction as their bombs hit the ground beneath them. But there was no time to speculate about the war on the ground for there was also a battle in the air to contend with as flak continued to harass the bomber crews. Following "bombs away" each group continued to the Rally Point where the 2nd Combat Wing's lead, highright and low-left group positions were reassembled.

The flak faded and the gunners on *Corky* scanned the blue sky for enemy fighters. They were glad to see so many American fighters airborne that day, escorting the bomber crews all the way to Brunswick and home again. The Luftwaffe failed to make much of an appearance that day. A formation of FW190s was seen although none approached the 453rd Group's aircraft closer than 2,000 yards, and a few dog fights were observed from a distance. On the return flight the 453rd's crews encountered more flak. This was particularly intense at the Dutch coast, where some of the aircraft were damaged.

The Liberators crossed the North Sea and the English coastline at Lowestoft. After seven hours and four minutes flying time *Corky's* wheels touched down on the tarmac runway, and by two o'clock all aircraft had landed back at Old Buckenham. Back at their dispersal points, exhausted crews climbed out of their aircraft, went off to debriefing, then to the mess halls to eat before returning to their billets to rest amid a myriad of emotions and thoughts as they tried to comprehend the events of the day. Many of them, including *Corky*'s crew, anticipated another mission the following day.

At mission briefing on Thursday 16 March, Crew 25 learned that for their second mission they would be returning to Germany, this time to the south of the country. The assigned primary target was the Dornier aircraft factory, a mission that flight engineer and waist gunner Perry Roberson later described as "One long trip to Friedrichshafen."

Twenty-four aircraft departed Old Buckenham that morning between 0715 and 0742 hours and climbed through an icy overcast, eventually finding *Wham Bam* high over the base. The 453rd Bomb Group assembled into two sections. *Corky* joined the first section and took position in an element led by Lt. William Bertrand in *Hollywood & Vine*, with Lt. Robert Swigert's crew in *Valkyrie* as left wingman. Lt. August "Gus" Bergman's crew were forced to return to base because *Blondes Away* seemed to be consuming too much fuel.

After crossing the English Channel the 453rd Bomb Group reached the enemy coast at 1015 hours. The bomber stream continued over northern France and Pete Veilleux looked down from the nose turret at his ancestral homeland for the first time. The Liberators crossed over the Ardennes and continued on to a snow-covered Germany, eventually approaching Friedrichshafen, located close to Lake Constance and the Swiss border. Again the bomber crews were reassured by the presence of American fighter aircraft that remained in view until fifteen minutes before reaching the primary target.

Of the twelve aircraft in the first section of the 453rd Group's formation, eleven were still in group formation while of the twelve aircraft flying in the second section, five had strayed and only seven remained in their briefed positions. The continuing eighteen aircraft maintained their briefed course until reaching the Initial Point of the bomb run. As bomb bay doors rolled open, the Liberators turned and proceeded over the northern end of Lake Constance. A second turn led them down the lake until they were south of the target. Bombardiers caught occasional glimpses of the Dornier factory off to the left, through a layer of altocumulus.

Six red flares fired from the leading PFF aircraft announcing that the target sighting would be made using radar and that all other bombardiers would drop their bombs on the leader's sighting. Nearing the target it was clear that the Liberators were flying off course and so the PFF ship led the 453rd Group in a 360-degree turn over Lake Constance. As the Group approached the target on a northerly heading they encountered an intense barrage of flak that lasted until "bombs away"—the bombs disappeared into the thin layer of white cloud and the results of the drop were unobserved but were reported to have fallen on a point two miles east of the briefed target. The Group reached the Rally Point and following the "rally" the formation headed for home and made a gradual descent to 15,000 feet. An hour passed until friendly fighter aircraft returned to escort the bombers home. For the second day running, the Luftwaffe failed to make much of an appearance, although the flak was particularly accurate over the enemy coast en route back to England.

Eighteen Liberators from the 453rd remained together during the return flight. On board *Corky*, Perry Roberson went about his duties. As flight engineer, Perry was responsible for monitoring the engines, fuel levels, the four generator switches, ammeters, and voltmeters. He checked the fuel supplies and realized that they were running low—it seemed to him unlikely that they would make it back to Old Buck'. On the B-24, four valves could manipulate the fuel supply of each fuel cell, each with three shut-off ports—one port led to the assigned engine, the second to a set of fuel cells, and the third was a crossover port that interconnected the other three valves. In the event of an emergency, this configuration allowed each of the four engines to be fueled from any set of fuel cells, or for a burning or shut-down engine to be disconnected from the fuel supply. As *Corky* edged across the Channel, Perry distributed the limited fuel resource equally between all four engines:

Having parked their ambulances in readiness beside a grounded Liberator, medical personnel join the gathering to "sweat out" the return of the 453rd Bomb Group from the mission to Friedrichshafen on 16 March 1944. Note the distant airborne Liberator to the left. (USAF via Martin Bowman)

> Fuel transfer was my duty when needed. . . . We had the ability to
> transfer fuel while in flight and by carefully adjusting the levels in
> the tanks I was able to keep all engines going.

Eventually crossing the English coastline, Jack Nortridge headed directly for the emergency landing field at Manston, Kent. *Corky* touched
down on Manston's three-mile runway after eight airborne hours plus
nineteen minutes—the crew was relieved to have made it back to
England.

> We came back to England low on fuel and made an emergency
> landing in Southern England with all engines still going. . . . After
> landing I took off a fuel tank cap . . . and looked at the fuel in the
> tanks through the filler holes. I could see the bottoms of the tanks,
> and we realized how lucky we were!

After filling up with fuel, Jack Nortridge's crew returned to Old
Buckenham. They were stood down when the 453rd Bomb Group returned to Friedrichshafen two days later—on this occasion the Germans were ready and waiting. In *Blondes Away*, Gus Johnson's crew returned to Old Buck' from their third mission, but many others were not
so fortunate. Heavy flak had been encountered and intense fighter attacks plagued the Liberators for over one hundred miles causing heavy
losses for two Norfolk Liberator Groups—the 392nd Bomb Group at
Wendling lost fourteen aircraft and the 44th Bomb Group at Shipdham
lost eight. In total the 2nd Bomb
Division lost twenty-eight Liberators on 18 March.

From the 453rd Bomb Group,
Lt. Phillip Stock and his 733rd
Squadron crew failed to return.
The command pilot on this, the
formation's lead ship was Col. Joseph Miller, Commanding Officer of the 453rd Bomb Group.
Col. Miller had been responsible
for progressing the 453rd Bomb
Group through Phase training
and into combat operations within days of arriving in England.
Having suffered damage from
fighter attacks, Miller's ship *Little
Bryan* could not keep up with the
formation. On the way home
from Friedrichshafen the crew
bailed out and Miller was forced

Col. Joseph A. Miller, Commanding Officer of the 453rd Bomb Group,
was shot down on 18 March 1944. (Frank Kyle)

to crash land in a French field. At first he was assisted by the French Resistance, but he was soon captured by the Germans and became a prisoner of war.[1]

Lt. Seymour Cohen was assigned to *Corky*'s crew on a permanent basis as navigator in place of Donald Lawry. Seymour Cohen was Jewish, of Rumanian and Austrian descent, and so this was a significant motivating factor for him during his military service. His relatives in Europe

Lt. Seymour Cohen (right) caught in the lens of a street photographer in San Antonio, Texas, 1943. (Anita Cohen)

suffered terribly from anti-Semitism prior to and during the Second World War. Most, if not all of them, perished during the Holocaust. Although the scale of this horrific crime was unprecedented, violent anti-Semitism was not a new phenomenon. Indeed, Seymour's parents had immigrated to the United States many years previously in reaction to similar intolerance and hatred.

Throughout Eastern Europe during the nineteenth century, most Jews lived in small religious communities known as *shtetls*. Despite being poor, these close-knit communities provided an environment for focused religious practice, thus preserving the Jewish identity and way of life, and insulating them to a large extent from discrimination. Outsiders often viewed these Jewish communities with suspicion because of the religious and social differences and because the Jews spoke Yiddish (similar to German but written from right to left with Hebrew characters). Towards the end of the nineteenth century, the Jewish communities of Eastern Europe suffered terribly from anti-Semitism. In Rumania Jews were denied an education and barred from state service. Legally inferior, they were discriminated against economically.

Russian Czar Nicholas II attempted to convert one-third of Russian Jews to the Orthodox Church. Furthermore, he aimed to force another third of the Jews to leave Russia, while the remaining third he planned to eliminate through starvation. Organized and government-endorsed persecution and extermination of Jews began in Russia in the form of riots known as *pogroms*, in which Jews were subjected to stoning, beatings, and murder, while their property was pillaged. They were forced to sell their businesses and homes, which were otherwise destroyed in arson attacks.

Similar horrors were committed throughout Eastern Europe where Jews lived in fear for their lives. The end of the nineteenth century saw a mass exodus of Jews from Eastern Europe. From 1881 until the U.S. Immigration Act of 1924, approximately two and a half million Jews fled hostility and persecution and settled in the United States; many others migrated to Canada. Up to three-quarters of them came from Russia while the remainder came from Poland, Hungary, Lithuania, and Rumania. Unlike many other migrants during that era who were often seeking employment to earn money to support families back home, the Jews migrated as whole families—men, women, and children—for they intended to stay in the "New World" where they hoped they would be safe from persecution and violence.

Most of these Jewish immigrants were extremely poor, and one quarter could not read or write. Speaking Yiddish was sometimes associated with ignorance and poverty by the Western European Jews who had settled in the United States earlier in the nineteenth century. But Yiddish culture thrived in the United States, especially Yiddish theater, musicals, and newspapers. A daily Yiddish newspaper went into production in

1885 and along with several weekly papers, helped preserve the community's identity and ethnicity while helping them adapt as they were slowly, sometimes awkwardly, assimilated into American society.

Seymour Cohen's father, who as a young man left Rumania with his whole family in search of a better life free from oppression. They traveled to the United States in steerage class, so named because they were accommodated in the area adjacent to the ship's steering mechanism—it was noisy and crowded but also the cheapest way to travel. On their journey across the Atlantic the family decided to change their name from Baron to Cohen, which is Hebrew for priest.

Eventually, several of Seymour Cohen's uncles went to live in Canada, but Seymour's father stayed in the United States because his new bride wanted to remain in Brooklyn, New York, so she would remain geographically close to her older brother, her only blood relative in the United States. Born in Austria, at thirteen years of age she traveled with her brother to the United States. Years later, the rest of their family were murdered in the Holocaust.

Seymour's father found employment as an ironworker for a large company that had built the Brooklyn Bridge, and he was proud to be working for such a prestigious organization that had constructed one of New York's most celebrated architectural achievements. Mr. and Mrs. Cohen started a family—first a boy, then a daughter. Their third child, Seymour, was born in Brooklyn on 9 September 1916, and a little over a year later his younger sister was born. Seymour was barely two years old when his father was involved in an industrial accident, badly injuring his right thumb. Medical treatment was relatively primitive in those days and the injury resulted in the amputation of his right hand, leaving him with a compromising disability and unemployed.

Mr. Cohen was a very kind, gentle man, but determined. He taught himself to write and do practically everything else with his left hand, only encountering difficulties while trying to cut his food. One of his brothers in Canada assisted him financially, enabling him to buy a variety store, which later became a hardware store, in Bayonne, New Jersey. The Cohen family relocated to Bayonne, a city on a peninsula located just south of Jersey City, close to Manhattan and just north of Staten Island (which became accessible by the Bayonne Bridge in 1931, one of the longest steel arch bridges in the world).

The last thee decades of the nineteenth century were Bayonne's formative years, when New Yorkers and members of America's upper classes visited Bayonne to enjoy the resort hotels and beaches. The area was known for boat building and yachting, and its farmers and fisherman supplied New York. By the time the Cohen family moved there, Bayonne had significantly urbanized and industrialized. By the 1920s the Standard Oil Company employed over six thousand of the city's residents, and Bayonne was one of the largest oil refinery centers in the world. During the Second World War, a large shipping terminal was built on the east side of Bayonne, adjacent to New York Bay, along with a massive dry dock and naval supply center. Bayonne was home to thousands of European immigrants including many Jews, and the city's first synagogue was constructed in 1905.

In 1908 a play called *The Melting Pot* became one of the most successful productions in Broadway's history. Borrowing the theme from *Romeo and Juliet*, British playwright and Zionist Israel Zangwill told the story of two lovers from Russian Jewish and Russian Cossack families in America and in doing so he gave the immigration experience a metaphor. Zangwill wrote that God was melting Europe's barbarian tribes into a metal from which he can cast something new — "Americans." The message was simple; there was no place for old hatreds in the "New World."

Eastern European Jews and their descendents, among them world-famous composers Irving Berlin and George Gershwin, made a profound contribution to the United States, especially in the entertainment industry and with the creation of Hollywood. Thousands prospered as doctors, academics, journalists, playwrights, and lawyers. In 1927 there were some twenty thousand lawyers in New York, and two-thirds of them were Jewish. Having struggled out of poverty in the face of tremendous criticism that they did not work hard enough, American Jews soon received criticism for working *too* hard.[2] Anti-Semitism was prevalent throughout American society, including the government and in academia. But the main consolation for American Jews was that, whereas in Eastern Europe their families had suffered violent persecution, in the United States it was not legal to beat or murder Jews.

Jews were succeeding in the American dream and this led others to resent and fear them. The manifestation of this fear was discrimination. Quotas were implemented restricting the number of Jews that could be admitted to trades and universities, especially law schools, regardless of qualifications and academic success. Furthermore they were excluded from joining non-Jewish country and social clubs in what was described as "five o'clock anti-Semitism." Other Americans would work alongside Jews but would not socialize with them afterwards — Anglo-Saxon resistance to the melting pot.

The immigrants were devout orthodox Jews who followed tradition and custom, but their offspring were often keen to assimilate into the American mainstream that they were often excluded from. The Jewish women wanted to be liberated American women and the men and women wanted to dress like Americans. Becoming less apparently Jewish sometimes meant that they were better accepted and less alienated, and many changed their names to sound more "American."[3] As the years passed, many second-generation Jewish Americans began to forsake their Yiddish language, and at times became culturally estranged from their parents.[4] Just as in the Eastern Europe ghettos, education was

recognized as the only way out of poverty, in America the Jewish immigrants viewed education with similar importance. Jewish children were
under pressure to succeed in the education system.

The Cohens were determined that their children be Americans, successful Americans, and they were determined that they each receive a
good education. Seymour's brother became an accountant and his two
sisters became teachers. Seymour attended public school in Bayonne
and later graduated from the John Marshall School of Law in Jersey
City (now Seton Hall), despite official restrictions on the number of Jews
that were allowed to study in law school. Seymour passed the New Jersey bar in 1938 and set about starting his own law practice. A couple of
years later he was drafted for military service.

Seymour had been sixteen years old when he first heard about the
shocking events taking place in Europe. German Chancellor Adolf Hitler publicly blamed Germany's Jewish people for the country's economical struggles and in 1933 began policies of anti-Semitism. Jews lost their
German citizenship and were gradually forced out of work and into
ghettos. During the following four years over one hundred thousand
Jewish refugees left Germany and then in June 1938 Hitler ordered the
destruction of synagogues in three German cities. In both Germany
and Austria during November 1938, Nazi mobs burned two hundred
synagogues, destroyed more than eight hundred Jewish-owned shops,
and looted more than seven thousand others. Jews themselves were subjected to physical violence and murder. An estimated twenty thousand
Jews were arrested and sent to concentration camps where they became
forced laborers.

President Roosevelt recalled the American ambassador to Germany
and made available its quota for twenty-seven thousand Jewish immigrants. However, the United States failed to increase this number as such
an act of Congress in favor of the Jewish people of Europe was unrealistic considering the climate of institutionalized anti-Semitism then prevalent in the land of the free.[5] Germany conquered Austria and Czecho-
slovakia in 1938, and the large Jewish communities of these two countries
were under serious threat. Meanwhile, millions of Jews in Poland, Rumania, and Hungary were suffering under brutal anti-Semitic regimes.

The American public was aware to some extent of the suffering inflicted upon European Jews, but nobody could imagine the extremity of
the horrors—Hitler's "final solution." The reality of Nazi war crimes
were not brought to light until the end of the war, by which time six million Jews had been murdered during the holocaust. Furthermore, five
million Gypsies, physically and mentally disabled people, homosexuals,
Communists, and those involved in resistance movements met the same
horrifying fate in the death camps.

But even from the limited information that was available during the
late 1930s and early 1940s, for Jewish Americans from Eastern European

backgrounds, the situation was reminiscent of what they had been told of their family history, and the pogroms of the late nineteenth century. It seems that in their absence, things had not progressed or become more civilized in the "Old World."

It was still peacetime in the United States when Seymour Cohen became an army private stationed in the south. After several months a recruitment officer asked if any of the troops were interested in joining the Army Air Corps. Seymour volunteered and was then transferred. He loved a challenge and new experiences, and made the most of any opportunity to learn. Furthermore, Seymour was motivated by strong convictions—with war on the horizon he became dedicated to the task of serving his country and as a Jew with family in Austria, he felt a significant responsibility to all those suffering oppression in Europe at the hands of the Nazis.

Intelligent, educated, and extremely confident at twenty-six years of age, Seymour was destined to become an officer, a Second Lieutenant in the United States Army Air Force, and to be selected for navigator training. It seems that Jews were disproportionately represented through the range of aircrew roles; a far higher proportion of Jewish cadets were selected for navigator or bombardier training than as flight engineers and gunners. One common theory suggests that prejudice and ignorance were prominent factors: Jews were widely perceived to be "good with numbers" and that a navigator could be considered to be a "flying accountant"![6]

After graduating from navigation school Lt. Seymour Cohen was assigned to the 733rd Bomb Squadron, 453rd Bomb Group, which was undergoing Phase training at Pocatello, Idaho. For a while he was appointed the position of assistant squadron navigator and was then assigned to Crew 37. His pilot was Lt. George Wear from Louisiana.

After the completion of Phase training in California, Lt. Seymour Cohen navigated Lt. George Wear's Liberator, the *Golden Gaboon*, from San Francisco to Old Buckenham along the same route flown by Jack Nortridge's original crew. Upon arrival in England, Seymour didn't escape the cold and flu epidemic at Old Buckenham, and he was subsequently grounded for a week or so. Meanwhile, tragedy struck Crew 37, as former pilot George Wear recalled more than half a century later:

> We were devastated because of the loss of seven of my crew members. I flew my first mission on February 21, 1944. It is probable that Seymour Cohen flew this mission with me. The next group mission was on February 22, 1944. I was not scheduled to fly that mission but I went to the briefing and found that three of my crew members were scheduled to fly with Lt. Richard Ingram's crew, when I was available to fly! I insisted that I fly the mission with my crew instead of breaking up crews, but to no avail. My crew members did not return from this mission.

Golden Gaboon. Lt. George Wear's crew flew this Liberator from San Francisco to England, with Lt. Seymour Cohen as navigator. (Mike Bailey/Donald Olds, 453rd BG Association Collection)

March 6, 1944, a mission to Berlin was scheduled for the group. I was available to fly and again went to the briefing [where I found that five of] my crew members were scheduled to fly with other crews. I again objected to the refusal to let me fly the mission, to no avail.

Four out of five of Lt. George Wear's crew members assigned the Berlin mission were killed; one was lost with Lt. Patrick Tobin's crew, and three were killed when Lt. Elmer Crockett ditched in the North Sea. Furthermore, Lt. George Wear's original copilot, Lt. Ray Gilbreath, who had been transferred to another crew prior to leaving California, had also been lost on the Berlin mission while flying with Lt. Patrick Tobin. Lt. Seymour Cohen returned safely from the mission. George Wear recalls:

Of the ten men in my crew there were only three survivors after only a limited period of combat. Our only choice was to fly as replacement [crew members to make up full crews]. The bombardier was so upset with that arrangement he was [temporarily] taken off flying status.

Lt. Col. Ramsay D. Potts became the 453rd Bomb Group's Commanding Officer on 19 March 1944. A CO was traditionally referred to as the "old man," but Ramsay Potts was just twenty-seven years of age when he arrived at Old Buckenham. (Maj. Gen. Ramsay D. Potts)

However, soon Lt. George Wear, his bombardier, Lt. Ralph Swafford, and navigator, Lt. Seymour Cohen, were given more consistent assignments. Everything was in a constant state of flux at Old Buckenham, and following the loss of Col. Joseph Miller on 18 March 1944 the crews at Old Buckenham anticipated the arrival of a new commanding officer. They didn't have to wait long to find out who their new leader would be, as the following day twenty-seven year-old Lt. Col. Ramsay D. Potts arrived at Old Buckenham as the new 453rd Bomb Group CO.

Born in Memphis on 24 October 1916, the son of a Tennessee cotton broker, Lt. Col. Ramsay Potts had studied economics and English at the University of North Carolina. He graduated with a bachelor of science degree in commerce, went to work for his father in the cotton business, became a professor of economics at Memphis Junior College and then decided on a future as a lawyer—but that would have to wait. In 1940 it seemed that sooner or later the United States would be drawn into the war in Europe, and in September the Selective Service Act was passed. Ramsay Potts was obliged to register for the draft, volunteered for the Army Air Corps and was called to active service early in 1941. In 1942 he arrived in England and was assigned to the 93rd Bomb Group at Hardwick, Norfolk, becoming the commanding officer of the 330th Bomb Squadron, and later Group Operations Office. He survived the legendary low-level raid on the Ploesti oil fields in Rumania on 1 August 1943, on which he was a flight leader, and completed a tour of combat missions before serving as chief of staff at the 2nd Combat Wing Headquarters.

Upon being appointed the role of 453rd Bomb Group CO, Ramsay Potts discovered that Gen. Edward "Ted" Timberlake, 2nd Combat Wing CO and former 93rd Bomb Group CO, had persuaded 2nd Bomb Division commander Major General Hodges in favour of Potts. Hodges was considering one of two West Point colonels currently on their way from Washington, but Timberlake's persuasion worked; Hodges agreed and Potts accepted the challenge. Hodges looked at Timberlake and said, "I give him six weeks." Potts knew that the 453rd Bomb Group had been suffering from hard times and that the pressure was on him to do something about it, fast. Following his arrival at Old Buck', Ramsay Potts instantly became a popular leader and is remembered as being an excellent CO. His experience brought vital combat knowledge to the group from which the crews were to benefit tremendously.

George Wear:

> I was fortunate to meet Lt. Col. Ramsay Potts a few days after his arrival, when I was called for a maximum effort mission. The officer that had assigned seven of my crew members over my objection was there but had not communicated that fact to the new officer. I agreed to fly the mission if a crew could be available. Ramsay Potts, with my bombardier, came to the plane I flew as soon as I landed. He said he was pleased that I made it back, understood the problems I and the bombardier faced and that he had a solution. One of the better crews needed a pilot because their pilot had been injured and would be off flying for a month or more. I would be assigned pilot of that crew and my bombardier, Lt. Ralph Swafford, would remain as my bombardier. I flew over ten missions with that crew and in total flew thirty-one missions as a replacement pilot with other crews or with a composite crew when a maximum effort was required.

Meanwhile, George Wear's navigator, Seymour Cohen, had been assigned to Crew 25. Seymour was a veteran of three combat missions when he joined *Corky*'s crew. His first mission was to Achmer, Germany, on 21 February 1944; his second mission was on 5 March when the 453rd Bomb Group went to Cazaeu, France, and then he flew again on 6 March 1944 on the first major raid on Berlin. It is not known with which crews he flew these missions.

Jack Nortridge was still only twenty-six years of age; Seymour Cohen was twenty-seven and became the eldest member of *Corky*'s crew. He was a competent navigator and he soon became a reliable friend and crew member. All the guys on the crew had great respect for Seymour. They were aware that he was Jewish and had volunteered to fly combat missions over Nazi-occupied Europe. There were of course several thousand Jewish flyers in the 8th Air Force but it was understood that in the event of being captured by German civilians or the military and taken prisoner, they might not have the same chances of survival. Jewish prisoners were more likely to be subjected to physical violence than were the other captured airmen—and all airmen, whatever their religion, were vulnerable to lynching if captured by German civilians who sought revenge for Allied bombing.

Prior to each mission, American airmen were issued escape kits that included a compass and maps, local currency, morphine syringes, and Dextrose tablets; they had .45 caliber pistols and they carried false identity cards with photographs of themselves in civilian clothes. For identification in the event of their death they wore dog tags that stated not only their serial number and blood group, but also their religion. Christian airmen wore dog tags with a "P" for Protestant or "C" for Catholic—Jewish airmen's dog tags were stamped with an "H" denoting Hebrew. Therefore, after baling out of a crippled airplane, usually the first thing that many Jewish airmen did upon reaching the ground was to bury their dog tags. However, for some this was a dilemma— better to fall into the hands of the Gestapo or S.S. wearing the dog tags and be shot as a Jew, or better to discard the dog tags and be shot as a spy? If captured and interrogated by the Germans, in compliance with the Geneva Convention prisoners were obliged only to provide their name, rank and serial number. But in the case of the Jewish airmen, their names usually revealed their religion.

There were over eight thousand RAF and USAAF prisoners of war incarcerated at Stalag Luft I alone. Two to three hundred of them were Jewish airmen. One survivor later testified that when the Nazi Gestapo leader Heinrich Himmler visited the camp, he gave the order that all the Jewish prisoners were to be separated and shot. But when the other prisoners threatened to riot the death sentences were not carried out.[7] However, in January 1945, segregation was implemented and the Jewish prisoners at Stalag Luft I were alarmed to find themselves moved to barracks

in an isolated compound. Chilling rumors circulated that they were to
be marched to death camps, but thankfully this did not happen. Meanwhile, the Jewish prisoners lived in constant fear.

On 23 March 1944 the 453rd Bombardment Group flew a mission
to attack Handorf airfield near Münster, Germany, but when
the weather interfered they resorted to the secondary target, the railroad marshalling yards in Münster. One Liberator, piloted by Lt. James
Hamilton of the 733rd Bomb Squadron fell victim to enemy action. Despite injuries from flying glass to the left side of his face (the original Liberators assigned to the 453rd Bomb Group did not have bullet-proof
glass in the cockpits), James Hamilton kept the Liberator airborne long
enough for most of his crew to bail out. Eight of the crew survived but
Hamilton and his ball turret gunner, Sgt. John MacKenzie, were both
killed. Hamilton's flight engineer, Sgt. Pasqual "Pat" Gicale, who had
been a passenger on *Corky* from San Francisco to England, was not airborne on the mission that day.

In less than seven weeks the 453rd Bomb Group had flown twenty-
three combat missions from Old Buckenham and had endured severe
losses of aircraft and personnel. A significant number of the original
crews had either been killed or were now prisoners of war. Replacement
crews and crew members were continually arriving from training units
in the United States and many of them were also being lost. The survivors frequently found themselves sleeping in half-empty huts as the
memories of names and faces grew forever hazy. Bill Eagleson recalls the
hut that was home to the officers of *Corky*'s crew and three other crews:

> We lost many of our early-on friends during the month of Febru-
> ary and early March. . . . As I remember, Johnson's crew was in the
> hut, and I don't recall too much about the other crews, because it
> seemed that the other eight spaces were sort of transient. The
> crews came in and the crews went out, some of them never to be
> seen again.

Towards the end of March, weather conditions hindered missions
deep into Germany and so the 8th Air Force focused its attention on *Noball* targets and airfields in France. Jack Nortridge's crew flew their third
mission on Friday 24 March, their first mission with Seymour Cohen as
navigator. The primary target was the airfield at Nancy in northwest
France where *Corky*'s bombs fell. However, as a result of weather interference, some of the 453rd Group's aircraft proceeded to St. Dizier,
where they bombed an airfield. All fifteen aircraft returned to base and
Corky's wheels touched down after an exhausting seven hours and seven
minutes.

The crew flew again on Sunday morning when they were dispatched
to a *Noball* target near Domart, France. Clouds prevented observation of

the bombing effects, and all twenty-eight aircraft returned to Old Buckenham. *Corky* landed after four airborne hours plus forty minutes. On this day Capt. Robert Kanaga and Capt. Robert Coggeshall's duties were switched—Kanaga became group training officer and Coggeshall took over as 733rd Squadron CO.

On Monday 27 March the 453rd Bomb Group dispatched twenty-three aircraft to bomb the Luftwaffe's training airfield near Pau in southwestern France, close to the Spanish border. The 453rd Bomb Group's aircraft took off at around ten o'clock that morning. For Jack Nortridge's crew it was their fifth mission, however they were soon forced to turn back when the number one engine on *Corky* began to leak oil and eventually the engine failed. *Corky* landed at Hethel airfield, approximately eight miles from Old Buckenham, after more than three hours flying time.

Meanwhile the rest of the group continued on the mission and bombed their primary target with effective results. They encountered moderate flak over France; however, the lead ship, *Cabin in the Sky*, received a direct hit. There were eleven crew members on board; Lt. Alvin Lien and eight men from his usual 735th Squadron crew, the 453rd's Group Operations Officer Maj. Curtis Cofield flying as command pilot,

B-24 *Cabin in the Sky* (nearest the camera) departing English skies on the fateful morning of 27 March 1944. A crew member poses for the photograph at the open waist position (where for some reason no gun is mounted). All eleven crew members were killed. (Mike Bailey)

Above: Pau airfield; a Luftwaffe training base under attack from the 453rd Bomb Group on 27 April 1944. (Frank Kyle)

Right: 733rd Bomb Squadron CO Capt. Robert Coggeshall (left) and Lt. Samuel "Sammy" Borenstein, 733rd Bomb Squadron Command Navigator. Sammy Borenstein was killed on what should have been the twentieth birthday of his friend Donald Lawry. (Donald Olds, 453rd BG Association Collection)

and the 733rd Squadron's Command Navigator Lt. Samuel "Sammy" Borenstein. He had been a good friend of Donald Lawry's and had gone with Bill Eagleson to buy a wedding present and card for Donald and Dorothy prior to attending their wedding in California—the day of Sammy's fateful mission to France should have been Donald's twentieth birthday.

Witnesses counted as nine parachutes appeared from the burning *Cabin in the Sky,* just before it plummeted into the Bay of Biscay, five miles off shore near Isle d'Oleron at 1559 hours. Five of the crew were seen to be picked up immediately, presumably by enemy surface craft. However, no member of the crew was ever reported to be a prisoner of war and none of them was seen or heard from again. The remains of the ball turret gunner were recovered by the enemy and were allegedly interred at sea. The remains of six others including Maj. Cofield were later washed ashore adjacent to La Rochelle, France. The other four members of the crew were not accounted for, and it was concluded that they were lost at sea.

CHAPTER TWELVE

Jimmy Stewart, Leadership, and the Liberty Run

T he 453rd Bomb Group's Commanding Officer Lt. Col. Ramsay Potts had been at Old Buckenham for just eight days when Maj. Cofield was killed in action. Meanwhile, the twenty-seven-year-old CO was facing the challenges of taking over leadership of the 453rd. In a 1999 interview with the *Bar Report*, Ramsay Potts, a retired attorney, reflected on both his civilian life and military service, and commented on his early days at Old Buckenham:

> I had a lot of trepidation because the squadron commanders were older than I was, and many were "West Pointers" [graduates of the prestigious West Point Military Academy]. I shuffled the structure of the group and asked for a new operations officer [to replace the deceased Maj. Cofield], somebody from the outside. Lo and behold, they sent an officer from another group—a guy named Jimmy Stewart. Jimmy Stewart, the actor, became my operations officer!

James "Jimmy" Stewart, the Hollywood movie star, was famous for his roles in films such as *You Can't Take It with You, Mr Smith Goes to Washington, Destry Rides Again, The Shop around the Corner,* and *The Philadelphia Story.* In fact he had appeared in almost thirty movies prior to commencing his military service. Therefore, on 30 March 1944 there was an atmosphere of curiosity at Old Buckenham when the thirty-five-year-old Maj. James M. Stewart arrived and assumed the very real role of group operations officer. Lt. Jim Kotapish, copilot on Lt. Ray Sears's crew, 734th Bomb Squadron, recalls:

> I was in the mess hall . . . as I was leaving this guy walked towards me, and we greeted each other. When I got back to the hut I mentioned that I had seen someone who looked like Jimmy Stewart and was informed that he had just joined the outfit.

Bob Bieck was at that time a 732nd Bomb Squadron pilot and recalls feeling less than enthusiastic about the news:

> Major Cofield was a former airline pilot, was very well liked, and we did not exactly jump for joy to have a celebrity take his place. Besides, we had heard enough of Clark Gable, a "gunner" with a B-17 Group. [Gable was making *Combat America,* a documentary

film about air gunners.] He flew five missions, got an air medal, and
was sent home to sell war bonds. I really don't recall when we
learned that Jimmy Stewart was with the 445th at Tibenham [prior
to being assigned to the 453rd]. Simply put, we just didn't care.

When the Selective Service Act was passed in September 1940, the
United States' first peacetime military conscription, James Stewart,
along with all other twenty-one- to thirty-six-year-old men, was legally
required to register for the draft. The first 900,000 inductees were chosen by a lottery broadcast live on radio at the end of October; Stewart
was one of those chosen. A year before Pearl Harbor, Jimmy Stewart
failed his medical inspection after weighing in at ten pounds under the
height–weight ratio requirement, and was given a deferment. He could
have gone on with life and movies in Hollywood, but instead he made
an appeal against the decision. Anticipating that America would be
drawn into the war, and following in both grandfathers' and his father's
footsteps (veterans of the Civil War, Spanish–American War, and the
First World War), Stewart believed that serving his country was more
important than making movies.

In 1935 Jimmy Stewart had realized a dream and learned to fly in
California, and had since accrued over three hundred hours flying time
in his logbook. He hoped that this experience would allow him to serve
in the Army Air Corps. Stewart embarked on a high-fat diet and allegedly either didn't go to the bathroom for thirty-six hours before returning for a second medical in February 1941, or persuaded the officer in
charge not to weigh him at all. Jimmy Stewart was accepted in the
Army Air Corps.

In March 1941, just days after winning his Academy Award, an
Oscar, for *The Philadelphia Story*, Jimmy Stewart became a private in the
Army Air Corps. His salary plummeted from $1,500 a week to $21 a
month. But as biographer Lawrence J. Quirk noted, Stewart went from
being a private on KP duty, peeling potatoes, to officer duty in a relatively few months. As far as Stewart was concerned, making movies was
what he *used* to do. After two years of military service, he found himself
serving as operations officer in a squadron assigned to the 29th Bomb
Group at Gowen Field, Boise, Idaho. There he trained pilots on four-
engine bombers, the B-17 and B-24. There were in fact a number of pilots at Old Buckenham who had been instructed by Jimmy Stewart during the spring and summer of 1943.

Frustrated by being a Phase One training instructor, Stewart desper-
ately wanted to be sent overseas to combat. Soon he was transferred to
Sioux City, Iowa, and assigned the role of squadron operations officer,
and then commanding officer of the 703rd Bomb Squadron, 445th
Bomb Group, and sent to England where he arrived in November 1943.
At Tibenham airfield in Norfolk, Jimmy Stewart soon gained the reputation as a "lucky" pilot. The 445th's crews noted that Stewart's missions

Jimmy Stewart, Holly-
wood movie star and com-
bat veteran, on the control
tower at Old Buckenham
in 1944. (Bill Eagleson)

were not limited to the "milk runs," the easy missions, but that he invariably flew the more arduous missions to major targets in Germany,
such as Kiel, Bremen, Brunswick, and Berlin. Stewart flew twenty-two
bombing missions with the 445th and 453rd Bomb Groups.[1]

Within nine weeks of commencing operations, the 453rd Bomb
Group had lost two of its key leaders, Col. Miller and Major Cofield.
Both were graduates of the West Point Military Academy. In place of
the "West Pointers" came combat veterans, first the twenty-seven year

old replacement Group Commanding Officer Lt. Col. Ramsay Potts, and then Operations Officer Maj. Jimmy Stewart.

Bill Eagleson recalls:

> We did have some hard luck. We lost our leadership. I believe the "West Pointers" were hard luck guys, if there were such a thing as hard luck guys. I do remember that for a time just before Jimmy Stewart [was assigned to the group] we wondered *who* we would have in command . . . I don't recall the arrival of Jimmy Stewart in any special manner. I do know that at the time of his arrival our group was short on leadership and he came on as group operations officer. His effect as a movie star did not have any particular concerns as far as our crew was concerned.

Despite earlier cynicism, 732nd Bomb Squadron pilot Lt. Bob Bieck soon became impressed by Jimmy Stewart's presence in the 453rd Bomb Group, simply because of Stewart's unremarkable professionalism:

> Stewart, from the start, maintained a low profile. He was never aloof nor arrogant. He simply did his work as the group operations officer just like any other Major was supposed to do.

Lt. Abe Wilen was a navigator in the 732nd Bomb Squadron and first became acquainted with fellow Pennsylvanian Jimmy Stewart soon after the movie star arrived at Old Buckenham. Abe Wilen was one of four airmen from Pennsylvania chosen to pose for photographs with Jimmy Stewart, standing in front of the B-24 *Male Call*, on board Stewart's Jeep and acting out a mission debriefing scene. On the whole Jimmy Stewart avoided media attention during his military service. Sometimes press photographers and female admirers were known to gather outside the base hoping for a glimpse of the Hollywood star.

Jimmy Stewart's presence at Old Buckenham was closely observed by the future movie star Walter Matthau, then known as Sgt. Walter Matthow, who served with the 453rd Bomb Group as an instructor on the Link Trainer, by modern standards a rather primitive flight simulator. The son of Russian-Jewish immigrants, his acting career was in its infancy when the war broke out. At Old Buck' Sgt. Matthow was just a regular guy, although one who was enjoying a winning streak—on one occasion he won several thousand dollars at a card game and took everyone in his barracks for dinner at the Palace Hotel in Norwich. At Old Buckenham, one of Jimmy Stewart's responsibilities was mission preparation, necessitating him to stay awake through the night working alongside his assistant, Capt. Andrew Low, and an intelligence officer, and then briefing the crews early in the mornings prior to missions. Walter Matthau sometimes crept into the mission briefings just to see and hear Jimmy Stewart address the flying personnel. As an aspiring actor, Walter Matthau got a kick out of being so close to one of his heroes. Years later he told a CNN reporter: "I used to like to go to the briefings, because I'd like to hear him do his 'Jimmy Stewart.' I used to watch the way people would relate to him. They would relate to him as if he were a movie star—for a while—then they would forget all about that and realize he was one of the boys. He was marvelous to watch."

Bob Bieck recalls:

> Stewart usually gave the mission briefing each morning. His delivery was right out of *The Philadelphia Story* or *Mr. Smith Goes to Washington.* He spoke slowly with very good pronunciation, with sort of an "Aw shucks" presentation.

Lt. Nick Radosevich had been instructed by Jimmy Stewart in flying B-17s and B-24s at Gowen Field, Boise, Idaho in 1943. He completed his thirty-second and final mission in July 1944 and taxied back to the hardstand where Jimmy Stewart had parked his Jeep, and was waiting to welcome the crew home.

> I personally know that Jimmy Stewart cared about the crews under him, and maybe the trust and confidence in his leadership contributed to morale. Lt. Robert Witzel [another first-pilot in the 453rd] and myself flew ten missions in eleven days. We were scheduled to fly the eleventh when Jimmy Stewart took us off and sent us to Scotland for a ten-day R&R. I don't think you could find anyone that was as good a group operation officer as Jimmy Stewart. He simply did his job very well and watched out for all the crews in the group.

Sgt. Robert Victor was the radio operator on Lt. Nick Radosevich's crew. While serving in the 29th Bomb Group in 1943, Robert Victor flew as Jimmy Stewart's radio operator on many training flights out of Gowen Field, Boise, Idaho. He recalls the presence of Stewart at Old Buckenham in 1944:

> Maj. Stewart did impart a sense of camaraderie by just being there and I believe that many of us wanted to perform better just because he was there. I will always remember him as a very fine officer and a very talented pilot.

Jimmy Stewart was often seen in the mess hall at breakfast before missions; he usually gave the mission briefings; he was on the flight line when the mission was launched, sometimes he flew the colorful assembly ship, *Wham Bam,* and led the 453rd into formation. Later he would join the gathering that waited near the control tower to see the group return. Several times he led the 453rd on missions to Germany. Many of the officers got to enjoy Jimmy Stewart's piano playing in the Officers' Club. Sometimes he sang a rendition of his favorite song, *Ragtime Cowboy Joe.* When dance parties were held on the base, to which girls from the local towns were invited, Stewart kept his distance and didn't dance with any of them but, as Bob Bieck recalls, he always could be counted on to play the drums.

Initial curiosity soon faded and the majority of the crews at Old Buckenham soon became unfazed by Jimmy Stewart's Hollywood status. They regarded him not as a celebrity, as the household name that he was, but as Maj. Stewart, a combat veteran and a competent and dedicated operations officer. His presence undoubtedly had a positive effect, but this can be attributed as much to his leadership skills as his popularity as a Hollywood movie icon. He was always friendly, approachable, and unassuming and was very well liked, but he was not close to anyone except the commanding officer, Lt. Col. Ramsay Potts, and the assistant group operations officer, twenty-seven year old West Point graduate Capt. Andrew Low. These three leaders shared a billet at Old Buckenham; Stewart and Low bunked at one end of the hut while Potts had a bedroom at the other end. In the middle of the hut was a seating area for reading and relaxation. More often than not the hut was uninhabited at night; Stewart and Low invariably worked from dusk until dawn preparing missions at Operations. The crews soon learned to trust Jimmy Stewart, just as they trusted Ramsay Potts. Far from being star-struck, the flying personnel were preoccupied by their missions and surviving their combat tours.

Many years later, Jimmy Stewart reflected on his military experience:

> I tried with all my might to lead and protect them [the aircrews of the 445th and 453rd Bomb Groups]. I lost a few men—all my efforts, all my prayers couldn't stand between them and their fates, and I grieved over them, blamed myself, even. But my father said something wonderful to me when I came home after the war. He said, "Shed all blame, shed all guilt, Jim. You know you did your very best, and God and Fate, both of which are beyond any human being's efforts, took care of the rest."[2]

In 1993 Jimmy Stewart was interviewed on British television, and was asked about his experiences in the Second World War:

> I think that whole military experience that I had, is something that I think about almost every day . . . one of the great experiences of my life. Much greater [than being in the movies].

Soon after the war Jimmy Stewart returned to the movies with *It's a Wonderful Life*, for which he received his third academy award nomination. It also became Stewart's favorite of his own films. But the media wanted a war story, some glamor and heroics. Stewart, a modest man, would not oblige beyond a few words:

> I saw too much suffering. It's certainly not something to talk about—or celebrate. Sherman said "War is Hell"—how right he was; how truly he spoke!

With the exception of a few general comments, Jimmy Stewart never talked much about the war to television interviewers, historians, journalists, or even to his own family. So unfortunately his experiences, his "war story," has mostly been left for others to interpret and portray. Some biographers have glamorized, perhaps celebrated, an assertion that at the time of Jimmy Stewart's arrival at Old Buckenham, the 453rd Bomb Group was a "hard luck" unit with "a morale problem that was among the worst in the 8th Air Force." Furthermore, the airmen in the 453rd were refusing to fly![3] Once setting the scene, enter Jimmy Stewart center stage, the solution to the 453rd Bomb Group's problems. Biographer Roy Pickard stated that Jimmy Stewart did the "lion's share of the rebuilding" in the 453rd, and fails to mention the other key leaders. Rather than telling the story of Jimmy Stewart's wartime service, such distorted portrayals seem to echo the script of the compelling 1949 movie *Twelve O'Clock High* in which Gregory Peck starred as General Frank Savage, sent to replace the CO of a failing bomb group infested with morale problems.

A fictional account, *Twelve O'Clock High* was based on a real B-17 Bomb Group and its commander. In the film, the general's predecessor had shown too much sympathy for his men and allowed them to believe that they were a "hard luck" bomb group. Peck's character takes the tough approach and tries to whip the group into shape, refusing to allow them to feel sorry for themselves, although ultimately, despite his successes, the general suffers a breakdown. But whereas the fictional commander is initially met with resentment and requests for transfer, legend has it that at Old "Buckingham" or at "Buckinghamshire" airfield, as biographers have erroneously renamed the base, Operations Officer Jimmy Stewart was met with adoration. One day he discovered that someone had written the words "Death Takes A Holiday" across his Jeep—an indication that the 453rd Bomb Group was winning and its alleged morale problem had been resolved.

To illustrate this, biographer Donald Dewey states, "within a couple of months of the arrival of Potts and Stewart, the 453rd's proficiency rate on raids rose from near the bottom to near the top among 8th Air Force units." This is a simplification of the developments within the 453rd Bomb Group; the term "proficiency rate" is somewhat ambiguous, especially when used to quantify morale. If it means more aircraft reaching the target or fewer aircraft having to abort then aircrew morale is one of many contributing factors. This could also be attributed to ground crew competence and the supply of spare parts needed to repair aircraft. Bad winter weather created havoc for the ground crews working round the clock and exposed to the elements; bad weather and mechanical problems frequently interfered and forced bombers to abandon missions and return early (yet the 8th Air Force was never once turned back by the enemy). If an increased "proficiency rate" means improved bombing accuracy, this could be attributed to clear spring and summer weather conditions as well as increased experience and expertise of navigators and bombardiers. If improved proficiency is a reduction in aircraft losses and aircrew attrition, it might be fair to say that there was a correlation between an increase in morale and the decline of the Luftwaffe.

The majority of crews throughout the 8th Air Force were occasionally forced to abort missions and return to base with numerous problems such as engine or supercharger problems resulting in a loss of turbo power, leaking engine oil, oxygen supply failure, or crew members suffering from air sickness or anoxia. But occasionally whispers of suspicion spread around each base regarding certain pilots and crews who had returned seemingly unnecessarily, almost routinely from several consecutive missions; furthermore in some instances the ground crews couldn't identify the alleged technical problems, and morale was brought into question. One pilot in the 453rd Bomb Group aborted on five consecutive missions and was then grounded; his thoroughly demoralized crew was assigned to another pilot. But such cases were exceptions to the norm within the 453rd, with the vast majority of individual mission aborts clearly justified. Nonetheless, the number of aborts was one of many factors that determined the reputation of a bomb group.[4]

Another cause for controversy was the number of 8th Air Force aircraft landing in neutral territory where the crews could only sit and wait out the rest of the war. In the event of aircraft enduring serious battle damage or suffering from technical malfunctions that would endanger their return to England, both neutral Switzerland and Sweden were seen as last resort destinations by not only aircrews, but also their leaders. In fact, one 93rd Bomb Group veteran recalled that during a mission briefing one morning at Hardwick airfield in November 1943, Ramsay Potts, who at that time was group operations officer in the 93rd Bomb Group, stated words to this effect:

> If you get into trouble . . . and you don't think you can make it back . . . here are the coordinates of places you can land in Sweden, and Sweden is neutral and they will intern you. But we don't know what's happened to the last crew that went in there . . . and I don't want you guys to start a parade into Sweden![5]

At times suspicions were aroused when there *did* appear to be a parade of 8th and 15th Air Force bombers heading for neutral territory. During the mission of 24 April 1944, for example, a total of fourteen England-based American bombers interned in Switzerland. By mid-1944 the increasing numbers of American bombers standing silently at Swiss and Swedish airfields led to questions being raised regarding morale and even desertion. But such suspicions were eventually disregarded when in 1945 the situation was assessed realistically—the battle damage to the interned aircraft was such that less than half of the aircraft interned in Switzerland were deemed repairable. Furthermore, battle damage assessments exclude those aircraft forced to land in neutral territory due to fuel shortages or with injured crew members on board in need of urgent medical treatment.

Regarding the issue of airmen refusing to fly, most bomb groups in the 8th Air Force did experience periodical morale problems of one kind or another during challenging times, and were often a result of fatigue and exhaustion. While some such incidents did occur at Old Buckenham in 1944, this behavior was not unique to the 453rd Bomb Group. In a letter written fifty-eight years after he took command of the 453rd Bomb Group, Ramsay Potts, who retired from the Air Force as a major general, reflected on his early days at Old Buckenham:

> When I took command of the 453rd, there was a serious morale problem in the group. Seven flying officers had refused to fly and no decisive action had been taken to rectify this situation. I immediately interviewed personally each of the seven officers and explained to them that they were volunteers; that they were expected to set an example; that, if they did not return to flying status, they would disgrace themselves and their families; and that, unless they returned, I was going to court-martial them and recommend the most severe punishment. All but one of the seven returned to flying status immediately, and the odd man out was sent by me to the Central Medical Board for evaluation.

Lt. Bob Bieck was a lead and then a Pathfinder pilot in the 732nd Bomb Squadron; in July 1944 he became the 733rd Bomb Squadron's operations officer following the loss of Captain Andy Boreske. Bob Bieck recalls:

> Lt. Col. Ramsay Potts was a no-nonsense man and his presence was felt at once. He was one of the most dynamic officers I have ever known. He was like a caged tiger chaffing to be released. He has subsequently claimed there were six or seven officers who had refused to fly. I would accept that; moreover, there may have been at least a dozen more who were on the edge of quitting. Please understand this feeling was endemic throughout the 8th Bomber Command. For example, the 44th, 93rd, and 389th Bomb Groups, to name just a few, had suffered drastic losses and were only now being rebuilt.

Evidently there was a minority of airmen in the 453rd who were suffering psychologically, who wanted out, and who were refusing to fly because, as Jimmy Stewart acknowledged, "War is Hell." But the majority of airmen at Old Buckenham *were* flying their missions, and many were dying, just like the aircrews of any other bomb group in the 8th Air Force. To casually claim that morale among the men of the 453rd was among the worst in the 8th Air Force, and to present an unbalanced picture synonymous with disloyalty and dishonor is, to the veterans, the ultimate criticism. It is all too easy to sensationalize, to paint a picture of the 453rd Bomb Group as an undisciplined, cowardly shambles, like a scene from *Catch-22*, and to portray Jimmy Stewart as some kind of savior. Although it would make a good Hollywood story, it doesn't sit comfortably with many of the veterans whose personal experiences were far more complex. The concept of "military morale" is itself ambiguous, open to interpretation and something that, as Mark K. Wells wrote in *Courage and Air Warfare*, resists quantification: "No simple yardstick of 'good' or 'bad' morale exists today; nor did it during the conflict . . . thousands of individual airmen each fought very personal battles . . . morale [was] a very personal experience."[6]

Consequently, testimonies vary but interestingly, the majority of the 453rd Bomb Group's veterans dispute that a serious morale problem ever existed at Old Buckenham and mostly seem to have been unaware of anyone refusing to fly. Pilot Lt. Nick Radosevich of Crew 41, 734th Bomb Squadron was at Old Buckenham from the beginning until July 1944:

> I was greatly surprised when I read your letter . . . [referring to an alleged] morale problem in the 453rd Bomb Group. This is the first time I have heard about any problem. My morale was okay because I was focused on the job we had to do. Some were afraid to die and that's normal.

Robert Victor, the radio operator on Crew 41 recalls:

> I am aware of the large number of casualties that we suffered from operations in February and March 1944 but I do not remember . . . [anyone refusing] to fly. I'm certain that the rumor mill would have been working very well with respect to that matter, if in fact there was any public knowledge of it then. If anyone had refused to fly for any reason other than health, Col. Miller would have court-martialed them and it all would have become public knowledge. Frankly I can't recall that any trials of that sort ever took place. That is not to say that there wasn't the usual griping about the food, the weather, the everlasting mud, the paucity of time-off leaves.

Lt. Eugene McDowell, the copilot on Lt. William Bates's crew, 732nd Bomb Squadron, recalls:

> I am not aware of any morale problem in the 453rd . . . After I finished my combat tour, I went to 2nd Combat Wing Headquarters, as an assistant to Jimmy Stewart and I never heard anything mentioned concerning this problem.

Lt. Richard Witton's crew assigned to the 732nd Bomb Squadron was lost on a mission over Brunswick on 8 May 1944; navigator Lt. Abe Wilen survived and became a prisoner of war. With regard to allegations of morale problems at Old Buckenham, he believes:

> Someone is overdramatizing . . . to my personal knowledge, I don't know of anyone refusing to fly. Nothing changed as a result of Stewart and Potts. We were there to do a job and it made no

difference who was calling the shots. Ours was a job of fighting and winning a war and surviving. Everything else was for books and the movies; all the intrigue, glamour, and heroics.

Lt. Jim Kotapish joined the 453rd at Boise, Idaho, and was assigned to Lt. Ray Sears's crew, 734th Bomb Squadron, and arrived at Old Buckenham early in 1944, prior to the group commencing operations. He flew his thirty-first and final mission early in August 1944 and remained at Old Buckenham until the end of the war, having been appointed the role of club officer, responsible for running the Officers' Club.

> I was quite surprised to hear that there were seven persons requesting an out from flying at the time that Col. Potts arrived. Having flown a tour as a squadron lead crew and also a group lead crew I can sympathize with them and their reluctance. You have to do some combat flying with all the fighters and flak perils to empathize with them.
>
> One of our original crew members of the Lt. Ray Sears crew, on which I was the copilot, quit after one mission. As far as I know there was no retaliation placed on our one-mission person. It was early in 1944. I suppose there was lots of new stuff happening. So he merely was grounded and assigned to ground duties. We also had a crewman who shot himself in the foot, literally, during our hop across the country to go overseas.
>
> I do know of one person, a pilot, whom I consider a hero. He had walked away from his plane when lining up for take-off for a mission. He also served Mass with me, and was being counseled by the priest who talked him into going back to flying missions. You've guessed it. He never came back from his next mission.

Nick Radosevich commented that he was "focused on the job we had to do" and this probably explains the different interpretations of the morale situation. Likewise, Group Commander Lt. Col. Ramsay Potts was focused on the job that *he* had to do and for him, seven refusals to fly did constitute a serious morale problem in the 453rd Bomb Group. As the CO, Ramsay Potts had to account for those seven individuals one way or another, and he also had to stifle the causes of the problem before it gained momentum and became contagious. Viewing the situation objectively, Ramsay Potts knew that the seriousness of the problem was not just what was happening, but what could happen if things continued on their current course. He did not want a mutiny on his hands. As it turned out, due to numerous factors including the efforts of Ramsay Potts, the feelings of seven men refusing to fly did not spread to the other flying personnel; the full potential of the morale problem remained dormant. However, from the perspective of the majority of flying personnel who did not refuse to fly, and even for those who momentarily faltered, that they continued to fly combat missions in the face of life-threatening danger does not correspond with *their* definition of a serious morale problem. Discontentment was rife, but as time would tell, this was not enough to undermine the morale of the majority. Regardless of frustrations, it seems that determination prevailed.

In order to understand the discontentment and frustration experienced within the 453rd Bomb Group during February and March 1944, it is imperative that all the complexities of the situation are considered, with a realistic perspective on the context in which the 453rd Bomb Group existed. In early February 1944 the 453rd reached peak flying strength as the crews completed their tiring South Atlantic flights and arrived in the European Theatre of Operations only to be hit by a cold and flu epidemic on the base. The flying personnel were young men, far from home, and homesick. Conditions at Old Buckenham were not easy to adjust to—the weather was dreadful, it snowed and it rained; the billets were cold, drafty, and damp, each with two insufficient potbelly stoves yet not enough fuel to keep them burning. Initially the food was unappetizing English rations; and everywhere on the base there was deep, liquid mud. As Bill Eagleson remarks:

An army is entitled to bitch—*That's* morale!

Furthermore, when the last of the original crews arrived at Old Buckenham, the 453rd commenced missions and had since endured heavy combat losses. According to the alphabetical system of group identification markings, the 453rd flew with a new marking on their tails—"circle-J" signified that they were the newest and least experienced group in the B-24 formations and were therefore potentially easy prey for the experienced Luftwaffe fighter pilots. Combat flying was physically and mentally exhausting, and the realities of warfare were not easy to adjust to. The 453rd's rookie crews had to come to terms with facing life-threatening danger and they had to learn to cope with fear and with the loss of their friends. Replacement crews arrived to fill the vacuum left by those who didn't make it back to base, but their very presence as "replacements" was an unsettling reminder of their transitory and volatile existence. Then, like a real kick in the head, their tour of duty had been increased from twenty-five to thirty missions, thus increasing the odds against their survival.

Having been at Old Buckenham just eleven days when Jimmy Stewart was assigned to the 453rd Bomb Group, Lt. Col. Ramsay Potts was already in the process of taking decisive action to strengthen morale and consolidate the unit's leadership. When looking to replace the deceased Maj. Cofield as group operations officer, Ramsay Potts specifically requested "somebody from the outside" in order to renew the spirit of the 453rd. Prior to the arrival of Potts, he believes, "there simply hadn't been much leadership" and perhaps this had been the fundamental problem at Old Buckenham, while discontentment was one of the symptoms.

According to some sources, Potts's predecessor, Col. Joseph Miller had not been popular among some of the flying personnel. On 18 March 1944 when returning from Friedrichshafen, Miller's aircraft endured severe battle damage and was in trouble. The ship lost airspeed and altitude; clearly Miller was not going to make it back to England. When the 453rd returned without him, there was a great deal of speculation regarding what had happened, and who would replace him. Jim Kotapish remembers hearing a rumor later that day, according to which, someone on the mission broke radio silence upon witnessing Miller's fate, and declared "Good for you, you son of a bitch; you got what you deserve!" Whether the rumor was based on fact or fiction, it illustrates the feelings of at least some of the airmen and the state of morale. Apparently this resentment towards Miller stemmed from a mission briefing when Miller concluded his speech by unintentionally announcing to the crews that he would be there to welcome them back—*if* they got back! Perhaps it was a Freudian slip, but the airmen were becoming increasingly superstitious and such remarks hardly inspired confidence.

Furthermore some of the 453rd Bomb Group's personnel felt that Miller was responsible for their troubled initiation into combat. A graduate of the United States Military Academy at West Point, Miller had served in the military for thirteen years prior to becoming CO of the 453rd Bomb Group. It has been suggested that he pushed the 453rd through Phase training rather rapidly because he was so eager to get into combat.[7] In fairness to Miller, it's worth considering that the 452nd Bomb Group, a B-17 unit based at nearby Deopham Green airfield, had been activated on the same day, and later flew its first mission on the same day as the 453rd Bomb Group. The 458th Bomb Group's activation to debut mission time period was approximately the same.

The majority of the 453rd Bomb Group's veterans remember Col. Joseph Miller favorably and would dispute the existence of bad feeling and rumors against him. Abe Wilen claims, "I had no knowledge of anything negative about Col. Miller." Robert Victor recalls:

> Shortly after the 453rd was formed [Col. Miller] met with all of us, officers and enlisted men, but thereafter he maintained a strictly business attitude with little or no fraternization. He let it be known that he expected the best that we could be from everyone. As far as I could determine he was respected by everyone. In England, he flew as group leader in whatever rotation that required. In short, I personally thought highly of him as a commander and do not recall any other criticism of his command.

Assigned to the 7th Tow Target Squadron based at March Field, California, back in 1943 Lt. Bob Bieck was a pilot dragging moving targets for air gunners to shoot at. When the 453rd Bomb Group arrived at March Field, Lt. Bieck observed the sense of urgency and understood Miller's predicament:

They had much training to do, and they did not have enough aircraft. Everybody seemed rushed. I learned that Col. Miller was
under constant pressure to get his group out of March Field and en
route to England irrespective of their degree of preparedness.

Although he had never even flown a B-24, in November 1943 Bob
Bieck was happy to be transferred to the 453rd since he hated target
towing with a passion. Regardless of who or what was responsible,
Phase Three training was rushed through in three weeks with a scarcity
of training aircraft; upon arrival in England practice missions were
flown but still the group was insufficiently trained in formation flying.

Bill Eagleson recalls:

> We were [at first] "sitting ducks"; loose formation for the experi-
> enced Nazi foe — *We had to learn* — We did.

On his first mission early in February 1944, 734th Bomb Squadron
pilot Lt. Ray Sears lost the group in cloud and then tagged along with
another formation. Over the target he experienced difficulties with his
electrically heated flying suit and was, as copilot Lt. Jim Kotapish recalls:

> Freezing his butt off. . . . Ray yelled for me to take over, which I did
> and found myself in the midst of the bombers on the bomb run. . . .
> I had never experienced any B-24 formation flying prior to that
> time. I was so mad at this point that I had to start learning forma-
> tion flying under these circumstances, that to this day I don't know
> if there was any flak or fighters, since I was so busy trying to avoid
> a collision when the group peeled off after the drop.
>
> We [the 453rd Bomb Group] were pulled out of combat to
> practice formation flying, which we never received back in the
> States. It just wasn't the introductory flights we took [prior to the
> first combat mission on 5 February]. . . . I believe that the group
> was stood down about the first part of March 1944.

Indeed, the group was stood down from flying missions for five
consecutive days at the end of February into early March. Then, soon
after Lt. Col. Ramsay Potts arrived at Old Buckenham the 453rd spent
ten out of eleven days without flying any combat missions (28 March
to 7 April inclusive with one exception, 1 April, when the 453rd was
dispatched to Germany). But the primary factor for the 453rd's absence from enemy skies at that time was the weather — other groups
were grounded also. Meanwhile, the 453rd's crews flew practice missions over England under the supervision of their new CO, Lt. Col.
Ramsay Potts:

> I made it my task to fly as soon as possible with the crews from each
> squadron in order to assess their proficiency and to compliment
> them on their skills. It turned out that the pilots and aircrews of the
> group were first-rate and, with this base to build upon, the 453rd
> Bomb Group became one of the primary bomb groups in the 8th
> Air Force.

Then I went to work on some of the people who had allowed the situation to fester for so long. We didn't have a morale problem after a little while.[8]

Under Ramsay Potts's command, Maj. Jimmy Stewart, Capt. Andy Low, along with the four squadron commanders (including the 733rd Squadron's CO Capt. Robert Coggeshall and 733rd Squadron Operations Officer Capt. Andy Boreske), became a strong team that

Left to right: Lt. Milton Stokes (735th Bomb Squadron pilot) and Maj. Robert Sears (735th Bomb Squadron CO who had flown as Command Pilot on Milton Stokes' aircraft) discuss the events of the mission with Lt. Col. Ramsay Potts and Maj. James Stewart. Robert Sears was soon to be promoted to lieutenant colonel; on 29 April he failed to return from a mission but survived as a POW. (Frank Kyle)

was successful in turning the 453rd Bomb Group around. Ramsay Potts welcomed the arrival of Jimmy Stewart, admired his credentials, and valued his support in reestablishing the leadership of the 453rd:

> [Jimmy Stewart] was one hundred percent as a pilot. And he also had a tremendous rapport with the men—that languid, humorous way he had of settling them down in some pretty stressful situations. But, just as important to me, he grasped immediately what I said to him once about agreeing with Field Marshall Montgomery's view of war. Monty used to go up to a soldier and ask him what was the most important thing he had. And when the soldier would invariably answer something like his rifle, Monty would jump all over him and say, no, it wasn't, it was your life, so you better hold on to it. I told the 453rd the same thing until it was coming out of their ears. From a military point of view, that meant they better fly in close formation [thus maximizing their combined defensive firepower in the face of the Luftwaffe] if they expected to return to base. Jimmy understood that, too. He impressed them with living as well as winning, and more than that an officer can't do.[9]
>
> We hit it off very well, even though he was eight years older than I was. He was a wonderful addition to the group and had the same languid style as in his movies. Everyone loved him. We whipped that group into tip-top shape and it quickly became one of the best groups in the Air Force.[10]

As a 732nd Bomb Squadron lead pilot, and later a Pathfinder pilot, Lt. Bob Bieck found himself working in close contact with Jimmy Stewart. Bieck reflected on the impact that Jimmy Stewart's presence had on morale in the 453rd:

> While I was never a close friend, he did call me Bob. . . . There is no question that morale improved; however, I am not sure that he alone was the key. The war was gradually going our way, and our losses were diminishing considerably.

Certainly the 453rd Bomb Group sensed the demise of the Luftwaffe; the 733rd Bomb Squadron later received a citation for flying eighty-two consecutive missions without losing a single aircraft. However, in March 1944 there were still many hard times ahead for the 453rd Bomb Group. Two missions to Brunswick in April and May resulted in particularly heavy losses of crews and proved to be the most significant challenge for morale that the 453rd would ever face. But as the weeks progressed, the reality of some fortunate airmen completing their combat tours and being sent home to the United States provided a big boost.

In addition to addressing leadership and morale issues, Lt. Col. Ramsay Potts focused on aspects relating to discipline and sought out those enlisted flying personnel who, through boredom between missions, were gaining notoriety by congregating in some empty huts, drinking alcohol, and gambling. Ramsay Potts recalls:

Another problem reared its ugly head . . . gunners from the four squadrons had been placed in one of the Nissen huts near the road that went by the base. They had become somewhat rowdy and undisciplined, and I decided that the gunners from each squadron should be returned to their squadron areas where they would be intermingled with the more mature crew chiefs [ground crew leaders] and armament personnel. This turned out to be good for morale both among the gunners and among the squadrons and crews.

Perhaps the next initiative was an inspired incentive for some of the enlisted men to become more disciplined (or even a consolation for the abandonment of their unauthorized social club!). Certainly it reduced the number of officer/enlisted inequalities:

Another question arose when the club officer came to me to say that he had arranged for beer to be provided for the Officers' Club. Much to his dismay, I told him that we would not allow beer to be served in the Officers' Club until we could have it for the [enlisted men in the] Airmen's Club and the NCO Club. He was finally able to arrange that and this also helped morale throughout the group.

Bill Eagleson concludes:

Should anyone be credited for pulling our group together it would be Ramsay Potts and Andy Low. . . . Ramsey Potts brought combat knowledge to us. Jimmy Stewart—finest, dedicated leader.

I could not say enough about the leadership that we had at the 453rd Bomb Group command level. . . . Ramsay Potts, he was an amazing person—very young. He was a favorite of Timberlake's [Gen. Edward "Ted" Timberlake, 2nd Combat Wing CO and former 93rd Bomb Group CO], as they had flown together on Ploesti. Captain Robert Coggeshall was the finest of flyers. He took over the 733rd Bomb Squadron from Robert Kanaga [one of many initial changes initiated by Ramsay Potts]. Coggeshall was quite a guy; he was a very skilled, accomplished aviator; told great stories, kept the morale going. Crews always felt comfortable when he was flying with them or leading them—a good squadron CO.

But even with new leadership I conclude that warm spring days that dried the mud, daylight takeoffs, *experience*, were all survival factors. We were not the "worst group"—never did we belong in this category! Our crew morale was *high*!

Just the mud around us reminded that big things were happening at Old Buck'. Namely the 453rd was into operations, we were going through another learning phase, and we had faith in our crew and in the guys that were flying left and right of us and up and down from us—just a determined lot out to do a job.

Early morning on Saturday 1 April, Jack Nortridge's crew taxied out, not in *Corky*, but in the B-24 *Blondes Away*. Twenty-three Liberators left Old Buckenham's main runway, assigned to bomb chemical works at Ludwigshafen, Germany. The 453rd Bomb Group led the 2nd Combat Wing, with the 445th flying high-right and the 389th low-left. The B-24s proceeded into southern Germany where thick cloud rose to above 20,000 feet causing navigation and formation confusion.

Relying on the radar-equipped lead aircraft the majority of the 453rd Group's Liberators bombed the railway marshalling yards at Pforzheim, Germany, from 21,000 feet; the Nortridge crew were credited on their mission records with an attack on Mannheim, close to the primary target. The group flew home via Dunkirk where light flak was encountered. Crossing the English Channel it became apparent to Perry Roberson that the fuel supply on *Blondes Away* would not last them to Old Buck', and so Jack and George took *Blondes Away* into Manston, Kent, after an exhausting seven hours and forty-eight minute flight. All other aircraft returned safely to Old Buckenham.

Between combat missions, if practice missions were not scheduled, often the flying personnel had little time or energy for anything other than eating or sleeping. A few days on the ground might provide some free time for leisure activities or writing home to families, friends, and girlfriends, as Bill LeRoy recalls, "I wrote home as often as possible (not nearly enough)." Others spent time in the base gym or played for their squadron in softball, baseball, and basketball games. There was also a base cinema that showed mostly old movies, a library, a Red Cross club, and the Officers' Club. On the communal site there was a PX (Post Exchange) that sold weekly rations of cigarettes, razors, toothbrushes, chocolate (Hershey bars), peppermints, and chewing gum— the English children took a particular liking to chewing gum, as Bill Eagleson recalls:

> We often shared our PX rations with friends (British). Kids liked our gum. We were greeted, "Any gum, chum?"

The combat crews were issued bicycles and with the arrival of spring, bike rides became popular, as this was a good way of investigating the local villages and pubs. After a pint or two of warm beer, navigating and steering one's way back to base in the darkness of the blackout conditions provided a challenge.

Perry Roberson:

> Transportation on base was walking or bicycles. We did have trucks to take us to and from the plane.

Bill Eagleson:

> The road to the Officers' Club was surrounded by mud. The road to the Combat Mess site, *that* was surrounded by mud; that road was most frequented by all our personnel going to and from the flight lines. We were assigned Raleigh bicycles, and sometimes it was quite challenging to ride your bike along that concrete slab

with mud on each side with "six-bys" and all the traffic that was going to and from the flight lines. But that was the way it was.

Our journeys usually took us into Attleborough because we'd get down [along Miller Road] to site three, we'd take a right there, go north [along Buckenham Road] and west a little bit to the beautiful town of Attleborough, which I remember very vividly.

Attleborough was on the doorstep, but for many an off-duty GI the city of Norwich, eighteen miles from Old Buck', was the favorite place for an evening of entertainment. Norwich is a city originating in Saxon times and full of historic buildings. The cathedral dates back to 1096 and its tower and spire are second only to Salisbury's in height. There is a Norman castle built in 1100 and ruins of the thirteenth-century city wall, which had once enclosed an area larger than medieval London. There were old cobbled streets and Tudor buildings. According to historical accounts, half the population of the city had been wiped out during the Black Death of 1348. And now a new era of history was being added to the centuries of history that had gone before—four and a half years of war had taken its toll on Norwich, and many Americans were shocked by their first impressions, such as the wrecks and shells of burned out buildings.

During the First World War, Norfolk had endured aerial attacks from German Zeppelins, and so during the months that led up to the Second World War the prospect of aerial bombardment was a very real

Norwich Castle, built in 1100. (Will Lundy)

Norwich Cathedral. In the autumn of 1944 the spire was almost struck by a low-flying B-24 lost in cloud over a blacked-out Norwich at dusk. The battle damaged B-24 had previously made a forced landing in a farmer's field; a repair team lightened the aircraft and all radio equipment was removed before it was flown out of the muddy field by a 3rd SAD pilot. The weather made a sudden turn for the worse but the Liberator eventually landed safely at Watton. (unknown)

London Street in the city of Norwich, looking towards the clock tower of the City Hall. (USAF via Martin Bowman)

fear for the people of the city, and on the day that war was declared, air-raid sirens rang through the city. There were many more false alarms during the months ahead, but in the summer of 1940 enemy aircraft attacked Norwich, causing damage to residential areas. More Intruder attacks followed, often by lone German aircraft, and by the end of 1940 the death toll was sixty-one. Similar attacks continued until the summer of 1941.

Late one night in April 1942 the sirens sounded around the city as formations of German aircraft approached Norwich for a raid that lasted over an hour. Most of the bombs fell in residential areas and missed the historic buildings of the city center. One hundred and sixty-two civilians were killed and several hundred others were injured in the Blitz attack. Two nights later another intensive raid was launched against Norwich, killing sixty-nine more, destroying a couple of churches and many more civilian buildings. The effects of these raids had a devastating effect on the city and the citizens of Norwich, and many women and children were forced to escape to the countryside at night to sleep in open fields to avoid the danger. Others found temporary accommodation or stayed with relatives in the rural villages and towns and waited out the war.

Similar raids were launched against other cities such as Exeter, Bath, Canterbury, and York. None of them were military targets but all contained historic architecture. For this reason these raids of 1942 became known as the "Baedeker Raids," because allegedly the targets were selected from the famous prewar Baedeker guidebooks to Britain that listed places of cultural heritage. During a third large-scale Blitz attack on Norwich in June the Germans seemed determined to destroy the cathedral. Several churches were among the many buildings that were gutted by fire or reduced to rubble by high explosives, but somehow the cathedral and the castle and several other historic landmarks survived this attack. Norwich endured a fourth such raid in August 1942.

That year over 250 Norwich residents lost their lives in German bombing raids, and in October King George VI visited Norwich to inspect the damage and raise the morale of the people. By the end of the war the death toll was 340 people killed. Over 1,000 more were injured. Eighty-five percent of the buildings were damaged, of which two thousand were destroyed.

In 1944 the air-raid sirens still sounded most days, but these were invariably false alarms. By this time there were something in the region of one hundred thousand USAAF personnel based within a thirty mile radius of Norwich, and for many of them Norwich was the nearest "Liberty Town." Most evenings truckloads of off-duty GIs were shuttled from their Norfolk bases on what they called the "Liberty Run," an evening of entertainment in the city. The trucks would park on the concrete-surfaced cattle market site beside the castle, and the Americans would be free to explore Norwich. After closing time the Americans would mostly return to the cattle market to find their army transport to carry them back to base.

The American Red Cross Club at Bishops Palace, adjoining Norwich Cathedral, provided food, entertainment, and lodgings at a reasonable cost for the American airmen. There was also a popular Red Cross Club in Bethel Street. Although over one hundred public houses had been destroyed or badly damaged during the air raids of 1942, there were still many places for the Americans to drink warm beer in 1944—Norwich was famous for having a public house for each day of the year and a church for each Sunday. There were also dance halls, cinemas, and theaters. When the *Daily Mirror* newspaper turned its "Jane" comic into a production that toured the country's theaters, the real-life Jane was a success. In the cartoon version, Jane was famous, or rather infamous, for taking her clothes off—in the theater performances she didn't disappoint the audience, who saw a silhouetted Jane as she stripped behind a screen.

Bill Eagleson:

> Our fun was had in Norwich town, particularly in the Hippodrome Theatre watching your risqué lady, Jane, of the *Daily Mirror*. She was quite a hit with the troops. And when we had a free evening on a Liberty Run we'd go into the Hippodrome and listen to Janey sing a few songs. I do remember going to the Odeon Theatre; it was upstairs, in Norwich. I believe I saw *A Guy Named Joe* there, with Spencer Tracy.

In Norwich the Americans had the opportunity to get to know more British people, and some of them found English girlfriends and war brides. East Anglian folklore has immortalized many of the first impressions of the American airmen. Overcoming their initial differences and misunderstandings, the English and their American cousins soon learned to get along. One memorable first impression of the American GIs was their apparent relaxed attitude towards certain military formalities, namely the fraternization between officers and enlisted men. This behavior bemused the English, who noted that the Americans related to each other as equals with supposed disregard for appropriate military protocol, as the distinctions of rank and status became blurred by friendship.[11]

Indeed, officers and enlisted men would be seen socializing and drinking together in English pubs, and when given forty-eight- or seventy-two-hour passes, a whole inseparable aircrew might make a trip to London together. The English reaction at the time was often: "Imagine going to war and treating your officers as 'buddies.'"[12] In fairness, this was equally true of RAF aircrews, but in many of the towns and villages where Americans were based, the locals never encountered RAF aircrews and believed this behavior to be uniquely American. Sometimes

even the regular American Army soldiers, many of whom were awaiting the Allied invasion of Europe and the opportunity to play their part
in the war, were equally perplexed by the attitudes among their winged
contemporaries:

> Of interest we had problems of understanding—our "ground
> pounders" living the good life in London did not appreciate our
> nonchalance, often lack of military decorum, and of course the
> wearing of ribbons. Our British friends sometimes thought we
> were sinking their Isles with manpower and equipment. Our
> trained and psyched-up land combat parachuters were difficult to
> contain—they wanted Germans. Our combat crews on leave gen-
> erally stayed together, officers and enlisted men. This custom was
> not understood by all.

It is important to remember also that the overall majority of these
young flyers were not "professional soldiers" or ambitious military men.
They were "civilian-soldiers" who, due to the circumstances of the war,
had volunteered for the Army Air Force either before or after they had
been drafted for regular army service. Originally the aircrew selection
processes were based on the scientific methods of evaluation tests and
examinations for general intelligence and mechanical aptitude. These
were supplemented by a series of written and physical "Stanine" tests
(Standard Nine, graded one to nine), as well as interviews regarding
backgrounds and interests. The grade requirements for pilots, navigators, and bombardiers varied according to fluctuating manpower demands for each role—therefore, this was a key factor in determining
whether an individual would serve as an officer or an enlisted soldier.

Certainly during crew training in the United States, officers and enlisted men were discouraged from socializing together and lived in separate quarters. It was recognized as important to instill in the enlisted
men a sense of discipline, to encourage the necessary respect for their
officers so they were able to follow orders. But by the time they reached
England and began flying their combat missions, while fraternization
between officers and enlisted men was to some extent discouraged, it
was inevitable. Both the flying officers and enlisted men understood the
importance of chain of command, but the emphasis had shifted as a result of shared experiences and challenges.

Generally speaking, both the army "ground pounders" and the English people who encountered the American airmen in East Anglia
lacked a real understanding of the nature of the aircrew experience.
The pilot was always recognized as the crew leader and commander,
even though he was often only two or three years older than the youngest man on the crew. Each man was trained to fulfill a crucial role that
was imperative for the survival of the other nine men. As the Army Air
Force commander Gen. Arnold stated, "Nowhere in the world are the
lives of men as interdependent as in a bomber on a mission."

At twenty thousand feet, teamwork was frequently the most important factor for their common survival. In combat conditions where seconds could mean life or death, where the drone of aircraft engines, exploding flak, and machine gun fire could seriously restrict communication, intercom dialogue needed to be specific and concise, warranting a first-name relationship—it followed that this became evident both in the air and on the ground.

On one occasion, Lim Wing Jeong was walking through the base when he saw his pilot from afar. The sergeant hollered, "Hey! Jack!" Although Lt. Nortridge had always insisted that his crew call him Jack, a senior officer within earshot reprimanded Sgt. Jeong, reminding him to always address an officer by his rank.

Within crews, shared experiences led to close friendships, dependencies, and a sense of solidarity that often seemed to overshadow, although never actually replace the class distinctions between officers and enlisted men. On the base there was a clear division between barracks facilities for officers and enlisted men. At most American bases there were different mess hall facilities, serving different food for officers and enlisted men. There might be two lines for the base movie theater, and due to the officer/enlisted men ratio, it was usually the enlisted men who had to join the much longer queue and wait in line. The officers enjoyed the Officers' Club, and an Aero Club was opened at Old Buck' in April for the enlisted men. The officers could leave the base area at will during their off-duty hours, while the enlisted men needed to obtain a pass. At Old Buckenham however, measures were taken to relax the aircrew officer/enlisted men distinctions, especially in preparation for missions as Bill Eagleson recalls:

> Later on, probably when Ramsay Potts took over in mid-March, we were moved to a Combat Mess site and we ate with our crews. . . . We enjoyed that, being with the crews for breakfast as we gathered to get down to the flight line and go together. That was a good concept to bring us into a common mess hall before missions. It wasn't "officers/enlisted men" or "officers/airmen"—it was *aircrew,* and that spirit prevailed.

Crews were typically a diverse bunch of individuals thrown together by fate and circumstances. Under other circumstances crew members might not have chosen each other as friends, but friends they became and they learned to appreciate their differences and work together. Crew 25 was no exception to this. Bill Eagleson remembers:

> What a democratic crew we had in *Corky* . . . thinking back we had Jeong in the tail . . . a Chinese tail gunner. We had Pete Veilleux up in the nose; he was a Frenchman from Maine. We had DeMay . . . and he was a Russian as I remember . . . he was a Russian from Brooklyn. . . . Seymour Cohen [a Jewish navigator] from New Jersey. . . . He replaced Donald Lawry as our navigator.

For the airmen at Old Buckenham, combat experience soon influenced their daily outlook. At the time of volunteering for the air force their motivations tended to be based on altruistic ideals:

> At that time of life, I believe we were motivated by the bigger problem of America's survival and the survival throughout the free world—I really believe we felt that way. When it came down to flying our missions, we were motivated by our own thoughts for survival and we did try our best to take care of each other. The aircrew was a completely different concept—the aircrew feelings were not experienced by other military groups. In the air corps our crew was our family, and we hung in there together. We went on leave together, we *thought* together, we worked together, and we *fought* together. And we had a high respect for each other.
>
> I know that nowhere could you find a cooler cat at a quay than Bill LeRoy; nowhere could you find a more diligent flight engineer than Perry Roberson; nowhere could you find a leader more concerned for his men than Jack Nortridge—and that's the way our aircrew dealt with the challenges of survival.

Jack Nortridge's crew remained good friends with Gus Johnson's crew and others in the 453rd Bomb Group but often aircrews mixed only with their own crew and learned to be cautious about making too many other friends. This insulated them to some degree from the implications of the inevitable reality when another aircraft in the formation was lost, taking with it one's close friends.

Often local English people, many of them missing their own sons and daughters, befriended the American visitors, opened their doors to them, served them dinner, and made them feel welcome. Regardless of any earlier Anglo-American misunderstandings, Bill Eagleson recalls:

> We were treated well by the locals in Old Buck and Attleborough. . . . I attended the local village church at Attleborough. . . . My dear friend was the village vicar, Stephen Dennett—he was of great help bringing our members closer to the English people and customs. When free I used to straddle the Raleigh and wheel past Gaymer's Cyder Mill to Sunday vespers. You people were so strong and overly patient with our sometimes-difficult customs. Sunday vespers were heartening and a source of support—people friendly—and from my point we learned well each others customs. . . . Afterwards, restful conversation at the Rectory.

On Good Friday, 7 April the 453rd Group was grounded. However, that evening some of the crews were alerted for a mission the following morning. Often some of the airmen would go down to their dispersal point and talk with mechanics who were busy repairing and preparing the aircraft. An early night was the preferred option for many, while those not on alert would go to Attleborough for a pint or take the Liberty Run to Norwich. Bill Eagleson:

St. Mary's Church in Attleborough, where Bill Eagleson regularly attended services. Immediately to the right of the church is the Griffin Hotel, where *Corky's* crew often drank warm beer or Gaymer's Cyder. (Terry Woods)

Days not on missions were spent training, "soldiering," and surviving a bitter cold environment—scrounging coal was a priority. Blackouts were more like "brownouts" and pale yellow rays filled our off-base gathering spots; Red Cross, Norwich; Hippodrome Theatre, the Bell pub, and dating a wonderful English lass, for dancing at the Samson & Hercules ballroom. . . .

Those Liberty Runs to Norwich were maddening. Imagine flying in from a mission, tired, cold, change into Class A's. Dark hard ride in covered "six-bys." Sometimes very somber, searching out your young lady at the cattle market; sometimes consoling young friends whose aircrew man still had not or might not return. Then penetrating the yellowish haze at the Bell to share a pint or two of Gaymer's; thence to Samson & Hercules, for a few hours humanity—*I'll be seeing you*—*Will call soon*—*Night, love*—*Work tomorrow*—the convoy rumbles out, blue black-out lights through your countryside. Arriving at the base we listened for engine run-ups. Sometimes hopped on our bikes to check our ship at the hard-stand—*Bombs in the bay?*—*What word crew chief?*—"*Fuel Load 2600*"—*Damn!*—*Where? Let's do it: One mile plus, back to the Nissen*—*Lights out*—*Thoughts from today*—*A prayer for all hosts in the sky*—*and final shivers.*

CHAPTER THIRTEEN

The Battle of Brunswick

O
n Good Friday, thirty-six crews at Old Buckenham were alerted for a maximum effort mission scheduled for the following day, 8 April 1944.
Bill Eagleson:

> Sometimes we did know the day before and would suspect that we were going to fly, as I can remember in the evening going down to the aircraft and checking around. So I guess . . . we were on an alert, and if the CQ woke us that morning we knew we were going to fly.

After breakfast, some of the enlisted men from the Nortridge and Johnson crews walked together to the Technical Site. Bill LeRoy and Salvatore Giombarrese, an Italian American from Johnson's crew, walked together on their way to attend the gunners' and then radio operators' pre-mission briefing. Giombarrese was in good spirits that morning, chatting, joking, and singing. In the main briefing hall, the officers waited for their target to be announced, as Bill Eagleson recalls:

> Combat experience—it was a "sweating-out" process from beginning to end. It seems we would start by sweating-out the target. We would try to interpret the target by questioning the crew chief and the armorer on the type of load and the gas that was on the aircraft . . . [then] into the mission briefing where we'd sweat-out that curtain being drawn, to find the target for the mission.

With so many crews crowded into the briefing hall, clearly something big was on, such as a maximum effort to Germany. The target was revealed: the aircraft industry plants at Brunswick. Some of the airmen calmed themselves by reflecting that the 453rd Bomb Group had been to this German city twice before and the losses were minimal—one aircraft had failed to return from the 20 February mission, and a few others made it back with battle damage. Indeed, the Nortridge crew's first mission together was a raid on industrial areas in Brunswick on 15 March— of course the flak was distressing but at least the Luftwaffe had kept its distance. Parked beside the control tower at dispersal point number forty four, *Corky* was within easy walking distance of the squadron operations rooms and the briefing hall. Bill Eagleson:

B-24 flight deck. (Frank Kyle)

> Getting out to the airplane, checking the crew's stations, communications, oxygen, etc., and then we in *Corky* sort of all huddled together in our flying clothes up in the flight deck .

As the gunners checked their weapons, Jack Nortridge and George White conducted their extensive preflight checks. Then with ignition switches set to "Off," the ground crew pulled through the propellers by hand. At the flight engineer's position on the left side of the flight deck behind Jack's seat, Perry Roberson turned the fuel tank valves to the "On" position and George responded by switching on the main line and battery switches.

Perry switched off the generator switches and then stepped down onto the bomb bay catwalk and reached into the left side of the nose wheel compartment to start the auxiliary power unit (APU), a small gasoline-fueled engine, similar to a lawnmower engine and nicknamed the "put-put" after its distinctive sound.[1] Besides flooding the aircraft with fumes, the "put-put" ran a generator that powered the electric auxiliary hydraulic pump, providing hydraulic power to start the engines. George set the four ignition switches and master switch to "On" and

Jack checked that the parking brakes were applied. With a myriad of switches and dials to contend with, there was no time to dwell on the nerves associated with a mission to Germany.

> Instrument AC power switch: "On"
> Supercharger: "Off"
> Automatic pilot: "Off"
> Wing and prop de-icers: "Off"
> Intercooler shutters: "Open"
> Cowl flaps: "Open"
> Propellers set to high RPM
> Altimeters: "Set"
> Mixture controls set to "Idle Cut-Off"[2]

George checked the airplane fire extinguishers and then signaled through his side window to the fireguard standing by with a fire extinguisher. Engine number three was always started first as it drove the aircraft's main hydraulic pump. He then switched on the four electric fuel booster switches for pressure to prime the engines, held down the number three start energizer to "Accel," opened number three throttle approximately one third, and primed number three engine by pressing the corresponding primer switch intermittently. He then threw the meshing switch to "Crank" and with a whine the starter motor began to turn the propeller—just as the engine shuddered and fired into life the mixture control was set to "Auto-Lean," allowing fuel to the carburettor jets.

Engine number four was next, followed by number two and number one—the inboard engines were always started first so that in the event of an engine fire, the fireguard would not step into the arcs of the spinning outboard propellers. With all four engines warmed up, Jack released the brakes and steered *Corky* out of the dispersal point. Bill Eagleson:

> [During] the taxi . . . make certain the plane didn't run off the taxi strips, which sometimes they did. Looking at that taxiway I marvel at how old Nortridge and the others could pilot a plane in almost darkness—how they could taxi the aircraft out to the runway, usually on the outboard engines, and usually in the cold, cold mornings. That was quite a sight, quite an experience.

The crew squeezed onto the flight deck behind the cockpit as George monitored communication from the control tower on the command set, a small VHF radio with preset channels. At 1015 hours, a green flare was fired from the tower and the first of thirty-six aircraft turned into the main runway for takeoff. Bill Eagleson recalls:

> We were huddled on the flight deck . . . and Nortridge—Jack was noted for his takeoffs—he was at full power turning *in* to the runway! He really could fly that airplane.

Lt. Gus Johnson's crew in front of the B-24 *Stolen Moments* at Old Buckenham. Back row, left to right: Lt. Olson (navigator), Lt. Johnson (pilot), Lt. Bebenroth (bombardier), and Lt. Griffin (copilot, replacement for Lt. Stonebarger). Front row, left to right: Sgt. Becker (engineer/waist gunner), Sgt. Giombarrese (radio operator/waist gunner), Sgt. Cleary (tail turret gunner), Sgt. Eihausen (top turret gunner), and two unidentified replacement crew members. Becker and Giombarrese were both injured on the 8 April 1944 Brunswick mission. (Gloria Johnson)

Jack and George set the flaps and ran up the four Pratt & Whitney radial engines to a combined maximum of 4,800 horse power, before releasing the brakes.

> That was a good feeling to see Nortridge look back down at his crew on the flight deck, and sort of smile and then throw full power to it—and boy, we banged a right and off we went!

Above the deafening noise, Perry called out the increasing airspeed directly into Jack's right ear—Jack's eyes were focused on the shortening runway ahead as he kept the nose wheel firmly on the ground.

> He'd hold that plane down, all the way down the runway. He wanted plenty of air under the wings before he pulled back on the controls.

Reaching one hundred miles per hour, the end of the runway was in sight and together Jack and George pulled back at the controls with all their strength. *Corky* climbed away from Old Buck' almost reluctantly at first, weighed down with bombs, fuel, guns, ammunition, and men. To avoid potentially lethal drag to the rising aircraft, George raised the landing gear at the first opportunity. Often at this stage of the mission the bombers would be climbing through a treacherous overcast.

> Sweat-out the overcast, getting into your formation, finding *Wham Bam*, finding the flares. Finally the bomber stream all headed wherever we were going.

But conditions were clear on 8 April, and the 453rd Bomb Group formed into three sections over Old Buckenham. The Nortridge crew in *Corky* took their position in the 453rd Bomb Group's second section formation. Gus Johnson's crew took off in *Cee Gee II* borrowed from the 735th Squadron instead of the scheduled B-24 *Curly*, and found their position in the third section. Meanwhile, *Ken-O-Kay II* had failed to take off for the mission; *Old Butch* aborted early in the proceedings due to engine failure, and *Queenie* returned to base early with two runaway propellers.

Bill LeRoy was seated at his small table behind the flight deck on the starboard side of the aircraft. He had already turned on the IFF, which automatically transmitted a signal that allowed radar stations to establish the aircraft's identification: Friend or Foe (IFF). The IFF set would be switched off soon after crossing the English coastline. Voice communication was only used in emergencies and otherwise a policy of radio silence was strictly adhered to. Having been assigned specific frequencies to monitor, LeRoy listened in on his liaison set (a transmitter and receiver), keeping a log of all receptions.

The 2nd Combat Wing formation was assembled with the 445th Bomb Group in the lead position, the 389th as the high group and the 453rd as the low group. A radio compass mounted on the top of each aircraft received fixed radio checkpoints from the *Buncher* (medium frequency) and *Splasher* (direction finding) beacons on the ground. Radio operators communicating by Morse code could obtain a fix on their position if requested by the pilots or navigators.

On the way out, the 453rd Bomb Group formation was approximately one to one-and-a-half miles behind and 2,000 feet lower than the wing leaders, the 445th Bomb Group. The formation proceeded across the North Sea en route to Germany. Lt. William Bertrand experienced technical difficulties, jettisoned his bombs in the North Sea, and returned to base. Lt. Mark Neary lost two engines over the North Sea while transferring fuel and also returned. Thirty-one aircraft assigned to the 453rd Bomb Group continued towards Germany—in each heavily loaded Liberator it took all of the pilot and copilot's strength to keep in a tight formation. On the way to Brunswick the 453rd Bomb Group formation became spread out and it struggled to keep up with the lead group. In order to maintain a tight and compact group formation, vital for maximum defensive firepower, the leading 453rd aircraft slowed down to allow the stragglers to catch up. Gradually the group climbed to 18,000 feet en route to the target.

Half of the 8th Air Force's bombers dispatched that day were B-24s of the 2nd Bomb Division. This force of 350 Liberators crossed the coastline into enemy occupied Europe, flying directly into the sun. Weather conditions remained clear, providing ground visibility throughout the mission and allowing navigators to employ pilotage navigation. Looking out for landmarks through the side windows, Seymour Cohen was reassured to see dozens of friendly fighters that were tagging along for the bomber crews' protection.

When Bill Eagleson arrived at Santa Ana Air Force Base, California, for preflight training in January 1943, all the cadets received a welcoming letter from the base commander that referred to their facing the enemy. The letter included emotive remarks such as, "Our enemies are cruel, vicious, ingenious, trained and disciplined, and hard in the extreme." Bill Eagleson compares that letter with real combat experience:

> The combat flying was a strain and it was not fun. I guess that letter from Santa Ana, about us facing the enemy—at *that* time we were younger and I guess we were able to feel the need for our going to war and for the survival of our nation, and I really believe that we were ready to go to any extreme to accomplish whatever mission was laid on us.

In the United States during the early 1940s, the mass media and the Hollywood film industry had been significantly influential in determining what Americans understood about the Germans. But in combat, many of the American airmen gained an impression of the enemy they encountered that differed significantly from that view of the foe provided by the American media in its patriotic crusade.

On board the Liberators in the aerial battlefield high above Europe, the gunner's time was divided between extremes of mind-numbing boredom and sheer terror. And there were two types of terror to confront, two deadly enemies to encounter. Firstly there was the flak, four or five miles removed from the human lives of the gunners who fired it. The Liberator crews could only stare helplessly at the flak—random little clouds of black smoke in the distance that all too rapidly grew closer and more intense as the formation became immersed. The low-pitched rumble of the exploding flak shells was particularly unnerving, as one veteran recalls of flak, "When you can hear it, it is too close."[3]

The cessation of flak often coincided with the arrival of the other enemy—the Luftwaffe. But at least the American air gunners could respond to the fighter attacks by shooting back. The enemy fighters that fearlessly swept through the bomber formations provided an occasional blurred and fleeting glimpse of the pilot inside. Sometimes they would fly in so close that the American gunners could "see the whites of their eyes"—they would be staring the enemy right in the face and they didn't look all that different from themselves. Somehow they were just as young, dedicated, and humanly vulnerable, not to mention subject to patriotism and propaganda. Regrettably, it seems that the Luftwaffe fighter pilots were ignorant of, or had at least turned a blind eye to the reality of Hitler's "final solution" as six million Jews were murdered.

At the end of the war a Luftwaffe fighter pilot wrote: "Disgusted and indignant, the German fighting soldiers and officers turn away from those whose brutal war crimes and atrocities are now exposed. These criminals, whose activities were . . . restricted to the concentration camps and labor camps . . . have dishonored the name of Germany."[4]

In the spring of 1944, the 8th Air Force was trying to pound the Luftwaffe into submission. Nobody was convinced that the Allies had already achieved victory in the battle for air superiority. The Luftwaffe pilots were clearly skilled and courageous. Spinning upside down in inverted attacks from high above, they would descend upon the bombers from the blinding glare of the sun, before the American air gunners had even seen them. After attacking in a dive, they would then pull away and disappear within the blink of an eye. From the top turret Harvey Nielsen spent most of his time staring into the sun, waiting for fighters to emerge from the glare. When they did appear he could rotate the electrically operated turret at normal or high speed through a 360-degree field of fire to fend off the higher attacks. Although the top turret guns had interrupters to prevent damage to the vertical twin tail fins, it was possible to fire into the propeller arcs!

The pilots, navigators, and bombardiers objective was getting the bombs to the target. The air gunners' role was to keep the Luftwaffe at a distance—if they succeeded in shooting down or damaging enemy aircraft, this was considered to be a bonus. In reality, most aircrew gunners were not expert marksmen and, unskilled in deflection-shooting techniques, most relied on the "zone system" of aiming at the enemy aircraft and filling that "zone" of sky with bullets.[5]

On the way to Brunswick, the P-38 and P-47 fighter escort had so far been excellent and they became engaged in dogfights with the enemy in the distance, outside the flak barrage, but soon the little friends were outnumbered. Fifty miles before the Initial Point of the bomb run the flak eased.

Bill Eagleson:

> Flak usually came first. If it stopped we had to expect German fighters. They would sometimes wait outside of the "box barrage"—I remember the yellow nose Focke Wolves of Dummer Lake raising hell with us over Brunswick—early German fighters effective, well trained, fearless . . .

Lt. Joe DeJarnette's crew—all were killed on 8 April 1944 Brunswick mission. The B-24 *Blondes Away* was assigned to the Nortridge crew for missions on 1 April and 9 April 1944. (Frank Kyle)

Dummer Lake was not only a key landmark for navigators, but it was significant also for the concentration of Luftwaffe fighters stationed close to it. Suddenly waves of enemy fighters swept in towards the Liberators. Accounts varied—some crew members on the American bombers counted a total of twenty-five, others guessed seventy-five, some even estimated up to ninety FW190s and Me109s attacking the 453rd Group formation. In the chaos of the violent attacks, the Liberators' intercom systems often became blurred by distorted voices as gunners gave running commentaries of the attacks. Electrically operated nose, top, ball, and tail turrets rotated in all directions with their guns firing frantically to ward off the enemy.

From the first section of the 453's formation, Lt. Joe DeJarnette's aircraft, *Little Joe (Son of a Beach)*, was hit—the aircraft crashed at Salzwedel, Germany, killing all ten men on board. Lt. James Bingamen's ship, *Rooster,* crashed at Wessendorf, Germany; of the twelve men on board, eleven of them escaped death but were subsequently captured by the Germans. Lt. Fred Brady and his crew were also in trouble—their Liberator, *Lil' Eight Ball,* crashed at Elmendorf; six were killed and four survived to become prisoners of war.

Stationed in the Emerson power turret in the nose of *Corky,* Pete Veilleux defended his crew with the twin machine guns, as waves of twelve to twenty enemy aircraft swept through the second section formation in head-on attacks. He recalls:

> I think Brunswick was the most memorable mission. . . . Well that
> was a tough one. I can see the German pilot now, coming in
> through the formation and giving me the finger. . . . I can see him
> giving me a great big grin and giving me the finger on the way by!

While over enemy territory, radio operator Bill LeRoy and flight engineer Perry Roberson spent most of their time standing up, back to back, at the gun positions in the waist section of the aircraft as they tried to remain balanced in the often erratically moving aircraft. When they fired their guns in response to enemy attacks, spent .50 caliber brass cartridges piled up around their feet. Following the waves of head-on attacks, the enemy fighters turned to make individual attacks from the rear and *Corky*'s Chinese American gunner, Lim Wing Jeong, responded from the tail turret. As the enemy dived away under the aircraft, Joe DeMay fought back from the ball turret—his left foot on the range control enabling him to frame the enemy fighters with his optical gun sight. But Joe needed plenty of warning from Jeong, LeRoy, and Roberson, since the gun barrels and ammunition feed restricted his peripheral vision. Other attacks came in from below, firing directly towards the undersides of the Liberators.

Meanwhile, nose turret gunners witnessed twelve FW190s attacking with a barrage of rockets from a distance of over two thousand yards, before pressing home their attacks with 20mm cannon fire. Directly to the left of *Corky*, Lt. Robert Swigert's ship (42–11076) was hit and went down in flames. The Liberator crashed at Tylsen; nine were killed and one survivor became a prisoner of war.

In the third section of the 453rd Bomb Group formation, Lt. Jack Dixon's flak-damaged aircraft (41–29571) was in trouble—easy prey for the enemy fighters that went in to attack. The Liberator crashed at Uelzen, Germany; three were killed and seven survivors were later reported to be prisoners of war. Meanwhile, Lt. Jay Wells's aircraft (42–64453) was knocked from the formation. It crashed at Henningen, Germany; there was just one survivor from the ten-man crew.

Flying at the rear of formation were good friends of *Corky*'s crew—Gus Johnson's crew (in *Cee Gee II*) and Lt. August "Gus" Bergman's crew (in 42–64464). Lt. Gus Bergman's enlisted men lived in the hut next door to the one shared by the enlisted men from the Nortridge and Johnson crews. Bergman's radio operator, Sgt. Vince "Sparks" Pale from Philadelphia, had celebrated his twenty-first birthday on the previous day; he had trained in radio school with Bill LeRoy.

On the Brunswick mission, Bergman's crew had a newly assigned navigator, Lt. Richard Crown, as 2nd Lt. Bill Myre had been promoted to First Lieutenant two days previously and was now navigating the lead

Lt. August "Gus" Bergman's crew. Back row, left to right: Sgt. Dick (flight engineer/waist gunner), Sgt. Whitehurst (tail gunner), Sgt. Cullinan (waist gunner), Sgt. Cole (nose turret gunner), Sgt. Pale (radio operator), and Sgt. Fisher (ball turret gunner). Front row, left to right: Lt. Myre (navigator), Lt. Bergman (pilot), Lt. Durborow (copilot), and Lt. Goff (bombardier). Myre was transferred to another crew prior to the Brunswick mission on which this crew was shot down; Pale was the only survivor. (John P. Durborow)

ship to Brunswick. For Bill Myre, it was a fortunate promotion, but for Richard Crown, a fateful crew assignment. Vince Pale never even met the newly assigned navigator—Vince didn't even know what Lt. Crown looked like, for when the officers climbed aboard for the mission, the gunners were attending to their guns and ammunition and Vince was checking his radio equipment.

To their frustration, Bergman's crew witnessed about nine fighters appear off the port side but out of range of their .50 caliber guns. At first the gunners fired at the enemy only to see their tracers arcing downwards. It seemed like the enemy fighters were taking their time, pacing along, picking out their targets, knowing the .50 calibers couldn't reach them. Then they turned and attacked. From the flight deck of their ship, Gus Bergman, copilot John Durborow, and radio operator Vince Pale saw a B-24 ahead of them get hit by a rocket. Bergman and Durborow both exclaimed, "Look at that!" and then within thirty seconds it was their turn—a rocket from a German fighter made a direct hit on Bergman's Liberator, blowing a large hole in the underside of the ship.

A damaged oxygen supply in the back of the plane created a momentary fireball that swept through the fuselage in seconds and then it was extinguished when the oxygen was consumed, leaving Vince Pale with burns to the left side of his face. Then another fighter attacked with 20mm cannon fire—strafing the cockpit, shattering glass, piercing metal, and hitting Bergman and Durborow in their legs. Vince Pale witnessed the whole bloody episode from inches away, while patting his clothes to dampen the flames. The pilots lost control and the Liberator went into a spin—Vince was pinned to the wall by the centrifugal force, certain that he was about to die!

Miraculously, the injured pilots somehow pulled the plane out of the spin and ordered the crew to bail out. Vince Pale looked up and saw the top turret gunner unbuckling himself from his seat, and Vince was certain that the gunner was right behind him as he dived through the jagged hole in the floor that had been created by the rocket. Vince pulled the ripcord and drifted earthwards. On his way down he saw five or six other parachutes, perhaps from other crews, and then heard the Liberator explode when it hit the ground at Sistedt. The rest of his crew perished—but somehow Vince Pale survived, albeit with injuries. He was captured and became a prisoner of war. For the copilot's family, it was the first of two such tragedies—less than four months later, John Durborow's brother was killed while flying as a navigator on a B-17 from Thorpe Abbotts, Norfolk.

On board *Cee Gee II*, Gus Johnson's waist gunners, radio operator Salvatore Giombarrese and flight engineer Peter Becker both were injured by enemy fire. Giombarrese, who had been in such a carefree mood that morning, was badly wounded. Becker was shot in his right hand by a 20mm shell but was otherwise okay; he pulled off his glove and stuck his hand out the waist window to freeze his hand, allowing the blood to congeal. Twenty-four Old Buck' Liberators continued towards Brunswick as gunners defended their ships, navigators continued plotting and calculating their course, and pilots took evasive action.

Bill Eagleson:

> The physical strain of flying was on the pilot and copilot, particularly flying in tight formations under fighter attack, calling out fighters and trying to nose-in to the fighters with the rest of the formation; and trying to avoid mid-air collisions—called for a lot of skill, and these guys were really competent in handling that plane. I can't say enough for my pilot.

Just before the IP and amid fighter attacks, the 453rd had made a sharp right turn to close the gap on the rest of the Wing but now seemed to be overtaking the 445th and 389th Bomb Groups. Subsequently, the three sections of the 453rd Group's formation became dispersed—the second section flying high right position (including

8 April 1944. Brunswick Mission. 453rd Bomb Group formation.

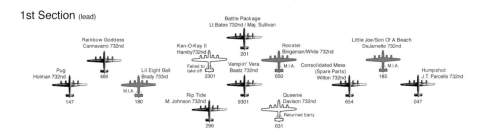

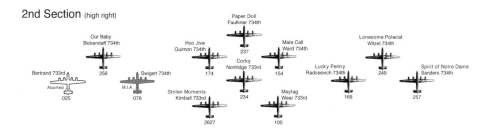

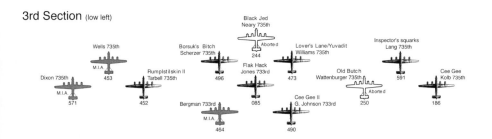

Lt. Hamby did not take off for the mission; Lt. Davison returned to base early; Lt. Bertrand, Lt. Neary, and Lt. Wattenburger aborted the mission. Seven of the 453rd Bomb Group's aircraft were shot down by enemy fighters over Germany.

Corky) actually overtook the first section. But Lt. Bickerstaff from the "second" section had dropped back to the "first" section during the approach to the target. The third section flying low-left became especially scattered—Lt. Jones and Lt. Kolb ended up in the now-leading "second" section over the target. Meanwhile Lt. Tarbell, Lt. Lang, and Lt. Williams found themselves in the relegated "first" section over target. *Corky*'s bombardier had a front-row seat of the view ahead:

> If you were under fighter attack you looked up ahead and you
> could see the barrage flak and you knew that the fighters weren't
> going to bother you when you were flying through that stuff.

Close to the target the fighters disappeared, but the tension remained. The box barrage flak over Brunswick was extremely dense
while the tracking flak seemed to be very accurately sighted.

> And now you're sweating out barrage flak into the target, and so it
> went. And along with that you're sweating out the survival of your
> crew—*How are they doing? How's the oxygen? How are the elements treating
> them? How is everybody holding up?* It seemed to be a constant form of
> pressure.

The disjointed group formation continued its attempt at a straight
and level bomb run at 18,000 feet. A slight ground haze and very ineffective smoke screen partly obscured the target although visibility was
otherwise exceptionally good. From the leading "second" section of the
formation, Bill dropped *Corky*'s bomb load "on the leader" at 1415
hours. Jack and George immediately took extreme evasive action—at
21,700 feet the 389th Bomb Group Liberators were almost directly overhead and their bombs were falling through the 453rd Bomb Group formation! From the tail turret, Jeong could see the trail of bombs and
clouds of smoke bellowing from the vicinity of the aircraft factory.

Maintaining an altitude of 18,000 feet, the 453rd Bomb Group's survivors headed for home. Over the North Sea they descended to 5,000
feet and the crews were able to take off their oxygen masks and relax a
little, although the pilots, navigators, radio operators, and flight engineers still had work to do. Eventually Old Buck' came into view, distinguished from the surrounding bases by the windmill at Carleton Rode.

Gus Johnson's crew were in trouble. Peter Becker, one of two injured
crew members on board, didn't let the 20mm cannon shell injury to his
right hand distract him from his duties as flight engineer. When the nose
wheel on *Cee Gee II* could not be lowered hydraulically, Becker set about
cranking the wheel down by hand—for this he was to be rewarded the
Silver Star. *Cee Gee II* landed safely and all returnees were back on the
ground by five o'clock. *Corky*'s flying time that day was five hours and
fifty-nine minutes.

Ambulances rushed out to gather the casualties who were brought
home in battle-damaged Liberators. Peter Becker and Salvatore Giombarrese were rushed several miles to the 231st Station Hospital at Mor-
ley Hall near Wymondham, where they were treated for their injuries.
Becker spent several days in hospital and was soon back at Old Buck'
and flying missions again. However, Giombarrese was injured so badly
on that mission that he was never seen again by his friends at Old Buck'.
The memory of Giombarrese's high spirits on the morning of 8 April
1944 would remain with Bill LeRoy forever.

In all, 190 aircraft, including those of the 453rd Bomb Group, dropped their bombs over Brunswick's aviation factory with what were officially regarded as "excellent" bombing results. Over one hundred other Liberators sought targets of opportunity. But the battle of Brunswick had cost the B-24 groups dearly. Besides the seven aircraft and seven crews that failed to return to Old Buck' that day, the 93rd Bomb Group at Hardwick and the 458th at Horsham St. Faith each lost one aircraft; the 446th at Bungay lost two; the 392nd at Wendling lost two plus a third which crashed at the Norfolk coast; the 466th at Attlebridge lost six; and the 44th at Shipdham lost a staggering eleven aircraft.

Saturday 8 April was a day that the crews of the 453rd would not forget and they came to fear Brunswick, probably more than any other target. Of those missing in action that day, twenty-five men were later reported to be prisoners of war and forty-seven were dead. Some ships had returned with dead or injured on board. To date these were the 453rd Bomb Group's heaviest losses for a single raid. There were more than seventy-four empty beds in the huts at Old Buckenham that night.

O n Easter Sunday, crews were awakened again for another mission to Germany, this time to bomb an airfield and aircraft factory at Tutow. *Corky* was undergoing repairs of damage caused by flak and fighters over Brunswick, and so the Nortridge crew were for the second time assigned to fly *Blondes Away*. However, Jack and George battled with supercharger problems and after rapidly losing airspeed were forced to return early. They landed at the first base they could find—Rackheath, near Norwich, after more than five hours flying time. Having turned back before reaching the enemy coast, *Blondes Away* would not be classed as "dispatched" and the crew knew that they would not be credited for the mission. Jack Nortridge filled out the required Form-1, detailing the aircraft's mechanical problems and the crew waited for a ride back to Old Buck'.

Meanwhile, many others aborted the mission due to weather interference. Those that continued were attacked by as many as thirty Me109s— thankfully, the German pilots seemed to be inexperienced, although the rudder cables on one B-24 were shot out, forcing the crew to return to base early. Lt. Keith Hamby and Lt. Mark Neary's ships were seen to turn off and head north; later these crews were reported safe in Sweden. Eleven of the 453rd's aircraft bombed Tutow where they encountered meager flak response and were escorted home by P-38 Lightnings.

On Monday 10 April, the 453rd Bomb Group briefed twenty-six crews for a mission to an airfield at Tours in central France. In their repaired *Burgundy Bomber*, the Nortridge crew left Old Buck' just after seven o'clock that morning. The 453rd led the 2nd Combat Wing, flak was encountered upon reaching enemy territory, cloud became solid, and the airfield at Tours was not visible. The group proceeded to the secondary target, the airfield at Bricy located seven miles northeast of

Orleans. Visibility there was good and most of the aircraft dropped their bombs on this airfield while others reportedly bombed the hangar area at Romorantin airfield. Friendly fighter cover was excellent; however, crews witnessed one 389th Bomb Group ship being shot down by enemy fighters. Meager flak was encountered on withdrawal from the target areas. *Corky* landed back at Old Buck' after a flight lasting two minutes short of six hours.

Two days later the 453rd Bomb Group was assigned Zwickau, Germany, as its target. Twenty-six crews were briefed for a midmorning takeoff in light winds with restricted visibility at 20,000 feet. The Nortridge crew was forced to abort the mission when two engines began overheating and the couplings were blown. *Corky* landed at Old Buck' after a two-hour flight. The rest of the group became dispersed in cloud over the North Sea when another formation of B-24s flew directly through the 453rd Bomb Group's formation. The mission was abandoned due to unfavorable weather, and the group returned to base.

The 8th Air Force statisticians measured the success of bombing missions in terms of bombing results—the accuracy and the effectiveness of the bombing raids regardless of aircraft losses and aircrew attrition. It was believed that accurate bombing results meant winning the war; aircrew casualties were seen as inevitable. However, achieving what was regarded as effective bombing results depended upon the airmen, their training, their abilities and morale. Besides the obvious dangers of injury from enemy action, long hours at high altitude in subzero temperatures were physically and mentally challenging for the aircrews. They relied heavy flying clothing, electrically heated suits and oxygen systems and were highly susceptible to frostbite and anoxia, as well as the effects of low air pressure such as aeroembolism, otherwise known as "the bends." They also had to deal with constant noise and aircraft vibration. All of these combined factors intensified the mental stresses of combat exposure, leaving the airman vulnerable to physical and emotional exhaustion—nervous breakdowns were not uncommon.

The flight surgeons at each base monitored the well being of the aircrews, and they recognized the pressures of combat conditions. One of the responsibilities of the flight surgeon was to prescribe aircrews periods of relaxation on rest leave at one of the dozen or so rest homes in the United Kingdom. Among aircrews, a flyer suffering with the severe symptoms of combat fatigue was referred to as being "flak happy." Subsequently the rest homes became known as "flak houses" or "flak farms." Some aircrews were routinely given up to seven days rest leave partway through their combat tours as a preventative measure. The "flak houses" were mostly old manor houses, mansions, or hotels in the countryside and were staffed by Red Cross workers who provided varying leisure pursuits and an atmosphere of "rest and recreation." The

Nortridge crew were given five such days of R&R in April and they adjourned to the Palace Hotel in Southport, Lancashire, as Perry Roberson recalls:

> Partway through our missions, we got a rest leave to a resort near Liverpool. This was a welcome break from missions every three to four days.

Bill Eagleson:

> I remember a large red brick hotel building that we stayed in and behind that was an amusement park—and we had a hell of a time riding the "dodgems" as a crew. It was fun!

When the crew returned to Old Buckenham they found that they had missed the opening of the base Aero Club on 14 April, which offered the enlisted men facilities on a par with those provided in the Officers' Club. The official opening had been a celebration enjoyed by many of the enlisted men along with some of the top brass at Old Buckenham and from the 2nd Combat Wing headquarters. Among those present at the party was Maj. James Stewart, who on the previous day had led the 453rd to Germany on his first mission with the group.

On Tuesday 18 April the Nortridge crew got back to work when *Corky* and twenty-five other aircraft departed Old Buckenham for a mission to Germany. Two hundred and seventy-five aircraft of the 2nd Bomb Division were assigned one of two primary targets in Germany, both aviation industry plants. With half the division assigned the target of Brandenburg, the 453rd Bomb Group headed for the Heinkel aircraft parts plant at Rathenenow, located less than fifty miles west of Berlin. Weather and visibility were excellent, although the Luftwaffe failed to make much of a presence. Flak too was meager, and the 453rd bombed the Heinkel plant as briefed. All aircraft returned safely. *Corky* landed after seven hours and twenty-eight minutes flying time.

CHAPTER FOURTEEN

"Our Prayers That Night Were Shared"

Saturday 22 April 1944 became a disastrous day for the 2nd Bomb
Division. Forty-four years to the day later, Bill Eagleson put pen
to paper to record his memories of his ninth combat mission:

> According to my notes, 22nd April was not a happy day for
> "Libs"—we went to Hamm on a spring day—that morning no
> alert. We slept late, sat behind the Nissen huts, enjoying—then a
> mission alert and briefing call. The bikes roared to Operations.
> Everyone thought: *Late take-off—"milk run"; let's get this one in!* We
> were going to fly rested, in full daylight.

At the mission briefing a wave of silence washed over the room as
the briefing officer entered and walked to the front of the hall. Faces
stared at the curtain that concealed today's target—the curtain was
drawn and revealed colored ribbons pinned to a map of Europe.
Aghast, all eyes followed the blood-red ribbons leading into Germany to
the target—the marshaling yards at Hamm!

> When the target came up, experienced faces expressed
> wonderment—the Ruhr Valley with diminishing daylight . . . the
> irony of that mission was, we couldn't understand what we were
> doing at three o'clock waiting for a briefing, and then we figured,
> this is gonna be a *Noball*, a "milk run"—just over the channel and
> then we'll be back. And then we got to the briefing room, we
> looked at that red line that took us right over the Ruhr Valley and
> I said "Oh . . . !"

Anticipating the imminent Allied invasion of Europe, the 8th
Air Force was eager to take advantage of every opportunity to destroy
the German transportation and communications systems. When bad
weather over the continent cleared during the day of 22 April the 8th's
commanders figured that a late mission would catch the Germans off
guard. Ironically, it was the American aircrews who were most surprised by the late mission and, as it turned out, it was the Luftwaffe
who achieved the upper hand in surprise tactics that day. The raid on
Hamm was set to be a "maximum effort" involving over eight hundred
American bombers and the participation of more than eight thousand
American flying personnel. Following the B-17s of the 3rd and 1st Bomb

Divisions, the eleven B-24 Bomb Groups of the 2nd Bomb Division were to fly in four combat wing formations at the rear of the huge bomber force.

At mission briefing, reconnaissance photographs of the target area were projected onto a screen and the crews were briefed on the significance of the target: as the largest rail junction in Germany, the marshaling yards at Hamm provided a major route of rail traffic between the industries of the Ruhr Valley and northern Germany. Each day ten thousand wagons rolled through Hamm, making it one of the busiest, most vital, and, at a scale of three miles in length, the largest rail junction in Germany. The mission scheduled for 22 April was to be the first major American raid on Hamm.

Navigators noted escort fighter rendezvous times and locations. Most of the 8th's fighter groups would be airborne to escort the bombers as well as conducting strafing sweeps of Luftwaffe airfields. A few squadrons of RAF fighters were also expected to participate in the escort duties. However, the little friends would not be able to save the bombers from the flak that was expected in the Ruhr Valley, one of the most heavily defended regions of Germany often referred to as "flak alley." Briefing information covered enemy defenses and then "Questions?" and "Time hack"—all airmen synchronized their watches and filed out of the briefing hall.

Out on the field, as usual *Corky* was at dispersal point forty-four. Lt. Elmer Crockett's crew boarded the *Golden Gaboon* at forty-five and Lt. Gus Johnson's crew found their assigned aircraft *Stolen Moments* parked at thirty-seven. A green flare was fired from the control tower and the pilots started their engines and taxied out at 1610 hours. After a second green flare at 1625, one by one the bombers began to roll along the runway at Old Buck' just thirty seconds apart, and in turn each became airborne. All twenty-six aircraft had departed Old Buck' by 1646.

The 453rd Bomb Group formed over the base behind their assembly ship *Wham Bam* from which green flares were fired at 3,000 feet. The 734th and 735th Squadrons were assigned the first section; the 732nd and 733rd Squadrons composed the second section where *Corky* took up position. The second section was to remain high-right of the first section until reaching the English coast. The 453rd climbed to 15,000 feet for combat wing assembly. Meanwhile the 445th Bomb Group formed to green and red flares over Tibenham before climbing to 14,000 feet, and the 389th Bomb Group formed to red flares over Hethel before climbing to 13,000.

These three groups then assembled into the 2nd Combat Wing formation over *Buncher 6*, the radio beacon at Hethel. The 453rd flew as two high-right sections above the 445th, whose lead aircraft, piloted by Col. Robert Terrill, was in turn to lead the 2nd Combat Wing and the entire 2nd Bomb Division of almost three hundred airborne B-24s. As the 2nd Wing crossed the coastline at Lowestoft at 15,000 feet, the 453rd Group's second section (including *Corky*) dropped back to the high-right position above the 389th Bomb Group. The 2nd Combat Wing formation was now in shape and the rest of the division followed. Reaching the Dutch coastline the 453rd's second section trailed the first section by approximately one-and-a-half miles. Lt. Louis Scherzer's aircraft began leaking oil from the number three engine and returned to base; Lt. Elmer Crockett also returned to base after the number one engine on the *Golden Gaboon* cut out. Meanwhile, as Bill Eagleson remembers:

> Missions did not leave time for thought about what was coming next. Early flak, usually at the coast, very accurate tracking, evasive action difficult for tight formation—*Good* navigation was the key. Our S-2 [Intelligence] gave us enemy flak installations. It was important to avoid warships and large towns—military installations, unless targeted.

The briefed course should have taken the Liberators north of the anti-aircraft defenses at Amsterdam before commencing a consistent heading to the target area. However, the 2nd Wing had crossed the enemy coastline south of the briefed course and later the navigational error was exaggerated with the failure of the radar and the flux-gate compass on board the lead ship, piloted by Col. Terrill. As this was the 2nd Bomb Division's lead ship it carried two navigators, and they allegedly disagreed over their position at this point of the mission.

The 2nd Wing erroneously turned south. Flying off course, Terrill's ship missed the correct IP of the bomb run and led the 453rd and 389th Bomb Groups and the 14th Combat Wing formation over the Ruhr Valley, notorious for its fierce anti-aircraft defenses. Four Liberators were lost to flak while many others sustained serious damage. The 14th wing's lead navigator calculated that a 300 mph groundspeed had carried them beyond their wing's IP and directed the 14th Wing on an approach to Hamm from the west. Meanwhile the 20th and 96th Wings had recognized the navigational errors in the formations ahead and escaped the Ruhr Valley by continuing along an approximation of the briefed course to Hamm.

The 2nd Combat Wing (including *Corky*) continued to run the gauntlet over the valley of death, the Ruhr Valley. The navigation error was realized but the wing was already thirty miles off course. Different formations of the 2nd Bomb Division were scattered far and wide, making it impossible for the little friends to concentrate their escort duties.

> That was a difficult mission. I do not recall the navigational error. . . . I do not remember becoming that scattered—of course we *were* under fighter attack, we were under flak attack and, I think we [the 453rd] were all happy to be going in the same directions in a tight formation. . . . Flak—tracking—barrage. Vicious. Old *Corky* caught the measles.

With both hands on the controls and using all of his strength to maintain formation, Jack found his visibility impaired by his essential but uncomfortable steel helmet, which was sliding forwards over his eyes. Bill Eagleson was up on the flight deck between the pilots, his usual position on missions before and after the bomb run, and so Jack asked Bill to adjust his steel helmet for him. Bill joked, "Adjust your own damned helmet," before pulling at the back of Jack's helmet to maximize the pilot's vision. Seconds later a piece of shrapnel from a flak burst ripped into the flight deck, hitting Jack's steel helmet, spinning it round on his head, slicing a hole in the sleeve of George's flying jacket sleeve, and cutting the cord of his electrically heated flying suit. It narrowly missed Bill's oxygen mask hose and Jack's face. It was a close call for Jack, George, and Bill:

> We joked regarding my possible loss of hand while holding his helmet—the minute the helmet spun I had just taken my gloved hand off the helmet.

Perry Roberson:

> It was the most flak I saw on any mission—"the black clouds of smoke were thick enough to walk on," is the usual expression, and on that one you could almost believe it.

The 2nd Wing somehow split into two formations when the 445th Bomb Group and the first section of the 453rd made a left turn and headed in a northeasterly direction towards Hamm via Dusseldorf. Meanwhile, the 389th led the second section of the 453rd (including *Corky*) to Hamm by making a right turn and circling back into the course of the briefed route. But then the 389th's lead ship was hit and badly damaged with one engine on fire. Most of the crew bailed out while four men remained on board and continued to lead the 389th and half of the 453rd towards Hamm—eventually the 389th's lead ship fell from the formation.

The confusion and chaos continued as different formations of B-24s approached the target at Hamm simultaneously from different headings. Most of the 20th Wing managed to bomb Hamm with what were regarded as "reasonable" results but the 96th Wing approached the target on a 360-degree heading (rather than the 136-degree briefed heading) and ended up on a collision course with the 445th Group and the first section of the 453rd Old Buckenham Liberators. To avoid disaster the 445th turned away from Hamm and followed the Rhine to the secondary target, the marshaling yards at Koblenz.

Subsequently not only did the 453rd Bomb Group's first section become detached from the lead group, but four aircraft from the second section (including *Corky*) had at some point joined them. These aircraft bombed Hamm at 1940 hours. The sun was beginning to set and not much could be seen of the ground.

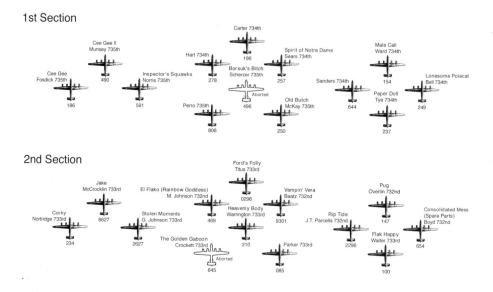

22 April 1944. Hamm Mission. 453rd Bomb Group formation during assembly.

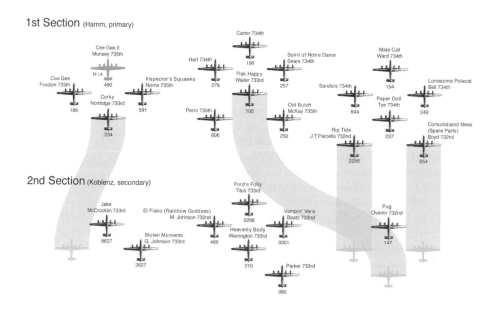

22 April 1944. Hamm Mission. 453rd Bomb Group formations over targets.

The railroad marshaling yards at Hamm, Germany, under attack on 22 April 1944. (USAAF via John Archer)

Meanwhile, following their full circle turn from the Ruhr Valley defenses, the 389th Bomb Group and what was left of the 453rd's second section were now on their straight and level bomb run. Gus Johnson's crew in *Stolen Moments* remained in their briefed position, high-right of the 389th Bomb Group's formation. One minute from the bomb drop, the 389th's troubled lead aircraft with a burning engine and remaining four-man crew slipped out of the formation. Another 389th aircraft took over the lead position, and seconds later, "bombs away"—the 389th Group dropped their bombs on Hamm's marshaling yards on their leader's sighting.

However, the 453rd Group's second section found that their sights were focused on B-24s of the 389th flying below them and so they held their bombs and instead attacked Koblenz, at 2008 hours. The Liberators rallied and picked up speed for the return flight. Somewhere along the way *Corky* and *Stolen Moments* were reunited as Bill Eagleson recalls, and as for the flak:

> It just never stopped until after "bombs away." It seemed we were pretty well scattered. We joined up with B-24 *Stinky [Stolen Moments]*, Pilot Gus Johnson. . . . [1]

Pete Veilleux remembers an aircraft in trouble over Hamm:

> I felt pretty bad for a guy—this guy was flying high-right, it seemed
> like he was from another outfit. This B-24 was flying high-right and
> the airplane got a fire and the guy bailed out . . . the parachute
> blossomed, and just the minute the parachute opened, the fire
> went out on the airplane and they went on back to England.

As the Hamm mission unfolded and the returning Liberators flew
home into headwinds and the setting sun, one thing became clear—the
restful springtime morning enjoyed by the crews at Old Buckenham
that day was not such a blessing. Flak was encountered as the formations approached the Belgian coastline. The Liberators began to lose altitude over the North Sea and the crews removed oxygen masks and disconnected heated suits.

As daylight dissolved into dusk the Americans looked ahead to low-
hanging clouds above England. They were all too aware of their inexperience in night flying, and with so many aircraft in formation they
were forced to fly home with their navigation lights switched on. *Corky*
and *Stolen Moments* remained together across the North Sea and without
expectation the crews began to relax, as Bill Eagleson recalls:

> *Corky* survived the North Sea crossing—we enjoyed a smoke, shud-
> dered at twilight's last gleaming—then it started all over again.

The Germans had attempted to take advantage of the twilight. A
force of aircraft was dispatched from airfields along the French coast
and the Luftwaffe followed the Americans back to England. Bill Eagleson looked out at the tracer bullets streaming through the darkness from
the tail turret of *Stolen Moments:*

> What a ride home. Below it was darkening and enemy fighters
> were hitting us from six o'clock-low. Tracers like laser beams rose
> from darkness. Our gunners could only fire when fired at—Sgt.
> Cleary on *Stinky [Stolen Moments]* burned out everything—we were
> tucked in so close I could read his dog tags. . . . He had a solid
> stream of fifty-calibers going out of those two guns. . . . All the ac-
> tion was from the waist and tail guns.

Perry Roberson was at the right waist gun position on *Corky:*

> When we were coming back in, it was getting dark, and these fight-
> ers followed us in—and Jeong was giving it to them with the tail
> turret, and I was shooting at them whenever I could, whenever I
> thought I saw one of them.

Lt. James Munsey of the 735th Squadron was flying back to Old
Buckenham in *Cee Gee II* (a name derived from the initials of his three-
year-old daughter Carole Geane). Fifteen miles from the English coast,
a JU-88 made just one frantic, but devastating pass on the Liberator. As

cannon fire struck the tail of *Cee Gee II* the tail gunner was blasted from his turret and thrown into the aircraft (he survived as a result of having left the turret doors open). One of the waist gunners was knocked unconscious, or had been killed, but nobody was sure which so in the hope that he was still alive, two crew members attached a parachute to his harness and opened the escape hatch to throw him out of the doomed

Back from the Pas de Calais on 20 April 1944. Lt. James Munsey (left) inspects the battle damage to B-24 *Queenie*. On that day, Munsey had flown as an instructor pilot with Lt. Ed Perro's crew, a new crew on their first mission—tragically, the tail gunner, Sgt. Oren Dierdorf, was decapitated. Two hundred flak holes were counted on the aircraft. Listening to the account of the mission is group CO Col. Ramsay Potts (second from the left). The waist gunner, Sgt. Walter Thomas (second from the right), was killed a few weeks later; James Munsey had only two more days to live. (Estate of Col. Frank Russell Webster, courtesy Mark Forlow)

aircraft; but just then the two men were blown out of the open hatch, while a wall of fire swept through the bomb bay.

The number-two engine was in flames, the hydraulic system was shot out, and the radio operator had been blinded. With fire taking hold of the cockpit, Lt. Munsey and his copilot Lt. Robert Crall held the Liberator long enough for others to escape but at landfall the wing tanks ignited and the aircraft exploded and crashed in coastal marshland at Reydon, Suffolk. Five of the ten-man crew escaped death—James Munsey was posthumously awarded the Distinguished Service Cross.

At the Norfolk coastline, British anti-aircraft fire was thrown up among the American and German aircraft as the chaos and panic escalated both in the air and on the ground. One B-24 returning to Horsham St. Faith became the victim of anti-aircraft fire over the city of Norwich. The Luftwaffe shot down several more Liberators as the Americans tried to find their bases in darkness. Meanwhile, RAF fighters arrived to participate in the chaos.

Bill Eagleson:

> Technicolor flak, calls for IFF [Identification Friend or Foe], confusion, enemy aircraft all the way to Old Buck'. . . . All hell broke loose because we had the German fighters, we had the British anti-aircraft opening up, and we also had our own planes firing at excess. . . . It was harassing and rather scary. . . . Everybody was shooting at everybody else. Fireworks in the sky!

When the Liberators tried to land at their Norfolk bases the Luftwaffe began strafe attacks at targets on the ground. At Rackheath two B-24s were shot down while attempting landing approaches and a third was attacked as it touched down on the tarmac; another B-24 that was undergoing repairs on a floodlit hardstand was hit. At Seething there was a pileup on the main runway involving five aircraft as they came in to land—the beacon of wrecked Liberators burned through the night. Unable to find a blacked-out Old Buckenham, Lt. Fred Parker and Lt. William "Mac" McCrocklin both managed to get safely on the ground at Seething. Lt. James Workman, the copilot on McCrocklin's crew commented in his flight log that, "the sky was a madhouse," and wrote the following in his diary:

> It started getting good and dark as we left Belgium, on coast. I could look out the window and see tracers from fighters attacking us, rockets, flak, flares, and goodness knows what else, all at one time, thought my time was up. God took care of us. . . . Lost more over England than over enemy territory. It was awful, I'm several years older now.

Old Buck' was mostly in total darkness to avoid enemy attack; momentarily the runway lights would be switched on and then off again. Radio operators called out to "Flame Leap," the call sign for the 453rd Bomb Group's control tower at Old Buck', for landing instructions. As

the 453rd Bomb Group circled in the landing pattern and attempted to
land, the German fighter attacks continued. When the lights came on at
Tibenham, three Liberators from the 453rd hopped over to the neighboring base. American, British, and German aircraft—everything in
the sky over Old Buckenham encountered fire from the defense guns on
the ground. Bombs that had been stuck in the bomb bay of one B-24
since Hamm eventually fell free, landing on Old Buckenham's main
runway without exploding.

> It did take us a while to find Old Buck' in the dark, and the runway
> lights to my recollection were going on and off as things were
> pretty hectic on the ground also . . . the landing lights were turned
> out while we were in the [landing] pattern . . . two .50 caliber ma-
> chine guns were active on the runway and also one unexploded
> armed bomb was on a runway. . . . Blinking field lights—pattern
> confusion—landing lights brought reaction from our Me109
> escort—We brought some of the war back with us.

At 2306 hours *Corky* landed safely at Old Buckenham, six hours and
twenty minutes since takeoff. The last crew to get back on the ground at
Old Buck' was Gus Johnson's crew in *Stolen Moments* who landed at 2327.
The next morning the Nortridge crew looked over *Corky* to assess the
damage and realized how lucky they were.

Perry Roberson:

> On examination in daylight we found that a 20mm shell had hit
> the rear edge of one aileron and just frayed it out, the tip of the
> aileron set off the shell causing minor damage.

Bill Eagleson:

> I remember very vividly the Hamm mission and the escort we
> had home by German fighters. That was a real sweat-out mis-
> sion, probably had a more lasting effect on my memory than any
> mission that we flew. . . . The crews were not happy over this mis-
> sion . . . I would like to know how they ever planned a mission to
> Hamm down the Ruhr Valley, with a take off in late afternoon. It
> was disappointing enough to get to the briefing room before the
> mission to learn that we *weren't* in for a "milk run," that we *were* in
> for a trip down the Ruhr Valley and we *were not* prepared nor
> trained for night flying. . . . It was rough!
>   The RAF drew our admiration for their night-flying skills and
> techniques—to my knowledge henceforth we stayed with our
> training and mass night missions were not attempted.

Considering the ferocity of the flak fire and the nature of the Luftwaffe attacks, the 453rd Bomb Group's losses might easily have been
much greater. The 2nd Bomb Division began to count the cost of the
mission. Besides the seven aircraft lost over Europe and the North
Sea, fourteen Liberators were either shot down over Norfolk or had

crash-landed at their bases as a result of enemy action and ground fire. Another fifty-nine B-24s returned to Norfolk with battle damage. Of the 2nd Bomb Division's personnel, sixty-four were missing, twenty-eight were wounded, and forty-six were killed. Despite considerable damage to the marshaling yards at Hamm, trains were running through Hamm and Koblenz within a few days. In all, only one German aircraft was destroyed during the Luftwaffe's intruder attack, shot down by a gunner on board a Liberator on its return to Seething. The B-24 groups were stood down the following day.

> That's the way it was 22 April 1944—some sadness, some gratitude—our prayers that night were shared.

CHAPTER FIFTEEN

Paris and London

On Tuesday 25 April the 453rd Bomb Group was assigned the railroad marshaling yards at Mannheim as its primary target. After the briefing, a dawn chorus of droning aircraft engines reverberated across the field as *Wham Bam* and twenty-six battle-ready Liberators left their dispersal points, alternating the power on their outboard engines to assist their steering, bobbing slightly on their nose wheels to the occasional squeal of brakes. Each aircraft had its bomb bay doors ajar to rid the bay of lethal fumes, and the stench of aviation fuel fumes drifted across the flight line. *Corky* negotiated the narrow taxi track and joined the single-file traffic parading past the control tower in the half light en route to the main runway. By 0620 hours the 453rd Bomb Group was airborne and circling over its base.

Old Buckenham appeared to gradually shrink in scale amidst the patchwork of meadows and green fields of growing wheat, lined with hedgerows and trees that cast long, lazy shadows as the sun began to rise. Soon the triangular layout of runways was reduced to miniature proportions, several thousand feet below. Just a few miles on the Raleigh bicycle often seemed like such a slog, yet from the air the same distance appeared to be insignificant. Seemingly just a stone's throw from Old Buck' the base at Tibenham came into view, over which the Liberators of the 445th Bomb Group were circling. Hethel airfield also became visible as the 389th Bomb Group was launched into the new morning. The outlines of the American bases at Snetterton Heath and Deopham Green could also been seen, where the aircrews were still on the ground preparing to climb aboard their Flying Fortresses for the day's mission.

With so many aircraft airborne in a concentrated area of sky, formation assembly was always a potentially hazardous venture. Now that spring had arrived, bringing with it many bright, clear mornings, assembly was a less dangerous affair and the crews were not quite so nervous during this stage of their missions. With their home base still in view the 453rd Bomb Group's aircraft formed as two sections, each comprising three-plane elements. Setting out for their tenth mission, the Nortridge crew in *Corky* joined up with their assigned three-plane element leader, a nameless Liberator (42–95019) flown by Lt. Elmer Crockett, while in the element's left position was Lt. Donald Jones in *Flak Hack*. In the element to the right of *Corky*, Lt. Gus Johnson's crew was airborne in *Stolen*

Moments. Johnson had two stand-in crew members that day, including a copilot named Lt. Griffin. Johnson's regular copilot, Lt. Gilbert Stonebarger, was assigned to fly as Crockett's copilot while Sgt. Frederick Derolf flew as ball turret gunner on Crockett's aircraft on this mission.

The 453rd Bomb Group led the 2nd Combat Wing with the 389th flying high-right and the 445th flying low-left. The wing crossed the south coast of England at Beachy Head but three of the 453rd's aircraft aborted the mission with gas leaks and fuel transfer problems. The bomber stream crossed the French coastline at 20,000 feet in the vicinity of Dieppe and then four more Liberators returned to Old Buckenham due to various malfunctions (oil leaks, engine failure, and instrument failure). Nineteen aircraft remained in the 453rd's formation.

The mission that spring morning turned out to be yet another memorable one. It was a classic example of a *snafu* affair—situation normal: all "fouled" up! A serious navigational error, compounded when the clear skies were transformed to patchy cloud, led the 2nd Combat Wing far off course as the Liberators headed southwards into France, where the Old Buckenham aircraft received a welcome from German antiaircraft fire. The bewildered aircrews looked out through the flak-filled skies as the Eiffel Tower came into view. Pete Veilleux, the nose turret gunner on *Corky* recalls:

B-24 Liberators stream contrails en route to their target. (USAF via Martin Bowman)

> The lead navigator brought us over Paris. We weren't supposed to
> be there . . . and I often wonder whatever happened to Crockett's
> crew . . .

The flak from the anti-aircraft defenses around Paris was fierce, and
the clear skies enabled accurate aiming. Having survived the 6 March
Berlin mission, seven weeks previously, when half his crew were killed,
Elmer Crockett once again became a victim of misfortune. At 0834
hours Crockett's ship suffered a direct hit. Pete Veilleux witnessed the
incident from the nose of *Corky*:

> I remember seeing the aircraft come up, seeing the aircraft explode
> right there, and the airplane going up about thirty feet in the air . . .
> we were pretty damn close. . . . When the airplane went down—I
> can see it go down now, on fire—we were supposed to move right
> into their spot [as element leader]. That was what we were sup-
> posed to do but I don't think we moved into that exact spot because
> the shells were coming right underneath the airplane *[Corky]*, they
> were bouncing the airplane up in the air.

The Nortridge crew could do nothing but agonize at the sight of
Crockett's rapidly descending aircraft. Crockett managed to keep the
Liberator flying fairly stable just long enough for the crew to escape—a
few small figures were seen to leap from the burning ship, eight or nine
chutes were counted, one of them was on fire! Another Liberator ahead
was hit and lost an engine; another close by was hit, causing damage
to its aileron control cables; yet another, named *Battle Package*, was hit,
causing a serious fuel leak and engine failure. These three ships all
pulled out of the formation and returned to base. Then *Corky* shuddered
as a burst of flak knocked out number-three engine. Shrapnel had
ripped a hole in the propeller's spinner dome from where engine oil
began to spew out, as well as from the engine oil tank, with an alarming
risk of igniting as it streamed across the hot exhaust. Things weren't
looking too good for *Corky*'s crew.

These experiences, challenges, and life-threatening circumstances
could not be compared to any other life experience encountered by the
crew, before or since. One day way back when Perry Roberson was ten
years old he had taken an oxcart loaded with farm produce (such as
milk, eggs, homemade cakes, cookies, vegetables, and the locally celebrated "Roberson Sausage") to a store two miles from the Roberson
farm. On the way home a severe thunderstorm blew in and Perry pulled
the oxcart under a shelter at an unused storehouse—he crawled under a
bench to hide from the lightning and wait out the storm. A couple of
years later on a trip in the family car with his uncle, aunt, and three cousins, the brakes caught fire while driving down a mountainside in Tennessee. Using their initiative the four boys leapt out of the car and attempted to put out the fire by peeing on it! But the situation over Paris

was beyond such simple action. Perry was a responsible crew member; certainly his experience of growing up as the eldest child in a large family of brothers, sisters, and double-first cousins, each with their own responsibilities on the farm, provided a good grounding for his future experiences and challenges as flight engineer on an aircrew.

From the right waist hatch of the B-24, Perry could see the oil pouring from the engine. Leaving Bill LeRoy to man the waist guns, Perry disconnected his oxygen mask hose from the fixed outlet and plugged it into a portable oxygen bottle. Restricted by his bulky flying clothes and flak jacket, Perry clambered towards the flight deck, stepping awkwardly along the narrow seventeen-foot bomb bay catwalk, squeezing between the bombs. All the while Jack and George battled to maintain control of the aircraft as the flak continued to explode around them.

It was a race against time and this is where Perry's role was vital. The danger of the leaking engine oil catching fire was potentially fatal. The engine needed to be shut down immediately but first Jack and George had to "feather" the propeller by adjusting the pitch of the blades by 90 degrees thus allowing the propeller to cut through the air with minimum resistance and without windmilling uncontrollably. This was known as a "runaway" propeller resulting in a over-speeding engine and would cause severe drag to the aircraft, hindering the crew's return to England. Furthermore, a runaway propeller caused vibration and without oil pressure, bearings would dry out and the engine would seize; these factors combined could cause the propeller shaft to break loose from the engine.

Besides being essential to the engine lubricating system, the leaking oil now leaking was also used to provide hydraulic pressure to control the gearing inside the propeller's spinner dome, which in turn enabled the propeller to be feathered. The propeller had to be feathered while there was still enough oil in the engine oil tank to do so, before all hydraulic pressure in that engine was lost and the engine would have to be shut down before the leaking oil ignited and set fire to the airplane.

Perry reached the flight engineer's station behind the Jack's seat, where fuel gauges, engine gauges, generator switches, voltmeter, and ammeters were mounted on the bulkhead. Harvey Nielsen, top turret gunner and assistant flight engineer, had already climbed underneath the flight deck and started the auxiliary power unit (APU), the "put-put" engine which ran the electric auxiliary hydraulic pump. Perry was then able to maintain hydraulic pressure to the number-three engine just long enough for the propeller to be feathered. The damaged engine was then immediately shut down—the Pratt and Whitney Twin-Wasp coughed and spluttered in disagreement as its life was terminated.

Meanwhile things went from bad to worse when the persistent flak knocked out *Corky*'s number-one engine and the propeller feathering process was repeated. With greatly reduced airspeed, *Corky* fell behind the formation. Pulling away from the flak barrage over Paris, Jack turned for home on two engines. Selecting an area of deserted farmland, Bill Eagleson prepared to salvo their ten 500-pound general purpose bombs in a field, lightening the load and increasing their chances of survival. The number-three engine drove the main hydraulic system, which enabled the opening and closing of the bomb bay doors, movement of the gun turrets, and so on. But with that engine shut down, the APU and the auxiliary pump provided hydraulic pressure backup. This would be essential for lowering the landing gear, operating the flaps and utilizing the power brakes—that's if *Corky*'s crew was lucky enough to make it back to England.

With the bombs gone and the load lightened, it was Seymour Cohen's turn to perform miracles. Seymour continued with pilotage navigation, but backed it up with some dead reckoning navigation, just in case they ran into some cloud that might obscure key landmarks. Perhaps checking to see that the pilots were still in their seats and that it wasn't time to bail out yet, Jack and George saw Seymour's face appear once or twice inside the domed window in front of the cockpit.

Still in view, the Eiffel Tower was his initial checkpoint—they had lost so much altitude that Bill Eagleson recalls they were practically looking *up* at the Paris landmark! Seymour navigated a route to the French coast, and on two engines, Jack and George used all their strength to keep *Corky* on course. Alone at low altitude, the crew no longer had to rely on their oxygen masks to breathe. With no little friends in sight to offer protection, the crew knew how vulnerable they were to prowling Luftwaffe fighters searching for battle-damaged stragglers such as *Corky*. All eyes were peeled as gunners' fingers rested nervously on gun triggers. An aircraft was seen in the distance . . . a fighter . . . the gunners held their fire until they could identify it or until it was in range . . . the crew cheered—a P-51 Mustang!

Many bomber pilots envied the men who flew the fighters, especially those who flew the P-51 Mustang, the "Cadillac of the Sky." A fighter pilot was his own gunner and his own navigator, yet despite his solitude he seemed to enjoy independence and freedom beyond the experiences of bomber pilots. Bomber pilots had to fly in tight formation, sweating out the flak and the fighters on straight and level bomb runs. It was an overwhelming test of nerves for all the crew. But fighter pilots, they could at least respond to their fight-or-flight instincts when the going got tough and they found themselves outnumbered by the enemy.[1]

On board *Corky* the crew was reassured to know that they had a P-51 flying at their left wing, escorting them home. *Corky* and the little friend crossed the French coastline and headed out across the English Channel. Remembering all too vividly the events of the Hamm mission three days earlier, the gunners kept watch at their guns, with the exception of Bill LeRoy who went up to the radio operator's position on the flight deck. He switched on the IFF set that automatically transmitted a signal to radar systems on the ground in England. *Corky* sluggishly crossed the Channel and Seymour Cohen called out the coordinates of the emergency landing field at Manston. The English coastline was a welcome sight as Perry continued to adjust fuel levels and managed to keep two engines running smoothly. Nearing the field, George White radioed in to the control tower using the Command Set and received permission to land.

Corky landed safe and sound after their six-hour-and-ten-minute flight. The P-51 followed them in, and *Corky*'s crew discovered that the little friend was also battle damaged as a result of some daring treetop-level ventures while strafing an airfield flak tower—six inches of each propeller blade tip were twisted back. While *Corky* and the P-51 remained at Manston for repairs, the 453rd sent a plane to collect the crew, and the shaken P-51 pilot went along with them for the ride. His name was Lt. Henry R. Kayser and he was assigned to the 357th Fighter Group. Two weeks previously he had shot down an Me109 and shared a one-quarter credit on a He111. But he must have been slightly shaken by his lucky escape on 25 April, for he hugged his parachute all the way to Old Buck', as Bill Eagleson recalls:

> We brought the P-51 pilot home with us and he wouldn't let go of
> his parachute!

Back at Old Buck' the Nortridge crew were updated on the events of the mission. Fourteen aircraft from the 453rd Bomb Group had continued towards Mannheim having reestablished their course. In the target area, an intense barrage of flak was hurled at the bombers, and bombardiers found the target obscured by solid cloud. Low on gasoline the group jettisoned their bomb loads in a field and returned to base.

Within a few days the status of Elmer Crockett's crew was reported. His aircraft crashed at Chatenay and thankfully all ten crewmembers survived. Bill Eagleson notes:

> Elmer Crockett was a favorite friend—Great pilot, solid original
> crew . . .

Nine of the crew became prisoners of war but copilot Gilbert Stonebarger (usually from Johnson's crew) evaded capture and eventually made it back to England. Stonebarger came from California, but his parents were German immigrants. One night while at Old Buckenham, he wrote to his father to say that he had just got back from a mission to Germany on which they had bombed his hometown.

A second aircraft failed to return to Old Buck'—*Borsuk's Bitch*, piloted by Lt. Louis Scherzer of the 735th Squadron, was seen to peel away from the formation over the target area. Badly damaged, this aircraft limped into neutral Switzerland from where the crew were later reported to be safe.

"Bombs away" over Germany. (Frank Kyle)

On 26 April the Bomb Groups of the 2nd Bomb Division were again dispatched to Germany. *Corky* was held up at Manston, undergoing repairs to the damage sustained over Paris and so Jack Nortridge was assigned *Stolen Moments*. Twenty-four aircraft departed Old Buckenham between 0610 and 0638 hours for the airfield at Gutersloh. Formation assembly was conducted using instrument procedure due to limited visibility. One aircraft, *Becky*, was forced to return to Old Buck' when one crew member passed out due to lack of oxygen, and later *Ken-O-Kay II* lost the formation.

Friendly fighter cover was good and no enemy fighters were encountered on the mission. Reaching the target area, a dense ten-tenths of cloud cover obscured all target sightings and an absence of radar-equipped pathfinder aircraft prevented the Liberators from finding their primary targets. The 453rd Bomb Group resorted to their secondary target but this was also covered. All aircraft returned to Old Buckenham, jettisoning their bomb loads en route. *Stolen Moments* touched down on the main runway after a flight that had lasted five hours and two minutes. The Nortridge crew would have three days rest before their next mission—despite being exhausted it was worth making the most of a thirty-six-hour pass and taking in the sights of London.

For British aircrews, a forty-eight- or seventy-two-hour pass usually provided the opportunity to go home to see family and friends. But for American crews, far from home and family, their thirty-six-hour leaves were often spent seeing some of the sights of Britain. *Corky*'s crew went on a few such jaunts to England's capital city, taking a train from Attleborough station, making a connection at Norwich or Ely, and later arriving in London at Liverpool Street or Kings Cross station, from where they took the London Underground, known as the "tube." They would stay at the Mayfair Hotel or at the Grosvenor House Hotel which had an exclusive restaurant for military officers called the Willow Run. However, *Corky*'s crew, both officers and enlisted men, tended to spend their time together.

Far from being a city of bright lights, the blacked-out conditions of a war weary London were something of a culture shock. The American tourists were faced with the sight of unimaginable bomb damage. German bombs had wiped out huge areas of the city. But despite the effects of war, there was still more to see and do in London than a thirty-six-hour pass allowed. Sightseeing included the River Thames, Houses of Parliament, St. Paul's Cathedral, and Buckingham Palace. Then the Americans would stop in at the Rainbow Corner Red Cross Club, located near Piccadilly Circus on Shaftesbury Avenue. They visited the pubs, met English girls and drank warm beer with other American and British troops, went to nightclubs, and enjoyed London theater such as the Palladium or the Windmill. Some members of *Corky*'s crew even sheltered from air raids in the tube stations.

Bill Eagleson:

> It was quite interesting to go to the Windmill, one of your downtown theaters, and have a purple alert come on and all of a sudden have a notice that the bombs were getting closer, and then the theater evacuation and then [after the air raid everyone would] come back into the show. . . . The people in London were very friendly towards us.

In London we enjoyed Bebe Daniels, and a great male singer Anton Wallbrook, and he was very good. He sang "Home Is the Place Where Your Heart Is," and our hearts were home.

An army base named Camp Rucker opened in Dale County, Alabama, in 1942. To earn extra money to support the family, Perry Roberson's father worked there later in the war, guarding German POWs, while Perry's mother worked for a while in the base laundry. Meanwhile Perry's uncle and aunt continued to look after the family farm. At the time of the opening of Camp Rucker, in May 1942 the base finance officer's fifteen-year-old daughter was invited by a neighbor to attend a church service at Echo. During the service, Elizabeth "Libby" Fields immediately noticed Perry Roberson, the "Greek God," and when he got up to take his noisy baby brother outside, Elizabeth gave him an unforgettable smile. After the service, one of Perry's friends dared him to ask Elizabeth out for a date and that afternoon the couple went to see an Abbott and Costello comedy. When Elizabeth's mother asked her how she liked Perry, the response was, "I like him fine. When I get old enough, I'm going to marry him."

Mail across the Atlantic during 1944 seemed to take forever, and Perry longed for letters from his family and from Elizabeth. On Saturday 29 April Perry wrote home:

Perry Roberson married Elizabeth upon his return to the United States. (Ruby Jo Roberson Faust)

> Dear Mother, Just got back from London. Had a pretty good time. They had only one raid while I was there but I was so tired that I didn't wake up until the all clear. It's really a big town and pretty crowded now. Some of the areas have been bombed pretty bad. I have eleven missions in now and I think we have to put in thirty in all. Some of the fellows that came over with me already have twenty in now.
>
> I haven't had a letter from you in several days and haven't heard from Libby but twice since I got over here.
>
> You ought to see the cigarettes they have over here, they are a dry, cheap tasting cigarette. I like the bread they have for it is something like our whole wheat bread.
>
> Well I better close. Love, Donald
> [Perry McDonald Roberson]

Of course, Perry didn't alarm his family by mentioning how many of the original crews had failed to return from missions, and instead decided to "Ac-cent-tchu-ate the Positive" just as the 1944 hit song recommended—and in the true style of Crew 25. When *Corky's* crew went to London that April, Peter Becker, the flight engineer on Johnson's crew, asked Lim Wing Jeong to get a ribbon for his silver star. Becker had been awarded this following the 8 April Brunswick mission. Sgt. Jeong recalls getting back from that trip to London:

> One night when we came back from London, we passed this farm-house where this man had some chickens. We asked him to sell us some chickens and he wouldn't sell them, so that night we went back—Pete and I and Cleary [Bill Cleary from Johnson's crew]—we went back there and stole six chickens.

In hindsight he regrets that they didn't leave any money behind to pay for the chickens, but knows that the farmer would still have been angry with them.

> The next day the policemen, or "bobbies," came out and they questioned the soldiers. . . . Anyway, the chicken feathers were fly-ing all over the air base!

It seems that the enlisted men from the Nortridge and Johnson crews were notorious, even legendary. Certainly some pilots wouldn't stand for such antics from their crew members. But Jack Nortridge knew that his crew were all good-humored, that they were mostly just kids after all, and that when it came to doing their jobs and flying their missions they were all responsible and efficient crew members. And anyway, Jack Nortridge had quite a sense of humor himself.

Early each morning the crews assigned to fly would be awoken by a CQ officer, whose job it was to disturb the crews from their slumber. Barging open the hut door he would shine a flashlight around the dark-ened billet, loudly announcing the names of those assigned to fly along with breakfast and briefing times, occasionally ad-libbing a little banter or sarcasm to the procedure.

One morning the CQ officer entered the hut occupied by Jack Nort-ridge, George White, Bill Eagleson, and Seymour Cohen among others, and announced, "Jack Nortridge's crew, time to get up and go get your asses shot at! Breakfast at 0600, briefing 0630 . . ." and so on. This greet-ing became a daily wake-up call until Jack decided to put a stop to it, but he made sure that the occupants of the hut had the last laugh. Jack loaded his .45 with a blank cartridge and placed the gun under the pil-low of his bed, which was conveniently situated right next to the hut door. The next morning the CQ officer stormed in and announced, "Crew 25—time to go-get your asses kicked . . ." Jack reached for the gun and fired it across the hut! Needless to say, from then on there was a polite knock on the door before all future wake-up calls.

PART FOUR

Fear/Faith

CHAPTER SIXTEEN

Milk Runs and
Maximum Efforts

O n Sunday 30 April 1944, eighteen Liberators were dispatched
from Old Buckenham on a *Noball* mission to the V-weapon
site at Siracourt near St. Pol, France. It had become routine
that the 8th Air Force flew missions to *Noball* targets along the Pas de
Calais coast, as part of *Operation Crossbow*, whenever the weather was unfavorable over more distant, strategic targets. Just weeks later, during the
summer months and beyond, these rocket installations would be used to
launch the notorious V.1 Doodlebugs against England.

Due to the relatively short duration of flying time required for missions to the V.1 sites and the proximity of these targets and the French
coast, a *Noball* mission necessitated minimal time over enemy-occupied
territory and so the aircrews endured limited exposure to enemy action.
Therefore this was initially considered to be a "milk run," an easy mission in comparison with a long-haul mission to Germany. At the end of
1943, the 8th Air Force attacked V.1 launch sites from an altitude of
12,000 feet. But antiaircraft defenses were increased and by March 1944
the American bombers had been pushed up to 20,000 feet in the face of
intense flak opposition, equal in ferocity to that at the German targets.
Although still preferable to the prospect of a deep penetration mission
to Berlin, a *Noball* mission was no longer assumed to be an easy ride.

Jack Nortridge and his crew flew in *Corky*, which had been returned
from Manston after undergoing repairs following the Paris incident five
days earlier. A small bomber force of fifty-five B-24s from Old Buck',
Hethel, Tibenham, and Hardwick located their primary target, where
all but three aircraft were effective. All Liberators returned to their Norfolk bases, and *Corky* landed at Old Buckenham after four hours and
twenty-three minutes.

On Monday 1 May the 8th Air Force briefed its crews for missions to
twenty-three V-sites in the Pas de Calais area. Twenty-one crews departed Old Buckenham for a target at Watten; among them were the
Nortridge crew in *Corky* and their hut mates, the Johnson crew (in 41–
29447). In the Watten area the bombardiers found dense contrails and
ground haze that interfered with their sighting. Following the failure of
the bombsight in the lead aircraft, the bombs were dropped to the left of

the target. All aircraft returned to Old Buck', and *Corky* landed safely after four hours and fifty-seven minutes.

The crews attended debriefing, went to the mess halls to eat, and then retired to their huts to rest. But for twelve crews at Old Buckenham the day was just beginning, as for only the second time ever, the 8th Air Force dispatched two bombing missions in one day. Not a moment could be wasted. With the Allied invasion of Europe imminent, undermining Germany's frontline fighting strength was of primary concern to the Allies and a prerequisite to the invasion. Therefore, the 8th Air Force's strategic bombing campaign was scheduled to broaden its scope. While continuing its campaign to rid the skies of the German Air Force, the 8th was to begin to target French and Belgian railway networks, sharing this objective with the U.S. 9th Air Force and RAF Bomber Command.

There were tremendous moral implications associated with such targets, because without doubt such attacks would result in the loss of French and Belgian lives. General Dwight Eisenhower, Supreme Allied Commander of the Allied invasion forces, later stated: "The initial attacks upon the communications systems in France were undertaken at the result of an extremely difficult decision for which I assumed the full

Bomb damage to railroad marshaling yards weakened Germany's front line fighting strength and was therefore significant to the success of D-Day. (USAF via Martin Bowman)

responsibility. I was aware that the attacks upon the marshaling yards and rail centers would prove costly in French lives. In addition, a very important part of the French economy would for a considerable period be rendered useless." General Koenig, Commander of the French Forces of the Interior, asked Eisenhower to reconsider, but had resigned himself to the reality of the situation when he confessed, "It is war."[1]

On 1 May the primary targets assigned to the 8th Air Force were railway marshaling yards in France and Belgium. The 453rd Bomb Group was assigned a marshaling yard at Brussels where according to reconnaissance photographs, all twelve Liberators were accurate in their bomb drop. On two missions that day, the 453rd dispatched thirty-three aircraft and all returned safely.

For several days during the first week of May, bad weather over the continent hindered missions to industrial targets in Germany or railway targets in France and Belgium, but the 8th Air Force was successful in targeting the V.1 launch sites along the French coast. On Tuesday 2 May, the Nortridge flew *Corky* to the Pas de Calais region on a *Noball* mission. The 453rd Bomb Group found its primary at Siracourt masked by cloud and so the group's leading pathfinder ship reverted to radar for the bomb run. The mission reports claimed that the bomb drop was accurate. It turned out to be a milk run; the bombers were greeted by only moderate flak while the Luftwaffe failed to make an appearance — perhaps they knew that the fifty airborne bombers were being escorted by one hundred fighters, both P-47 Thunderbolts and P-51 Mustangs. All Liberators returned safely to Old Buck' where *Corky* landed after just three hours and thirty-four minutes.

For three days the 453rd Bomb Group was stood down. Occasionally an aircraft would leave Old Buck's main runway for a practice or test flight, observed momentarily by ground crews who were going about their labors of repairing and servicing the Liberators on the concrete hardstands. The ground crews' working hours were long and unglamorous and were under constant pressure from the group's commanders to "keep 'em flying." Usually they worked through the night and only found time to sleep when their aircraft were airborne on missions, but even then they mostly slept by the aircraft dispersal points in tents and shacks made from the crates of replacement engines and spare parts. They rarely found enough time to sleep in their barracks quarters. Often they waited in vain for their ships to return.

With four mechanics working with him, Technical Sergeant Hand-verger is remembered as the crew chief responsible for *Corky* and one other B-24. The Nortridge crew's lives were dependent upon the work accomplished by their ground crew. Technical Sergeant James E. Straub was a line mechanic on a 733rd Bomb Squadron ground crew. One of his crew's responsibilities was the B-24 named *Star Eyes*, a new natural metal finish Liberator that was assigned to Gus Johnson's crew as their regular ship towards the end of May. James Straub recalls:

> Most of my time at Old Buckenham was spent working on our air-
> craft, gassing them up, and "pre-flighting" them before each mis-
> sion. This was done in the very early hours of the morning. Then
> after takeoff on their missions, we would go to sleep in our tent out
> by our hardstand and wait for the aircraft to return from the mis-
> sion, and then do whatever had to be done to get it ready for the next
> day's mission. Sometimes this meant changing an entire engine.

At some time or another over recent weeks winter had finally given way to spring. The muddy areas around the aircraft dispersal points had dried out. From across the field the water tower could always be seen, a black metal tank raised high on four legs above mess site number two, where a number of stray cats living in the vicinity of the base would often congregate outside the kitchens waiting for leftovers. No doubt some of them had lost their owners on missions and were left to fend for themselves. Set within the peace of the countryside, the dispersed living and communal sites were becoming surrounded by a scene of serenity as the adjacent fields were carpeted by new crops and the once skeleton-like trees and hedgerows became clothed in green foliage. The base at Old Buckenham became a more hospitable environment.

On days when no missions were scheduled the aircrews were able to catch up on sleep—in fact they were often so exhausted they did little else between missions. As the weather grew milder, even the concrete-floored huts became almost tolerable. The thick brown mud around the accommodation sites and communal areas had dried out and became restored by grass. "Overshoe Lane" (named because of the overshoes the troops were issued in order to help them cope with the muddy conditions on the base during the winter months) was no longer a dirt track, and had been covered with concrete. New shrubs and trees had been planted around the living areas, and the grass area in front of the Station Headquarters site became a sports field for softball and football.

The post theater showed movies almost daily, while the Aero Club was now operating at full swing and providing entertainment and relaxation for the enlisted men. A snack bar run by the Red Cross was the focal point of the Aero Club, and this was open late, allowing the enlisted men to eat something at almost any hour that their hunger dictated (irregular routines of early morning missions interspersed with days off often resulted in irregular eating hours). There were also games facilities such as ping-pong and billiards and tables for letter writing or card games. The 453rd's very own orchestra, the "G.I.VERS" had already made several appearances in the Aero Club, performing their Glenn Miller–influenced music to an enthusiastic audience of GIs and girls invited from the surrounding area. Usually each fortnight a dance was held at the Officers' Club. Signs would be posted in and around Attleborough inviting local girls to attend these dances and others came

from as far as Norwich and were provided
round-trip transportation in army trucks.
Inspired by the "big band" sound, English
girls soon forgot what seemed like anti-
quated dance steps and learned to Jitterbug.
To them the GIs were exciting, rich, glamorous, and they epitomized the illusion of
America as portrayed by Hollywood.

   During the spring of 1944, the city of
Norwich seemed to be suspended beneath
barrage balloons, packed in tightly to deter
enemy air attack. The Liberty Run now arrived in Norwich during daylight hours, but
as always the evening would begin with a
search for friends from home, maybe from
school, college, or early military training, and who were also stationed in
Norfolk. Often the first target for *Corky*'s crew was the bar at the Bell, a
hotel and public house near Norwich Castle, where they would check
with friends and acquaintances in other groups to find out who had and
who hadn't made it back from recent missions. The next stop was often
the Samson and Hercules dance hall in Tombland, or one of the Red

The public bar at the Bell Hotel in Norwich was usually the
first stop for *Corky*'s crew while on a Liberty Run. (Will Lundy)

GIs and English women in a Norwich dance hall during 1944; believed to be the Samson & Hercules where Bill
Cleary's pet skunk was set free! (author's collection)

Cross meeting places at either the Bishop's Palace adjoining Norwich Cathedral or at Bethel Street where they would enjoy hamburgers and Coca Colas while socializing with friends from Old Buck'.

The enlisted men from *Corky*'s crew, along with their cohorts, the enlisted men from Lt. Gus Johnson's crew, soon earned themselves quite a reputation. On one occasion Johnson's tail gunner, Bill Cleary, decided to take his pet skunk on a Liberty Run—and he let it loose in the Samson & Hercules ballroom! Oranges were like gold dust in the war-rationed England of 1944, and one evening the enlisted men from Johnson's crew caused quite a commotion when they decided to share some of their rations with English civilians at the Hippodrome Theatre.

As the evenings grew longer and warmer, relaxation was often centered on the locality of the base, as an alternative to the Liberty Runs to Norwich. Cycling was particularly popular during the peaceful spring and summer evenings, and many of the Americans cycled into Attleborough to visit its public houses, especially the Angel and Griffin hotels.

Bill LeRoy:

> While in England I spent many a day touring the country; Oxford, London, Norwich, and drank many a beer in Attleborough (Angel Hotel). The English people at all times treated us as old friends, from young to old. We had fresh eggs from local farmers. Lt. Johnson's crew . . . we were in the same hut. I do recall going to town (Attleborough) many a night with their crew, especially Sgt. Albert Eihausen and Sgt. Peter Becker.

Perry Roberson:

> When on leave in Attleborough, Norwich, or other towns we learned to drink warm beer and Scotch instead of cold beer and bourbon.

A little more strenuous was the ride from the base to Old Buckenham village, where cottages, trees, the village church, and a couple of pubs encircle the large village green. Others ventured even further on their bicycles, to more distant villages. To many an American who rode his Raleigh bicycle along mile upon mile of narrow Norfolk lane, lined with overgrown verges of grass and wild hemlock plants, past thickets, woodlands, fields, and meadows where cattle grazed lazily in the evening sunshine, cycling was the ideal way to enjoy the English countryside. Often a village on the horizon provided an incentive for another mile or two, even if it meant finding one's way back to base after closing time and a few pints of warm beer or Gaymer's Cyder, along darkened lanes with no signposts to guide the way.

Bill Eagleson:

> Late spring, your long summer evenings would find us cycling to nearby pubs, until "Time, Gents!" There we had opportunities to know and appreciate your folks, sing songs; "Roll Out the Barrel,"

"There'll Always Be an England," "Six Pence," "White Cliffs of Dover," "Oh, That B-24," "Berkley Square."

Pete Veilleux:

> We did bring home a few heifers from Attleborough at the auctions. We'd buy them for seven bucks apiece and drag them home—we almost had to drag them home, 'cause you try to push an animal and he doesn't want to go—I'm telling you, that it's quite a job, but the steaks were good!

Bill LeRoy:

> Colonel Potts found out so we had to get rid of the evidence. Gave some steaks to Operations officers.

The enlisted men assigned to the Nortridge and Johnson crews were known throughout the base for their good-humored antics, their sharing their hut with Harvey Nielson's monkey, Pete Becker's dog, and Bill Cleary's skunk; for going to the auctions and taking cattle back to Old Buck'; and for the chicken feathers flying around the base. Bill LeRoy remembers that "Somebody killed the skunk, and I think the dog died too." and as for the monkey:

> It got sick and Harvey sold it to another gunner, and the monkey died about two days later . . . and boy, the guy was raving mad about that. But Harvey said "Well, I can't do nothing about it," so that was the last of our animals. Harvey was crazy over monkeys for some reason, he spent a lot of money on monkeys!

Pete Veilleux explains the mysterious fate of Stinky, the skunk belonging to Bill Cleary:

> Jeong got up one morning—we weren't flying, but he slept in—and it seems like the other crew's mascot had got out of the pen and it relieved itself by Jeong's bed, and Jeong planted both feet in there that morning. Well, needless to say that .45 immediately went into action!

Bill Eagleson:

> Now it can be told—Jeong shot the skunk!

On 6 May the 453rd Bomb Group participated in a *Noball* mission and the following day the 8th Air Force dispatched over one thousand bombers from the English bases on a "maximum effort" mission to Germany. The B-17 groups were assigned primary targets in the vicinity of Berlin while the B-24s of the 2nd Bomb Division headed for Münster and Osnabrück. Jack Nortridge and his crew flew *Corky* in a formation of twenty-nine Old Buckenham aircraft, which dropped their incendiary bombs through the cloud cover and into Osnabrück's industrial area on the sighting of a radar-equipped lead aircraft. The flak was once again moderate and the Luftwaffe absent. The 453rd returned to base, and *Corky*'s wheels touched down on the tarmac after five hours and five minutes.

On Monday 8 May the 453rd Bomb Group was assigned to fly a maximum effort mission to aircraft factories in Brunswick, Germany, where exactly one month previously the group had lost seven aircraft to enemy fighters. The Nortridge crew was not assigned to fly the 8 May mission, but remembering the carnage they had witnessed over Brunswick in April, they sweated out the return of the rest of the Group with heavy hearts. And they were right to worry. The mission echoed the "Battle of Brunswick" of the previous month; facing an opposition of an estimated two hundred Luftwaffe fighters, eight crews were lost.

Badly damaged by fighter attacks, the Liberators flown by Capt. John Banks and Lt. Dean Hart collided, and just a few men escaped alive. Lt. Endicott Lovell's crew in *Gypsy Queen*, Lt. Ray Keith's crew in *Pug*, Lt. Thomas Stilbert's crew in *Lucky Penny*, Lt. Richard Witton's crew in *Choo Choo Baby*, and Lt. John Mackey's crew all failed to make it back to Old Buck'. One crew from the 733rd Bomb Squadron was lost, piloted by Lt. Fred Parker. Seven members of this crew were killed and three became prisoners of war. They had flown only five combat missions, having been at Old Buckenham for less than one month—they arrived on 13 April as a replacement for one of the crews lost over Brunswick on 8 April. Bill Eagleson has vague recollections of this crew:

> I believe Parker's crew were in our hut, but that's difficult to accurately recall.

If that recollection is correct, then the officers of the Nortridge, Johnson, and Parker crews shared their hut with the Jones crew. Lt. Donald Jones's crew was returning from their nineteenth mission, this time in a severely battle-damaged Liberator with one wheel up and one wheel down, a punctured nose wheel tire, no brakes, and no flap control. To avoid blocking the runway, the control tower at Old Buck' advised Jones to continue to the Liberator repair depot at nearby Watton airfield. The crew bailed out, with the exception of Jones and his copilot who managed to crash-land safely at Watton.

After bailing out, navigator Lt. Fred Stein landed in a field somewhere between Old Buck' and Watton, where he was greeted by a Home Guard posse carrying pitchforks and shotguns. Exhausted by his flight and disoriented from his parachute jump, Lt. Stein addressed the Englishmen with the exclamation, "Am I glad to see you guys!" The problem was that he said it in German! Stein was a Minnesota farm boy from a town whose inhabitants were mostly German speaking, and he had convinced himself that if he were ever forced to bail out over enemy territory then his life might depend on communicating in German. He was hurriedly marched to the nearest police station, believed to be a German spy![2]

The officers from the Jones crew were glad to get back to Old Buck', but it was unnerving to see the four empty beds in their hut that night where twenty-four hours previously had slept Fred Parker's crew; where one month plus one day before had slept Fred Brady, his copilot, navigator, and bombardier—also lost over Brunswick. The next crew to occupy those beds was lost on their first mission.

Capt. William "Mac" Mc-Crocklin (left) surveying the battle damage with Sgt. Curtis "Tex" O'Neal, nose turret gunner, on 8 May 1944. Copilot James Workman wrote in his diary, "How Tex got out I'll never know." (James N. Workman)

Capt. Mac McCrocklin's
top turret gunner, Sgt.
Marty Sasala (left), and
navigator, Lt. Harrison
"Harry" Cassel, inspect-
ing their aircraft's battle
damaged tail. (James N.
Workman)

Capt. William "Mac" McCrocklin's crew nearly didn't make it back
from Brunswick. The nose turret was so badly shot to pieces that for a
moment the crew assumed that the nose turret gunner, Sgt. Curtis
"Tex" O'Neal; navigator, Lt. Harrison "Harry" Cassel, and bombardier, Lt. Raymond "Bee" Behymer, were dead. But somehow all three of
them were alive. The copilot, Lt. James Workman, later wrote in his

diary, "Thought for sure that Tex, Harry, and Bee were gone. How Tex got out I'll never know." McCrocklin's ship was covered in bullet holes and their oxygen system was damaged, the radio was shot out, a propeller was damaged, the throttle cable to the number-two engine was severed, the left elevator was badly damaged, and a fuel cell, fortunately of the self-sealing variety, was punctured.

The flight engineer, Sgt. Johnnie Doyle, had part of a 20mm shell in his arm. Waist gunner Sgt. James "Little Robbie" Roberts's hand was nearly frostbitten and he had a sprained ankle—a 20mm shell exploded under his foot but the damage was minimized because (fortunately) he was standing on a flak jacket for extra protection. The pilots feathered the number-two engine on their landing approach at Old Buck'. A flat tire caused them to "ground loop"—they swerved 180 degrees to the left and onto the grass. In his diary, the copilot declared, "Just by the will of God we are alive."

Meanwhile the whole drama was observed by a visitor to Old Buck', an American airman stationed at another airfield in England. He was waiting for the return of his brother, Lt. Abe Wilen, the navigator on Lt. Witton's crew. But when it became evident that this crew was "missing in action," one of their friends and hut mates, Lt. Eugene McDowell, somberly assisted Abe Wilen's brother as they packed Abe's personal belongings. He was later reported to be a POW.

Lt. Robert Catlin's crew was returning home in a battle damaged *Valkyrie*, which they were forced to abandon over Norfolk. However, flight engineer and waist gunner Sgt. Ray Bates had been wounded in three places on the mission and allegedly would not bail out because of the injuries to his legs. Another crewmember was slightly injured and his parachute had been damaged, and so Bates gave him his own parachute—when McCrocklin's copilot heard about this incident he commented in his diary, "Just the same as saying 'you live, I'll die.'" *Valkyrie* plunged into a thicket at Morningthorpe near Long Stratton. Bates was miraculously thrown clear when the aircraft exploded—he emerged from the wreckage with further injuries but he was very grateful to be alive.

Twenty-seven aircraft had left Old Buck' on the morning of 8 May and only seventeen returned to base; forty-two men had been killed in action, thirty-six were later reported to be prisoners of war, and three remained in the "missing in action" category. The cost of two missions to Brunswick, a month apart, was a high price paid by the Liberator men of Old Buck'.

The 8th Air Force's bomber crews had completed vigorous, extensive training schedules in the United States, which had been effective in providing them with the skills necessary for proficiency at their assigned duties. However, the training did not cover the emotional aspects of warfare, of dealing with the loss of friends and facing one's own death or the anxiety at the prospect of being injured or captured by the enemy.

Lt. Robert Catlin's Liberator crashed near Long Stratton, Norfolk. The crew had bailed out, with the exception of the flight engineer—miraculously, he walked away from the wreckage! The following day, members of Catlin's crew visited the scene of the crash. (Donald Olds, 453rd BG Association Collection)

Besides the obvious encounters with flak and fighters, there was also the reality of their own actions to contend with—aerial bombardment. With the vision of falling bombs and the consequential death and destruction imprinted on their minds, not everyone could sleep soundly after missions. Despite the inevitabilities of war, aircrews were emotionally unprepared for the intensity of their experiences, the horrifying fears they faced and the tragedies they witnessed.

Perry Roberson:

> One of the sadder things I saw was a B-24 going down with a parachute caught on the tail assembly. The plane seemed to be on autopilot but was on its way down.

The ground personnel at Old Buckenham also witnessed scenes that would haunt them for life. When aircraft came home with dead or seriously wounded on board, the medics, firemen, and even the mechanics would have to deal with unthinkable horrors—treating injuries and sometimes removing the body of a decapitated gunner from his turret. When a crew was lost on a mission, their belongings would immediately be removed from their billets to reduce the reminder for other crews so that the events would have minimal effect on morale.

Bill Eagleson:

> The personnel in our hut . . . four crews, we did lose two of them . . . and after that we had several crews come in. I remember distinctly one crew came in; they didn't get their bags unpacked. They were flown maybe two days after they arrived in our barracks and they didn't get back from the mission. . . . [It is] very difficult to describe the feelings but somehow or another when replacement crews arrived, it was just a little different feeling.
>
> We really felt for these guys, but we didn't know how to express it I guess. It could even have been modesty. We were to them "combat veterans." We had flown some arduous missions, we knew what they had to face, and we knew that they would have to work out their doubts and fears just as we were trying to work out *our* doubts and fears. Maybe it would take some "flak juice" from one of the "flak houses" that we visited twice, once in Southport and once in the Lake District.

Short periods of time spent on rest leave at rest houses (flak houses) at least acknowledged the need to reduce the anxieties and stresses that might otherwise lead to nervous exhaustion or even emotional breakdown—"operational fatigue." Each bomber unit was assigned a flight surgeon who was responsible for both the physical and mental well-being of aircrew. At Old Buckenham it was flight surgeon Maj. Harvey Lloyd's job to determine whether or not each airman was fit to fly, and he had the authority to recommend to the squadron commanders cases for furlough and rest leave. As well as being present for mission briefings and interrogations he also met with individuals to discuss personal problems, and he attended social gatherings on the base to keep a watchful eye over the crews.

The ten young airmen who flew in *Corky* shared a strong belief that, whatever happened, they would always make it back to Old Buck'. This is something Jack Nortridge regularly assured his crew. Prior to flying missions the feelings of apprehension were, according to the bombardier:

> Hard to compare or equate with any other of life's challenges . . . thanks to a very confident pilot things always were altered to the positive side, starting with faith of plane and crew, down to the last mechanic on the hardstand. We also had English friends with the same strong faith.
>
> Combat stress and exhaustion, if it was a factor—I can speak for my crew—we sort of laughed it off and hung in together and talked each of our problems out with one another. I think we dealt with it ourselves pretty well.

Many of the aircrews were notably superstitious and such idiosyncrasies would surface in a variety of ways, some almost indiscernible and others seemingly eccentric. The former variety of behavior might include carrying out simple daily procedures habitually, precisely, the same as the day before and the day before that. This included walking to the mess halls, the briefing, and the aircraft in the same way each morning, taking the same route, lighting up a cigarette at the same point of the journey; the logic being that, *something* seemed to be keeping them alive, and they didn't want to change anything, *just* in case.

Some aircrew members would disappear round the back of their plane to urinate on the tail wheel prior to a mission as this was considered to be a lucky ritual. However, superstitious airmen at Old Buck' were less inconspicuous since the B-24 didn't have a tail wheel, and often there were other crew members, mechanics, and armorers congregating around the nose wheel at the front of the aircraft making final preparations.

Occasionally, during off-duty hours the crews might find themselves tuning into a German propaganda station on their personal radios. Music chosen to appeal to British and American servicemen would be interspersed with well-informed dialogue referring to individual groups, sometimes naming an individual group or squadron CO, occasionally naming individual aircraft.[3] Some pilots would not name their aircraft or have nose art painted on it for fear of it somehow attracting bad luck—in case the enemy fighter pilots decided to single out specific aircraft in the same way as they sometimes seemed to concentrate on certain units, recognized by the identification markings.

The pre-mission ritual! (Estate of Col. Frank Russell Webster, courtesy Mark Forlow)

Then of course there was a certain crew that hung corks around the inside of their plane for good luck to the amusement of a replacement crew who borrowed *Corky* for a mission. Of course, the new crew had been intrigued by the name before they climbed aboard, but as each crew member checked in over the intercom there was laughter as someone said, "What have we got here?" Someone replied instantly, "Hey, I've got one too!" and someone else said, "Me too! That crew must've been really inspired when they decided what to name this ship!'

Spirituality and religion played an important part in the lives of many young Americans at Old Buckenham. At first, in the absence of a base chapel, religious services were held in one of the mess halls. Then in May a large Nissen hut was converted into a chapel under the supervision of the group's Protestant chaplain, Capt. Lester Liles. Many of the personnel volunteered their free time and set about converting the hut and using salvaged material such as the wood from bomb crates they constructed an altar, kneeling benches, pedestals, and a confessional for the Catholic airmen. Services were held on Sunday mornings and evenings for the Protestant troops, and each Thursday morning a visiting chaplain or local minister would give the sermon, providing each man the opportunity to occasionally hear a chaplain of his own denomination. Bill Eagleson:

> As I remember we did have a spiritual leader in Chaplain Liles with the 453rd. We had excellent rapport with Chaplain Liles. As a matter of fact Chaplain Liles married Don [and Dorothy] Lawry just before we left March Field. Later on we did get a Catholic Chaplain. Also we had a vicar that traveled onto the base quite frequently in a rather beaten down old car.

Initially, visiting chaplains held Catholic services at the base and Chaplain Quinlan from the base at Tibenham held Mass each Sunday morning at Old Buckenham until Father Healy was assigned to the group as Catholic chaplain. Meanwhile Jewish services were held each Friday evening but often in the absence of a rabbi, Capt. Liles attended these services and gave a sermon. Protestant and Catholic services were also conducted prior to missions, and often held in the briefing hall following mission briefing. Some of the Americans attended religious services in the local communities during their free time, and Bill Eagleson was among the regular American guests at the Sunday evening vespers at St. Mary's Church in Attleborough.

> Spirituality was more or less a personal factor, as was superstition. The belief that our crew developed was a belief that we *were* going to come back and that we would stick together to see that everybody got back, and I think our pilot John Nortridge preached that many, many times, "If you stay with me I'm going to get you home"—and we believed that, so perhaps you could call that faith.

Following the calamitous mission to Brunswick, the crews at Old Buckenham were awakened in the early hours of the following morning, Tuesday 9 May, for a mission to Belgium. On board *Corky* that day there were two unfamiliar faces among the crew in place of two absentees. Following a recent visit to the base dentist, Bill Eagleson had been grounded for a couple of days while Seymour Cohen was not assigned to fly this mission, having already flown one mission more than the other officers on the crew. A navigator and bombardier from another crew were assigned to fly the mission with Jack and the others.

The Liberators flew through clear skies to the German night fighter base at Florennes. Friendly fighter support was excellent upon crossing the enemy coast but limited over the target area, where the Liberators dropped their bombs on the Luftwaffe airfield with what the official mission reports would state as accurate and effective results. Lt. Edward Perro's crew, flying in *Cee Gee*, was lost to enemy fighters over France; five of the crew were killed and five became prisoners of war. The friendly fighter presence increased on the return journey, and dogfights between American and German fighters were observed in the distance.

At Old Buckenham that morning, the hours leading up to the estimated return time of the 453rd Bomb Group passed slowly. The atmosphere and the expectant feeling at the flight line intensified as ground and air personnel who had not been assigned to fly that day began to congregate in the vicinity of the control tower. Eager to see the group return, they waited patiently with their eyes fixed on the horizon, as Norfolk's flat terrain appeared to be overcast by polythene skies. Bill Eagleson recalls waiting for his crew to return that morning:

> My one time when I missed flying with my crew. . . . I had a tooth extraction so I was grounded . . . and it was kind of a lonely feeling being on that airfield without my crew or *Corky*, just waiting, sweating them back home.

At eleven o'clock the sky was filled with aircraft circling the base. *Corky* landed safely after four hours and thirty-seven minutes, taxied around the field towards the tower, and back into the dispersal point where Bill Eagleson and Seymour Cohen waited to greet the crew.

On Thursday 11 May the 2nd Bomb Division was assigned marshaling yards in France as their targets, with the 453rd Bomb Group destined for distant Belfort near the Swiss border.[4] During a late morning takeoff, twenty-four aircraft had departed Old Buck' by eleven o'clock. Jack and his crew flew *Corky* alongside Gus Johnson in *My Babs* and a B-24 named *Rainbow Goddess*. The formation crossed the English coastline at Beachy Head and crossed the English Channel and then the French coastline at Le Havre. Flak and fighter opposition was moderate; visibility was limited due to cloud, haze, and aircraft contrails. The primary target at Belfort was obscured beneath the cloud and so the

453rd continued one hundred miles to their secondary target at Chaumont, France. The 453rd bombed Chaumont's marshaling yards at 1623 hours. Returning home low on fuel, Jack Nortridge landed *Corky* at an airfield in southern England after an eight-hour-and-forty-seven-minute flight. After refueling they continued home to Old Buck'.

Following the 11 May mission, both the Jack Nortridge and Gus Johnson crews were stood down for two weeks rest and relaxation. Meanwhile, on 12 May the 8th Air Force launched its first attack on synthetic oil production in an attempt to deprive the enemy of fuel and therefore rid the skies of the Luftwaffe. The 453rd Bomb Group was assigned the oil plant at Zeitz in central Germany. The 8th Air Force had been attacking the Luftwaffe "in the air, on the ground, and in the factories," and with the assault on oil production, the enemy air force would be starved of fuel and it would fall further toward demise. It was imperative that the Luftwaffe was further weakened before the Allied invasion of Europe commenced. The invasion was imminent and the tide was turning.

CHAPTER SEVENTEEN

Flame Leap

I n May 1944 both the Jack Nortridge and Gus Johnson crews were
given thirteen days rest from combat flying. Bill Eagleson had got
word that a friend from home, Frederick Christensen, was now a
P-47 pilot with the 56th Fighter Group. Nicknamed "Rat-Top" by the
other pilots in the 56th, Lt. Frederick Christensen had arrived in England during the summer of 1943 as a replacement pilot. He completed
his training in England in August 1943and was then assigned to the 62nd
Fighter Squadron, 56th Fighter Group, which was now operating its
P-47 Thunderbolts out of Boxted airfield, in the county of Essex. Under
the pretext of a navigation and orientation practice flight, the Nortridge
crew set off on a pleasure flight in *Corky* and headed for Boxted.

Bill Eagleson recalls:

> We went down and visited the 56th Fighter Group, specifically one
> of my high school classmates, Fred Christensen—one of the lead-
> ing "aces" in the 56th.

The Nortridge crew were honored to meet several recognized
fighter aces at Boxted that evening, including Francis Gabreski, Walker
Mahurin, and the group's commanding officer, Hubert Zemke. Officially, an ace was a fighter pilot who had shot down at least five enemy
aircraft. The 56th Fighter Group, along with the 4th Fighter Group,
were the 8th Air Force's leading two fighter groups, in terms of the
numbers of fighter aces assigned to them. The 4th Fighter Group was
now equipped with P-51 Mustangs, while the 56th Fighter Group was
still flying the heavier and less maneuverable P-47 Thunderbolts. The
56th had become known as the "Wolfpack" because they were known to
hunt like wolves.

Twenty-two-year-old Lt. Fred Christensen was born in Watertown,
Massachusetts, and had attended Watertown High School along with
Bill Eagleson; although Fred was two years younger, they had known
each other well during high school days. By May 1944, Fred had fulfilled
the ace criteria and he was to prove himself further within a couple of
months—he set a record in the 8th Air Force when he became the first
pilot to shoot down six enemy aircraft on one mission. He flew a person-
alized P-47 named *Rozzi Geth* after his girlfriend Rosamond Gethro. Bill
Eagleson recalls:

Lt. Fred Christensen in his P-47 *Rozzi Geth* at the peak of his "fighter ace" status, having shot down twenty-two German aircraft (later revised to twenty-one-and-a-half). Fred was a graduate of Watertown High School in Massachusetts, where he had been friends with Bill Eagleson. (Col. Fred J. Christensen)

> It was quite an evening with the fighter boys, and they made a
> point later on when they could—Fred made a point to come up
> and see us while we were flying over the Channel, flying into
> enemy territory, with his P-47 named *Rozzi Geth*.

As well as getting an insight into the experiences of the fighter pilots, the Nortridge crew also made a trip to the county of Somerset, in southwest England where Bill Eagleson's cousin Everett was based as a C-47 crew chief. All across southern England, thousands of Allied soldiers were camped out in readiness for the Allied invasion of Nazi-occupied Europe. At the airfields there were similar scenes of activity as C-47 Skytrains and troop carrier gliders were being prepared. *Corky* landed at Weston Zoyland, the home of the 442nd Troop Carrier Group, where over seventy C-47s and one hundred gliders were dispersed around the airfield.

Little Friends—six P-47 Thunderbolts from the 56th Fighter Group escort a B-24. (Jim Sterling)

> I did have a cousin based in Somerset. He was flying C-47s as a crew chief; later he flew gasoline with the B-24s. At one time just before D-Day we brought our bomber down to his base. . . . It was a very pleasant experience talking to those guys that were getting ready to cross the Channel for the first time.

Seymour Cohen's older brother, Albert "Al" Cohen, was a sergeant in the army and assigned to the tank corps. Although Seymour was four years younger than Al, Seymour had been drafted into the army first, before volunteering for the Army Air Force. On one occasion prior to the Allied invasion, Al visited Seymour at Old Buckenham and stayed in one of the vacant beds in the Quonset hut with the officers of *Corky's* crew. Seymour and Al took a train to Norwich and had their photograph taken by a professional photographer. They sent it home to their mother—it was surely a distressing feeling for her, having two sons in the army and both of them fighting in Europe. The photograph was proudly displayed in the window of their father's hardware store in Bayonne, New Jersey. The Nortridge crew was also assigned their second seven-day rest leave, this time at a Red Cross flak house in the Lake District, Northern England. Bill Eagleson:

> We did have two seven-day rest leaves at flak houses in Southport and the Lake District—the Red Cross ran these and did their best to provide super comforts.

The Cohen brothers in Norwich, England, 1944. Sgt. Albert Cohen (left) visited Seymour at Old Buckenham soon before D-Day. This photograph was sent home to New Jersey where it was proudly displayed in the window of their father's hardware store. (Anita Cohen)

In the tranquil surroundings of the Lake District the crew enjoyed a quiet and relaxing break, then at the end of the week they returned to Attleborough by train, with two additions—two Windermere Terriers. They named the black puppy Flak and his brown brother Corky, the namesake of the crew's Liberator aircraft.

Back at Old Buck' they found the 2nd Bomb Division's aircraft identification markings had been modified to improve unit identification at long range. On the vertical tail fins of the 453rd Group aircraft, a black tail (denoting the 2nd Combat Wing) with a diagonal white band (signifying the 453rd Bomb Group) had replaced the original "circle-J" insignia. On the white diagonal band *Corky*'s new identification letter, "N," appeared with a black bar that signified the 733rd Squadron.

On Thursday 25 May the Nortridge and Johnson crews were awakened for a return to missions when the 8th Air Force ordered visual attacks on rail installations and airfields in France and Belgium. The target for the 453rd Bomb Group that day was the marshaling yards at Troyes, France. Jack's crew climbed aboard *Corky*, and Johnson's crew prepared themselves for their first mission in a new natural metal finish B-24 J named *Star Eyes*. The waist gunners much preferred these new J-model aircraft, for their guns were mounted in sealed, Plexiglas waist windows, eliminating most of the freezing cold drafts that they were subjected to in their original aircraft with open waist hatches. Gus Johnson's crew flew twelve different aircraft during the course of their missions, but *Star Eyes* became their "regular" aircraft, and the crew's names were painted in small writing on the fuselage.

In total, twenty-four Liberators, each carrying ten 500-pound bombs, took off from Old Buck' for the mission. It was a fine spring morning with exceptional visibility over the base and the group formed into two sections of twelve aircraft, led by Maj. James Stewart. Over the continent the first section overran Troyes due to weather interference, and bombed Terrennes instead, while the second section bombed Bretigny airfield, the group's secondary target. The 453rd encountered moderate but accurate flak, but no enemy fighters, and all aircraft returned to England. *Corky* touched down at base after six hours and thirty-two minutes, and Johnson took the silver-winged *Star Eyes* into the emergency field at Manston.

The 453rd Bomb Group rested the following day and then *Corky*'s crew was among those assigned the mission the next Saturday 27 May. Twenty-eight aircraft were dispatched to bomb the railroad marshaling yards at Saarbrucken, Germany; however, Jack and George were unable to change the position of the flaps on *Corky* despite attempting all emergency procedures, and were forced to abort and return home.

Three more Liberators returned early and twenty-four continued and bombed the target area with what the mission report described as "effective" results. Flak that day was reported to be moderate but accuracy was hindered by chaff released from the bombers to jam the flak gunners' radar sights. Again, the Luftwaffe failed to make an appearance for the seventh consecutive mission flown by the 453rd. On this day the Group's Commander Lieutenant Colonel Ramsay Potts was promoted to full Colonel.

Jack Nortridge's crew rested on the following day, while their hut mates, Johnson's crew, set out in the B-24 named *Flak Hack* for a mission to the synthetic oil plant at Merseburg, Germany. The group encountered inaccurate flak over Dummer Lake, usually notorious for the concentration of enemy fighter units, and intense and accurate flak in the target area. One of the group's gunners shot down an attacking Me410 fighter while some of the crews reported no Luftwaffe sightings at all—other 8th Air Force bomb groups were not so lucky. On this day a 734th Squadron gunner with two enemy aircraft credits became the first 453rd Group crew member to complete a tour of duty.

On Monday 29 May *Corky*'s crew was awakened for a long-haul mission to occupied Poland. Flying in two sections, the 453rd Bomb Group was assigned an oil refinery as its primary target, located at Politz, near Stettin, seventy miles northeast of Berlin. Twenty-five aircraft departed Old Buck' and Jack Nortridge's crew in *Corky* took up their position as an element leader in the second section. Two radar-equipped Pathfinder Force (PFF) aircraft from Hethel joined the 453rd Group formations. They would act as radar pathfinders if weather conditions prevented visual bombing. Visual bombing was usually more accurate, but radar bombing was considered preferable to abandoning the mission. Lt. Alfred Tolley was at the controls of one of the pathfinder aircraft. Lt. Tolley had been one of the original 453rd Group pilots prior to being selected as a PFF pilot and assigned to the 389th Bomb Group at Hethel. On this mission to Politz, Lt. Tolley was to lead the 453rd Bomb Group, and in turn the entire 2nd Bomb Division on the mission.

The Liberators crossed the North Sea, proceeded over Northern Germany past Hamburg, where two of Harvey Nielsen's aunts lived, and continued over Denmark, where Harvey's parents and three of his siblings were born. The formation crossed a corner of the Baltic Sea before turning south into northwest Poland. Jack's crew were comforted to know that their P-47 friends in the 56th Fighter Group were out there among the escorting fighters.

Copilot George White and bombardier Bill Eagleson often assisted Seymour Cohen with pilotage navigation by keeping track of landmarks and passing details on to Seymour, who plotted their course on a map and worked on dead reckoning navigation. Seymour also kept a log of times and events that occurred on the mission. It was important to remember the information provided at mission briefing regarding flak defenses and areas where enemy fighters were concentrated—all the places they needed to avoid. Although they were flying in formation following a lead ship, if they became separated for any reason then Seymour would need to know exactly where they were and how to get home. The small observation windows in each side of the nose of the aircraft provided some visibility, but it was all too easy for a navigator to turn away to view his maps and notes and miss a vital landmark. Seymour could use all the help he could get.

The bombardier's primary role was undertaken during just a few minutes of the mission, between the initial point of the bomb run and "bombs away." The rest of the time Bill Eagleson was able to assist Jack and George on the flight deck and call out for oxygen checks every few minutes to make sure that the whole crew was breathing and conscious. Bill Eagleson recalls:

> Regarding crew positions, the bombardier's station was not always in the nose on *Corky* . . . our crew stations varied with missions. As I recall most of the time I was on the flight deck between pilot and copilot . . . doing pilotage navigation, just a lot of coordinating things. . . . When General LeMay's "lead crew" concepts were

brought forth, the bombardier was really the tenth man on the crew.

It is ironic that Bill Eagleson should feel that he was the "tenth man on the crew." After all, the bombardier's role was primary in the whole course of the mission. Without him there would be no need for the pilots to fly the bomber, no reason for the navigator to direct it or the gunners to defend it. However, following the excitement of being trained on the top secret Norden bombsight and the feeling of prestige associated with the "Bombardier's Oath," finding Sperry bombsights in their assigned aircraft came as a big surprise and disappointment to the bombardiers of the 453rd Bomb Group.

As the first section of the 453rd Bomb Group's formation approached the Initial Point of the bomb run they were attacked by up to thirty FW190s. And then they attacked the second section, in which *Corky* was flying. Pete was perched on the nose of the aircraft in his turret with his guns blazing, and Harvey's too, up in the top turret. Jack and George attempted to "nose in" to the incoming Luftwaffe fighters, thus shortening each attack by forcing the enemy pilots to pull away in order to avoid collisions. If the fighters attacked from around one- or two-o'clock level then Jack would say, "You take it, George!" George would use all his strength to turn *Corky* into the fighters, all the while checking to his right to avoid colliding with other bombers. If the enemy planes came in at around ten or eleven o'clock then George White would say, "You take it Jack!" Bill Eagleson was usually up on the flight deck behind the two pilots' seats, and if he saw fighters coming in from the twelve-o'clock level he would call out, "SOMEONE take it!" Fighter attacks from one- or two-o'clock high-right were usually aimed at the number-three engine and the copilot's position. Crippling the engine that controlled the main hydraulic system and injuring or killing the copilot would certainly put the aircraft and crew in serious trouble. Lim Wing Jeong watched from the tail turret as a huge air battle took place before his eyes—an estimated two hundred enemy fighters attacked the Liberator formation flying behind the 453rd Bomb Group.

Approaching Politz, Bill Eagleson took a portable oxygen bottle and crawled through the tunnel under the flight deck, past the nose wheel (careful not to lean on the nose wheel doors, for they were sprung to open with approximately seventy pounds of pressure), and into the nose compartment of *Corky*. At the initial point of the bomb run, indicated by colored flares fired from the lead ship, all bombardiers pulled one of two levers to the left of their Sperry sights, opening the bomb bay doors. Meanwhile, all pilots reduced airspeed and began a straight and level flight into the target area; between the IP and the bomb drop it was imperative that altitude and airspeed remained stable regardless of the flak that enveloped the formation.

Underneath the nose turret, Bill was crouched uncomfortably over the bombsight, staring down through the flat glass window. Every burst of flak that exploded in a cloud of black smoke underneath the aircraft was magnified by the optical part of the bombsight. Trying not to be distracted by the flak, each bombardier in the formation attempted to apply some precision to the bomb run. The first section of Liberators dropped their bombs on the oil refinery at Politz, and within a few minutes smoke was seen to rise from the target to an altitude of 10,000 feet. As a result of the first section's bombing, Bill could see a heavy smokescreen covering the oil refinery, and he waited for the bombs and colored smoke markers to fall from the lead plane. With his left hand on the lever that released the bombs, he talked Jack through the last few seconds of the bomb run:

> PDI centered. . . . Oh Boy! Jack, keep it steady . . . steeeaddy . . . bombs away! *Let's get the hell out of here!*

The Liberators immediately turned, gathered speed, and proceeded to the Rally Point. The flak soon faded away but the enemy fighters returned, continuing their attacks until after the Liberators had rallied, when wing formation was restored. All of the 453rd Bomb Group's aircraft arrived safely at Old Buckenham by around four o'clock. Other groups were not so lucky—the 8th Air Force lost thirty-four bombers that day, eight of which were interned in neutral Sweden. In addition to these losses, the 489th Bomb Group from Halesworth lost two B-24s when they collided and crashed near Tibenham, Norfolk.

Corky touched down at base after seven hours and forty-two minutes flying time. A war correspondent looking for a story approached Bill LeRoy and asked him about the mission, and Bill described how they had been attacked by some 150 enemy fighters. Incidentally, three weeks previously he had written and told his mother that he had completed seventeen missions. She had written back and said, "That's nice, son," not really having any idea exactly what it was that he was doing. Following the Politz raid, the war correspondent asked Bill, "Where are you from?" and Bill replied, "St Louis." The next morning over breakfast, Mrs. LeRoy was enjoying the *St. Louis Post* over breakfast, when she turned the page and to her amazement saw a photograph of her son staring her in the face. The caption read: "In Today's Raid: Tech. Sgt. William G. LeRoy, who participated in today's raid over Germany." Mrs. LeRoy read the account of the mission to Politz and the reality of what her son was doing hit home. Worried to death, she immediately wrote to Bill to say, "Son, please be careful!"

On Tuesday 30 May, *Corky*'s crew rested while thirty-four other crews were assigned to fly a mission to an airfield at Oldenburg, Germany. The bombs were dropped on the German airfield with accuracy, but the Liberators encountered vicious flak, intense and accurate, which caused serious battle damage to six aircraft. However, all aircraft crossed the North Sea en route home to Old Buck'. Lt. George Wear, the 733rd Squadron pilot from Louisiana whose twenty-sixth birthday was on this day, was among the personnel gathered on the flight line to sweat out the return of the mission.

One by one the ships came in to land, and then George Wear watched as the *Golden Gaboon* went out of control. He had a particular fondness for this ship, having flown it from California to England with Seymour Cohen as his navigator. But the *Golden Gaboon* had suffered severe battle damage on the mission to Oldenburg, and the pilot, Lt. Wilbur Earl, lost control as the aircraft became caught in the slipstream of the preceding plane. The *Golden Gaboon* crashed on the main runway as fire fighters raced to the scene. As they battled with the inferno, a huge pillar of black smoke drifted skyward, visible for miles around. Miraculously, Lt. Wilbur Earl's crew escaped with only minor injuries.

Lt. Lester Baer's battle-damaged Liberator, *Zeus,* had lost airspeed and altitude and subsequently became separated from the formation. He continued back to England on two engines, eventually reaching Old Buck' where he found the main runway blocked by the burning *Golden Gaboon*. With two propellers feathered, two engines still running, the

The battle damaged *Golden Gaboon* crashed and burned at Old Buckenham on 30 May 1944, but miraculously Lt. Wilbur Earl and his crew escaped with only minor injuries. Seymour Cohen had navigated this aircraft to England while assigned to Lt. George Wear's crew. (Donald Olds, 453rd BG Association Collection)

left landing gear still enclosed under the wing and refusing to move, Lt. Lester Baer approached one of the shorter auxiliary runways into a strong crosswind. Those 453rd personnel gathered at the flight line watched anxiously and with bated breath as *Zeus* touched down on just the right wheel from the main landing gear and the nose wheel . . . skillfully Lt. Baer managed to keep the left wing horizontal for several moments until finally it gave way—the left wing tip and prop from the number-one engine struck the tarmac and violently swung the aircraft onto the grass.

Seconds later the drama was over as *Zeus* came to a standstill amid a cloud of dust and dirt and engine fumes. The crew climbed out uninjured. Later that day in the lounge of the Officers' Club, in the company of Group CO Col. Ramsay Potts and Group Operations Officer Maj. James Stewart, Lt. Lester Baer was awarded the Distinguished Service Cross by Brig. Gen. Timberlake, the commander of the 2nd Combat Wing.

On Wednesday 31 May, the assigned target was the railroad marshaling yards four miles east of Lumes, France. Twenty-seven Liberators were dispatched from Old Buckenham; Jack Nortridge's crew flew their ship *Corky*, while their friends and hut mates, Gus Johnson's crew, was assigned *Archibald* for the mission. They encountered inaccurate flak over the French coast and then encountered cloud fronts rising up to 26,000 feet in some areas. The weather conditions were not as briefed, and there were fears that this might result in inaccurate bombing and the casualties of civilians in nearby residential areas. Therefore the 2nd Bomb Division was recalled before reaching the target area. *Corky* touched down at base after four hours and forty-five minutes flying time.

German radio propaganda later announced over the airwaves that they had fought off the Americans and the 8th Air Force had been defeated on the mission that day. In truth the 8th Air Force was sometimes defeated by the weather, but not once was a mission recalled due to enemy action. In the combat mess hall that evening, a grand dinner was served in honor of Lt. Charles Ward's crew of the 734th Squadron—the first crew in the 453rd Bomb Group to complete their tour of duty. This event was encouraging for all at Old Buck'.

The month of June was to have particular significance. The Allies had already begun misleading the Germans into believing that the anticipated Allied invasion would occur in the Pas de Calais region of France. German photographic reconnaissance aircraft were intentionally allowed to wander over southeastern England to view the buildup of troops and armament there, the wooden tanks scattered across the farmland of Kent and Sussex, the ships and landing craft on the coast, the dummy landing craft in the Thames estuary. Furthermore, Allied fighter-bomber attacks were made against Pas de Calais region, where the heavy bombers continue to pound the V.1 launch sites. The Germans became convinced that the invasion force would be coming via the Straits of Dover. Meanwhile, speculation among the American aircrews was increasing daily—some called it "invasionitis."

On Friday 2 June, the 453rd was assigned, not a strategic target such as an airfield, an aircraft factory or marshaling yard, but for the first time a tactical target. Twenty-three crews set out from Old Buckenham to bomb a German gun position near Berck-Sur-Mer in the Pas de Calais region. However, *Corky*'s crew was not assigned the mission. The following day the group was assigned a similar target. Meanwhile, Major James Stewart, who recently celebrated his thirty-sixth birthday, was promoted to Lieutenant Colonel.

CHAPTER EIGHTEEN

"Great Crusade"

Soldiers, Sailors, and Airmen of the Allied Expeditionary Force! You are about to embark upon the Great Crusade. . . . The eyes of the world are upon you. The hopes and prayers of liberty-loving people everywhere march with you. In company with our brave Allies and brothers-in-arms on other Fronts, you will bring about the destruction of the German war machine, the elimination of Nazi tyranny over the oppressed peoples of Europe, and security for ourselves in a free world. . . . Much has happened since the Nazi triumphs of 1940–41. . . . The tide has turned! The free men of the world are marching together to Victory!

Pre-D-Day address by
General Dwight D. Eisenhower,
Supreme Allied Commander-in-Chief,
Allied Forces of Liberation.

After three days of rest, Jack Nortridge's crew was alerted for the mission of Sunday 4 June, when the 8th Air Force was assigned targets in France. A force of nearly two hundred 2nd and 3rd Bomb Division Liberators were ordered to attack airfields in the Paris area while the Flying Fortress Groups of the 1st and 3rd Divisions were assigned railroad bridges as their targets. Following the mission briefing at Old Buckenham, Captain Andy Low received news of his promotion to major. Low was to fly as command pilot on board Lt. Milton Stokes's Liberator that day, leading the group to an airfield at Romorantin located one hundred miles south of Paris. It was a late mission and between 1530 and 1609 hours, twenty-six aircraft departed Old Buck'. The Nortridge crew in *Corky* led Lt. Miller in *Maid of Fury*, Lt. Fisher in *Hard T'Get*, and Lt. Osborn in *My Babs* as the high-right four-plane element in the second section. Gus Johnson's crew flew *Archibald*, visible to the left of *Corky*.

The 453rd Bomb Group's leading section of thirteen aircraft flew high-right of the 389th Bomb Group, who were leading the 2nd Wing during this mission. The Liberators received a welcoming of intense and accurate flak as they crossed the continental coastline halfway between Cherbourg and LeHavre, but subsequently no more flak was encountered on the mission and the Luftwaffe failed to make an appearance. The 389th Bomb Group led the wing on a southeasterly course, eventually reaching the target area at Romorantin where adverse weather conditions interfered. From the IP at 17,000 feet, everything seemed to be going according to plan. However, the lead bombardier on Maj. Low's aircraft mistook an ordnance depot two miles southeast of the briefed MPI (Mean Point of Impact) for the assigned target.

Meanwhile, in trail of the first section, the 453rd's second section of thirteen aircraft flew high-right on the 445th Bomb Group. The Nortridge crew in *Corky* were flying in this second section and were now approaching the target area. Upon reaching the IP they began what at first seemed to be a routine bomb run. However, as the lead bombardier of this section was making a sighting on the airfield below, in the confines of the nose turret above him, the nose turret gunner was dealing with an urgent call from nature, and when he accidentally knocked over a can of urine it leaked down from the turret, poured across the bombardier's

Crew 25 with their B-24 *"Corky" Burgundy Bombers* at Old Buckenham. Back row, left to right: Joseph DeMay, Harvey Nielsen, Lim Wing Jeong, Bill LeRoy, Aurèle "Pete" Veilleux, and Jack Nortridge. Front row, left to right: Bill Eagleson, Seymour Cohen, George White, and Perry Roberson. (Bill Eagleson/Anita Cohen)

sighting window, and froze. The bombardier's detailed vision of the ground 17,000 feet below turned to a blur and frantically he spent the last few vital seconds of the bomb run trying to scrape the ice from the window. Subsequently he made an inaccurate bomb drop and according to the official mission report, "A gross error resulted."

Bad weather and consequential navigation problems caused confusion for the 453rd Bomb Group's aircraft on the way back to England. Some of the Liberators became separated and lost, and a few of them, including *Corky*, were dangerously close to Paris and the city's anti-aircraft defenses. *Corky* struggled back across the Channel into thickening cloud over England where, with a sense of desperation, the crew found themselves roaming what they eventually realized was Salisbury Plain.

Bill Eagleson recalls:

> That was the day that we almost bought it! We were coming in low, and we had an undercast and we saw some green through the undercast. . . . I was standing between Jack and George on the flight deck and we looked out and we could just see a sort of a greenish effect in front of the aircraft and we all yelled together!

Jack immediately applied full throttle and it took all of his and George's strength to pull *Corky* up the side of the hill. The crew was lost and looking for somewhere to land. Seymour Cohen managed to navigate them back to Norfolk where they attempted to land at RAF Downham Market. George White made radio contact on the command set and the RAF responded by firing rockets through the low cloud to indicate the location of the runway. With limited visibility, the weather getting worse by the minute, and time running out . . . Jack began an almost blind landing approach and the rest of the crew sweated out his skills. But realizing his approach was too high, at the last moment Jack decided to go round again.

With a very low fuel supply they knew they had only a few chances to get *Corky* down on the ground. Anxiously, Bill Eagleson began to count their attempts and momentarily held up one finger, and then two fingers as Jack began a second approach. But again, Jack felt uneasy and aborted in favor of making a third pass. Meanwhile the RAF continued their firework display to welcome in their American visitors. Bill Eagleson held up three fingers, fearing that they were running out of time. On the third pass Jack confidently put *Corky* down on the runway at Downham Market and the crew breathed a sigh of relief. It was Sunday afternoon; the crew had survived the mission and arrived at an RAF airfield, as Bill Eagleson recalls, "just in time for tea!"

The crew were to remain at Downham Market overnight, and were assigned billets for their stay. As they relaxed in their quarters they were visited by some British WAAFs (Women's Auxiliary Air Force) who brought them tea and snacks, much to the crew's pleasant surprise.

They knew that the WAAFs' American counterparts, the WACs, wouldn't dare go within one hundred yards of flying crews' billets!

Although the 453rd Bomb Group suffered no losses that day, several other aircraft were forced to land at other bases on the way home. Gus Johnson took his crew into Gravely airfield in Kent and Lt. Miller's crew made it into Halesworth, Suffolk. The following morning, Jack Nortridge's crew flew back to Old Buckenham, where they found an overwhelming sense of anticipation amid heightened speculation. No missions had been dispatched that morning, and early in the afternoon the Liberty Run to Norwich was canceled. Much earlier than usual, the metallic voice from the base Tannoy system made an announcement—"Standby, everyone alerted!" All movement was confined to base and all telephone calls were suspended. In addition, on their return to Old Buck', the Nortridge crew discovered that their two mascot Windermere Terriers, Corky and Flak, were badly ill with distemper.

> Old Buck' looked like a combat zone. Troops were armed with carbines, colts, helmets and carrying gas masks. Before getting shut up on the ground we had to get our pets to a Norwich vet. . . . The only way we could get off the base was through the kindness of our flight surgeon, Major Lloyd, who gave us an ambulance to take the two dogs, Corky and Flak, to the veterinary.

Jack and Bill cleared the base in the ambulance with the puppies and headed for Norwich. Every lane around Old Buckenham and all roads to Norwich were clogged with troops, tanks, jeeps, and armored trucks, but the ambulance ensured priority through the military traffic and eventually they reached the city.

> Being an ambulance, MPs waved us through—A crowd gathered at Norwich market place. We parked near a mews—"What's happening?" on the faces of all assembled. The back door opened, Jack Nortridge and I stepped out with two "pups" wrapped in GI blankets. The gathering was astonished. . . . Leaving our pups with a Norwich vet, Jack and I returned to base for involvement in the big war.

Back at Old Buck' the restless flying crews confined to their base were under orders to stand by with their gas masks and .45 caliber handguns at the ready. Expectantly they tried to pass the time up until the scheduled late dinner. Bill Eagleson cycled out to the dispersal point to check on their B-24, *Corky*. Each serviceable Liberator around the field was now being readied with fuel, bombs, and ammunition in preparation for a maximum effort mission. There was an atmosphere of excitement in the air at Old Buck' that evening and the crews got the impression that their most significant mission was about to commence. At eight o'clock that evening the Tannoy system around the base updated the group's personnel with these instructions: " All combat crews check with operations immediately. . . . Waves number 1, number 2, number 3, 4, 5, and 6 of A-Flight, briefing at 2300; B-Flight all waves, briefing at 0300; C-Flight, all waves, briefing at 0400."

Combat crews made their way to their assigned squadron's operations buildings situated within the base technical site. The new terminology of "waves" and "flights" had been introduced in preparation for *Operation Overlord*—the Allied invasion of occupied Europe. The role assigned to the 8th Air Force was to support Allied ground forces by "neutralizing" the enemy defense installations along the Normandy coastline in the invasion area between Le Havre and Cherbourg, and as far inland as the city of Caen. Briefing was scheduled for 2300 hours for the first D-Day mission, 8th Air Force No. 394, which would be flown at first light on the morning of the invasion.

At 2315 hours the briefing room doors were locked and the roll was taken. Col. Ramsay Potts commenced the mission briefing with a wire from 8th Air Force Commander Gen. Jimmy Doolittle, which began: "We are summoned to participate in a history-making invasion." At midnight it became a certainty that 6 June 1944 would be D-Day. A message from Gen. Hodges, commander of the 2nd Bomb Division, was read next: "The enemy defenses must be destroyed . . . the success of all men of all nations participating will be profoundly affected by our efforts . . . we must not fail them now."

A large map focusing on the French coastline replaced the familiar map of Europe. Lt. Col. James Stewart briefed the crews on their assigned formation positions and then Lt. Col. Harris added further specific details relating to the first mission of the day. Takeoff was to commence at 0200 hours when thirty-six Liberators, each carrying fifty-two 100-pound "anti-personnel" bombs, would depart the base at intervals as six "waves" of six aircraft, thus eliminating confusion and reducing the risk of collision in the cloud and darkness. The purpose of the 453rd Bomb Group's mission, the crews were told, was the direct support of American troops who were being transported across the Channel in landing craft to Omaha Beach. One of five Normandy coastal sectors designated for the deployment of Allied landing forces, Omaha Beach was a four-mile stretch of sand between Colleville-sur-Mer and Vierville-sur-Mer. The target assigned to the 453rd was a tactical target, a defense position guarding Omaha Beach that was located near St. Laurent, Normandy; zero hour would be 0628 hours; code word: *Maisey-Doats.*

Capt. Crowley and Lt. Friedman of S-2 (Intelligence) elaborated on target details. Located one mile north of St. Laurent, the primary target was one of many gun positions just three hundred yards from the shore with an estimated complement of forty men with machine guns, two- or three-inch mortars, and antitank guns. Due to the landing of Allied troops along the coastline in the target area below, it was stressed that precise timing would be of utmost importance. Secondary targets would be any railroad, enemy troop concentration, or road junction further inland. With mission briefings completed the crews collected their flying equipment and boarded transport to their aircraft dispersed around the field.

Meanwhile, the first American parachutists of *Operation Overlord* had landed in the Normandy countryside at 0020 hours, while simultaneously a battalion of British infantry troops and Royal Engineers landed in Horsa gliders. During the next three hours a further one hundred U.S. gliders and two U.S. Army Divisions landed, and a British Airborne Division carried by over three hundred aircraft and almost one hundred gliders. These Allied airborne forces were successful in disorganizing German communications, neutralizing defenses, and seizing two bridges, despite the strain of high winds, initial navigational confusion, and losses of personnel and equipment.

Out on the darkened airfield at Old Buckenham, crews of the 453rd Bomb Group prepared themselves for the mission and climbed aboard their aircraft for the briefed "stations" time of 0100 hours. Jack Nortridge's crew went through the preflight checks in *Corky* at their dispersal point close to the control tower. Thirty-six bomb-laden Liberators taxied out with their navigation lights switched on. Takeoff commenced, as briefed, at 0200 hours. Within a couple of minutes the first wave of six aircraft had departed. Ten minutes elapsed between each wave of six aircraft until finally the last ship left the base at 0327 hours.

Bill Eagleson:

> We took gas masks onto our plane. We were under orders to fly with gas masks due to the possibilities of the Germans retaliating with gas. . . . This mission was gratifying—we realized a cause. The most difficult part of that day for the fellows on the plane, and [particularly for] Jack and George, was instrument conditions— taking off at night in the dark . . . into thick, maximum, nail-biting overcast.

At 9,500 feet *Corky* broke out above the cloud and the crew found the sky filled with aircraft illuminated by the light of the full moon, multicolored arcs of identification flares and blinking navigation lights. When clouds continued to build up underneath the aircraft, the waves of 453rd Bomb Group aircraft formed into two sections at 2,000 feet higher than briefed. *Corky* took up the assigned position in the first section, behind Johnson's crew in *Star Eyes*. Formation assembly for this mission was particularly nerve-racking because of the increased likelihood of midair collisions, and for most of the pilots it was their first real experience of night-time formation flying.

Some 1,800 8th Air Force heavy bombers were airborne over Eastern England in preparation for the first mission. Led by a 389th Bomb Group Pathfinder aircraft, the Bungay-based 446th Bomb Group was the first formation of B-24 Liberators over the Normandy beaches. Following the

2nd Bomb Division's Liberator formations were B-17 Flying Fortresses of the 1st Bomb Division and the Fortresses and Liberators of the 3rd Bomb Division. Thirty-six squadrons of P-51 Mustangs and P-47 Thunderbolts were also taking to the skies, briefed to escort the bombers to France before peeling away to strafe ground targets.

The formations turned to the south and eventually crossed the English coast and proceeded across the Channel. The aircrews had anticipated seeing the Allied Navy off the French coast firing their shells at the German gun positions while landing craft waited to slide onto the beaches—but instead, many of the American aircrews looked blankly at cloud, while others caught occasional glimpses of action through broken cloud. Disappointed that they could not see much of the great spectacle below, they knew nevertheless that beneath them was a seaborne armada of more than 2,700 vessels spread across the Channel from England to the beaches of Normandy. Besides the huge 8th Air Force formations leaving southern England that morning, there were also 9th Air Force medium bombers and RAF fighters and bombers. An estimated 11,000 Allied aircraft were sent into battle on D-Day; the weakened German Air Force was not expected to pose much of a threat. Confidently, Gen. Eisenhower had told his forces that if any aircraft were seen overhead, they would be Allied aircraft.

Before the Allied Armies crossing the Channel by boat were able to land on the beaches, the German defenses would first be assaulted by a combined attack of naval and air bombardment which began at 0530 hours. While the Allied Navy force fired their guns at the coastline, waves of 8th Air Force heavy bombers and 9th Air Force B-26 and A-20 medium bombers approached Normandy. As the formations of 2nd Bomb Division Liberators began their bomb runs, the aircrews knew that directly below them were American soldiers who were anxiously waiting to fight their way onto Omaha Beach. With the exception of occasional flashes from the naval barrages, Jack Nortridge's crew in *Corky* could not see too much of the coastline or the action below them, but they saw just enough to confirm that the Allied invasion was on.

Perry Roberson:

> We knew it was for real when we could see those battleships pouring shells into the beach . . . the awesome thing is the fate of our country was in the hands of nineteen- and twenty-year olds.

The limited light and restricted visibility meant that bombardiers were briefed to drop their bombs on the sighting made by the radar-equipped Pathfinder aircraft that were leading each group. For the 453rd Bomb Group it was "bombs away" at 0628 hours. Just two minutes later the first of thousands of landing craft plowed onto the sand as the American troops of two U.S. battalions fought the bloody battle of Omaha Beach.

Caught in the currents of rough seas, many of the landing craft were wrecked by underwater obstacles and damaged by German fire. Most of the American amphibious tanks became swamped and sank. Regrettably, there were extremely high numbers of casualties even before reaching the shore. The American troops became engulfed in clouds of dust from the naval shelling of the beachheads, and many became caught between enemy fire and rising tides. In the chaos of the treacherous conditions, one of the battalions landed half a mile from its scheduled point and became the target of heavy fire from the concrete gun fortifications.

The American bombers had bombed through an undercast and consequently much of the initial aerial bombardment at Omaha Beach had been ineffective in its objectives and a high proportion of the enemy coastal defenses had remained operational. The aircrews were acutely aware that American troops were present so very close to the targets and consequently bombs were dropped with particular caution, many of them falling too far inland. But even where bombs fell accurately, the thickness of concrete protecting the gun fortifications cushioned the impact. Up to an hour after the first Liberators attacked the Omaha sector, B-17 Fortresses continued the attacks. The sea-to-shore naval bombardments were also largely inaccurate due to the low ceiling level and the clouds of dust that restricted visibility.

While the landings at Omaha Beach may almost have turned into disaster, the American landings to the west at Utah Beach were regarded as a success. The water was calmer and the area less exposed, and the 9th Air Force's B-26 medium bombers managed to neutralize the beach defenses prior to the landings at Utah. In the British landing sectors, the assault on Sword Beach followed successful RAF attacks while movement inland was delayed at Gold Beach when RAF aircraft were unsuccessful in attacking some of their targets. Canadian troops were late in landing at Juno Beach, which gave the Germans time to prepare, following the Allied air attacks.

For the Old Buckenham aircrews, the first *Operation Overlord* mission turned out to be something of a milk run, regardless of the huge scale and significance of the mission. Both flak and fighter opposition were nonexistent. The 453rd Bomb Group returned to Old Buck' after the first mission of D-Day with no losses. *Corky* landed back at Old Buck' after five hours and forty-two minutes flying time. The crews were tired from the mission and from having been awake for more than twenty-four hours. *Corky*'s crew was able to go to their huts to sleep while for others the day was only about to begin. Despite deteriorating weather, final preparations for a second mission of D-Day were almost complete, as the 8th Air Force launched assaults on railroad bridges and airfields in the Normandy area. On that day the 453rd Bomb Group dispatched a total of seventy sorties from Old Buckenham, although twelve Liberators dispatched on the second mission returned early due to the unfavorable weather conditions.

The 8th's fighters flew patrols over Normandy and attacked ground targets throughout D-Day, while other Allied aircraft protected the shipping lanes and provided support for the assault troops. That night nearly one thousand RAF bombers flew missions to block enemy transport routes into Normandy, and by the early hours of Wednesday 7 June, it was clear that the Allies had secured a foothold in Europe — *Operation Overlord* had so far been a success. On D-Day the bloodiest battles were fought by the thousands of Allied ground soldiers and paratroopers who landed on Normandy's beaches and fields before fighting their way inland. However, the RAF and USAAF's concentrated bombing campaign during 1943 and the first half of 1944 had led the Allies to attain air superiority over Europe. The Luftwaffe failed to make much of an appearance on 6 June 1944, and this absence was significant to the success of D-Day.

CHAPTER NINETEEN

Hamburg and Berlin

T he news of D-Day reached the U.S. almost instantly. That evening, Harvey Nielsen's sister-in-law wrote to Harvey's niece:

Dear Iris and everyone, the big Invasion started last night and
I hope finished quickly and successfully. I wonder where Harvey
is . . .

During the week following D-Day the 8th Air Force continued flying
tactical missions, weather permitting, in support of the ground troops
who were fighting their way further into France. Communications systems, rail networks, and Luftwaffe airfields continued to be the targets
for the American bombers. On the morning of Wednesday 7 June,
D-Day-plus-one, twenty-three Liberators departed Old Buckenham to
bomb a vital communications center at Argentan, forty miles south of
Le Havre. *Corky*'s crew returned to Old Buck' safely after their five hour
and thirty-eight minute flight. They rested the following day while other
crews flew, and then on Friday all 8th Air Force operations were prevented by unfavorable weather.

On the morning of Saturday 10 June, the 453rd Bomb Group dispatched two missions simultaneously. Mission number one was assigned
the airfield at Evreux, forty miles west of Paris, as its primary objective;
the second mission was assigned the airfield at Dreux, twenty miles
southeast of Evreux. A total of thirty-four aircraft left Old Buck' and
formed into two sections, but confusion resulted from both missions trying to form in overcast using the same flare signals, at the same time and
altitude over Old Buckenham. Fourteen aircraft returned to base early
and three aircraft bombed Illier airfield with the 93rd Bomb Group.
Jack Nortridge's crew in *Corky*, flying with the second formation,
bombed the airfield at Dreux before returning to base and landing after
five hours and twenty-six minutes flying time.

Again on Sunday 11 June the 453rd Bomb Group dispatched two
missions to France. Mission number one was to bomb a railroad bridge
over the Loire River at Le Port Boulet, some fifty miles southwest of
Tours. Weather interfered and twenty-four aircraft were forced to return to base without completing the mission. Jack Nortridge's crew had
been awakened at 0130 hours for mission number two. Twelve crews
were assigned the mission with the objective of a visual attack on the

German fighter base at Cormeilles-en-Vexin, northwest of Paris. *Corky* was undergoing maintenance and so Jack Nortridge was assigned to fly *Sweet Sue*, a new silver Liberator. Following the mission briefing, the crew was driven out to dispersal point number seventeen in the 735th Squadron dispersal area on the far side of the airfield. Twelve Liberators started their engines at 0500 hours, and began to taxi out.

Nortridge in *Sweet Sue* led the right three-plane element; to the left was a shiny new B-24J named *Stinky* and to the right was another new B-24J named *Mary Harriet*. One of the group's Liberators returned to base early and eleven continued to the target area, reaching the IP at 0746, nine minutes behind schedule. Over the target they found broken cloud and were greeted with flak and ground rockets. The lead ship suffered a malfunction, accidentally dropping its load too early and eight other bombardiers dropped their bombs simultaneously, believing the lead bombardier had sighted the target. Reconnaissance photographs revealed that the main bomb fall had been twenty-six miles short of the target! Two bombardiers held their bombs, certain that they hadn't yet reached the target—ten minutes later they both made sightings with their Sperry bombsights and dropped their bombs directly on the Luftwaffe airfield. The Group returned to base, and *Sweet Sue* landed after a four-hour-and-twenty-three-minute flight.

Following the pattern of the past two days, the 453rd Bomb Group dispatched two missions to France on Monday 12 June. Weather was clear over the targets, a railroad bridge at Montford and an airfield at Conches. The Nortridge crew was not assigned to fly that day, although their hut mates, Gus Johnson's crew, flew *Star Eyes*. The Luftwaffe made their strongest presence since before D-Day, costing the 8th Air Force six B-17s and two B-24s. A battle-damaged, Norfolk-based B-24 became the first heavy bomber to land on a Normandy airstrip—no longer did battle-damaged aircraft have to recross the Channel before finding refuge. On this day Hitler unleashed his newest weapon on London—the V.1 flying bomb. Launched from the Pas de Calais coastline, it became known to the Londoners who lived under its threat as the Doodlebug.

On Thursday 13 June the crews at Old Buckenham were woken just half an hour after midnight, but the mission was subsequently called off and then rescheduled. Twenty-two crews were briefed at three o'clock for two targets in France, twenty-five miles apart, a railroad bridge at La Vicomte-sur-Rance, northeast of Dinan, and the railroad bridge at Montford that had been attempted by the Group on the previous day. Twenty-two Liberators each carrying ten 500-pound bombs formed over the base in two formations of eleven and were joined by two radar-equipped PFF lead ships from Hethel.

The Nortridge crew in *Corky* and the Johnson crew in *Star Eyes* both took their positions in the second formation and headed for Montford. Official records suggest that *Corky* ended up in first formation over La

Vicomte-sur-Rance; however, the combat mission records for the members of *Corky*'s crew credit them with a mission to Montford. The first formation allegedly made a visual drop on their target and apparently partially hit the bridge, while the radar equipment in the second formation's lead aircraft failed and results were deemed to be poor. All aircraft returned safely to Old Buck' and *Corky* landed after five hours and thirty-eight minutes flying time.

On Thursday 15 June, three of the four squadrons assigned to the 453rd Bomb Group were assigned a mission to France. *Corky*'s crew joined the group formation as it departed to bomb a bridge just thirty-five feet wide at LePort Boulet. The 453rd Bomb Group dropped over one hundred tons of bombs onto the bridge, and reconnaissance photographs later revealed that although the bridge was not broken, it was severely damaged. *Corky* landed back at base after this five-hour-and-fifty-four-minute round trip. Due to unfavorable weather all Liberators remained on the ground at Old Buck' for the next two days.

Some time in June 1944, the 453rd Bomb Group began to remove the ball turrets from its Liberators when the defensive value of this turret was brought into question. Because of the drag and reduction in airspeed resulting from the lowered turret, often the turret would only be lowered during fighter attacks, and sometimes by the time it was lowered the attacks were over. Bill Eagleson recalls the primary reason for the reduction in the B-24's defences:

> The Germans were running out of aggressive, experienced combat fliers, fighter pilots. We noticed that someplace early on in May, their usual aggressiveness of hitting us at 12 o'clock, rolling through the formation, and taking a B-24, was not happening. . . .
> They were not the aggressive-type fighter pilots that we experienced early on in the days of our Group's initiation to combat conditions over Europe.

The Luftwaffe could not train pilots as quickly as they were losing them. Sometimes, such as the missions to Brunswick on 8 April and 8 May and the mission to Politz on 29 May 1944, the Luftwaffe appeared to be as strong as ever. For many months ahead the German fighter pilots remained a threat, often mustering the strength and resources to attack the American bombers with notable prowess. In July 1944 the Luftwaffe launched a new fighter into operations—the Me262 was the world's first operational jet; however, Hitler was preoccupied with offensive rather than defensive investment and at first insisted the jet be employed as a bomber.

In September 1944, although air superiority clearly belonged to the Allies, the Luftwaffe proved that it could still inflict devastation upon the American bomber formations. On a mission to Kassel, Germany, the Luftwaffe managed to shoot down twenty-five Liberators from the 445th Bomb Group formation during an attack lasting just three minutes. Two more Liberators crash-landed in France, two landed at the emergency base at Manston in Kent, and another crashed at Old Buckenham. Of the thirty-seven Liberators dispatched from Tibenham that morning, only seven made it back to base. But such incidents were rare, and mostly the Luftwaffe appeared to be weak. While the flak never ceased and continued to be a deadly menace to the bomber formations, more often than not the Luftwaffe would be represented by just a small number of fighters and it was apparent from their tactics that they were inexperienced and less determined. Increasingly on missions the Luftwaffe failed to show up at all.

In removing the ball turrets on the B-24s, aircraft weight was reduced, air resistance was minimized, and cruising speed increased. The 453rd Bomb Group crews were generally unaffected by the removal of the ball turrets and continued their missions with ten men on each crew. On *Corky*, Joe DeMay flew the rest of his missions as a waist gunner, sharing these duties with flight engineer Perry Roberson and radio operator Bill LeRoy.

Following the tactical missions of recent weeks in support of *Operation Overlord*, the 8th Air Force and RAF were preparing to return to strategic targets in Germany, with oil targets being given priority. The effects of Allied bombing on the German synthetic oil industry were profound. Germany had produced 175,000 tons of aviation oil in April 1944 but during June production had been reduced to 55,000 tons; later, in September the figure would be just 7,000 tons.[1] With fuel reserves running low, the Luftwaffe's fighter operations were being continually reduced while training units were either operating in a state of disarray or were disbanded. For the Allied aircrews, the chance of survival was increasing, while the Allied ground forces fighting further into Europe were less susceptible to enemy air attack. Meanwhile, German soldiers fighting on the ground declared, "If it's a silver aircraft, it's American; if it's black, it's British; and if you can't see it, then it's the Luftwaffe!"

On the morning of Sunday 18 June almost 1,400 heavy bombers were dispatched to bomb oil refineries and Luftwaffe control centers in the vicinities of Hamburg, Misburg, Bremen, Fassberg, and Stade. Forty-six crews at Old Buckenham were called just fifteen minutes after midnight for breakfast—the mess halls had never been so busy. Forty-six was so far the highest number of aircraft that the 453rd Bomb Group had dispatched on one mission. It was apparent that it would not be a milk run and that it would be a maximum effort to Germany. After breakfast the crews crowded into the briefing hall, where it was announced that due to the scale of the mission, the group was briefed to fly in four sections rather than the usual two or occasional three. The curtain was pulled back to reveal two targets in the vicinity of the great industrial city of Hamburg—important oil refineries and Stade airfield, located to the west of the city.

For Harvey Nielsen, top turret gunner on *Corky*, the mission was particularly poignant, for two of his aunts from Denmark lived in Hamburg. Jack Nortridge's crew in *Corky*, Gus Johnson's crew in *Star Eyes*, and
forty-four other crews made their preflight preparations and were all set
for an instrument takeoff at the briefed time of 0430. As they waited for
further instructions a yellow flare signaled them to standby. Slow, anxious minutes passed; an hour, and still they waited. Finally at six o'clock
the group took to the skies and assembled as four sections. *Corky* flew
with the other 733rd Squadron aircraft as the fourth section. Over the
North Sea the crews welcomed the arrival of their fighter escort, which
included the sleek-looking, twin-engine P-38 Lightnings. Over Germany the aircrews could see the horrifying effects of the Allied round-
the-clock bombing campaign, as Bill Eagleson recalls:

> That day in June . . . all of Germany seemed to be on fire. . . . We
> had smoke up to our bombing altitude. . . . You looked over Ger-
> many and there was a black pall that just said, "Hey you guys,
> you're close to having it!" We saw the columns of smoke rising up
> to twenty-two thousand feet. . . . You could see Germany burning.
> You could look to the south and you saw Brunswick and some of
> these other big cities were just tall columns of black, *black* smoke—
> just like a signal that said "Why? Why does this have to happen?"

As the 453rd Bomb Group approached the IP of the bomb run, the
weather deteriorated and the Liberators received a welcome from
Hamburg's anti-aircraft gunners, who fired concentrated flak into the
path of the bomber formation, causing considerable damage to a number of the aircraft. The sections assigned to bomb Stade airfield failed to
locate this primary target and therefore reverted to the secondary target.
No fighters were encountered, and the waist gunners busied themselves
by throwing bundles of chaff out of the rear escape hatches in the floors
of their bombers, to screen the bombers from the anti-aircraft gunners'
radar equipment. The fighter escort remained present throughout the
most potentially hazardous stage of the mission.

According to official records each of the four sections of the group
formation bombed either the oil refineries or the port area of Hamburg
through haze and smoke from altitudes between 22,000 and 24,500
feet. Maybe Pete Veilleux was remembering another mission when he
recalled:

> I think we came in at 12,000 feet that day and we could see the
> people scurrying on the ground, and we dropped the bombs. It
> kind of hurts your feelings in a way because needless to say, we
> killed a few innocent people. But that was war!

Following the bomb run on Hamburg, clouds and dense contrails
from aircraft engines hindered reorganization of the group's formation
at the rally point, but the formation was finally restored upon recrossing

the enemy coast. *Corky* touched down at Old Buck' after five hours and fifty-four minutes. All crews were back at base soon after midday. Other groups had not been so fortunate.

Although he didn't know it until many weeks later, Harvey Nielsen's second cousin, Martin From, was killed in action in France on 19 June. On 25 June his family in Nodaway County, Missouri, received a war office telegram announcing his death. This gave the Nielsens even more reason to worry for Harvey and his brother George, who were both overseas in the Army Air Force (George was an army nurse stationed in Africa).

Some time during June 1944, letters that had been written to George White by his parents were "returned to sender" by the U.S. Postal Service. The White family feared the worst, but in the absence of a telegram from the War Department, they could do nothing but wait for news. Fortunately, they had nothing to worry about and George was alive and well.

London and the whole of southeastern England was being victimized daily by Hitler's flying bombs. The V.1 launching ramps in the Pas de Calais region started receiving renewed attention from both American and British bombers. On Tuesday 20 June the 8th Air Force launched its largest force to date, dispatching bombers on a maximum effort to oil refineries and industrial targets in Germany and Poland, as well as V.1 launch sites in France. A single squadron of eleven aircraft left Old Buckenham for a return to the *Noball* target at Fienvillers, where a V.1 launch site was reportedly put out of action. Gus Johnson's crew in *Star Eyes* and eleven other crews set out for a second *Noball* target, the V.1 base at St. Martin L'Mortier.

Meanwhile, Jack Nortridge's crew joined twenty-three other crews in the briefing hall in preparation for a return to the synthetic oil plant at Politz, located in distant Poland. However, after his encounter with an estimated two hundred enemy fighters over Politz on 29 May, Bill LeRoy was not sorry that he hadn't been assigned the mission (his mission total currently exceeded the rest of the crew, having begun his tour standing in on Catlin's crew for two missions). A replacement radio operator was assigned to Crew 25 that day. Twenty-four Liberators departed Old Buck' at around 0500 hours destined for occupied Poland. Liberators formed into three-plane elements and elements formed into two sections; *Corky*'s crew found their assigned position right up at the front section, on the left wing of the lead ship, a B-24 named *Porky*.

Formation assembly continued as sections formed into groups and groups formed into wings—however, on this mission there were problems and delays when the B-24 combat wings failed to assemble as a division formation. Despite there being seven hundred fighters escorting the 8th's bombers that day, some of the B-24 wings were dispersed too far and wide, making it difficult for the fighters to provide adequate protection. As the Liberators proceeded to Poland one of the fighter groups was having technical problems jettisoning a new type of wing-mounted drop tank, leaving just one Mustang Group to cover the dangerously loose 2nd Bomb Division formation of over three hundred B-24s. And when the Liberators found themselves without cover, the Luftwaffe intercepted. As the leading 14th Combat Wing crossed the Danish coast, Luftwaffe fighters struck over the Baltic Sea, costing the 492nd Bomb Group five Liberators.

From the 453rd Bomb Group's formation, crews witnessed two B-24s collide soon before 0900. Both were from the Hethel-based 389th Bomb Group, and only three parachutes were seen. Smoke screens and barrage balloons were visible at Kiel and Eckernforde, and a Liberator was seen heading toward neutral Sweden. At around 1000 the 453rd reached the IP and began the straight and level bomb run through flak-filled skies. *Corky* caught a few blasts of shrapnel but fortunately the damage was not serious. Two ships from the first section were not in their briefed formation position over the target area, but all twenty-four airborne Liberators of the 453rd dropped their bombs on the target as briefed.

Five minutes later, two more Liberators were seen heading for Sweden. Lt. Donald Kolb's crew, from the 735th Bomb Squadron, was in trouble. Their ship, *Becky*, had been hit by flak over the target and they were rapidly losing fuel. Clearly they were not going to make it back to Old Buck'. This crew was nearing the end of its combat tour and they found themselves in the face of adversity. They wanted to go home as soon as possible, but rather than risking their lives or risk being taken prisoner by the Germans by attempting to make it to England, they decided to hop over the Baltic Sea where they interned in Sweden. Better to be alive than dead; better to wait out the rest of the war in Sweden than in a German prison camp.

As *Corky* winged its way homeward, a plume of smoke reached up to bombing altitude from the burning oil refinery below and all around there were similar scenes of destruction. The bomber formations were engulfed in flak and when that ended the enemy fighters returned. Half an hour after the bomb drop, a B-24 was seen on fire and in serious trouble; it turned for Sweden. Bill Eagleson recalls that as well as flak and fighters, on the way home the sky was filled with

> The grey chutes of the Germans and the white chutes of the American Air Force hitting into the North Sea. That was quite a mission.

Corky landed at Old Buck' after seven hours and fifty-three minutes flying time. The exhausted crews attended "interrogation" (debriefing) where they recalled the details and events of the mission for Intelligence—of particular importance were the locations of the flak defences encountered during the mission; at what point enemy fighters intercepted; details of where Liberators were lost, and how many parachutes were seen. Having kept extensive notes in his logbook, Seymour Cohen was able to provide detailed information.

Mercifully, the 453rd Bomb Group lost just one Liberator on this mission, an aircraft from the 735th Squadron last seen heading towards neutral Sweden, from where Lt. Donald Kolb's crew was later reported safe. In total, forty-eight American bombers failed to return to England, twenty of which landed in Sweden. The majority of the losses were Liberators and crews from the Norfolk bases. Worst off was the 492nd Bomb Group at North Pickenham—fourteen Liberators and their crews were missing in action.

That night, *Corky*'s crew was again put on mission alert. This would be their thirtieth mission (Bill Eagleson's twenty-ninth, having been grounded on 9 May following a tooth extraction), but they anticipated that it would not be their last, because combat tours had recently been extended to thirty-five missions! However, because the crew had already completed the majority of their missions when this change occurred, they were expected to fly only one or two missions beyond thirty. George White and Bill LeRoy were not assigned the 21 June mission. They hoped for their crew's sake that it would be a milk run.

Little more than an hour past midnight, crews were awakened at Old Buckenham. In the combat mess hall they tried to fill up on food that they could barely face at that ungodly hour, but they knew a long day was ahead and this was their only chance to eat. Following breakfast they congregated in the briefing hall to learn of the "target for today" and they were unhappy to learn that they were headed for "Big B"—Berlin!

Corky's crew was particularly anxious, as they had hoped for something a little less like suicide right near the end of their combat tour. Maybe the selected target explains why George and LeRoy were not assigned the mission. After all, both of them had already completed thirty missions, as both of them had flown with other crews on the 6 March mission to Berlin. But then, Seymour Cohen had flown that mission too—and now for his thirtieth, approaching the end of his tour, he was being sent back to bloody Berlin! Enraged, Seymour sat through the briefing and tried to contain his dissatisfaction.

There was expected to be between eight-tenths and ten-tenths cloud cover with contrails at twenty-four thousand feet. The 453rd Bomb Group's target was the Diesel works at Nordban, a Berlin plant that was believed to be manufacturing the engines for V.1 flying bombs. Following the mission briefing, Seymour stormed into the office of the 733rd Squadron CO, Major Robert Coggeshall, and with his loud, booming voice he demanded to know, "Are you trying to kill us?"

Thirty-four Liberators departed Old Buck' and formed into three sections. *Corky* had taken a hammering during the Politz mission on the previous day and was undergoing repairs. The Nortridge crew along with a stand-in copilot and radio operator was assigned the B-24 named *Rag Doll* and were briefed to fly with *Partial Payment* and *Ford's Folly* as a three-plane element in the third section of twelve aircraft. Meanwhile, Lt. Robert Catlin's crew in the B-24 named *My Babs* was forced to abort the mission when they discovered a leak in the oxygen supply.

The 453rd Bomb Group crossed the North Sea and proceeded towards Denmark until north of Wilhelmshaven, then turned onto a southeasterly course. The carpet of cloud below began to break up. Hamburg became visible to the right, but slightly obscured by a dense plume of smoke that rose up to the Liberators' altitude from the burning oil refineries bombed three days previously. Over one thousand American bombers were airborne; the ratio of bombers to escorting fighters was almost one to one. This was to be the biggest raid Berlin had so far endured. But the presence of one thousand P-38s, P-47s, and P-51s didn't discourage the Luftwaffe from defending their capital city. Prior to the IP of the bomb run approximately twenty Me410s intercepted the 453rd Bomb Group's formation.

Bill Eagleson recalls:

> Hell of a place to go on one's 29th mission. It was quite a show. German fighters, Me-109, -210, -410, queued up for attack about twenty minutes from target . . .

Pete, Harvey, and Jeong in their turrets and Perry and Joe at the waist guns rattled off round after round of .50 caliber shells. Jack and the stand-in copilot tried to nose into the fighters as the head-on waves approached. Seymour tried to ignore the chaos around him to continue his navigations and soon announced that they were nearing the IP. Bill Eagleson crawled under the flight deck into the nose compartment of the Liberator and prepared for the bomb run. Several waves of enemy fighters plagued the 453rd; their retreat was followed by heavy flak. As the Liberators circled in cloudless blue skies for an approach from the east of Berlin, the 2nd Combat Wing lead, high-right, and low-left structure was replaced by an in-line trail of aircraft following the IP. Airspeed was reduced to a crawling pace and the bomb run commenced.

One of the 453rd Bomb Group's aircraft, *Archibald (What Da Hell)*, had been damaged by flak and then attacked by enemy fighters. The pilot was Lt. Melvin Williams of the 735th Squadron. His crew was one of the original 453rd Bomb Group crews from Idaho, and they were flying their twenty-eighth mission—they were looking forward to going home very soon. But just before reaching the target they were attacked by nine JU88s and their Liberator was riddled with 20mm cannon shells. The propeller spinner dome of the number-one engine was badly damaged and immediately all the engine oil was lost from that engine. With no hydraulic control the pilots had no control over this engine and were unable to feather the propeller. Another shell passed through the cockpit en route to the radio compartment, where it caused a fire. A shell fragment hit the radio operator in the forehead, removing the skin down to the bone the whole width of his head. The entire crew managed to escape the burning bomber and were later reported to be prisoners of war.

On board the B-24 *Rag Doll*, Bill Eagleson was focusing the bombsight on the ground below, trying to ignore the magnified flak shells exploding beneath the aircraft. The minute the flak ceased, the Luftwaffe immediately returned and just seconds later Bill Eagleson announced, "Bombs away!" From thirty-four Liberators, the bombs rained down in the vicinity of the factory and according to the official report, "the great majority of them hit as briefed."

The sequence of enemy fighters, flak, and then more fighter attacks lasted for the duration of over fifteen minutes, which seemed like an eternity to the bomber crews. The 389th from Hethel lost six and the 445th from Tibenham lost two Liberators. Over the target area, P-51s and P-38s arrived and offered some assistance to the bomber crews. Rather than gathering airspeed after the bomb drop, the 453rd Bomb Group proceeded to the rally point at a slow pace to allow some of its crippled aircraft to keep up. Consequently, the group was late for the rally and the 2nd Combat Wing formation was not fully reassembled. Meanwhile, at Old Buckenham George White and Bill LeRoy awoke and discovered that their crew had gone to Berlin. The 453rd made it back to Old Buck' low on fuel, and the Nortridge crew landed after a grueling eight hours and nineteen minutes.

On Saturday 24 June, George White and Bill LeRoy were back with their crew for their thirty-first mission. The 453rd Bomb Group's assigned primary target was an airfield at Bretigny, France. *Corky* was still under repair following the mission to Politz four days previously and so Jack Nortridge's crew was assigned *Star Eyes*. This aircraft had become the regular aircraft of Gus Johnson's crew, who were not assigned to fly on this day. Following an early morning briefing the Nortridge crew collected their flying equipment and rode out on trucks and jeeps to *Star Eyes* at dispersal point number forty-nine. Twenty-four ships left Old Buck' that morning and assembled as two sections. The Nortridge crew took up the briefed position in the first section.

Flying over France at 0800 hours the aircrews saw flak exploding to the right of the formation. Ten minutes later the 453rd Bomb Group was flying high over the target area, which was obscured by ten-tenths cloud cover. In the absence of radar lead aircraft, a bomb run was not attempted. Instead, the bombers circled the town of Dreux, thirty miles west of Paris, before heading twenty miles to the northwest to Conches where they located an airfield as a last resort target. The group endured flak on the bomb run and at 0846 hours the lead bombardier of the first section made a visual sighting and bombed an aircraft dispersal area on

B-24 *Star Eyes* with all engines running and ready to taxi out for a mission. Although usually assigned to Lt. Gus Johnson, on 24 June 1944 this ship was assigned to Jack Nortridge's crew for a mission to France. *Star Eyes* was shot down on 10 April 1945, just one day before the group's final mission. (James Straub)

the airfield. The second section's lead aircraft was hit by flak just before reaching the target, knocking out the superchargers on one engine. As it tried to abort from the bomb run the other ships in the section followed. This section then fell in behind the 446th Bomb Group and bombed another aircraft dispersal area on Conches airfield. By 1100 the 453rd Bomb Group was back at base. *Star Eyes* landed after five hours and twenty minutes flying time.

Other crews from the Group participated in a second mission that day, the bombing of a power station at Pont-à-Vendin, which was understood to be supplying electricity to several of the V.1 flying bomb bases. On this mission Capt. George Baatz's aircraft received a direct hit from a mobile flak battery. Capt. Baatz was the pilot of one of the original stateside crews subsequently assigned as a 732nd Squadron lead crew. They were flying their twenty-sixth mission on this day. In the copilot's seat was Maj. Edward Kemp, the group adjutant, who was not required to fly missions but had volunteered when the assigned copilot became violently ill. Baatz's B-24 disintegrated and fell into the Channel off

Dunkirk. Nine crewmembers were killed and the lone survivor was captured and became a prisoner of war.

Having completed thirty-one combat missions, on Sunday 25 June Jack Nortridge's crew was assigned to fly to a power station at Beuvry in the Pas de Calais region of France. This power station was believed to be supplying electricity to one of Hitler's V.1 flying bomb launch sites. Jack's crew boarded *Corky*, and Gus Johnson's crew climbed aboard *Star Eyes*. Twelve aircraft departed the field at Old Buckenham soon after nine o'clock that morning, assembled into formation and headed for France. However, *Corky* experienced further mechanical problems (the *Burgundy Bomber* had been under repair since the Politz mission five days previously) and Jack was forced to abort the mission. *Corky* landed back at Old Buck' after a two-hour-and-twenty-minute flight. Jack taxied round past the control tower for what would be the last time, and turned the Liberator into dispersal point number forty-four. The crew climbed out of their beloved ship and stepped back onto terra firma. It was all over.

CHAPTER TWENTY

Homecoming

T he evening of Sunday 25 June was a time of celebration for Jack Nortridge, Gus Johnson, and their crews—both crews had officially completed their combat tours. Jack's crew was credited with thirty-one missions on their combat records, with the exception of Bill Eagleson who had completed thirty missions, and between 184 and 189 hours combat flying time. Johnson's crew had completed thirty missions without a single abort. Both crews were automatically inducted into the infamous club of veteran aircrews—the Lucky Bastards' Club.

It had been an intense and grueling five months, but the two crews had survived, despite regretful losses of personnel from each crew. From *Corky*'s crew, Donald Lawry had been killed in action and James Witmer was a prisoner of war. From Gus Johnson's crew, Salvatore Giombarrese was hospitalized following the 10 April mission to Brunswick and never seen or heard from again by any of *Corky*'s crew. Two other members of Johnson's crew failed to return after a mission with Elmer Crockett on 25 April—Frederick Derolf was a prisoner of war but Gilbert Stonebarger had evaded capture and had miraculously made it back to England. On his return he was sent home to America.

For the survivors of the Nortridge and Johnson crews, it was a euphoric feeling to have made it through their combat tours, with the realization that they could now look forward to going home to America for a few weeks rest and recuperation. They anticipated that on their return to America they would receive orders for further assignments, though regretfully without the unity of their crews. The war was to continue for many months to come, but at least for *Corky*'s crew, this part of it was over.

There were also several other celebrations expected at Old Buck'. On 29 June the 453rd Bomb Group celebrated its first anniversary and to celebrate the occasion a dance was held at the Aero Club. Col. Ramsay Potts, the group's commanding officer, cut a large cake and the G.I.VERS orchestra performed. On 4 July there were Independence Day celebrations.

Bill Eagleson:

> Reverend Dennett [of Attleborough] set up correspondence with my family and it continued long after I went home. He was a

frequent visitor to our base. We had a Fourth of July party at the parsonage. That was quite an affair.

The Americans also played some baseball in Old Buckenham on that Fourth of July, upon the invitation of Old Buckenham Hall School to use the school's cricket ground. A mixed crowd of Americans, school kids, and locals watched the event.[1] Bill marveled:

> The Old Buckenham cricket ground—How did we Yanks ever get near such hallowed ground?

The following evening a dance was held at the Aero Club in celebration of the group's one hundredth combat mission.

Many changes were taking place at Old Buckenham at this time. On 2 July, Lt. Col. Jimmy Stewart was relieved from his duties as operations officer and transferred to 2nd Wing Headquarters at Hethel. Maj. Andy Low, former assistant operations officer and then 735th Bomb Squadron CO, became the new operations officer, but not for long—on 31 July he was shot down and taken prisoner. Capt. Milton Stokes, a lead pilot of the 735th Squadron (and friend of Jack Nortridge's since training together in Florida flying B-26 Marauders) became assistant group operations officer. On 7 July the 453rd Bomb Group's Commanding Officer, Col. Ramsay Potts, was transferred to wing headquarters at Hethel, where in August he took command of the 389th Bomb Group. Regrettably, on 11 July Captain Boreske, 733rd Squadron operations officer was reported missing in action.

Jack's crew took some time out and went for a final trip to London together, but this time the V.1 Doodlebugs, also known as Buzz-bombs, were plaguing the city.

> On our last crew trip to London following mission completion we were chased all over town by Buzz-bombs.

Previously in the Windmill Theatre in London, the crew had experienced the interruptions to the shows during air raids, but now:

> When the Buzz-bombs were flying around London we just got the purple alert, and the show went on. I do vividly remember going down into the tubes in Piccadilly and seeing the people laid out there for the night and the feeling of the German bombs, the V.1 rockets hitting above. It was quite an experience. . . .
>
> We were in the Regent Palace [Hotel] and a Buzz-bomb went off on the roof right close by, and we decided we'd get out of London. So we went to the southwest country for a couple of days where the Buzz-bombs didn't chase us around . . . we resorted to the quiet English countryside of Cornwall and Devon . . . we figured if

we'd done our missions then it was time to take care of ourselves
and get away from the war.

Back at Old Buckenham the time finally came to pack up their few
belongings and bid farewell to the 453rd. Bill Eagleson put the
crew's two mascot terriers, the black puppy Flak and his brown brother
Corky, in the hands of a new keeper, Major Hamilton, who had recently
taken over as the 733rd Squadron Operations Officer.

By the summer of 1944 the majority of the 453rd Bomb Group's
aircraft were shiny silver J-model B-24s. When Crew 25 finished their
missions, *Corky* was just a war-weary old olive drab H-model Liberator,

Prior to returning Stateside
in July 1944, during an official ceremony Bill Eagle-
son prepares to hand over
his dog, Flak, to Maj. Lee
Hamilton (second from the
left). (Bill Eagleson)

with myriad patches covering the areas damaged by shrapnel and bullets, but with new engines, and would remain at Old Buck' as a spare. But the *Burgundy Bomber* had been a reliable airplane; it had seen the crew through many harrowing times and had served them well, as Bill Eagleson recalls:

> So many, many memories of truly wonderful days—at times not realizing what anything was all about—but that B-24H, now she strained and worked and the more she worked the better she flew.

Perry Roberson:

> *Corky* had over two hundred patches from flak damage . . . our crew was broken up and most returned to the U.S. for flight training (B-29s). I stayed in the U.K. as a gunnery instructor until December 1944 when I returned to the U.S.

Bill LeRoy remained at Old Buckenham for an additional three months serving as a radio instructor. He returned home to the United States by sea in October, where he continued to serve as an instructor. Joe DeMay also remained in England a while longer, arriving back in

Departure day: four members of *Corky*'s crew gather for a photograph with a friend. Left to right: Jack Nortridge, George White, Pete Veilleux, Bill Eagleson, and Russell "Curly" DeMary (the navigator from Lt. Hal Kimball's crew). (Donald Olds, 453rd BG Association Collection)

the United States on 21 September. The rest of the crew went up to Liverpool from where they set sail on the steam ship SS *West Point* (a pre-war, five-star luxury liner then known as the SS *America*). There were several hundred wounded American troops on board, as well as over a thousand German prisoners of war in the hold of the ship. The German prisoners were en route to Miles Standish, the military camp near Taunton, Massachusetts. Some of the returning GIs played a little poker to pass the time. Soon before arriving back in America, Jack and the guy he was playing with ripped one of the cards in two, appropriately the dack of diamonds, and each kept half as a souvenir of their journey home.

For the first time, *Corky*'s crew had time to think, to try to comprehend the months gone by, to reflect on the loss of Don Lawry and so many other friends, and to contemplate the whereabouts of James Witmer. For the survivors, who had made it through relatively unscathed, that year or so of experiences was for them perhaps the most eventful, challenging, and defining twelve months of their whole lives. *Corky*'s crew had managed to keep it together through challenging and difficult times, and they had supported and depended upon each other with a tremendous sense of faith that somehow seemed to overshadow any real signs of "combat stress" or "operational fatigue" that might easily have defeated of them.

Bill Eagleson recalls:

> The stress came after we broke up as a crew and we found our-selves out there without our buddies from combat, at least that was my personal feeling.

After five days of zigzagging in convoy from Liverpool, the SS *West Point* began a direct route across the Atlantic. The ship was destined for somewhere on the East Coast of America—it turned out to be Boston, Massachusetts, to Bill Eagleson's delight:

> I woke up one morning, looked out the porthole, and there I was in my home town.

The SS *West Point* landed at Commonwealth Pier in Boston Harbor. Jack, Bill, and the others, with the help of dockhands with motorized "donkeys," rode out onto the street:

> Motorized donkeys driven by "V-Girls" got us through the gates at Commonwealth Pier—it was not legal.

Bill found a phone booth and called his folks to say that he was back in Boston; it was the first time he had heard voices from home in many months. Jack and Bill then continued with the flood of troops along Northern Avenue, across the bridge into downtown Boston. From South Station the crew caught a train to Camp Myles Standish in Taunton,

Massachusetts, a base staffed by Italian prisoners of war. The crew was there just a matter of hours for processing before being transferred to Fort Devens, Massachusetts. They spent a few days at Fort Devens but then as they were granted fifteen days R&R, several members of *Corky's* crew said their farewells and went their separate ways.

Jack Nortridge and Bill Eagleson headed into Boston together. They found themselves in the middle of a hurricane on Arlington Street outside the Hotel Statler (now the Park Plaza) where, no doubt, they had stopped for a traditional celebratory drink.

Bill recalls:

> A thought—Jack and I met on a Pullman east of Boise, Idaho (mid-August '43). We compared orders, decided if possible to team up. At Boise I flew through his check flights, admired his skill. Almost a year later we debarked in Boston, Massachusetts, where the SS *West Point* troop ship tied up at Commonwealth Pier—processing at Camp Myles Standish, Taunton, Massachusetts, and Fort Devens.

And then in hurricane rains outside the Hotel Statler in Boston, August 1944:

> Jack and I hugged, saluted . . . said "So long!" and walked to different subway stations—waving our customary good-byes—not knowing four decades would pass before another "Hi Buddy!" He was a great pilot, a great guy, and he *was* responsible for our coming home.

Jack caught a train from South Station to Chicago, eventually arriving home in Freeport, Illinois. Bill made his way to Park Street underground station and onwards to the Eagleson home in Watertown for the first time in a year. The experiences shared by those lucky, unlucky, but *always* "loveable bastards" of Crew 25 would last forever in memories of emotional lows and emotional highs:

> Should our guys ever get together to write "Attleborough tales"— the winter's walk from Old Buck' to the Griffin; shooting with the village vicar; or the infamous raid on the Gaymer's Cyder Mill; missing Liberty Runs from the Cattle Market; the night the crew of *Stinky* released a skunk in the Samson & Hercules; nights at the Bell to exchange missions with Stateside classmates assigned to other groups, oftentimes a search for a never-to-be-seen-again friend— that's the way I remember an emotional gauntlet.

Epilogue
Twilight's Last Gleaming

After Crew 25 departed Old Buckenham in the summer of 1944, that old *Burgundy Bomber* named *Corky* survived many more missions (more than seventy-five in total) and the rest of the war—but only just. On 8 September 1944 *Corky* was presumed to be missing in action when it failed to return to Old Buckenham from a mission to Karlsruhe, Germany. The pilot on Corky that day was Lt. Parks. The 453rd Bomb Group was over the target area, leading the 2nd Combat Wing, but ended up on a collision course with the last of the B-17 Groups which were behind their briefed schedule. *Corky* collided with a B-17 and allegedly lost a fourteen-foot section of wing. The B-17 was lost, but somehow Lt Parks and his copilot managed to maintain control of *Corky* until they reached France, where they landed in a field. *Corky* was repaired and flown back to England on 12 September.

The 453rd Bomb Group completed 259 missions from Old Buckenham. Fifty-eight aircraft failed to return and 366 were lost; many others survived as prisoners of war. With the European war winding down, the 453rd Bomb Group ceased flying missions from Old Buckenham on 12 April 1945 and prepared to return to the United States for redeployment as a B-29 Group in the Pacific Theater of Operations. But just three months after VE-Day, the war in the Pacific came to an end, and in September the 453rd Bomb Group was deactivated.

When the 453rd returned Stateside, its B-24 Liberators remained in England and were assigned to other units for the last few weeks of the war. *Corky* was transferred to the 446th Bomb Group at Bungay, Suffolk. At the end of hostilities *Corky* was flown to the 3rd Strategic Air Depot at Watton, Norfolk, and prepared for a trip back across the Atlantic, this time via the North Ferry Route, departing 22 June 1945. *Corky* was declared "surplus" and taken to Altus, Oklahoma, one of several vast aircraft graveyards, and disposed of as scrap on 13 September 1945.

Station 144 Old Buckenham was transferred back to the RAF in May 1945 but remained inactive until the station was officially closed in June 1960. Old Buckenham was the exclusive home of the 453rd Bomb Group—no other military flying unit ever occupied the base. The land

B-24 *"Corky" Burgundy Bombers* at the 3rd Strategic Air Depot, Watton, soon before being flown back to the United States. *Corky* had completed seventy combat missions and survived a midair collision with a B-17. (Bill Eagleson)

was subsequently sold, and over the years the majority of the buildings were demolished, hangars dismantled, and sections of runways, taxiways, and aircraft dispersal points were torn up and returned to agricultural use. The control tower was demolished in the mid-1970s. The Touchdown Aero Centre flying school operates from the remaining section of the main runway. A memorial stone in the shape of a B-24 tail fin and dedicated to the 453rd Bomb Group and the 366 young Americans who lost their lives flying from the airfield, is located adjacent to the flying club on the southern side of the old base.

Bunns Bank light industrial estate occupies two of the old communal and mess sites where a few Nissen huts remain. On a few of the dispersed living sites, clusters of forlorn and derelict huts still stand. Elsewhere, amid fields and hedgerows, narrow concrete pathways along which aircrews once walked in the early morning half light en route to breakfast and briefing prior to their missions, are the only reminders of this wartime history. In Old Buckenham village hall there is a room dedicated to the 453rd Bomb Group, containing photographs, memorabilia, and the roll of honor. Donald C. Lawry is listed on this brass plaque along with the names of the other young Americans who gave their lives flying from Old Buckenham.

On completion of his missions from Old Buckenham, Jack Nortridge was awarded the Distinguished Flying Cross for great courage, determination, and exceptional skill, and for being an inspiring example to his fellow flyers. At the end of the war he was discharged from military service and returned to Freeport, Illinois, where his wife, Evelyn, gave birth to two children. Jack declined the opportunity to fly as a copilot with American Airlines, later regretting this decision when he realized the financial rewards of a flying career. Jack never flew again after the war and for a while he was a success as a car salesman. When his marriage fell apart, he remarried and subsequently became the father of six more children, but sadly one of them lived to be just one year old and then died of meningitis. By this time Jack had began a career with the Fuller Brush Company and was living in Texas.

Deeply affected by his experiences, Jack never talked about the war to his family or anyone. His son John asked him on several occasions about the war but, "He always fluffed it off as something bad that had to occur to get rid of a larger evil. No big deal."

Following the war the veterans of the 8th Air Force typically pursued careers, ambitions, and raised families. They put their wartime experiences to the back of their minds and many, like Jack, hardly spoke about those days and just got on with living. The years went by until, finding themselves nearing retirement with kids having grown up and left home, they found time to reflect on their lives.

During the late 1970s and early 1980s, many of the veteran airmen began to retrace past experiences. They searched phone directories for their old crewmates, organized reunions, and planned trips back to England for "one last look" at their old home away from home, the bases from which they had flown. Jack Nortridge was instrumental in attempting to trace his old crewmates, who were dispersed all over the United States, and some of them were able to meet again and enjoy a reunion.

Bill Eagleson recalls:

> Jack Nortridge and I met in Palm Springs, California, for the last time. Jack had a rare form of cancer. He knew at the time that he was terminal. We all felt badly for Jack, but he had a great spirit, right up through the end.

With his wife, Clarinda, taking care of him through the diagnosis of melanoma up until his death, Jack's spirit of optimism, always turning the negative to a positive, certainly prevailed, as did

Bill Eagleson and Jack Nortridge reunited for the first and last time, Palm Springs, California, 1985. (Bill Eagleson)

his humor and his ability to lead others through times of crisis—while undergoing chemotherapy treatment he remarked to his eldest son, "Cool, I don't even have to shave or get a haircut." Jack died on 30 September 1985.

Back in October 1981, former navigator Seymour Cohen wrote an extremely colorful and articulate letter to Jack—it is a great tribute to the pilot of Crew 25:

> Dear Jack, I can't begin to express my deep inner joy and emotional satisfaction at seeing you again after all these years. The essential you has not changed at all. You are still the same genuine person.
>
> I still recall so clearly my respect and affection for you and your qualities of courage and good judgment under extreme circumstances of life threatening danger. That I am alive today is in no small measure attributable to you and your skill and courage.
>
> I see the same qualities in you now. The mark of a real man is his ability to accept success and failure as the creatures of chance that they are and the willingness to meet head-on the problems and disappointments of everyday life which confront us all. You have that mark. And you have my profound respect and affection.
>
> I don't know whether we will meet again. I fervently hope that we do. But, whatever may be in the future, I do not want any more time to pass without my telling you of my feelings for you over the past years and now.
>
> Yours in friendship and affection, Seymour Cohen.

In 1947 Seymour met Anita and the following year they married and settled in Fair Lawn, New Jersey, where they raised three daughters and remained through retirement. At last count, they had five grandchildren. Seymour was a very successful and prominent attorney during the postwar years, with his own general law practice in New Jersey. For a few years during retirement he was involved with reunions and kept up to date with the others from *Corky*'s crew. Seymour passed away in October 1997, not long before his golden wedding anniversary. Anita Cohen wrote:

> The time spent with *Corky*'s crew was a very important part of Seymour's life. No matter where we went, there was always some reference to his air force experience. . . . When we flew on a commercial plane during our travels, the memory of ten men crowded together on a B-24 was always there. . . . Having seen such destruction, having faced death every time he went on a mission, Seymour felt he was living on borrowed time, and so his attitude was always, "What will be, will be." He enjoyed helping people . . . and he passed that lesson on to his daughters.

Prior to joining the Army Air Force, Bill Eagleson had served in the U.S. Mountain troops, and on his return from England he became a mountaineering instructor with the Air Force's SAC Survival School.

Subsequently, Bill returned to Boston University and graduated with a bachelor of science degree in Education, followed by a masters degree in Education. He and his fiancée, Dorothea, were married on 26 December 1951 in the chapel at Boston University, and in the early 1950s Bill made the most of an opportunity to spend a year in London as an exchange teacher. In the absence of air raids and V.1 attacks, Bill and Dorothea enjoyed their stay on Edgeware Road, central London.

Bill continued his involvement in the ski world, both as a professional instructor and also working in ski retailing and wholesaling, and over the years he returned to Europe on many occasions with ski classes. He joined the faculty of Brockton High School, Massachusetts, where he coached sports for twenty-one years until his retirement in 1984. For many years Bill and Dorothea enjoyed summers along the New England coastline, on board their boat, the *DOBI FOUR* ("Do" for Dorothea, and "Bi" for Bill).

Bill LeRoy remained at Old Buckenham and served as a radio instructor until October 1944. Upon his return Stateside he became a radio instructor at Scott Field, Illinois, for the remaining months of the war; he left the service as a Sergeant Major ROM Division. Bill married and lives in Florissant, Missouri, where he retired in 1985 after forty years as a brick mason.

The war was a significantly traumatic experience for James Freddie Witmer, who wasn't at Old Buckenham long enough to fly a single combat mission with his own crew, *Corky*'s crew. James was lost on a mission to Berlin while flying with Lt. Patrick Tobin's crew—six of them were killed but James survived and endured the rest of hostilities as a prisoner of war. On his return home he worked with his father on the dairy farm. When his father retired, James and his wife, Hazel, bought the farm and raised a son and two daughters. After fifteen years owning the farm they sold it; James took a job selling insurance and later worked for the Pepsi-Cola plant in Texarkana.

James did not establish any connection with the other veterans of *Corky*'s crew, although Bill Eagleson was

James Freddie Witmer in 1995—fifty years after enduring the POW "death march." (Hazel Witmer)

happy to have had the opportunity to speak with him by telephone one day in 1996—it was the first time they had spoken since 1944. James did not like to talk to his family about his wartime experiences, especially his experiences as a prisoner of war, but occasionally he referred to being locked in railroad boxcars with bombs exploding all around, and being marched across Poland in the snow without Red Cross packages or food as the Germans retreated from the Allies. His sister Nadine recalls that, "When he finally returned home after the war, he was not the same person emotionally. He never recovered from the experience." Just a few weeks before his death, his nephew James Albert Gibson visited him. Witmer said, "I have never talked about it, but I know you want to know." He talked for three hours, sharing his experiences. James Freddie Witmer died on 30 July 1997 after a battle with cancer.

Perry Roberson remained in England as a gunnery instructor until December 1944. On his return he married his girlfriend, Elizabeth, in January 1945 in Covington, Kentucky. Subsequently Perry completed B-29 flight engineer training and became an instructor until he was discharged from service in October 1945. He enrolled at the Alabama Polytechnic Institute (now Auburn University) in January 1946 and, funded by his GI Bill, Perry graduated in August 1948 with a degree in agricultural engineering. He then spent forty years in the designing and marketing of farm machinery, retiring in August 1988.

Following retirement, Perry and Elizabeth moved to Pampa in the Texas panhandle to be near their daughter, Anne. Perry soon began a new career as a volunteer worker in a local hospital, and was later elected president of the hospital volunteer auxiliary. He was quoted in a newspaper article: "It makes a person feel like they're doing something for somebody when they don't have to . . . and it's a satisfying experience."

At the time of celebrating their fiftieth wedding anniversary in January 1995, Perry and Elizabeth were blessed with three children, nine grandchildren, and three great-grandchildren. Perry remained active until being diagnosed with what was at first believed to be influenza, then pneumonia, and finally as lung cancer in an advanced stage, complicated by a massive stroke just a week before his death—Perry passed away on 11 February 2000.

Pete Veilleux returned to Maine and married his girlfriend, Eleanor—*Miss Ella Mae*, whose name was featured on *Corky*. They raised a family

Perry Roberson and George White reunited in 1990. (White family)

and Pete ran a very successful construction business after the war and is now retired and residing in Hampden, Maine.

After completing his tour of duty with *Corky*'s crew, Harvey Nielsen returned to Missouri on leave and married Bonnie Lou Smith in St. Joseph. He was then stationed in Florida, where he trained as a B-29 gunner alongside Lim Wing Jeong. Then for a while, Harvey was stationed in Biloxi, Mississippi, where he lived with Bonnie until he was discharged from the military in 1946.

Harvey and Bonnie then moved to Mankato, Minnesota, where Harvey's brother Oage employed him as truck driver. Eventually Harvey bought his own truck and moved to Denver, Colorado, in 1949 and soon after, Harvey and Bonnie got divorced. Harvey then lived in Superior, Wisconsin, and then returned to Minnesota and worked for his brother Hans who owned a grain haulage company. Harvey and Hans took up flying as a hobby and between them bought a small airplane. Harvey eventually moved to Texas where he lived near Corpus Christi and continued to work as a truck driver. There are no reports to suggest that he ever owned any more monkeys—however, one Christmas he went home to Missouri and placed a number of toy monkeys under the tree for all the children in the Nielsen family!

In the 1970s, Harvey was involved in a bad road accident. He "totaled" his truck but lived to tell the tale, although he relied on crutches for a while and later walked with a cane. Sadly, he became a heavy drinker and suffered from a weight problem. Following a brief illness, Harvey died in a hospital in Mission, Texas, on Saturday, 27 June 1981. At the time of his death he was living with a woman named Dorothy in a run-down trailer and was apparently broke. The picture of Harvey and his aircrew standing in front of their B-24 *Corky* was hung on the wall of the trailer, a constant reminder of his pride in his wartime experiences and his companions. Harvey is buried at White Oak Cemetery in Pickering, Missouri, not far from his place of birth.

Jack Nortridge's attempts to trace his former tail gunner, Lim Wing Jeong, proved unsuccessful due to confusion regarding his name—military service records listed him erroneously as Lim W. Jeong, the result of an error made by U.S. immigration upon his arrival from China. He changed his name to Wayne Lim after the war, Lim being his family name, not Jeong. So everyone was looking for L. W. Jeong not W. J. Lim. When their searches proved unsuccessful, they started to think that they would never find him. So they were all the more delighted when Wayne managed to track *them* down!

Wayne reflected:

> It's too bad I didn't know about the 453rd [Bomb Group Veterans'] Association sooner. Sure would've loved to see John Nortridge again.

On his return to America in 1944, Wayne trained as a B-29 gunner in Florida alongside his friend and former crewmate, Harvey Nielsen. For a while it looked like Wayne might be assigned to the Pacific Theater on a B-29 crew to help fight the Japanese, his original motivation for enlisting in the Army Air Force. However, within days of Wayne's graduation from B-29 training in August 1945, the Japanese surrendered and the war was over.

Wayne's mother had died during the war and his stepmother died after childbirth from malnutrition as a result of the Communists' rise to power. Wayne later paid for his father, brothers, half-sisters, and a half-brother to travel to the United States. They had escaped the Communists in China and fled to Hong Kong after his father was tied up and displayed in a pigpen as a humiliating punishment for having owned property and failing to embrace the ideology of the People's Republic of China.

In 1950 Wayne married an American-born Chinese American woman named May. She refers to Wayne's old crew as the "international crew" due to their diverse backgrounds and ancestry. Wayne and May raised four children and they are now proud grandparents, residing in Houston, Texas. Wayne ran his own Chinese restaurants until his retirement. He has never returned to Europe and if he needs to travel in America, then he drives—he says he hates flying!

Around the time when Wayne Lim made contact with others from *Corky*'s crew, he saw a letter in a veterans' newsletter written by Joseph DeMay's sister. She was trying to locate *Corky*'s crew on Joe's behalf. Joe at this time was in a VA hospital, but by the time Wayne saw the article and called to speak to Joe it was too late; Wayne was told that Joe had passed away.

Whatever happened to Frank Conlon, originally the copilot on Crew 25? There were rumors that he crashed in the Atlantic Ocean en route to Europe, but he may have been last seen in Marrakech, Morocco. When Frank was transferred, he became a first pilot and was assigned to the 464th Bomb Group, 15th Air Force. On his third mission, 10 May 1944, his B-24, *Sleepy Time Gal*, was hit by flak over Austria, and Frank was wounded when a piece of shrapnel knocked his hand off the throttle. The copilot and flight engineer flew the aircraft back to their base in Italy and Frank was sent home to America where he was hospitalized for seven months. After the war he returned to Dubuque, Iowa, where he married and raised four children.

On his return from England, *Corky*'s copilot, George White, spent his rest and recuperation time at Redondo Beach, California, before being assigned the role of B-24 training instructor. Later he trained crews on B-29s and served at various bases around the United States between September 1944 and 1947. In the meantime, George married Artie Jones in October 1944; both were twenty-one years old. By the time

George was twenty-three he had reached the rank of captain and served as a training officer at Smokey Hills Air Force Base in Kansas. He was also the proud father of a daughter, Jackie.

With the responsibility of raising a family, George decided that he could make more money in the aircraft industry and left the Air Force. But allegedly his wife told him that she wanted the Air Force life and everything that went with it—a husband in uniform, the social circuit at the Officers' Club—and she divorced him. When George's daughter, Jackie, was eleven years old, Artie disappeared with a new man in her life, and George never saw his daughter again. He was devastated.

Meanwhile, George owned his own small plane and continued to enjoy flying. He returned to Oklahoma and completed a course in air-frame engineering and then worked for United Airlines for eighteen years in Washington, D.C., before finding employment with Boeing in Seattle. But when the work dried up he worked for his brother in con-struction and then for a while he moved back to Oklahoma where he owned a boat shop; later he worked for the post office and then returned to the aviation industry, working for TWA.

Meanwhile, in 1963 George had remarried—George and Barbara were to spend thirty-six very happy years together. He was very close to his stepdaughter, Francie, and encouraged her to get her glider pilot's license. George and Barbara retired in Bernice, Oklahoma. Barbara nursed George through several years of health problems—respiratory failures, lung disease, and emphysema—and he passed away peacefully on 7 November 1998 with his family around him. Whenever they had asked him about his wartime experiences, he had always just said, "We just went over there and dropped a few bombs and then came home, that's all."

In October 1994 the 453rd Bomb Group held a reunion at Rapid City, South Dakota. Five surviving members from *Corky*'s crew were reunited—Bill Eagleson, Bill LeRoy, Wayne Lim, Perry Roberson, and Pete Veilleux. The bombardier wrote down some of his thoughts in a letter following the reunion:

> I sure am proud of the guys that flew on *Corky*—I wish that we were geographically close now, to share today's challenges and this retirement. . . . I know we all would enjoy being together often.
>
> So we are not hesitant with prayers of thanks for each day of a new life. Whatever is ahead we must draw on the past experiences to help overcome whatever the obstacle—this must be and if it cannot be then faith and trust prevails. . . . We have a better, more understanding world, with miles to go, yet the trail has shortened.

Back in 1986, Bill and Dorothea Eagleson read a newspaper article about the restoration of an old B-24 Liberator in Massachusetts.

Five members of *Corky*'s crew reunited in Rapid City, South Dakota, October 1994. Left to right: Bill LeRoy, Perry Roberson, Pete Veilleux, Wayne Lim, and Bill Eagleson. (Bill Eagleson)

This particular aircraft had served with the RAF in the Pacific in 1944–45 and was later abandoned in India prior to being restored and flown for twenty years by the Indian Air Force. Abandoned for the second time, a British collector purchased the wreck in 1981, shipped it to England, and subsequently sold it to the Collings Foundation in Stow, Massachusetts. So one day Bill and Dorothea drove to Stow to investigate. They found hundreds of B-24 parts overflowing from an open hangar door into the snow—at that moment they joined the growing team of volunteers dedicating time and energy to the project. Bill drummed up the support of the 453rd Bomb Group Association, and other veterans associations followed suit with fund-raising activities.

Eventually the semirestored B-24 was shipped to Florida where the work continued. Over one million dollars from private and corporate donations was spent on the aircraft; a restoration team, much of it volunteer, put in one hundred thousand hours of work. The wreck was transformed into a fully restored, *flying* B-24 Liberator! Complete with the name *All American* painted on its nose and a "circle-J" tail marking (in honor of the 453rd Bomb Group) the restored aircraft made its debut flight in 1990. Bill Eagleson wrote:

Bill and Dorothea Eagleson on board the Collings Foundation B-24, *All American*. (Bill Eagleson)

This has been a monumental, never to be forgotten month. On September 9 *All American* began its odyssey . . . we anxiously waited for it to arrive here in New England. While mowing my lawn I heard a familiar long-past sound. Looking skyward, there, before my very eyes and ears soared and sung *All American*.

About 0700 next a.m. Caroline Collings called to invite me to Grenier Field, Manchester, New Hampshire, for an 0830 briefing. About 60 miles, without breakfast, shave, I took off—a heavy foot and God's help put me on location. I was assigned to a C-47 for a local fly-by following the B-24—the plane fits only one adjective— *Beautiful!* Then a formation flight to the city of Boston to be met by press and dignitaries. At Logan [Boston airport] I left the '47 and found myself flying "waist" with Charles Huntoon [453rd Bomb Group veteran] in the B-24. I tell you, when those Pratt & Whitney's were run up it took all of the seat belt to keep me down. I have never experienced such an emotional "high."

A short hop to a military base (Hanscom) then back to New Hampshire for a two day air show featuring the *All American*. . . . Our plane, yours and mine, is back in its element receiving hundreds and hundreds of people in a glowing, cathedral, shrine-like atmosphere—sharing moments from crewmen of almost a half century. . . . I do believe in miracles provided they are worked on . . . my evening prayers reach out for everlasting endurance in flight— may it fly well for all.

Since 1990 the *All American* has spent ten months of each year on tour, barnstorming air shows, reunions, and special events across the United States alongside *Nine-O-Nine*, the Collings Foundation B-17. Each year many thousands of veterans, their families, aviation enthusiasts, and parties of school kids visit the planes. Fourteen years on, the *All American* odyssey continues, complete with colorful new artwork and name, *The Dragon and His Tail*. It remains the only fully restored, airworthy B-24 in the world, despite having been manufactured in greater numbers than any other American military airplane.

B-24 *All American* over the Golden Gate Bridge. (Patrick Bunce/Collings Foundation)

At the 2nd Air Division Association's Chicago reunion in the spring of 1998, Bill and Dorothea Eagleson were presented with a plaque in recognition and appreciation of their efforts to help bring the *All American* to reality.

Early in January 1996 I searched for the relatives of Donald Lawry, the navigator on *Corky*'s crew who was killed on a mission to Germany in February 1944. There were only two clues with which to begin my search: the names "Lawry" and "Wisconsin." I wasn't certain that I would succeed in finding Donald's relatives, but I had a strong feeling that I would, that there would be a relative somewhere in Wisconsin. And it was only by a twist of fate that Donald's sister, Betty, received a letter from me. After all, there are no longer any known Lawry's in Wisconsin related to this particular family, and for most of her adult life Betty has been married with the surname Allen. One of my many letters written to Lawrys in Wisconsin was sent on to Betty by the wife of a cousin who had since passed away—Betty did not even know that this cousin existed until a couple of years previously when, on a trip to her father's birthplace in England, her newly-found English cousins told her "You have another cousin in Wisconsin!" Receiving the first letter from Betty and then being able to share with her the story of *Corky*'s crew was certainly one of the most rewarding aspects of writing this book. She wrote:

> As I read your letter I was just amazed. You were restating all the facts I had heard about how my eldest brother was lost while standing in as navigator for a different crew in 1944. . . . I never expected to hear from anyone about Don and his experiences in the war after all these years. It pleases me to know he has not been "lost" entirely . . . we were supposed to make contact and I'm so glad you did!

In the fall of 1996, Betty visited Bill and Dorothea Eagleson in Massachusetts, and Pete and Eleanor Veilleux in Maine; and then a couple of years later I visited Betty and her family in Wisconsin, where I also had the pleasure of meeting Artie Sands, Donald Lawry's old school friend, and Dorothy Taplin, who had been married to Donald for just a few short months prior to his death.

In September 2002, Betty and her husband arrived here in London for a vacation. That evening I met them at their hotel with good news— a copy of the e-mail from the University of Wisconsin Press announcing that they wanted to publish this book! A few days later we drove up to Norfolk where my father and I took Betty and Don Allen to the 100th Bomb Group Museum in the old control tower at Thorpe Abbotts airfield, and then showed them around the remains of the airfield at Old Buckenham, where Donald Lawry spent the last few weeks of his life. It was a warm and sunny afternoon as we walked amid farmland along the narrow pathway that once led to the accommodation site where the officers from *Corky*'s crew had lived, as Betty recalled:

It was really a reality check to see the less than desirable conditions those men had while stationed there. I came home and re-read the last letters we had received from my brother. His description was of the cold buildings, it raining "like the devil" and mud everywhere. When I was there it struck me how very quiet and peaceful it seemed with only an occasional small private plane taking off or landing at Old Buckenham. I wish that Donald had experienced that side of the lovely English countryside.

In 1996 Bill Eagleson reflected:

Early this summer . . . I had occasion to clear out some papers in the attic, and lo and behold I found the cork from the burgundy bottle that Don Lawry and I split at Lake Arrowhead. I have that cork here and I look at it tonight thinking of those guys and those fearless, reckless, sincere days, of '43 and '44.

In celebration of their completion of crew training in 1943, the cork was signed: "Corky—Don and Bill—We cracked it." Actually, the crew celebrated with ten bottles of burgundy wine, and when Bill climbed out of *Corky* for the last time in June 1944, he took with him two of the corks, both his own and Donald Lawry's. In 1996 Bill gave one of the corks to Donald's sister, Betty.

Bill Eagleson:

I am very proud of *Corky*'s crew—their accomplishments never to be repeated. Once again define those "Loveable Bastards": Far from home—kids—tough and determined—without a whimper or loss of loyalty, always through humor able to find their way. To them I share deep gratitude.

APPENDIX
Crew Personnel

Crew 25: *Corky's Crew:* 1943

Pilot:	1st Lt. John "Jack" A. Nortridge Jr. (0663084), Freeport, Illinois
Copilot:	2nd Lt. George L. White (0744812), Sapulpa, Oklahoma
Navigator:	2nd Lt. Donald C. Lawry (0690455,) Evansville, Wisconsin (KIA 22 February 1944 on a mission with Lieutenant Ingram's crew)
Bombardier:	2nd Lt. William "Bill" A. Eagleson Jr. (0752558), Watertown, Massachusetts
Flight Engineer and Waist Gunner:	S/Sgt Perry M. Roberson Jr. (14182581), Ozark, Alabama
Top Turret Gunner and Assistant Flight Engineer:	S/Sgt Harvey Nielsen (37226261), St. Joseph, Missouri
Radio Operator and Waist Gunner:	S/Sgt William G. LeRoy (37410657), St. Louis, Missouri
Ball Turret Gunner and Assistant Flight Engineer:	S/Sgt James Freddie Witmer (18137430), Texarkana, Texas (MIA 6 March 1944 on a mission with Lieutenant Tobin's crew; POW at Stalag Luft IV)
Nose Turret Gunner:	S/Sgt Aurèle "Pete" E. Veilleux (31116139), Waterville, Maine
Tail Turret Gunner:	S/Sgt Lim Wing Jeong (Wayne Lim) (18218623), San Antonio, Texas

Crew 25: *Corky's Crew, March–June 1944*

Pilot:	1st Lt. John "Jack" A. Nortridge Jr. (0663084), Freeport, Illinois
Copilot:	2nd Lt. George L. White (0744812), Sapulpa, Oklahoma
Navigator:	2nd Lt. Seymour Cohen (0667254), Bayonne, New Jersey
Bombardier:	2nd Lt. William "Bill" A. Eagleson Jr. (0752558), Watertown, Massachusetts

Flight Engineer and
Waist Gunner: S/Sgt Perry M. Roberson Jr. (14182581), Ozark,
                                 Alabama
Top Turret Gunner and
Assistant Flight Engineer: S/Sgt Harvey Nielsen (37226261), St. Joseph,
                                 Missouri
Radio Operator and
Waist Gunner: S/Sgt William G. LeRoy (37410657), St. Louis,
                                 Missouri
Ball Turret and
Waist Gunner: Joseph "Joe" DeMay (32782022), Brooklyn, New
                                 York
Nose Turret Gunner: S/Sgt Aurèle "Pete" E. Veilleux (31116139), Wa-
                                 terville, Maine
Tail Turret Gunner: S/Sgt Lim Wing Jeong (Wayne Lim) (18218623),
                                 San Antonio, Texas

Richard Ingram's crew, 22 February 1944

All ten men flying as Lt. Richard Ingram's crew on the 22 February 1944 mission
to Gotha were killed in action. They are listed in Missing Aircrew Report 2895:

Pilot: 2nd Lt. Richard M. Ingram
Copilot: 2nd Lt. Arthur E. White
Navigator: 2nd Lt. Donald C. Lawry (from Crew 25)
Bombardier: 2nd Lt. Michael A. Boehm
Top Turret Gunner: S/Sgt Raymond J. Diederich (from Lt. Wear's
                                 crew)
Radio Operator: S/Sgt Charles F. Ross
Ball Turret Gunner: S/Sgt James Golbski (from Lt. Wear's crew)
Right Waist Gunner: S/Sgt McCalvin J. Robinson
Left Waist Gunner: S/Sgt Thomas P. Crumpler
Tail Gunner: S/Sgt Richard C. Anderson (from Lt. Wear's crew)

Nine of them are listed on the Wall of the Missing in the American Military
Cemetery in the Netherlands and were posthumously awarded the Air Medal
and the Purple Heart. Richard Anderson was posthumously awarded the Purple Heart and was buried in Plot B, Row 27, Grave 9, at the American Military
Cemetery at Ardennes.

Patrick Tobin's crew, 6 March 1944

Lt. Patrick Tobin's crew are listed in Missing Aircrew Report 2972. Six of the
crew were killed on 6 March 1944 and were posthumously awarded the Air
Medal and the Purple Heart. Their names listed on the Wall of the Missing at
the American Military cemetery in the Netherlands.

Pilot: 1st Lt. Patrick D. Tobin Jr., Birmingham, MI
Copilot: 2nd Lt. Ray Gilbreath, Andersonville., Tennessee
                                 (originally Lt. Wear's copilot)
Navigator: 2nd Lt. David H. Miller, Cleveland, Ohio

Top Turret Gunner:	T/Sgt Peter M. Cunniff, Cambridge, Massachusetts
Radio Operator:	S/Sgt Peter Santora, New York City (originally from Lt. Crockett's crew).
Left Waist Gunner:	S/Sgt James J. Meyers, Buffalo, New York (from Lt. Wear's crew).

The following four crew members flying with Lt. Tobin on 6th March 1944 survived and became Prisoners of War:

Bombardier:	2nd Lt. Thomas L. Underwood, Quincy, Massachusetts
Ball Turret Gunner:	S/Sgt James Freddie Witmer, Texarkana, Texas (from Crew 25)
Right Waist Gunner:	S/Sgt Clair Kreidler, Scranton, Pennsylvania
Tail Gunner:	S/Sgt Joseph V. Williams Jr., Charlotte, North Carolina

NOTES

1. Shadows on the Horizon

1. Hugh Brogan, *The Penguin History of the United States of America*, p. 261 (Penguin Books, London, 1985).

2. David J. Goldberg, *Discontented America: The United States in the 1920s*, p. 7 (Johns Hopkins University Press, Baltimore, 1999).

3. Maldwyn A. Jones, *The Limits of Liberty*, pp.412–13 (Oxford University Press, New York, 1995).

4. Goldberg, *Discontented America*, p. 6.

5. The letter to Edward Murrow was written by Archibald MacLeish, Head of the Office of Facts and Figures in Washington. Quoted from Juliet Gardiner, *Over Here* (Collins & Brown, London, 1992).

6. "Bundles for Britain" was the name given to the campaign in which the American public donated food, and even children's toys to the British. When British children were sent to the United States to escape German bombardment, they were referred to as "Bundles *from* Britain."

7. Raymond Seitz, *Over Here*, p. 87 (Phoenix, London, 1998).

8. Howard Zinn, *A People's History of United States*, p.294, chapter 12 (Harper Perennial, New York, 1995).

9. John K. Galbraith, *The Great Crash:1929* (Houghton Mifflin, Boston, 1972).

10. *America's War: WWII in Colour* (Warner Vision International 2002).

11. A 1939 public opinion survey statistics quoted from Gardiner, *Over Here*.

12. *It's Great to Be an American*, J. Crane/R. Muffs.

2. Boise, Idaho

1. In most of this text I have referred to Sgt. Perry M. Roberson as Perry, which is how the crew and in later years his wife knew him, even though his siblings called him Donald. In this section I refer to him as Perry Jr. to distinguish him from his father, Perry Sr.

3. A League of Nations

1. Stan Steiner, *Fusang: The Chinese Who Built America*, chapter 10 (Harper & Row, New York, 1979).

2. Following the war Lim Wing Jeong Americanized his name, changing Wing to Wayne and writing the sequence Wayne J. Lim. In this text, however, I have referred to him as either Lim Wing Jeong or Sgt. Jeong. The rest of his air crew knew him as either Lim, Jeong, or Sgt. Jeong, and this is reflected in the quotes in which they refer to him.

3. "The Chinese Texans," an article by the Institute of Texan Cultures at San Antonio, University of Texas, http://www.texancultures.utsa.edu/txtext/chinese/chinese.htm.

4. Mike Wright, *What They Didn't Teach You about World War II*, p. 30, chapter 3 (Presidio Press, Novato, California, 1998).

6. On the Road to the Big League

1. Skitch Henderson was a well-known American musician who volunteered for the RAF prior to the United States entry into World War II. He became an RAF Hurricane pilot and was later transferred to the USAAF.

2. Quote taken from a recorded message of 1995: diary excerpt dated 7 January 1944, additional bracketed comments made at the time of recording.

10. Prisoner of War

1. Quoted from an e-mail; Delbert D. Lambson, 390th BG veteran, MIA 25 February 1944, former POW and author of *When I Return in Spring*.

11. Hosts in the Sky

1. For an account of Joe Miller's remarkable experiences as a POW, see Martin W. Bowman, *Home by Christmas: 8th and 15th Air Force Airmen at War*, p. 33 (Patrick Stephens Ltd., Wellingborough, Northamptonshire, 1987).

2. Bill Bryson, *Made in America*, p. 180 (Secker & Warburg, London, 1994).

3. Horace S. Turell (445th BG veteran), *The Invisible Battlefield?* 1996, http://users.skynet.be/sky72940/hal.htm.

4. Maldwyn Allen Jones, *American Immigration*, p. 298 (University of Chicago Press, Chicago, 1960).

5. T. H. Watkins, *The Great Depression*, p. 320 (Little, Brown & Co. / Back Bay Books, Boston, 1993).

6. Fred Rochlin, *Old Man in a Baseball Cap* (HarperCollins, London, 1999).

7. An interview with Ira Weinstein, 445th BG veteran and former POW at Stalag Luft I. "Being Jewish Was an Extra Risk for This Kassel Survivor!" Larry Hobbs, Staff Writer, *Palm Beach Daily News*, 19 January 1996. Reproduced in the *2nd Air Division Journal*, Fall 1996.

12. Jimmy Stewart, Leadership, and the Liberty Run

1. According to some sources, Jimmy Stewart flew twenty bombing missions; other sources (including 8th Air Force historian Roger A. Freeman) state that Stewart flew twenty-two missions. It's generally believed that he flew approximately three-quarters of his missions with the 445th, however, according to records at the Jimmy Stewart Museum, he flew nine missions with the 445th and ten with the 453rd.

2. From an interview with Lawrence J. Quirk, *James Stewart: Behind the Scenes of a Wonderful Life* (Applause Books, New York, 1997).

3. Dewey, *James Stewart: A Biography* (Little, Brown & Company, London, 1997), p. 251. There is some truth in this sensationalized account, but unfortunately the complexities of the situation are overlooked. Incidentally, Donald Dewey erroneously claims that the 453rd lost fifty-nine aircraft in the two months prior to D-Day and stated that the "2nd Wing Division" Headquarters

("2nd Wing Division" did not even exist) was located at Old "Buckingham" (spelled like the English town and the Royal Palace in London). Roy Pickard, in *James Stewart: The Hollywood Years* (Robert Hale, London, 1992), called the base "Buckinghamshire" (a county located more than one hundred miles from Old Buckenham) and claimed incorrectly that upon his arrival there, Stewart's missions were over.

4. Mark K. Wells, *Courage and Air Warfare*, pp. 105–6 (Frank Cass & Co. Ltd., London, 1995).

5. Walter Stills, navigator 93rd Bomb Group, recalling the words of Ramsay Potts during an interview with Granada Television in 1989 for the documentary *Whispers in the Air*.

6. Wells, *Courage and Air Warfare*, pp. 89–90.

7. 453rd Bomb Group veteran Harold Hopkins, quoted from an article on a 453rd Bomb Group veterans' website.

8. Quoted from Dewey, *James Stewart: A Biography*, p. 251, and used here with permission from Ramsay D. Potts.

9. Quoted from Dewey, *James Stewart: A Biography*, pp.252–53, and used here with permission from Ramsay D. Potts.

10. Quoted from "Legends in the Law: A Conversation with Ramsay D. Potts" (*Bar Report*, August–September 1999) and used here with permission from Ramsay D. Potts. Available at www.dcbar.org/for_lawyers/resources/legends_in_the_law/potts.cfm.

11. See Wells, *Courage and Air Warfare*, pp. 93–94.

12. This quote taken from Jean Lancaster-Rennie, *And Over Here!*, p. 1 (Geo. R. Reeve Ltd., Wymondham, Norfolk, 1976).

13. The Battle of Brunswick

1. In 1944 some ingenious engineers at the 3rd Strategic Air Depot (SAD) at Watton (ten miles from Old Buckenham) used an Auxiliary Power Unit to create the world's first rotary lawn mower to cut the grass around their workshops. The 3rd SAD was responsible for repairs, modification, and salvaging of all 2nd Bomb Division B-24 Liberators when the required work was beyond the means of the ground crews at the bases. The 3rd SAD also operated sub depots at each of the B-24 bases and dispatched mobile repair teams to B-24 crash sites, on many occasions flying battle-damaged aircraft out of farmers' fields.

2. *Flight Manual B-24D Airplane* (Flight and Service Dept., Consolidated Aircraft Corporation, San Diego, California, December 1942).

3. Hubert Cripe's account of the 6 March 1944 mission to Berlin.

4. Heinz Knocke, *I Flew for the Fuhrer* (Evans Brothers Ltd., London, 1953).

5. Roger A. Freeman, *The Mighty Eighth*, p. 74 (Macdonald & Co. Ltd., London, 1970).

14. "Our Prayers That Night Were Shared"

1. Lt. Gustav "Bob" Johnson's crew flew a B-24 they named *Stinky* from California to England, but they never flew this aircraft in combat. It was named after the pet skunk that belonged to tail gunner Sgt. William Cleary. On the 22 April 1944 mission to Hamm, Lt. Johnson's crew flew aircraft 42–52627, named *Stolen Moments*.

15. Paris and London

1. Major James J. Carroll, "Physiological Problems of Bomber Crews in the Eighth Air Force during WWII," March 1997 (a research paper presented to The Research Department Air Command and Staff College).

16. Milk Runs and Maximum Efforts

1. General Dwight D. Eisenhower and General Koenig quoted from Humphrey Wynn and Susan Young, *Prelude to Overlord*, p. 99 (Presidio Press, Novato, California, 1984).

2. Lt. Donald Jones's crew account courtesy of a crew history by Roger Stein, as yet unpublished.

3. Most infamous was William Joyce, a.k.a. Lord Haw-Haw, a radio propagandist for Nazi Germany who broadcast nightly from Berlin. Born in Brooklyn, New York, his father was Irish, his mother, who allegedly lived in Hingham, Norfolk, during World War II, was English.

4. The combat mission records of Bill Eagleson and Perry Roberson credit them with a mission to Belfort on 12 May; this mission was actually flown on 11 May, as stated by Andrew Low in the *Liberator Men of Old Buck'* (which includes a reference to Jack Nortridge for this mission). Jack Nortridge's combat mission record is correct and credits 11 May: Belfort.

According to the combat mission records of George White and Bill LeRoy, they were not assigned the 11 May mission to Belfort, France, and were instead assigned Zeitz, Germany, on 12 May. This is incorrect. George White's flying time (8:47) for his alleged participation in the 12 May mission to Zeitz is identical to Jack Nortridge's flying time for the 11 May Belfort mission.

19. Hamburg and Berlin

1. Statistics from J. Ethell and A. Price, *Target Berlin. Mission 250: 6 March 1944*, p. 154 (Jane's Publishing, London, 1981).

20. Homecoming

1. In 1944 my father was an eight-year-old pupil at Old Buckenham Hall School and was a spectator at the Fourth of July event. The school's cricket ground was considered prestigious; prior to the war the Australian cricket team had played there.

GLOSSARY

AAF	Army Air Force
Abort	To return from a mission before reaching the target
Allies	Britain, France, USA, Canada, USSR; the countries fighting against the Axis powers
APO	Army Post Office
ATC	Air Transport Command
AWOL	Absent Without Leave
Axis powers	Alliance between Germany, Italy, and Japan (originally the Rome-Berlin Axis, from north-south line between the two capitals)
BD	Bombardment/Bomb Division (redesignated Air Division in January 1945)
BG	Bombardment/Bomb Group
BOQ	Bachelor Officers' Quarters
BS	Bombardment/Bomb Squadron
Buzz Bomb	Slang for German V.1 pilotless flying bomb
Capt.	Captain
Chaff	Metal foil strips dropped from aircraft to disrupt enemy radar
CO	Commanding Officer
Col.	Colonel
Crossbow	Allied code for the plan to destroy the V.1 launch sites
CW	Combat Wing
CQ	Charge of Quarters
DR	Dead Reckoning Navigation
D-Day	Disembarkation Day; the day of the Allied invasion of Europe (6 June 1944)
Doodlebug	Slang for German V.1 pilotless flying bomb
Element	Three aircraft forming an "element" within a formation of multiple elements
ETO	European Theater of Operations
EVD	Evaded/Evadee (Missing in Action personnel who escaped death and evaded capture)
Flak	Antiaircraft fire (from the German term *Fliegerabwehrkanone*)
Gen.	General
GI	Government Issue (relating to the uniforms issued to U.S. troops, GI became slang for a U.S. soldier)
IFF	Identification, Friend or Foe; radio signal that allowed

	radar stations to identify aircraft
IP	Initial Point (the start of the 'bomb run' when the bombardier commenced target sighting)
KIA	Killed in Action
Limey	Slang for English person
Little Friends	Bomber crew slang for friendly fighters
Lt.	Lieutenant (1st Lt. or 2nd Lt.)
Lucky Bastard Club	The unofficial award for airmen who survived a combat tour
Luftwaffe	The German Air Force
Mae West	Inflatable life vest named after the buxom Hollywood film star
Maj.	Major
MPI	Mean Point of Impact (relating to the bombing of a target)
MIA	Missing in Action
Milk Run	An easy mission
Noball	Mission against V.1 launch sites
NCO	Non-Commissioned Officer
Overlord	Code for the Allied Invasion of Northwest Europe, 6 June 1944 *(D-day)*
Pathfinder	A lead aircraft equipped with radar (utilized in the event of a cloud-covered target)
PFF	Pathfinder Force
POW	Prisoner of War
R&R	Rest and Recuperation
RAF	Royal Air Force
RP	Rally Point (the briefed point following bombing when the assigned Combat Wing formation was resumed)
SAD	Strategic Air Depot
Section	Part of a Bombardment Group's formation (often a group's formation was arranged in two or three sections)
Sgt.	Sergeant
SNAFU	"Situation normal: all fouled up!"
S/Sgt.	Staff Sergeant
Strafe	To attack ground targets with gunfire
Straggler	A battle-damaged aircraft, or one with technical or mechanical malfunction and unable to keep up with its formation
T/Sgt.	Technical Sergeant
Tour of Duty	From the spring of 1944 onwards, 8th Air Force bomber crews were assigned to fly thirty combat missions (tours were later extended to thirty-five missions)
Tracer	A pyrotechnic bullet, visible when fired; placed at intervals in ammunition supplies to enable a gunner to trace his line of fire
U-Boat	*Unterseeboot;* a German submarine
USAAF	United States Army Air Forces

V.1/V-Weapon	*Vergeltungswaffen 1* (Reprisal Weapon 1); pilotless flying bomb
VE-Day	Victory in Europe Day; the end of the war in Europe, 8th May 1945
WAAC	Women's Army Auxiliary Corps
WAC	Women's Army Corps
WIA	Wounded in Action
Yank/Yankee	Slang for an American

BIBLIOGRAPHY

1. 8th Air Force/Military and Aviation/Americans in Europe

AAF: The Official Guide to the Army Air Forces (Special Edition for AAF organizations) (Pocket Books Inc., New York, 1944).

Andrews, Paul M., and William H. Adams. *Project Bits and Pieces: Second Air Division* (Eighth Air Force Memorial Museum Foundation, Warrenton, Virginia, 1995).

Bailey, Mike, and Tony North. *Liberator Album* (Voyageur Press, Stillwater, Minnesota, 1998).

Benarcik, Michael D. *In Search of Peace* (Michael D. Benarcik Foundation, Wilmington, Delaware / Jostens Printing & Publishing Division, State College, Pennsylvania, 1989).

Bowman, Martin W. *8th Air Force at War: Memories and Missions, England 1942-45* (Patrick Stephens Ltd., Wellingborough, Northamptonshire, 1994).

Bowman, Martin W. *Fields of Little America* (Wensum Books, Norwich, 1977).

Bowman, Martin W. *Four Miles High: U.S. 8th Air Force in World War Two* (Patrick Stephens Ltd., Wellingborough, Northamptonshire, 1992).

Bowman, Martin W. *Home by Christmas: 8th and 15th Air Force Airmen at War* (Patrick Stephens Ltd., Wellingborough, Northamptonshire, 1987).

Bowman, Martin W. *USAF Handbook* (Sutton Publishing, Stroud, Gloucestershire, 1997).

Bowyer, Michael J. F. *Air Raid!* (Patrick Stephens Ltd., Wellingborough, Northamptonshire, 1986).

Brown, David, Christopher Shores, and Kenneth Macksey. *Guinness History of Air Warfare* (Guinness Superlatives Ltd., Enfield, Middlesex, 1976).

Burton, Hal. *The Ski Troops* (Simon & Schuster, New York, 1971; available at www.alpenglow.org/ski-history/notes/book/burton-1971.html).

Encyclopedia of Air Warfare (Spring Books, London, 1974).

Ethell, Jeffrey, and Alfred Price. *Target Berlin: Mission 250: 6 March 1944* (Book Club Associates / Jane's Publishing Company Ltd., London, 1981).

Flight Manual B-24D Airplane (Flight and Service Department, Consolidated Aircraft Corporation, San Diego, California, December 1942).

Freeman, Roger A. *Airfields of the Eighth: Then and Now* (Battle of Britain Prints International Ltd., London, 1978).

Freeman, Roger A. *The Friendly Invasion* (East Anglia Tourist Board, in conjunction with Terence Dalton Ltd., 1992).

Freeman, Roger A. *The Mighty Eighth* (Macdonald & Company Ltd., London, 1970).

Freeman, Roger A. *The Mighty Eighth War Diary* (Jane's Publishing Company Ltd., London, 1981).

Freeman, Roger A. *The Mighty Eighth War Manual* (Jane's Publishing Company Ltd., London, 1984).

Gardiner, Juliet. *Over Here* (Collins & Brown, London, 1992).

Goodson, James A. *Tumult in the Clouds* (Arrow Books Ltd., London, 1986).

Johnson, Derek E. *East Anglia at War* (Jarrold & Sons Ltd., Norwich, 1978).

Kaplan, Phillip, and Andy Saunders. *Little Friends* (Random House, New York, 1991).

Kaplan, Phillip, and Rex Alan Smith. *One Last Look* (Abbeville Press Inc., New York, 1983).

Lambson, Delbert D. *When I Return in Spring* (Delzona, Arizona, 1994).

Lancaster-Rennie, Jean. *And Over Here!* (Geo. R. Reeve Ltd., Wymondham, Norfolk, 1976).

Liberator (Consolidated Vultee / General Dynamics, Convair Division, 1989).

Low, Andy, ed. *The Liberator Men of Old Buck'* (453rd Bomb Group Association Veterans' publication, 1979).

McLachlan, Ian. *Night of the Intruders: The Slaughter of Homeward Bound USAAF Mission 311* (Patrick Stephens Ltd., Wellingborough, Northamptonshire, 1994).

Reid, Alan. *A Concise Encyclopaedia of the Second World War* (Osprey Publishing Ltd., Reading, 1974).

Rochlin, Fred. *Old Man in a Baseball Cap* (HarperCollins, London, 1999).

A Short Guide to Great Britain (War and Navy Departments, Washington, D.C., n.d.).

Siefring, Thomas A. *U.S. Air Force in WWII* (Chartwell Books Inc., Secaucus, New Jersey, 1979).

Sims, Edward H. *American Aces of World War II* (Macdonald & Co., London, 1958).

Tute, Warren, John Costello, and Terry Hughes. *D-Day* (Pan Books Ltd., London, 1975).

Wells, Mark K. *Courage and Air Warfare* (Frank Cass & Co. Ltd., London, 1995).

World War II United States Aircraft (Leisure Books Ltd. / Salamander, London, 1985).

Wright, Mike. *What They Didn't Teach You about World War II* (Presidio Press, Novato, California, 1998).

Wynn, Humphrey, and Susan Young. *Prelude to Overlord* (Presidio Press, Novato, California, 1984).

2. U.S. History and Culture / World History / Miscellaneous

Brogan, Hugh. *The Penguin History of the United States of America* (Penguin Books, London, 1990).

Bryson, Bill. *Made in America* (Secker & Warburg, London, 1994).

Chambers Dictionary of World History (Chambers, Edinburgh, 1994).

Coe, Jonathan. *James Stewart: Leading Man* (Bloomsbury, London, 1994).

Cotterell, Arthur. *China: A Concise History* (Pimlico, London, 1995).

Dewey, Donald. *James Stewart: A Biography* (Little, Brown & Company, London, 1997).

Dictionary of North American History (Larousse, New York, 1994).

Faust, Ruby Jo Roberson. *Roberson Reunion Kin, Southeast Alabama, 1800s-2002: A Family History* (privately published, Indialantic, Florida, 2003).

Fishgal, Gary. *Pieces of Time: The Life of James Stewart* (Scribner, New York, 1997).

Goldberg, David J. *Discontented America: The United States in the 1920s* (Johns Hopkins University Press, Baltimore, 1999).

Heller, Joseph. *Now and Then: A Memoir from Coney Island to Here* (Scribner, London, 1999).

Jones, Maldwyn A. *American Immigration* (University of Chicago Press, Chicago, 1960).

Jones, Maldwyn A. *The Limits of Liberty* (Oxford University Press, New York, 1995).

Middleton, Richard. *Colonial America: A History, 1607–1760* (Blackwell, Cambridge, Massachusetts, 1992).

Pickard, Roy. *James Stewart: The Hollywood Years* (Robert Hale, London, 1992).

Quirk, Lawrence J. *James Stewart: Behind the Scenes of a Wonderful Life* (Applause Books, New York, 1997).

Robbins, Jhan. *Everybody's Man: A Biography of Jimmy Stewart* (Robson Books, London, 1985)

Seitz, Raymond. *Over Here* (Phoenix, London, 1998).

Steiner, Stan, *Fusang: The Chinese Who Built America* (Harper & Row, New York, 1979).

Terkel, Studs. *My American Century* (Phoenix Giant, London, 1998).

Todd, Lewis Paul, and Merle Curti. *Rise of the American Nation* (Harcourt Brace Jovanovic Inc., New York, 1982).

USA: The Rough Guide (fourth edition, Rough Guides Ltd., London, 1998).

Visiting Our Past: America's Historylands (National Geographic Society, Washington, D.C., 1986).

Watkins, T. H. *The Great Depression: America in the 1930s* (Little, Brown & Co./Back Bay Books, Boston, 1993).

Watson, Jack. *Twentieth-Century World Affairs* (John Murray Ltd., London, 1984).

Zinn, Howard. *A People's History of United States* (Harper Perennial, New York, 1995).

Zinn, Howard. *The Zinn Reader: Writings on Disobedience and Democracy* (Seven Stories Press, New York, 1997).

3. Articles, Unpublished Accounts and Online Sources

"American Prisoners of War in Germany: Stalag Luft IV," prepared by Military Intelligence Service, War Department, July 1944 (compiled and presented by Greg Hatton, available at www.b24.net/pow).

Bell, Miriam Roberson. "An Experiment in Communal Living," from the *Heritage Book of Dale County, Alabama* (Heritage Publishing Consultants Inc., Dale County, Alabama, 2001).

Carroll, Maj. James J. "Physiological Problems of Bomber Crews in the Eighth Air Force during WWII" (research paper presented to The Research Department Air Command and Staff College, March 1997).

Chenard, Robert E. *Historical Perspective on Waterville's 19th Century Franco-Americans* (available at members.mint.net/frenchcx/frcanwtv.htm).

"Chinese," *Handbook of Texas Online* (Texas State Historical Association; available at www.tsha.utexas.edu/handbook/online/articles/view/CC/pjc1.html).

"The Chinese Texans," *Institute of Texan Cultures* (University of Texas, San Antonio; available at www.texancultures.utsa.edu/txtext/chinese/chinese.htm).

Cripe, Hubert. "Mission 250—Berlin 6 March 1944" (personal account).

Davis, Master Sgt. (Ret.) Al. *Camp Roberts* (The California State Military Museum—Historic California Posts; available at www.militarymuseum .org/campbob.html).

Dole, C. Minot. "Adventures in Skiing" (available at www.alpenglow.org/ ski-history/notes/book/dole-1965.html).

Louis Dawson. *Camp Hale and the 10th Mountain Division: Colorado's Tough Ski Troops Helped Win WWII* (available at www.wildsnow.com/articles/soldiers/ 10th_mountain_division.htm).

"1st Battalion—87th Infantry Regiment" (available at www.globalsecurity.org/ military/agency/army/1-87in.htm).

Frisbee, John L., and Col. George Gudderly. "Lest We Forget" (*Air Force Magazine*, September 1997, Vol. 80, No. 9).

Govan, Capt. Thomas P. *Training for Mountain and Winter Warfare: Study No. 23* (Historical Section, Army Ground Forces, 1946; available at www.army .mil/cmh-pg/books/agf/agf23.htm).

Hobbs, Larry. "Being Jewish Was an Extra Risk for This Kassel Survivor! An Interview with Ira Weinstein," *Palm Beach Daily News,* January 19, 1996 (reproduced in the 2nd Air Division veterans' association *Journal*, Fall 1996).

"Legends in the Law: A Conversation with Ramsay D. Potts" (*Bar Report*, August–September 1999); also at www.dcbar.org/for_lawyers/resources/ legends_in_the_law/potts.cfm

Meistrich, Philip H. *A Crew Goes to War—the Hard Way!* (2nd Air Division veterans' association *Journal,* June and December 1986).

Mullany, Stephen William "Bill" Sr. "Summer 1944" (a personal account of a combat tour with the 453rd BG and life at Old Buckenham, written in 1986; available at users.rcn.com/smullany/summer1944/summer1944 .html).

"The 1940s: Americans Make Many Tracks . . . and Much War—A History of Humour in Ski Cartooning" (available at www.skiinghistory.org/ SkiHumor6.html).

Plunkett, George. *The Plunketts Home Page* (Norwich in old photographs and the history of the Blitz; available at www.the-plunketts.freeserve.co.uk).

The Promise of Gold Mountain: Tucson's Chinese Heritage (available at www.library .arizona.edu/images/chamer/chinese.html).

Sapulpa Community Guide (available at www.community-guides.com/sapulpa/ history.html).

The Second Air Division in East Anglia (Second Air Division Memorial library publication, Norwich, 1963).

Sherman, Don. "The Secret Weapon: The Legendary Norden Bombsight" (*Air and Space,* Smithsonian, February–March 1995).

Smith, Starr. "Jimmy Stewart: His Most Demanding Role" (*The Retired Officer Magazine,* September 1998).

Stein, Roger. Unpublished history of Lt. Donald Jones's crew.

"Testimony of Dr. Leslie Caplan: The Evacuation of Stalag Luft IV" (available at www.b-24.net/pow/nardocs.htm).

Texarkana Chamber of Commerce Web site (available at www.texarkanachamber .com/history.html).

"Texarkana, Texas," *Handbook of Texas Online* (Texas State Historical Association; available at www.tsha.utexas.edu/handbook/online/articles/view/TT/hdt2.html).

Turbak, Gary. "Death March across Germany" (*Veterans of Foreign Wars Magazine;* available at www.b-24.net/pow/nardocs.htm).

Turell, Horace S. *The Invisible Battlefield?* (445th Bomb Group veteran's biography; available at users.skynet.be/sky72940/hal.htm).

Watkins, Claude. "A Prisoner of the Luftwaffe, Part II—A Realistic Look at a Long Walk" (*American Ex-POW Bulletin*, April 2000).

Yedlin, Ben. "In My Sperry Ball I Sit" (*Flypast,* October 1999).

Various Articles and Letters from the 453rd Bomb Group veterans' association newsletter (1995–2002) and the 2nd Air Division Association's *Journal* (1986–1999).

4. Television and Video Documentaries

America's War: WWII in Colour (Warner Vision International, 2002).

Behind the Wire (produced by A. Allen Zimmerman and the Eighth Air Force Historical Society, 1994).

James Stewart: The Last of the Good Guys (BBC Scotland, 1997).

Liberty! The American Revolution (Twin Cities Public Television Inc., 1998).

The Memphis Belle (William Wyler documentary, 1944).

Start Engines: Plus Fifty Years (The Eighth Air Force Historical Society, 1991).

Target for Today (wartime documentary; *After the Battle Magazine,* London, 1985).

The West (coproduction of Insignia Films and WETA-TV, Washington, D.C., in association with Florentine Films and Time Life Video & Television, 1996).

Whispers in the Air (Granada Television, 1989).

5. Primary Sources

Combat mission records: Jack Nortridge, George White, Bill Eagleson, Perry Roberson, and Bill LeRoy.

Correspondence with Bill Eagleson: letters from 1986 onwards; recorded messages, 1995–1998; and e-mails from 1999 onwards.

Correspondence with Perry Roberson, Bill LeRoy, Wayne Lim, Pete Veilleux, and the families of these and all other crew members, as well as other 8th Air Force veterans and families.

Diary excerpts: Bill Eagleson, James Workman, and Fred Stein.

Individual deceased personnel file: Donald C. Lawry (provided by the Department of the Army, Alexandria, Virginia).

Individual flight record: Bill Eagleson.

Missing air crew reports (available from the Air Force Historical Research Agency, Maxwell Air Force Base, and the National Archives & Records Administration).

2nd Air Division/453rd Bomb Group wartime records: microfilm held by the 2nd Air Division Memorial Library, Norwich (copies from the Air Force Historical Research Agency, Maxwell Air Force Base, and the National Archives & Records Administration).

Video: Bill Eagleson's crew interviews at 453rd Bomb Group veterans' reunion, South Dakota, 1994.

Wartime letters written by Harvey Nielsen, Perry Roberson, and Donald Lawry.

Wartime articles from *Evansville Review, Janesville Daily Gazette, Texarkana Daily News, Texarkana Gazette, St. Louis Post, Prisoners of War Bulletin.*

INDEX

Page numbers in italics refer to illustrations